WIN
AT

SCRABBLE™

BRAND Crossword Game

WIN

AT

SCRABBLE

BRAND Crossword Game

HarperCollins Publishers
Westerhill Road
Bishopbriggs
Glasgow
G64 2QT

First edition 2010

Reprint 10 9 8 7 6 5 4 3 2 1 0

ISBN 978-0-00-737468-7

SCRABBLE® and associated
trademarks and trade dress are owned
by, and used under licence from,
Mattel, Inc. SCRABBLE is a registered
trademark of J.W. Spear & Sons
Limited, a subsidiary of Mattel, Inc.
© 2010 Mattel, Inc.

All Rights Reserved.

Collins ® is a registered trademark
of HarperCollins Publishers Limited

www.collinslanguage.com

A catalogue record for this book is
available from the British Library

Typeset by Davidson Publishing
Solutions, Glasgow

Printed in Great Britain by Clays Ltd,
St Ives plc

Contents

CONTRIBUTORS

Essential Scrabble Strategy
Barry Grossman

A-Z Guide to Scrabble Words
Barry Grossman
Allan Simmons

FOR THE PUBLISHER
Gerry Breslin
Lucy Cooper
Kerry Ferguson
Elaine Higgleton

The publishers would like to thank Allan Simmons, for providing the basic concept for the *A-Z Guide to Scrabble Words*.

Introduction

Collins Win at Scrabble is a one-stop guide to the key elements of, and best words for, Scrabble, to help you score more points from the tiles on your rack, and so to win more games.

The *Essential Scrabble Strategy* section gives an introduction to playing beyond the basics, to help casual players learn some of the finer points of game, and so become better able to work out how to use difficult racks, and how to make the most of horrible board positions. It explains why the **S** is so important, how best to use the blank tile, how to find seven- and eight-letter words to score a 50-point bonus, and which types of words to learn to increase your Scrabble word power. This section also includes a range of Scrabble challenges, so that you can put your new-found knowledge to the test.

The second section, *A-Z Guide to Scrabble Words*, gives a letter-by-letter introduction to some of the best words for Scrabble. The word lists in this section are not exhaustive: the aim has been to provide the casual player with focused lists that can really help get you out of trouble (when you have a **Q** but no **U** or blank tile, for example) and so help improve play.

Scrabble remains the world's most popular word game; we hope this book will help you take your game to the next level, will help you score more points, and win *lots* more games.

ESSENTIAL
SCRABBLE
STRATEGY

Essential Scrabble Strategy

1 Introducing Scrabble

Games are strange things. Some, like chess and backgammon, look terribly complicated to an onlooker who doesn't know the rules. It seems that you must have to be some sort of expert to play these games. Scrabble is different somehow.

Even if someone had never seen the game in their life before, it probably wouldn't take them long to pick up the general idea if they watched a game being played. The scoring might take them a little longer but, fundamentally, it's easy enough – just place the letters on the board to form words, like in a crossword. This makes most people think that once they've grasped that, they know all they need to know – perhaps all there is to know – about the game.

This is very far from the truth. Scrabble, like chess, backgammon or bridge, has a high skill factor. And that doesn't just mean knowing lots of words. A strong player will certainly know a lot of words that the average person, even the average reasonably well-educated person, will never have heard of. But you have to know the right words. A professor of English will find it no help at all in Scrabble to know words like **CATACHRESTICAL** or **SOMNILOQUENCE**. You can beat the Prof. if you know words like **OURIE** and **ZAX**.

> *Scrabble facts* – *In 1985, two Royal Marines on a training exercise on Brabant Island, Antarctica, fell down a crevasse; luckily, one of them had a Scrabble set in his kit-bag and they passed the five days that they waited to be rescued playing Scrabble.*

Increasing your enjoyment

A game of Scrabble is basically a series of problems. How many times have you yelled in frustration at picking too many vowels or consonants, or cursed the fates for giving you an unwanted **J**, **Q**, **X** or **Z**? How often have you looked at the tiles on your rack and thought, 'I bet these make a seven-letter word', but not been able to work out what it was? How much more fun would the game be if you knew how to deal with these situations?

> *Scrabble facts* – *In a two-person game, most people playing with family and friends will average between 180 and 300 points per game. Stronger players can average more than 400 points.*

Making the most of 'good' tiles on your rack and limiting the damage from 'bad' ones is what makes your game more enjoyable, and improves your chances of winning. And that's what this book is all about.

> *Scrabble facts* – *The highest-ever score for a single word was 392 for* **CAZIQUES***, played by Karl Khoshnaw of Richmond, Surrey, in 1982. The highest score for a game is a massive 1049 by Phil Appleby of Lymington, Hampshire.*

It won't happen automatically. It'll take a bit of concentration, a bit of practice, a bit of memory work. But if you enjoy Scrabble already, reading this book and taking on board what it suggests will bring you a lot more success at the game, and – more importantly – a lot more pleasure.

Who invented Scrabble?

Alfred Butts was an architect, but in the 1930s he was unemployed as a result of the Great Depression. He was also a word-game enthusiast, doing crosswords and tinkering with anagrams.

First there was Lexiko

Hoping to make some money, he developed a game called Lexiko. This involved players drawing seven tiles, then simply taking turns to discard tiles and draw new ones until they could make a seven-letter word. The first player to do so won. There was no board, no points and no element of interlocking your word with what had already been played. No games manufacturer was interested in producing it, partly because in the Depression most people presumably had little money to spend on games, but partly, one suspects, because it sounds a bit boring.

> **Scrabble facts** – Early names for Scrabble included **Lexiko**, **Criss-Crosswords** and **It**.

Butts then introduced point values for the different letters. When a player had won a round by playing a seven-letter word, the others could play whatever words they could make from their hand, and lose the point values of the remaining tiles.

Determined as ever, Alfred tried again to have the game produced commercially, but still with no success. As an architect, Butts would have known that everything takes time, whether building a house or perfecting a game. He kept refining his invention, and eventually added the board, the premium squares and the crossword-style building up of words that we know from the game today.

Scrabble is born

By now, you might think that the manufacturers would have been falling over themselves to produce the game, but still Butts had no success. In 1939 he met James Brunot, a civil servant with an entrepreneurial streak. Brunot was immediately intrigued by the game. He played around with the idea, refined it a bit more and, like Butts, tried to get it onto the market. But it was now the early 1940s, and the world had more pressing matters to attend to. Finally, in 1949, Brunot formed his own business, the Production and Marketing Company, and the game – by now, after a few more name changes, called Scrabble – was finally ready to go into the shops.

> **Scrabble facts** – *Butts based the frequency of letters in the Scrabble set on how often each occurred in headlines in the* New York Times, *the* Herald Tribune *and the* Evening Post.

Unfortunately, even after 18 years or so of development, Scrabble was still no overnight success. Sales were slow, and Brunot was losing money. In the first three years, no more than 20,000 sets were sold. Things were looking grim for Alfred and James, and Scrabble might well have faded away there and then. Then Jack Strauss went on holiday.

Holiday success

Strauss was a shopkeeper, and he discovered Scrabble while on a summer break with some friends. He loved the game and, on his return to work, promptly placed an order and organized a major promotion for the game in the store. This might not have mattered much if Jack Strauss had just been any shopkeeper. In fact, he was the chairman of Macy's, one of the largest department stores in New York. With that kind of power to push it,

Scrabble was well and truly on its way. Sales in the low thousands were transformed into millions, and Brunot's and Butts' long struggle was over.

> **Scrabble facts** – *There are daily or weekly puzzles or columns based on Scrabble* in The Times, Daily Telegraph, Daily Mail and Daily Express.
>
> *Because its Orthodox readers cannot write on a Saturday, the* Jewish Chronicle *has a weekly crossword designed to be done by placing tiles on a Scrabble board.*

Scrabble around the world

Scrabble soon spread through the English-speaking world, and it wasn't long until the game was being produced in foreign languages too. Of course, this required a re-evaluation of the point values and frequency of each tile for every new language.

- If you struggle without an **E**, spare a thought for the Dutch, who are such **E** addicts that they have a whopping 18 of them in a set, but only 20 other vowels in total.
- A Russian set has 33 different letters plus two blanks. Not surprisingly all these letters cannot fit into 98 tiles, so Russian Scrabble has a mighty 126 tiles per set, including the blanks.

> **Scrabble facts** – *Amongst the languages you can play Scrabble in are:*
> *Afrikaans, Arabic, Danish, Dutch, Finnish, Portuguese, Russian, Yiddish*

Scrabble is now played by millions of people across the world, and it regularly tops the chart of best-selling games. About 100 million sets have been sold worldwide since it all started in 1948! Walk into any house in Britain, and there's a 50 per cent chance that it will have a Scrabble set lurking somewhere. The game is said to be popular in homes ranging from Buckingham Palace to prisons.

> *Scrabble facts* – *Kylie Minogue is a big fan.*
>
> *Snooker players use it to relax in the long intervals between matches – Steve Davis and James Wattana are reported to be particularly hot, clearly masters of the Q as well as the cue.*

Parents can introduce young children to the game with *My First Scrabble*, and then they can move on to *Junior Scrabble* when they are a little older. There is also a Braille version of the game, with raised dots on the tiles and the premium squares.

And nowadays, of course, no range is complete without the computer version. You can buy a CD-ROM to play against your computer, choosing an appropriate skill level so that you always (luck permitting) get a good, close game. But be warned, the computer version of the game is addictive. You can find out about other forms of Scrabble in Chapter 12.

> *Scrabble facts* – *To celebrate the game's 50th anniversary in 1998, two teams from the Army and the Navy played a game on the pitch at Wembley Stadium. The side of each tile was 1.25 metres (4 feet) and the side of the board was over 18.5 metres (60 feet)!*

Alfred Butts died in 1993, so he lived long enough to see the worldwide success the game had become. Millions of sets, addicts by the tens of thousands, even Scrabble clubs and World Championships – could he have dreamt of what he was starting when he came up with his curious little game, back in those dark, depressed days of 1931?

2 The rules of the game

Every Scrabble set contains a copy of the rules, but just in case you've lost yours, or you haven't actually got yourself a Scrabble set yet, this chapter gives you a quick guide.

Setting up the game

1   Open out the board and give each player one of the tile racks. The bag containing the tiles should be placed to one side of the board, within easy reach of all the players.

2   One player acts as score-keeper for all the players, and will need a pen and paper. (Alternatively, all players can keep score as a check.) See Rules 7 to 11 for more details about scoring.

3   Each player draws one tile from the bag. The nearest to the beginning of the alphabet starts. In the event of a tie, the tied players draw again. A blank beats an **A**. The letters are then put back in the bag and the bag is shaken.

4   The player who starts picks seven tiles from the bag, and places them on his or her rack without letting the other players see them. Passing to the left, the other players in turn also pick seven tiles and place them on their rack.

The first move

5   The first player makes a word from two to seven of his or her letters and places that word on the board, either across (from left to right) or down (from top to bottom). One letter must go on the centre square (in most sets this is marked with a star or similar marker). The player counts his or her score (the first word counts as a double word score, see scoring, below) and announces it. He or she then takes as many tiles from the bag as have just been played, thus giving seven tiles on the rack again.

Second and subsequent moves

6   Play passes to the left. Each player makes his or her move by adding
    from one to seven of their own tiles to those already on the board.
    The letters played, either across or down, must themselves form a
    valid word, and they must interlock with the letters already on the
    board, crossword-style, so that all additional words formed are also
    valid words. Again, the move is completed by the counting and
    announcing of the score, and the replenishment of the rack back
    to seven tiles by picking from the bag.

Scoring

7   The basic score for each tile is shown by a small number, from one to
    ten, printed in the bottom right-hand corner of the tile. The list below
    shows the score for each letter.

Letter	No. in set	Score		Letter	No. in set	Score
A	9	1		L	4	1
E	12	1		M	2	3
I	9	1		N	6	1
O	8	1		P	2	3
U	4	1		Q	1	10
				R	6	1
B	2	3		S	4	1
C	2	3		T	6	1
D	4	2		V	2	4
F	2	4		W	2	4
G	3	2		X	1	8
H	2	4		Y	2	4
J	1	8		Z	1	10
K	1	5		BLANK	2	0

8   The board contains a number of special scoring squares.

  • A letter placed on a *Double Letter* square has its value doubled.
  • A letter placed on a *Triple Letter* square has its value tripled.
  • If any letter of a word has been placed on a *Double Word* square the complete word has its entire score doubled.
  • If any letter of a word has been placed on a *Triple Word* square then the word has its entire score tripled.

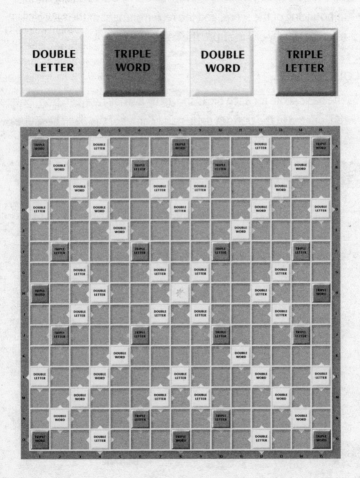

9   When two or more words are formed in one move, each is scored.
    The common letter is counted (with full premium values, if any)
    in the score for each word.

MOTIF = $(3 + 1 + 1 + 1 + (4 \times 2)) \times 2 = 28$
F is on a Double Letter square. M is on a Double Word square. The total letter score is added up first and then multiplied by 2 because of the Double Word square.

FIRM = $4 + 1 + 1 + 3 = 9$
Only the tile value of F is used. The Double Letter square only benefits the player who placed F on the board.

FIRMS = $(4 + 1 + 1 + 3 + 1) \times 2 = 20$

WRITS = $((4 \times 2) + 1 + 1 + 1 + 1) \times 2 = 24$

Total score = 44
The S is on a Double Word square so both FIRMS and WRITS score double. W is on a Double Letter square.

10 Premium squares are only counted in the move in which they are covered. If the word is modified in a subsequent move, tiles on premium squares count at face value only.

11 Any player playing all seven of his or her tiles in one move scores a **bonus** of 50 points in addition to the regular score for the move.

Miscellaneous

12 There are two blank tiles in the set, which may be used as any letter. When a blank is played, the player must nominate which letter the blank represents. The blank then remains as that letter for the rest of the game. A blank tile has a score of zero, but if a blank is placed on a Double Word or Triple Word square, the word is still doubled or tripled, as appropriate.

> *Scrabble tip – Another rule some people like to incorporate is to allow the blank to be lifted from the board and replaced with the letter it represents, allowing the player to re-use the blank. While not part of the official rules, this is a useful way to keep the game moving, and I would not discourage it, particularly for beginners.*

13 Rather than playing any tiles on the board, a player may instead choose to change any or all of his or her tiles. To do this, the player places the tiles to be changed to one side, picks the same number of new tiles from the bag, and then puts the old tiles back in the bag. A change counts as a score of zero, and a player cannot change and make a scoring move in the same turn.

14 Any other player may challenge a player's move, if he or she considers that any of the words made are not valid words. A challenge must be

made before the player has picked and looked at any of the replacement tiles. The word should then be checked in a dictionary or an official Scrabble word source. If the word is wrong, the player must take back his or her tiles from that move, and gets a score of zero.

> **Scrabble tip** – *Some 'house rules' allow players to consult a dictionary before playing their move, but most keen players do not favour this. It can be useful to have a dictionary around if a player challenges a word after it has been played. It's a good idea to have a dictionary that gives plurals and different verb forms (see page 175).*

Ending the game

15 When there are no tiles left in the bag, play continues until one player has used all the tiles on his or her rack. Every other player then has the total value of their unplayed tiles deducted from their score, and the player who has played all his or her tiles has the total value of all unplayed tiles added to his or her score. If no player can play off all their tiles, each player has the value of their unplayed tiles deducted from their score.

Some example moves

To help get you under way, follow through the moves shown on these boards.

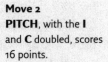

Move 2

PITCH, with the **I** and **C** doubled, scores 16 points.

Move 3
GLARED, with the **G** and **E** tripled, score 14, plus 6 for **AGATE**, scores 20 points.

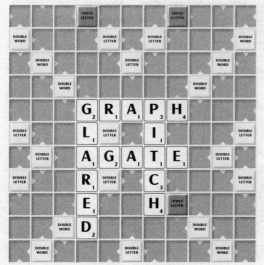

Move 4
GRAPH, with the **H** tripled, scores 19 points.

Move 5
BIOGRAPHER scores 18 points. (Note the **H** is not re-tripled.)

Move 6
OMIT scores 6 and **ID** scores 3, both doubled, making 18. **ME** scores 4 and **OR** 2, for a total score of 24 points.

Move 7
TENSILE, covering two double word squares, is doubled then redoubled, scoring 7 × 4 = 28, plus 7 for **AGATES**, scores 35 points.

Move 8
The **T** of **HONESTY** is doubled, then the whole word is doubled, scoring 20 (with the **H** as a blank scoring zero). Add 19 for **BIOGRAPHERS**, plus the 50-point bonus for using all seven tiles, for a total score of 89 points.

You may not spot words like **BIOGRAPHER**, **HONESTY** and **TENSILE** right away, but these moves have been shown to demonstrate the variety of ways you can 'build' a move within the basic rules, and how to score them.

Knowing if a word is allowed

It's very annoying when you play a word, only to have it disallowed by those you are playing with. Use *Collins Scrabble Lists* to adjudicate on any challenges. This lists every allowable word in strict alphabetical order, except that very long words, those with ten letters or more, are confined to a separate section at the end. No arguing about the plural of octopus or whether you can have **SUBLIMER** or **HONESTEST**.

If you haven't got *Collins Scrabble Lists*, you and your fellow-players will have to do a bit of adjudicating from time to time. Dictionaries will generally list only a base word, such as **TABLE** and will not specifically show **TABLES**, **TABLED**, **TABLING** or **TABLINGS**. Before starting play it's worth agreeing a few guidelines as to what you're going to allow and what you aren't. If you want to find out more, look at the section at the back of the book on allowable word forms.

> *Scrabble tip* – *By using the most recent edition of* Collins Scrabble Lists *the allowable word list stays up to date; new words are being coined or accepted into English all the time, and you don't want to be prevented from playing* **EMAIL**, **EURO**, **CHAV**, **ZIT**, **BIRYANI** *or any of a host of others.*

Using a large word source is the only way to bring into play the wealth of fascinating words which we will be looking at throughout this book, and which your own dictionary may not have. Some people feel that the more words are allowed in the game, the more it becomes just a memory exercise. Learning the words is certainly important, but having a large number of words at your disposal allows you to display a fuller range of Scrabble skills than would otherwise be the case.

> **Scrabble facts** – *It's difficult to assess how many words the average English speaker knows or uses, but estimates range from 40,000 to 75,000. Yet there are a whopping 267,633 words eligible for Scrabble in English!*
> *Lots to learn then...*

3 Two- and three-letter words

Now that we've got the rules sorted out, it's time to take a look at how you can improve your game. A major part of that consists of having a large armoury of useful words at your disposal. You may think the longer the word you know is, the more useful it will be, as it's likely to score more. However, in fact, the key to a good Scrabble vocabulary is a good knowledge of short words, particularly words of two and three letters.

Low scoring play
Adding the letters **F**, **A**, **R**, **E** to **TEAM** to give **AFTER** gives you a score of 7.

Short words are, of course, invaluable for helping you complete a game and to use difficult letters. They have another great use, which can really help you boost your score. You can use short words to join or 'hook' the word you want to play on to the board, by playing parallel to another word. You will usually make more than one word each turn and so make a higher score than just by crossing over another word. Look at the two different ways of playing on the two boards shown here.

Notice that the high scoring play has scored 18 more points than the low scoring play. This score was only possible because of the word **FA** (think musical scales).

High scoring play
Adding the letters **F**, **A**, **R**, **E** to **TEAM** to gives a score of 25.

Two-letter words

Here is the first, essential thing you have to know to improve your game: *know all the allowable two-letter words*. There are 124 of them in *Collins Official Scrabble Dictionary*, but to make the list more manageable, you can divide them into three groups:

- The ones you already know.
- The ones you already know, but may not have realized were words.
- The ones you probably don't know.

Commonly known two-letter words

Here are the words you most likely know and which will appear in most dictionaries:

AH	AM	AN	AS	AT	AX	AY
BE	BY					
DO						
EH						
GO						
HA	HE	HI	HO			
ID	IF	IN	IS	IT		
LA	LO					
MA	ME	MY				
NO						
OF	OH	ON	OR	OX		
PA						
SO						
TO						
UP	US					
WE						
YE						

Less well-known two-letter words

There are then a good selection of words that you probably know but were unsure whether they were allowable Scrabble words. As we enter less familiar areas, it is useful to know the meaning of the special words you use, not least so you can convince those you are playing with that the words are for real.

Contracted words

AD	advertisement
BI	bisexual
MO	moment
OP	operation
PO	chamberpot
RE	regarding
TA	thank you

Exclamations and interjections

AW	variant of **ALL**
ER	sound made when hesitating in conversation
HM	sound made to express hesitation or doubt
MM	expression of enjoyment of taste or smell
OI, **OY**	shout to attract attention
OW	exclamation of pain
OY	shout to attract attention (*or* grandchild)
SH	exclamation to request silence or quiet (*or used instead of* **SHILLING**)
ST	used to attract attention
UH, **UM**, **UR**	used to express hesitation or uncertainty in speech
YA	*variant of* **YOU**
YO	used as a greeting or to attract someone's attention

Then there are letters of the alphabet when spelt out. At the end of the list are some names for some Greek letters.

Letters of the alphabet

AR	letter **R**
EF	letter **F**
EL	letter **L** *or* an abbreviated version of **ELEVATED RAILWAY**, as in Chicago
EM	letter **M** *or* a standard unit of measurement in typography
EN	letter **N** *or* a unit of measurement that is half an em
ES	letter **S**
EX	letter **X** *or* a preposition meaning not including or an informal name for a former husband or wife
PE	letter **P**
TE	letter **T**

MU, **NU**, **PI** and **XI** are all Greek letters

Unfamiliar two-letter words

The third group of words will be less familiar, but, as a result, likely to be very useful once you have remembered them. They are listed below, and then some explanations follow.

AA	AB	AE	AG	AI	AL
BA	BO				
CH					
DA	DE	DI			
EA	ED	EE	ET		
FA	FE	FY			
GI	GU				
IO					
JA	JO				
KA	KI	KO	KY		
LI					
MI					
NA	NE	NY			
OB	OD	OE	OM	OO	OS	OU
QI					
SI					
TI					
UG	UN	UT			
WO					
XU					
YU					
ZA	ZO				

If all this looks a bit gobbledygookish, you may be surprised to know that even some of these are more familiar to you than you might realise:

- An **AB** is an abdominal muscle, as in toning up your abs and your pecs.
- **OM** is what Buddhists chant as part of their prayers.
- **AA** is a word from Hawaiian, meaning a rough volcanic rock. Its opposite, smooth volcanic rock, is called **PAHOEHOE**.
- **ZO** is a Himalayan cross-breed of a yak and a cow, also spelt **ZHO**, **DZO**, **DZHO** or **DSO**, useful Scrabble words every man-jack of them.

Just to help you along, here are a list of meanings for the rest of them.

AE	one
AG	agriculture
AI	shaggy-coated slow-moving South American animal
AL	Asian shrub or tree
BA	Ancient Egyptian symbol for the soul
BO	exclamation used to startle or surprise someone
CH	archaic form of **EKE** (to lengthen or stretch)
DA	Burmese knife
DE	of, from
DI	plural of **DEUS** (god)
EA	river
ED	editor
EE	eye (*Scots*)
ET	ate (*dialect*)
FA	fourth degree of any major scale (*music*)
FE	fee
FY	exclamation of disapproval
GI	loose-fitting white suit worn in judo and karate

GU	type of violin used in Shetland
IO	type of moth
JA	yes (*in South Africa*)
JO	sweetheart (*Scots*)
KA	spirit dwelling as a vital force in man or a statue
KI	Japanese martial art
KO	traditional digging tool (*in New Zealand*)
KY	cows (*Scots*)
LI	Chinese measurement of distance
MI	third degree of any major scale (*music*)
NA	no (*Scots*)
NE	nor
NY	near
OB	expression of opposition
OD	hypothetical force formerly thought to be responsible for many natural phenomena
OE	grandchild
OO	wool (*Scots*)
OS	mouthlike opening
OU	man, chap
QI	vital life force (*in Oriental medicine and martial arts*)
SI	seventh degree of any major scale (*music*)
TI	seventh degree of any major scale (*music*)
UG	to hate
UN	one
UT	the note C
WO	woe
XU	Vietnamese currency unit
YU	jade
ZA	pizza

Have a look back at the two-letter words every so often as you're going through the book. Once you're happy with the first two groups (i.e. the common ones, the contractions, the interjections and the letters), have a real go at mastering the unusual ones. They really are the essential first step to improving your game.

Three-letter words

But it doesn't end there. *Three-letter words are almost as important as the twos* for helping you build up your moves – and there are a lot more of them. Unless you have a lot of time and aptitude to study lists, or have a photographic memory, it will take you a few months to get to grips fully with the threes. Take them gradually, starting with the ones containing **J**, **Q**, **X** and **Z**. You won't need to know all of them before your game starts to improve.

Here are some of the most useful threes:

Containing **J**

GJU type of violin used in Shetland

JAP to splash

JEE mild exclamation of surprise

JIZ wig

JOE sweetheart (*Scots*)

RAJ British government in India before 1947

TAJ tall conical cap worn as a mark of distinction by Muslims

Containing **Q**

QAT evergreen shrubs

QIS plural of **QI** (*vital life force*)

QUA in the capacity of

SUQ open-air market place, e.g. in North Africa

Containing X

DEX dextroamphetamine

GOX gaseous oxygen

HOX to hamstring

KEX any of several large hollow-stemmed umbelliferous plants, such as chervil

RAX to stretch or extend

REX king

VOX voice

WEX wax

WOX wax

XIS plural of **XI** (*14th letter in the Greek alphabet*)

ZAX axe

Containing Z

You can remember some of the **Z**-threes in sets of two and three:

BEZ	part of a deer's horn	**BIZ**	business
CAZ	casual	**COZ, CUZ**	cousin
FEZ	tasselled cap	**FIZ**	fizz
MIZ	misery	**MOZ**	hex
SAZ	Middle Eastern stringed instrument	**SEZ**	informal spelling of 'says'
		ZIG, ZAG	to change direction sharply

Other useful Z-threes

ADZ tool with cutting blade at right angles to the handle

DZO animal that is a cross between a cow and a yak

JIZ wig

ZAX axe

ZEP type of long sandwich

ZOA independent animal bodies (*plural of* **ZOON**)

ZOS plural of **ZO** (*animal that is a cross between a cow and a yak*)

These lists are not exhaustive, but they will get you started. You won't always be able to fit in a **QUIVER**, a **ZEBRA** or an **ANNEX**, so you need to know a good selection of these shorter words to help you play your high-scoring letters – preferably for a more than face-value score.

Threes containing awkward letters

Other useful three-letter words are those that can help you get rid of awkward letters like **U** and **V**, or which allow you to use excess vowels. You should try to remember:

AIA	female servant, usually Indian or Malay
AUA	yellow-eye mullet (*Maori*)
AUE	Maori exclamation of pain or astonishment
AYU	small Japanese fish
EAU	river
UVA	grape
VAU, VAV	sixth letter of the Hebrew alphabet

Threes as 'hooks'

By 'hooks', we mean words which can be formed by adding one letter at the beginning or end of another word. Threes which are hooks of frequently used twos can be very helpful. You'll find that you play **ZO** fairly often now that you know it, which is why it's especially good to know **AZO**, **DZO** and **ZOA** – so that you can add the extra letter to an already-played **ZO**, making another word at right angles while you're doing it.

If you look back at the example moves shown in the previous chapter, notice that we didn't just add an **A** to **GATE** to make **AGATE** – we made a whole new word, **GLARED**, as well. This is why these hook-words of any length are so useful. The lists of useful **J**, **Q**, **X** and **Z** words above have been compiled partly with hooks in mind. Here are a few more commonly played twos with the threes you can make from them:

AA:	**AAH**	**AAL**	**AAS**	**BAA**	**CAA**	**FAA**	**MAA**
CH:	**ACH**	**CHA**	**CHE**	**CHI**	**ECH**	**ICH**	**OCH**
HM:	**HMM**	**OHM**					
KY:	**KYE**	**KYU**	**SKY**				

By now, you're no doubt wondering what these odd-looking words mean. As with the twos, some are more familiar than you might realize – **BAA** and **MAA** are the cries of a sheep and a goat respectively, **CHA** is tea, **ACH** and **OCH** are what you say in Scotland when you're annoyed, **HMM** is what you say if you're puzzled, and **AAS** is the plural of the rough volcanic rock **AA**. Here are some more meanings:

AAH	to exclaim in surprise
AAL	Asian shrub or tree
CAA	to call (*Scots*)
FAA	to fall (*Scots*)
CHE	dialect form of I
CHI	22nd letter of the Greek alphabet
ECH, ICH	to eke out
KYE	Korean fundraising meeting
KYU	in judo, one of the five grades for inexperienced competitors
OHM	unit of electrical resistance

Scrabble facts – *The only letter which does not feature in any two-letter word is* **v**. *There are no twos ending in* **C**, **J**, **K**, **Q** *or* **Z**.

Don't worry about meanings

A word of advice – don't get too hung-up on meanings. It's a familiar, plaintive cry when someone new to a Scrabble club has an unfamiliar word played against them: 'What does that mean?'. It only adds to their bafflement when, as often as not, the answer comes back, 'I don't know'. It comes back to what has been said before – it's not knowing lots of words that wins you games, it's knowing the right words.

Experienced players build up a stockpile of words that they know will prove useful to them again and again. Sometimes the words have interesting meanings which can help you remember them. But often it's just another fish or plant, or a word Shakespeare used, and which has lain, dusty and unloved, at the back of the cupboard of English words ever since. Until, that is, Scrabble players came along, blew the dust off and started using it. Some of the meanings worth knowing are given in this book, but there is no rule that says you have to know the meaning of every word you play and, at the risk of incurring the wrath of the purists, I would suggest that it's very often all right just to know the word because it's good for Scrabble and not to worry about the meaning.

Another reason it is not *de rigueur* to ask about meanings during a game is that you might seem to be fishing for useful information, such as whether the word is a noun, verb or adjective, and therefore whether you can put an **S** or some other letter after it. The time to ask about meanings is after a game, not during it.

> *Scrabble tip* – *You can get rid of excess* **I**s *and* **U**s *with* **IWI** *(a Maori tribe),* **ULU** *(type of knife) and* **UTU** *(a reward). You can then use hooks to turn them into* **KIWI**, **ZULU** *and* **TUTU**.

When you are ready, you can find complete lists of three-letter words on the internet. In the meantime, you will be doing fine if you learn the twos and make a start on the threes highlighted in this chapter. You'll soon wonder how you ever managed to play without **AIA**, **AUA**, **WEX** or **WOX**.

HAVE A GO
CHALLENGE NO. 1

First, work out the seven-letter word you have on your rack.
It shouldn't be too difficult – think of colours or fruit.
Then can you find two places to play it on the board shown?
Remember those two- and three-letter words.

Your rack is **A E G N O R S**

4 Dealing with J, Q, X and Z

Many players don't like to pick 'the big tiles' – **J**, **Q**, **X** and **Z**. They think that because there are fewer words in which to play them, they'll be hard to get rid of, and perhaps will even end up on their rack at the end of the game, costing them a handful of points. This is wrong. The big tiles are, *usually*, good tiles to pick.

The big tiles
You have already seen the two-letter words and some of the threes containing **J**, **Q**, **X** and **Z**. Right away you have an armoury of words that will help you play these tiles.

Get points with short words
The good thing about these small words is that they may well help you play a big tile for a worthwhile score. Remind yourself of the twos containing 'the big four':

JA	JO			
QI				
AX	EX	XI	OX	XU
ZA	ZO			

Have a look at this section of a board in play:

Your rack:
D E I K L Q U

You could play **QUITE** using the **T** on the board, scoring 16. But with your new-found knowledge of **QI**, you can play **QI** both ways, slotting in another two-letter word, **ID**, as well for a very healthy 65 points:

Playing **QI** scores 65 points.

In a similar way, how would you score more than 60 points with this board and rack?

Your rack:
A D F I J O P

You should see right away that the Triple Letter square is the one which is going to pay the dividend. Playing the **J** alone to make **JO** scores 25. But can you play a word downwards as well to get the **J** tripled again? **JO** doesn't fit in this case because you can't have **OTE**, but there's no problem with **ATE**. So play **JA** downwards, also making **JO** and **ATE**, and you're getting somewhere – 53 points for doing very little. Even better, add the **P** to the end of **JA** making **JAP**, turning **LATE** into **PLATE**, and you've bagged yourself another 10 – 63 for the move which is shown on the next page.

Playing **JAP** scores 63.

Always be on the lookout for these small but profitable moves when you have one of the big tiles. The **X**, which forms two-letter words with all the vowels (**AX EX XI OX XU**), is particularly useful for this tactic.

> *Scrabble tip* – *Always try to play the* **J**, **Q**, **X** *and* **Z** *tiles on premium squares for extra points.*

Get points with longer words

Another great way to get big scores with the big tiles is to look for 'double-letter–double-word' slots, or, even better, 'triple-letter–double-word' or 'double-letter–triple-word'. It works like this. Remember that if one of the letters in your word covers a Premium *Letter* square, and another covers a Premium *Word* square, the appropriate letter is doubled or tripled before the whole word. So it's another way of making a letter count for a mighty *six times* its face value. You need to make sure that it's a high-scoring tile that gets the six-times treatment.

With a rack of **E E I N O S** plus a **J**, **Q**, or **Z**, there are opportunities for multiple scores.

Look at the situation on the board shown above. On your rack you have **E E I N O S** plus one of the big tiles. Can you see where you could get your big tile doubled then redoubled, or doubled then tripled, or tripled then doubled, if it was a **J**, a **Q** or a **Z**?

Of course, you need to think here of rather longer words than the two- and three-letter ones we have been using up to now. There are plenty of common five- and six-letter words, even with the big tiles in them, and none of the words you are looking for here is unusual. The boards opposite show you some possible solutions.

JOINS scores 63

ZONES scores 75

QUINS scores 48

SNEEZE scores 75

Score with J, Q, X or Z on the Triple Word square

If no opportunities like the ones shown above present themselves when you have a big tile, you can often get a good score simply by mopping up a handy Triple Word square.

On this board use the Triple Word square for a high-score.

Look at the position on the board shown above. Ordinarily it wouldn't be worth much to use this Triple Word square. Low-scoring tiles will not score much and, if the left-hand row is usable all the way to the top or bottom, you could be opening a good place for your opponent to play a high-scoring bonus. But if you can slot in **JET**, **QAT** or **ZIT**, you pocket a handy 30 or 36 points, and you would be very unlucky if your opponent was ready to move in with an eight-letter word beginning or ending with the high-scoring tile you have provided. If your opponent does use the high-scorer to make a word that isn't a 50-point bonus, it would be most unlikely to score as many as yours just has. It would quite likely score no more than 12 or 14 points – a big net profit for you.

Useful four- and five-letter words with **J**, **Q**, **X** and **Z**

JUGA	plural of **JUGUM**, a small process at the base of each forewing in certain insects
JORAM	large drinking bowl
JORUM	large drinking bowl
AFLAJ	plural of **FALAJ**

FALAJ	water channel
AQUA	water
QUATE	fortune
QUINE	a young, unmarried woman or girl (*Scots*)
TRANQ	tranquiliser
IXIA	southern African plant of the iris family
PREX	US college president
SOREX	a shrew or related animal
XENIA	influence of pollen upon the form of the fruit that develops after pollination
ZEIN	protein occurring in maize
ZILA	administrative district in India
ZAIRE	currency used in the former Zaire

But the big tiles aren't always good

There are times when you don't want to pull one of these high-scorers out of the bag: when you're close to a bonus, and, sometimes, when you're close to the end of a game.

Breaking up a bonus word

If you have six low-scoring tiles, well balanced between vowels and consonants, and with not too many duplicates, you should be well on your way to making a seven-letter bonus word. Picking **J**, **Q**, **X** or **Z** at that stage just screws the whole thing up, unless you're lucky enough to pick, say, a **Z** to a rack of **A E I N S T**, which you can then arrange into **ZANIEST**. Usually you just have to play the high-scorer as quickly as possible for a low score, such as using the **Z** to make **ZO** for 11 points.

Pulling out a **Q** in such circumstances can be a real challenge. You need to know that there are some words that use a **Q** without a **U**, many of Arabic origin. Here are some examples of allowed words:

QI	vital life force (*in Oriental medicine and martial arts*)
QAT	white-flowered evergreen shrub whose leaves have narcotic properties
QADI	judge in a Muslim country
QAID	chief
QOPH	19th letter of the Hebrew alphabet
WAQF	religious or charitable endowment in Muslim law
FAQIR	Muslim who spurns worldly possessions
QANAT	underground irrigation channel
QIBLA	direction of Mecca, to which Muslims turn in prayer
TALAQ	Muslim form of divorce

Sometimes you are faced with the dilemma of whether to break up your promising combination (**A E I N S T** or whatever) for the sake of getting around 20 points for your high scorer rather than about 11 or so. How much easier if you had drawn an **R** for **RETAINS** or **G** for **SEATING**.

At the end of a game

The other time you may not want to see a big tile arriving on your rack is towards the end of the game. It depends on whether there is somewhere to play it for at least 20 points or so. If there is, it can win you a close game. If not, you either have to play it off for what you can (possibly giving your opponent a chance to play out and leave you with the rest of your letters on your rack), or conversely, get rid of the rest of your letters for whatever you can and perhaps be stuck with the biggie. In some cases, if the board is blocked, you might not be able to get rid of it at all.

HAVE A GO

CHALLENGE NO. 2

In the board shown, can you find a move that scores 45?
And can you find a move that scores over 55?

Your rack is **D E I J N O S**

HAVE A GO
CHALLENGE NO. 3

Using the board shown, can you score over 50 by playing six tiles?
In another part of the board, can you score over 60 by playing
six tiles?
Can you achieve a higher score by playing fewer tiles?

Your rack is **A E L M Q S U**

5 Using the S

Although **s** is only worth one point, it's much more valuable than you might think, because it can help you form seven-letter words and score 50 bonus points.

If you look at a game played between two good club players, and one between two less experienced players, a few differences will quickly be obvious.

- The stronger players will have played plenty of those unusual two- and three-letter words we have already looked at.
- There will be more parallel plays, resulting in solid blocks of tiles, rather than words which criss-cross through each other.
- There will be more seven- and eight-letter words played for 50-point bonuses.

This chapter will focus on the third of these, and in particular, how to use four of the six best tiles in the set – the four **s**s. The other two tiles, the two blanks, will be covered in the next chapter.

Why is the S so useful?

Look around you and come up with the first few words that come into your head. You might think of **CHAIR**, **TABLE**, **BOOK**, **SIT** and **READ**. Depending on who's in the room with you, you could come up with **MAN**, **WOMAN**, **HUSBAND**, **WIFE**, **BOY**, **GIRL**.

And what does every one of those words have in common? Yes, you can put an **s** at the end of all of them. Even **MAN** (he mans the lifeboat),

WOMAN (to act like a woman or to staff with women) and **WIFE** (to become a wife or take a wife) are verbs which can have **S** after them (or 'take an **S**', as Scrabble players tend to say). In fact, nearly every noun and verb in the English language can take an **S**. Many of the smaller words take S, and not always because of their status as a noun or verb – **DI** is a noun but is plural already (plural of **DEUS**, a god), but you can have **DIS**, teenage slang meaning to disrespect.

> *Scrabble tip – Some unexpected words that take an **s** (i.e. they can have an **s** put at the end of them):*
>
> | | | |
> |---|---|---|
> | **EROTIC** | **ERRATIC** | **MALTED** |
> | **PRY** | **TELLY** | **TRILBY** |
> | **WICKED** | | |

Even a lot of words that end in **S** take an **S** – **PRINCES** (to give **PRINCESS**), **POSSES** (to give **POSSESS**), **BRAS** (to give **BRASS**), **NEEDLES** (to give **NEEDLESS**) and indeed **DIS** (to give **DISS**, to treat with contempt). **ZEBRAS** can become **ZEBRASS** (a cross between a zebra and an ass), and if you're ever in a game where **DEADLINE** is played, then someone makes it **DEADLINES**, you could well and truly flabbergast your opponent by turning that into **DEADLINESS**.

> *Scrabble facts – Don't forget that there are four **s** tiles in a set, so there's a reasonably high chance that you'll get one at some point in the game.*

Using your S

The relevance of all this to the **S** on your Scrabble rack is twofold. Firstly, if you can make a six-letter word with the other six letters, the chances are you'll be able to stick an **S** on the end of it and, you've got a seven-letter word. So you've only got six letters to worry about manipulating. That means, assuming no blanks or duplicates, you only have 720 different ways to arrange your tiles which, while it might sound quite a lot, is a lot easier than the 5,040 ways you can arrange seven different tiles.

Of course, you may have a seven-letter word with an **S** in it, but the **S** isn't at the end. For example, with a rack of **I L N O R S T**, it may only be after coming up with wrong 'uns like *litrons* and *trinols* that you finally sniff out **NOSTRIL**. However, it's worth putting your **S** at the end of the rack and thinking around the other six to start with, and only if that fails, should you need to be more imaginative.

Secondly, once you've found your bonus word, you have a high chance of being able to fit it in. What can match the desolation of working out a splendid seven and then not being able to get it down? But with all those other words already on the board, most of them taking an **S**, you will usually have a couple of positions onto which you can hook your brilliant bonus.

It is worth stressing that you should not necessarily hang onto an **S** until you can get a bonus with it. Its usefulness for hooking means you can often get a good score without using it in a bonus word. Watch especially for positions where you can get two words doubled with the addition of an **S**. Look at the board opposite with a Double Word square next to **FIRM**.

If you have an **S** in this position, you should be looking to make whatever word you can with it, and use it to turn **FIRM** into **FIRMS**. If you can get a high-scorer on the Double Letter square, so much the better. Something like **WRITS**, coming down to also make **FIRMS**, would score 44 (see board on the next page).

A good board for playing an **S**.

Using the **S** to get down **WRITS** scores 44.

To summarize, the **S** can:

- Allow you to play a word, hooking an existing word, and thus scoring for both.
- Increase your chance of finding a seven-letter word.
- Taking 1 and 2 together, it can increase your chance of finding a playable seven-letter word.

You should expect to score at least 20 for an **S**, preferably more than 25.

The two **S**s problem

If one **S** is good, it follows that two on your rack at the same time must be twice as good. Right? Wrong!

Why? Well, quite simply, two of anything on your rack tends to weaken it (leaving aside blanks, which we'll come to in the next chapter). It's all to do with those different combinations again – you have far fewer separate ways of arranging your letters if you have a duplicate.

Two **E**s are usually alright, because **E** is such a common letter in English. And two **S**s are certainly better than some other duplicates; the dreaded duplicate **V** or **U** are real killers. But a second **S** has basically lost its advantage of being an **S** – its essential 'essness' (no, not a valid word). If you put one **S** to one side, hoping to make a word with the other six letters, and then stick the **S** at the end of it to make a seven, what has happened is that your second **S** has turned into just another letter. You're not really very likely to pick the letters for **ZEBRASS**, and your opponent would be amazed if you got all four **S**s for **POSSESS**.

As it happens, the most common initial letter for a word in *Collins Scrabble Lists* is **S**, and by quite a long way. So yes, there are lots of words, many of them seven- and eight-letter words, that begin and end with an **S**. Then there are armies of words ending in **–ISES** and **–ISTS**. So it's far from impossible to get a bonus word with two **s**s. It's just not twice as easy as getting one with one **s**.

Generally, the thing to do with a duplicate **s** is play one, hooking it onto a word already on the board, making another word at the same time, preferably using your higher-scoring tiles – you should be getting the hang of it by now – and then you're still left with one **s** and your lower-scoring tiles with which, fingers crossed, to get a bonus next time.

S at the beginning

As well as being an 'end hook' (going on the end of a word), the **s** is frequently also a 'front hook'; which means that it can be placed at the front of a word to form another word. You can often put an S at the front of words beginning with:

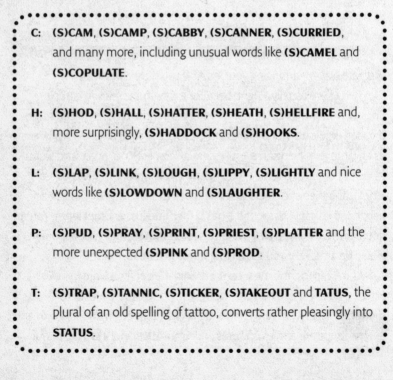

C: **(S)CAM**, **(S)CAMP**, **(S)CABBY**, **(S)CANNER**, **(S)CURRIED**, and many more, including unusual words like **(S)CAMEL** and **(S)COPULATE**.

H: **(S)HOD**, **(S)HALL**, **(S)HATTER**, **(S)HEATH**, **(S)HELLFIRE** and, more surprisingly, **(S)HADDOCK** and **(S)HOOKS**.

L: **(S)LAP**, **(S)LINK**, **(S)LOUGH**, **(S)LIPPY**, **(S)LIGHTLY** and nice words like **(S)LOWDOWN** and **(S)LAUGHTER**.

P: **(S)PUD**, **(S)PRAY**, **(S)PRINT**, **(S)PRIEST**, **(S)PLATTER** and the more unexpected **(S)PINK** and **(S)PROD**.

T: **(S)TRAP**, **(S)TANNIC**, **(S)TICKER**, **(S)TAKEOUT** and **TATUS**, the plural of an old spelling of tattoo, converts rather pleasingly into **STATUS**.

Scrabble facts – *Here are the meanings of some of the more surprising words that can be formed by adding an* **s** *at the start.*

S-CAMEL   Shakespearian word of uncertain meaning
S-COPULATE   of or like the small tufts of dense hair on the legs of some spiders
S-DEIGN   old form of disdain
S-GRAFFITI   ceramic objects that are decorated with patterns incised in to the top layer of the glaze to reveal parts of the ground
S-HADDOCK   edible yellow fruit that is a bit like a grapefruit
S-HOOK   set of parts ready for assembly
S-PINK   finch
S-PROD   young salmon

Words beginning with **M**, **N**, **W** and even **O** are also good to check for **s** front-hooks. And of course, like most other consonants, it will often go before a word starting with a vowel (**S-ADDER**, **S-EVEN**, **S-IRE**, **S-ODIUM**, **S-UNDRESS**). Add in exotica like **S-DEIGN** and **S-GRAFFITI** and you might almost start to think an **s** was as likely to go before a word as after it. It is, however, its power as an end hook that makes the **s** such a potent weapon to have on your rack.

HAVE A GO
CHALLENGE NO. 4

With the board position and rack shown below:

1. Can you find two seven-letter words – both fairly simple words ending in **S**?
2. Can you find one place where each fits on the board?
3. Can you see where you could play an eight-letter word (not ending in **S**) that would hit a Triple Word square?

Your rack is **A E L L R S U**

6 Using the blank

Sometimes a very inexperienced player will feel hard done by when they pick the blank, because it doesn't score anything. Wrong, wrong, wrong!

If you pick a blank, your heart should leap like a March hare on a trampoline. So long as there is an opening on the board somewhere, a blank should set you on your way to being able to play a bonus word, maybe not immediately, but reasonably soon.

Why? It's those combinations again. The larger the number of different ways you can form your rack into seven letters, the more likely it is that one of them will be a seven-letter word. We've already noted that a straightforward rack of seven different letters can be arranged 5,040 different ways. But six different letters plus a blank can be arranged in a massive 115,920 ways, counting the blank as each possible letter in each separate position. That's 23 times as many; picking a blank is like having 23 tickets in the lottery instead of just one.

> **Scrabble facts** – Don't forget that the blank has no value, whatever letter it is standing in for.

How to use the blank

You could try painstakingly working your way through all 115,920 combinations to find if you have a seven-letter word. At, say, 10 seconds per combination, that would take about 13½ days, assuming you don't stop for sleeping, eating or other essentials. Your opponent may get a tad restless. Happily, your brain will automatically shut out consideration of the vast number of these combinations that are obviously fruitless. In addition, the following will help you work at the challenge:

1   If some of your letters form a useful combination such as **–ING** or
    –ATE, put the blank with the other letters and see if any words suggest
    themselves. **G H I L N R ?** (**?** represents a blank) might look a bit of a
    mishmash. But make it **H L R ?** + **I N G** and it should immediately
    resolve itself into **HURLING**.

2   If there are no such handy combinations on your rack, go through the
    alphabet, making the blank each letter in turn. **D F I M N U ?** may not
    immediately look like anything, but once you try making the blank an
    L, **MINDFUL** might pop into your head.

3   Perhaps the blank will become the last letter in one of those useful
    combinations. **G H I L R U ?** also makes **HURLING**, even though you
    can't immediately isolate **–ING**.

4   You may be able to save a bit of time and mental energy by eliminating
    several possibilities for the blank:

    • If you have five consonants, one vowel and a blank, the blank is
      almost certainly going to have to be a vowel if you are using it to
      make a seven-letter word.

    • More obviously, with five bonus-friendly tiles (i.e. mainly one-
      pointers with a good vowel–consonant balance) plus a blank and a
      Q, there's really only one letter you need to think about making the
      blank. If you don't have a **U**, that's almost certainly what the blank
      is going to have to be if you are going for a bonus.

Play your blank with care

You must avoid the ultimate Scrabble crime of wasting your blank for a
low score. Don't just stick it into a four- or five-letter word for a few points,
even if you can't see anything else. Hold onto the blank and get rid of
some of your more awkward tiles, even for a lower score this time round,
and some bonus possibilities ought to start revealing themselves within
one or two moves.

In club and tournament Scrabble, the blank will rarely be played other than in a bonus move, unless the blank is picked right at the end of the game, when it may be too late to knock the rest of the rack into shape or there may be nowhere to play a bonus.

You may also be able to use the blank to get a move as good as a bonus, even if not an actual one. Remember we talked about getting a **J**, **Q**, **X** or **Z** on a Premium Letter square, at the same time as getting the word on a Premium Word square. Such a move can easily score 60–70 points or more, and could be well worth using a blank for.

> **Scrabble tip** – Do you ever feel the blank in the Scrabble bag? Mattel produce special tile sets for tournaments where every tile is smooth.

As a general rule, you should be looking to score at least 50 for a blank.

Two blanks

Even some quite experienced club players claim to dislike getting two blanks at the same time. The mesmerizingly high number of different combinations that can be made throws some people into confusion, and they say they 'just can't think', or even, appropriately enough, 'go blank'. This is a bit like people who say that being rich doesn't make you happy. It may be true, but you wouldn't mind giving it a try anyway.

The fact is that with two blanks you should be well on your way to making a bonus, unless the board is extremely blocked. If you find a double blank difficult to cope with, try thinking of one of them as the most useful letter it could be (bearing in mind your other five tiles) if it was not a blank. With a rack of, say, **A A C I P ? ?**, given that you have three vowels, at least one of your blanks is going to be a consonant. So think of it as one of those one-point, bonus-friendly consonants like **N** or **T**, and words like **CAPTAIN** and **CAPITAL** should soon start suggesting themselves to you. If you have **H O R T X ? ?**, make the rack more manageable by calling one blank an **E**, and **EXHORTS** suddenly becomes much easier to find.

However, with a rack like that, you may be able to play your **X**, perhaps with one of the blanks, for around 40 points, and still have a good chance of the bonus next turn. Unless you can play **EXHORTS** (or whatever) for a real stonker of a score – I would suggest at least 80 – a rack with lots of goodies like that should be good for two high scores.

Never change a blank

Above all, never change a blank. Why give your opponent the chance of picking it later? The only possible time you might want to try breaking that rule is if you are over 100 behind, and thus need two bonuses to come back. You could try putting a blank back in the hope of picking it later and getting bonuses with both of them. But this is an unwise tactic – particularly as by changing you waste a turn and fall even further behind.

HAVE A GO
CHALLENGE NO. 5

What type of letter is the blank almost certainly going to be to form a seven-letter word?

Can you find the seven-letter word? And where would you play it?

Your rack is **B D O R R S ?**

7 Finding the bonus words

Once you have mastered (and I do mean mastered) the twos, started learning some useful threes, lost your fear of **J**, **Q**, **X** and **Z**, and realized the value of the **s** and the blank, the next step on your road to being an accomplished Scrabble player is to be able to play bonus words; in other words, play out all seven of your letters in one go for that lovely, satisfying, game-changing, onlooker-impressing, opponent-shattering 50-point bonus.

Making bonus words

You may manage the occasional bonus now, but if you can get up to playing a regular one per game, then two per game, you will soon see your average score rocketing out of the sub-200 doldrums and into the stratosphere of 300+ and even 400+ (based on a two-player game).

So how is it done? Essentially, there are two keys to playing bonuses regularly: **managing your rack** and **knowing the words**. In this chapter we will look first at the various ways of managing your rack and then at how to form words through the use of **prefixes and suffixes** and by creating **compound words**.

Rack management

It's not just knowing words, it's knowing the right words that counts. There is no point in the random learning of seven-letter words. **PUPUNHA**, **MUNDIFY** or **THRUTCH** may just show up on someone's rack somewhere between now and the next millennium, but that's not the way to bet. Better by far to get familiar with words which, on the balance of probabilities, will come up on your rack with reasonable regularity.

Rack management essentially means knowing which letters to keep and which letters to get rid of to maximize your chances of a good score next time – preferably a bonus. Just as a good snooker player doesn't take a whack at the first ball he sees but tries to make sure he leaves himself an easy shot for next time, so should a Scrabble player have an eye to what he or she is storing up for the future.

Rack management: keep the right letters

The first thing to know when working out which letters to keep and which to play is the distribution of the tiles in a set. In other words, how many **A**s are there, how many **B**s, etc. Happily, many Scrabble boards actually list this distribution down one side of the board. We list them in Chapter 2. If your board doesn't, it's fairly easy to have a rough idea of how many of a particular letter are in the set by its point value:

> **Scrabble tip** – *Know the distribution of tiles in the set by point value.*
>
> | Point value | Number in set |
> | --- | --- |
> | 1 | 4‾12 |
> | 2 | 3‾4 |
> | 3‾4 | 2 |
> | 5‾10 | 1 |

Clearly, the fewer points a letter scores, the more there are of them. There are lots of the common letters to help you make words, but they don't score so much. There are fewer of the less common letters because they're harder to use, but they are worth more points.

This means a rack is going to tend towards having a lot of the one-point tiles: 68 of the 98 tiles (leaving aside the blanks) are worth one point. So the best bonus words to learn must be the ones consisting wholly or mainly of one-point letters.

Rack management: one-point letters

So which are the one-point letters? There are 10 of them: the five vowels **A E I O U**, plus five consonants, **L N R S T**.

Are these the 10 commonest letters in the language? A statistical analysis of over a million words of English covering newspaper reports, scientific and religious writing and general fiction concluded that the most frequently used letters, in order, were: **E T A O I N S R H L**.

So nine of our 10 commonest letters in the Scrabble set agree with this study. The rogue interloper in the study is **H**, but its frequency can be explained by the number of short, very common words in which it appears:

THE	THAT	THIS	THESE	THOSE
HE	SHE	THEY	HIM	HER
THEM	HIS	HERS	THEIR	WHICH
WHAT	WHO	HOW	WHY	

Thus the letter **H** appears in a passage of written or spoken English much more often than it would in a random collection of unconnected words.

The letter **U**

So the missing letter from our 'Scrabble Top Ten', the **U**, presumably came 11th in the statistical survey? Actually, it came 13th, behind **D** and **C**.

So why are there so many **U**s in the Scrabble set? Scrabble's creator, Alfred Butts, decided on the number of each letter by counting the frequency with which each appeared in three newspapers, the *New York*

Times, the *Herald Tribune* and the *Evening Post*. But it seems clear that he must have made some judicious adjustments after his mammoth count. He would have had to iron out the **H** problem, for one. And he also realized that there had to be a reasonable number of **U**s so that players could play the **Q**. (**QI**, **QAT**, **QADI** and the other non-**U** words would not have been part of his thinking at that time.) Four **U**s would be enough to give a reasonable chance of shedding the awkward **Q**, but not so many that players would be overburdened with a letter which, apart from **Q** duty, is not particularly helpful.

Rack management: the right vowels

The vowels have a fairly clear hierarchy of usefulness. **E** is the biggie. It's difficult (far from impossible, but difficult) to get a bonus without an **E**. As you may have discovered yourself, it can be hard playing any good move without an **E**. **A** and **I** come next, about equally useful, closely followed by **O**. As the ideal vowel–consonant split is three vowels and four consonants, it follows that the vowels you want on your rack are **A E I**. Even though our million-word analysis placed **O** above **I**, experience in Scrabble shows that the **I** is easier to work with.

> *Scrabble tip – In Scrabble **I** is more useful than **O**.*
> *It can be used in lots of suffixes:*
> **–ING**, **–IER**, **–IEST**, **–ISE**, **–IZE**, **–ISM** *and* **–IST**.

So do you try to keep **A E I** on your rack, and play any **O** or **U** that you have? Maybe, but it's not always quite that simple.

How to manage duplicate vowels

The problem of duplicated letters can easily come to haunt you with vowels, especially the **A** and **I**. You don't want two of either of these letters on your rack, because comparatively few words have two **A**s or two **I**s in them. Yes, there are all the words ending in –**ING**, thus giving **AIMING**, **BOILING**, **CHIDING** and lots of others, or the –**IER** and –**IEST** words – **DIRTIER**, **FIERIER**, **GIDDIEST**, etc., and no doubt you can rattle off a dozen words off the top of your head with two **A**s as well. However, duplicates radically diminish the number of different ways you can arrange the letters on your rack, and that constricts the number of useful moves you can make.

Tracking the letters played

For this reason, it is always a good idea to keep track of how many **A**s and **I**s have been played. Let's say it's about halfway through the game, with about 45 or 50 letters on the board. There are six **A**s on the board and two **I**s. You also have one of each on your rack. You can see that you are far more likely to pick another **I** than another **A**, so it makes sense to play the **I** if you can, but not be so concerned about ditching the **A**.

> **Scrabble facts** – *The distribution of vowels in a set is:*
> *twelve* **E**s   *nine* **A**s   *nine* **I**s
> *eight* **O**s   *four* **U**s

This should not take precedence over any really good move you can make that involves keeping the **I** and playing the **A**. But, other things being equal, play the **I**. A choice between **BAD** and **BID**? Go for **BID**. Wondering about **CARP**? Perhaps with a judicious reshuffle you could make it **PRIG** instead.

If you play bridge or poker, you will know the value of remembering the cards that have been played or folded. In poker, you don't try for the third six to go with your pair if both the other sixes are gone. In bridge, the king of trumps must win a trick if the ace is gone. We are using the exact same principle here in Scrabble. You use your knowledge of what has already been played to help you predict what will happen next. Except it's easier in Scrabble because you don't need to remember – the 'discarded' letters are all there face up on the board in front of you, so all you need to do is count them. (You might not even need to do that – in a later chapter, we'll look at the concept of tile-tracking, which shows you at a glance how many of each letter are still to come.)

The **E**, as we have already seen, is a sufficiently useful letter that to hold two of them is no bad thing. And there are plenty of four-letter words with a double **O** in the middle if you want to get rid of a couple of **O**s – but four-letter words with two **A**s or two **I**s are considerably thinner on the ground. Of course, you don't need to get rid of both your duplicates to alleviate your problem, as you only need to play one – but there is a comfort in having those double-**O** words available if you need them.

So, we have the apparently contradictory situation that one **A** or one **I** on your rack is better than one **O**, because **A** and **I** are commoner letters, especially for bonuses. But two **O**s are better than two **A**s or two **I**s, because they're easier to get rid of in short words.

An example

It's halfway through a game, there are four **A**s, four **I**s and four **O**s to come, and you have one of each on your rack.

Do you play **BID**, **BAD** or **BOD**?

The answer is, probably, play **BOD**.

The extra strength of **A** and **I** over **O** just about overrides the fear of picking a duplicate. But much would depend on other factors.

For example, if you have **–TION** on your rack, is it worth holding this useful suffix and playing the A? It could be, but you need to be aware that **–TION** is mainly useful for eight-letter bonuses; there are not many seven-letter words ending in **–TION**. So don't build your hopes up of getting a –**TION** bonus unless there are places on the board where an eight-letter word is playable.

If you think this is all starting to sound a bit technical, well, you're right. But that's the trouble with Scrabble racks – there is not always a clear-cut answer. It's like walking through a wood. This path is more overgrown, that one is muddier, a third goes uphill, and the fourth one looks pretty but there's a strange growling noise coming from its vicinity. Which one do you take? Hitting on the right one is a mixture of experience, common sense, instinct and luck.

Conclusion

We have established in general that **E** is the best vowel, **A** and **I** come next, **O** a little behind but with some points in its favour, and **U** the least useful. But even the humble **U** can be worth hanging onto if it is towards the end of the game and the **Q** hasn't appeared yet, especially if there are no handy places to slot in a **QI** or a **QAT**. So the distribution of vowels in Scrabble turns out to be about right. Well done, Alfred Butts!

Rack management: the right consonants

So what about consonants? Remember the one-point tiles, **L N R S T**. Holding on to these and discarding the rest is generally the quickest way to a bonus word. But as always, there are complications.

Below and on the next page we will consider each of these one-point consonants in turn.

The letter **L**

Of these five consonants, **L** is unquestionably the least useful. It should really be worth one and a half points. Hang on to it if you like but have no qualms about playing it away if you have a good move in which to play it.

The letter S

The **S** is a special case which we have already discussed in Chapter 5. If your rack is your afternoon tea-break, the **S** is a cream cake – great to have, but two are no better than one and might leave you feeling sick.

The letter N

The **N** is a common letter and is useful for forming words with –**ING**, –**TION** and –**SION**. But a word of warning about the **N** – it's a terrible letter for beginning words with. Try this little experiment: take your dictionary or *Collins Scrabble Lists*, and hold the '**N**' section between your thumb and forefinger. Look how skimpy it is. There are more words beginning with **W** than beginning with **N**. So if you have an **N** and you're trying to use it to start an eight-letter word for a bonus, my advice is – try something else, fast.

The letter R

Now, how about the **R**? Another useful letter, but again there's a catch. The **R** really needs an **E** to give it much value. It comes into its own because of the large number of words with the prefix **RE**–, or the suffix –**ER** (whether in its agent noun sense, e.g. **COUNTER**, **BUILDER**, or as a comparative of an adjective, e.g. **BLACKER**, **NEEDIER**). And it will not have escaped your notice that the one letter in both **RE**– and –**ER**, apart from **R**, is **E**. So if you don't have an **E**, and there aren't so many left that you're likely to pick one any time soon, don't bust a gut to hold on to an **R**.

The letter T

Which leaves the **T**. I am a **T** fan – apart from a blank, **S** or **E**, no letter gives me more comfort to hold on my rack than a **T**. The only trouble is, the statistics don't back up my enthusiasm as far as seven-and eight-letter words are concerned – the **N** and the **R** are slightly better, because of all those **–ING**s, **RE**–s, and **–ER**s. But that may be the point – the **T** is not dependent on specific other letters to make it useful, and my gut feeling is that its versatility makes it more valuable. A duplicate **T** is also far less of a handicap than a duplicate **N** or **R**. Cherish your **T**s, try not to play them unless you have no reasonable alternative, and a fair percentage of them will help you on the way to that elusive bonus.

I could analyse my games and try to produce statistics to back this up, but the trouble is that it would be something of a self-fulfilling prophecy. If I (generally) hold onto a **T** until I can make a bonus word with it, then I will obviously be able to count my bonuses and announce triumphantly that 50 per cent of them (or whatever) have a **T** in them, which wouldn't prove anything. But the **T** is a cheerful, sociable letter that will fit in with pretty much any rack it finds itself on, so if it knocks on your door, invite it in and make it comfortable. More often than not, it will reward your hospitality.

Rack management: the right balance

It goes without saying that if you've got a rack of **L N R S S T T** or **A E E I O O U**, then you haven't got a bonus. In fact, you haven't got much of a move at all. It's essential to maintain a balance of vowels and consonants, and we will look at what this means on the next page.

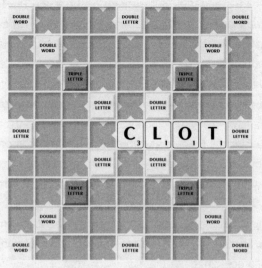

The right balance: your rack is **F I L N O U W**

An example

Let's say your opponent has started the game with **CLOT**, and your rack is as shown. Your first thought might be to play **FLOWN** through the **O**. That would get the high-scoring **F** on a Triple Letter square and net you an acceptable 21. But look what you've left yourself with on your rack: **I O U**. You may well pick at least two vowels among your four replacement tiles, leaving you with a vowel-heavy rack and little hope of a decent score next time.

You could still play **FLOWN**, but using the **L** on the board rather than the **O**. That only gets you 16 points, but leaves you with a more acceptable **I L U**. Still a bit too vowelly – ideally, if playing four tiles, you want to leave yourself two consonants and a vowel.

> *Scrabble tip* – *For good rack management the golden rule is that, where possible, you should leave yourself with either the same number of vowels as consonants, or one or two more consonants than vowels.*

FLOUT, using the **T**, would give you the desired two-consonants, one-vowel outcome, and also scores 16. The main disadvantage of **FLOUT** is that **O** next to the Triple Letter square; although you have to play your own game and not worry too much about what your opponent might have. On this occasion the pesky blighter only needs a **Z** and an **O** up his or her sleeve to score 65 points, leaving you with a disheartening deficit at this stage of proceedings.

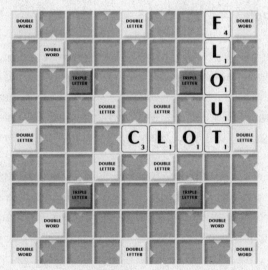

FLOUT scores 16,
but leaves a Triple Letter square next to the **O**.

Remembering that you should also be trying for **parallel** rather than **crosswise** plays, you might try **FOWL**. Not bad, scoring 18 points, though you are left with two vowels and one consonant. Pity about the **L** on the Double Letter square, rather than a higher-scoring letter. Hang on – how about **WOLF** in the same position? Now you score 21, the same as for **FLOWN**, and a more acceptable leave of **I N U**. (Scrabble players refer to the letters left on their rack after a move as the '*leave*'.)

Playing **FOWL** in parallel is another option – and **WOLF** performs even better.

As so often in Scrabble, there is no clear-cut answer. **WOLF** and **FLOUT** both have something to recommend them, and personally I would go for **WOLF**. But they're both a big improvement on **FLOWN**, because of the better leave – we have given ourselves a better chance of a balanced rack for our next move.

Rack management: keep letters that go together

It's not just a case of keeping **A E I** and **N R S T** and maintaining a good vowel–consonant balance. Often you'll have to keep some other letters as well – you may not have many of **A E I N R S T**, so you have to decide what else to offload. Again, much will depend on what good scores are available – never lose sight of the fact that that is the object of the exercise. But it will often be worth accepting a less than optimal score to give yourself that all-important optimal leave. If you have a rack **C D G K W** and two vowels, you don't want to leave yourself with incompatible letters like **G K W**, which are unlikely to combine together in a profitable way next time. Far better to play **G W**, probably along with a vowel, and leave yourself with **C D K**, a much happier combination, especially if you draw (or already have) an **E** to go with them.

Some Scrabble players refer to combinations like **C D K** as having better synergy than ones like **G K W**, although others just say that the letters go together, which is every bit as good.

Strategy and rack management

One of the most difficult things in Scrabble is when you know you're close to a seven-letter bonus but you haven't quite got one (or can't quite find it if you have). You are loath to play more than one or two of your tiles, because you don't want to break up a promising combination, such as **–ERING** or **–NIEST**. But that means you are scoring only a handful of points, while your opponent may be forging ahead with 20s and 30s. After three attempts, you may finally get your bonus for, say, 65 points, only to find that while you were scoring six or eight at a time, your opponent notched up 75 points altogether and you are no better off.

So what are we saying here? Do you or don't you hang onto a **A E I N R S T** combination like **A E N T**, or a suffix like **–ISH**? Do you just check to see if they can help you make a seven-letter word if you have them on your rack at the time, but if they don't, just play what you can for a decent score? Or do you hoard them, in the hope that next shot you will be able to put down that satisfying, opponent-demoralizing bonus?

There is no easy answer. Among the things to take into account are:

1   *The score*
    If you are appreciably behind, you may have no alternative but to go for a bonus.
    If you're ahead, try to keep your score moving along and don't worry so much about bonus-hunting.
2   *The state of the board*
    Are there places to play a bonus word if you do get one?
3   *Are there bonus letters left to come?*
    There is little point in trying for a bonus if the unseen letters are mainly **O**s, **U**s and higher-scoring consonants.

Remember that the extra 50 points from a bonus gives you such a powerful propulsion of points that it is worth devoting a lot of time to learning how to get them. If your rack is even starting to look as if it might make a bonus, and the board has openings or spaces where you can create openings, then it has to be worth considering.

Prefixes and suffixes

You should now be aware of the need to hold on to a reasonable balance of vowels and consonants and to keep the letters **N R S T** and **A E I** (think of the word **RETAINS**), as long as you are scoring reasonably in the meantime. When you keep other letters, you are trying to make sure they are compatible with each other. But the seven-letter words are unlikely to just turn up on your rack with all the letters in the right order. You still have to sort the letters out.

So how do you find the seven-letter word that may be sitting on your rack and earn those 50 lovely bonus points? The first things to check for are **prefixes** and **suffixes**.

Suffixes

Remember that some of these suffixes can do a double duty. **–ER** can form an *agent noun* (**BUILDER** from **BUILD**) or a *comparative adjective* (**SHORTER** from **SHORT**). **–ISH** can go after an adjective or noun to mean 'somewhat' or 'somewhat like' (**WARMISH**, **HAWKISH**). If you have an **F**, you could also try and catch one of the many available **FISH** which may be swimming around, such as **CATFISH**, **DOGFISH** or the rather unimaginatively named **FINFISH**.

Scrabble tip – *Here are some suffixes that will help you form seven-letter words:*

–ING	**–ED**	**–ISH**	**–IST**
–ISE *(or* **–IZE** *if you're holding the* **Z***)*			
–ER *and* **–EST** *(especially* **–IER** *and* **–IEST***)*			
–ABLE	**–AGE**	**–ATE**	**–ANT**
–ENT	**–MAN**	**–MEN**	**–LESS**
–NESS	**–LIKE**	**–TION**	**–LY**

Be careful about –ING

A quick word of warning about –**ING**. It's very tempting to hang onto these letters if you get them, come what may, in the expectation that they are bound to combine with almost any other four letters to form a seven-letter word. Well, sometimes they will and sometimes they won't, but it doesn't happen as often as you might think. In the meantime you are effectively trying to play with only your other four letters, drastically minimizing your potential score. And if and when you do get an –**ING** word, the double-consonant –**NG** can make it difficult to fit into a parallel play, so you may well not be able to get it down on the board.

Prefixes

The kings of the prefix world are **RE**– and **UN**–. A quick glance through the **RE**– and **UN**– sections of *Collins Scrabble Lists* might suggest that you can put either of these two pairs of letters before almost any word. You will quickly be disabused of this notion if you start trying to do so during a game. There are many, many words, some of which look perfectly reasonable, that cannot be formed in this way.

> *Scrabble tip* – *Not all* **RE**– *words are valid, even if you think they look right. You CANNOT play:*
>
> **RECLAMP**   **RECOACH**   **RESLUMP**   **RESTAND**
> **RETRICK**
> *any of which look as feasible as some words which are valid, such as:*
> **REVICTUAL**   **RESPLICE**
> **REEDIFY** *(hyphen not compulsory).*

Remember, Scrabble players didn't write *Collins Scrabble Lists*, lexicographers did. They will be able to cite examples of usage for all the words in their dictionary, and have excluded those for which they could find no examples. Fine, but it doesn't help you much when you're trying to work out whether to risk **REHAPPEN** or **UNSEXY** (the latter is valid, the former not).

> *Scrabble tip* – *Not all* **UN**– *words are valid either.*
> *The* Collins Scrabble Lists *does NOT allow:*
> **UNLIGHT   UNDARK   UNRUNG   UNHAIRY   UNSAD**
> *but does approve of:*
> **UNBRIGHT   UNHEARSE   UNHONEST   UNMELLOW**

So **UN**– and **RE**– are useful to remember, and well worth putting to one side of your rack to see whether they'll help you towards a bonus, but the frequency with which they can be used makes it all the more heartbreaking when they let you down when you need them most. There are lots of other common prefixes which can ease your path towards that elusive seven-letter word.

> *Scrabble tip* – *Watch out for these prefixes to help you towards a bonus word:*
> **PRE–   PRO–   ANTI–   DIS–   MIS–   OUT–   OVER–**
> **DE–   EN–   IN–   CON–   SUB–   UP–**

Using S

Apart from prefixes and suffixes, how else can we discover seven-letter words on our rack? We have covered the obvious one of words ending in **S** in Chapter 5. If you have an **S**, always pop it to the end of your rack, and see if your other six letters can make a six-letter word that your **S** might go on the end of to make a seven.

Compound words

Something else to watch for is **compound words**. This can often pay dividends even if you have higher-scoring letters on your rack. Does your rack divide into a three-letter word and a four-letter word? If so, they just might combine to form a seven. There are lots of examples:

> **PAYBACK**   **AIRLINE**   **MANHUNT**   **FOOTPAD**   **SEAFOOD**
> **REDCOAT**   **SUNTRAP**   **WARSHIP**   **HATBAND**   **KEYHOLE**

This technique may lead you to an eight-letter word (using a letter on the board) giving you to a 4–4, 3–5 or 5–3 compound word:

> **AIRTIGHT**   **WORMWOOD**   **BLUEBIRD**   **PAYCHECK**
> **CAUSEWAY**

Always look at your letters in as many different ways as you can. A word with a **Q** doesn't have to begin with a **Q**. Words can begin with vowels, or end with vowels other than **E**.

> *Scrabble tip* – *Some three-and four-letter words are particularly good for creating compound words, such as:*
>
> **AIR   FISH   MAN   MEN   SEA   SHIP   WARD   WOOD WORK**
>
> *and some colours such as* **RED** *and* **BLUE**.

A bonus-word challenge

Try and unravel these 20 teasers using the words shown below:

Five take unexpected letters before them to form other words.
Five take unexpected letters after them.
Five end with **A**, **I**, **O** *or* **U**.
And five have a **J**, **Q**, **X** *or* **Z**, *but where it comes in the word is up to you to discover.*

SIPRAIN	RAJTHING	CANTHEN	AIMSTRAP
QUARPET	THRIVEON	FLYWAUL	SHEISVAL
FILMNAG	IPLOTSEX	AIHOOTS	DRAWPLOY
AACEHUT	RUEPHONE	ZELEGAL	PLUMTILE
IMAPLOD	HATEDEER	ILOVAIR	ZREFEREE

Some will be compound words or will use prefixes or suffixes. The answers are given at the back of the book.

When you've got them, work out which 10 have the unexpected 'hooks' – and see if you can find them. For example, if the answer was **BRIDGES**, the hook would be **ABRIDGES**. For a hook at the end, **ELEVATOR** would become **ELEVATORY** (as well as the obvious **ELEVATORS**).

How to look for bonus words

The only other advice I can give in spotting bonus words is simply to look for them. Obvious, I know – but it's easy to get into the habit of playing that reasonable move for 20 points or so, or that word which will leave you a perfectly balanced and compatible rack, while all the time the seven-letter word is hiding in there somewhere. The more you play, the more you will develop a feel for whether a rack is likely to contain a bonus.

Have a look at these racks:

ACDEHIR	**ABINOPT**	**AELMNSV**
EEFGLOR	**AEINOST**	

First, without trying to work out what the seven-letter words might be, decide which combinations are likely to make a seven-letter word. Then, try and figure out the words. Let's look at them one at a time:

ACDEHIR

- The **C** and **H** might go together.
- And there's an **RE/ER**, in fact an **IER**, with other possibilities like **ED** and **IC**. **CHADIER**, **DACHIER** – nothing there.
- **CHAIDER**, **REDAICH** – the **RE** and **ER** don't appear to be much help.
- Maybe **IC** at the end – **HERADIC**? No, but a usable **L** on the board would give **HERALDIC**.
- A compound, perhaps – **ICEHARD**, **HARDICE**? **ICEHARD** sounds feasibly poetic but I haven't actually seen it anywhere, so it's a big risk.
- Finally, with the simple expedient of trying **ED** at the end to see if there might be a nice, simple past tense, and keeping our compatible **CH** together, we find the answer – **CHAIRED**.

A B I N O P T

- There is a **TION** in there but the only way the other three letters might go with them is **BAPTION** – not a word.
- No compounds suggest themselves.
- Nothing ending with **ANT**.
- The **ANTI** prefix likewise leads nowhere, unless someone who doesn't like dancing could be **ANTIBOP** – which is getting into the realms of fantasy.
- **BIOPTAN** sounds vaguely scientific but that doesn't make it a word.
- Finally, we correctly conclude that there is no seven-letter word here.

A E L M N S V

- Like **A B I N O P T**, it has five one-point tiles.
- It has an **S**, and both **MAN** and **MEN**.
- Any six-letter words from **A E L M N V** that the **S** might go after? **MALVEN**, **VELMAN**, **MENVAL** – all rubbish.
- **ELSV** doesn't combine with **MAN**, nor **ALSV** with **MEN**.
- The **A E L M N S** make a nice start and would go with various other letters to form a seven, but the **V** fouls things up – once again, regretfully, no seven-letter word.

E E F G L O R

- Not too promising on the face of it.
- **E F G L O** doesn't match up with **RE** or **ER** – **GEFOLER**, **REFLOGE**? Not a chance.
- **GOLFER** is in there but we have an **E** left over – still, it could be worth playing if we can get it on at least a Double Word for 20 or so.
- Any compounds? **EELFROG**? **LOGFREE**? **FOREGEL**? Hang on – **FORELEG**. The 4–3 split, using the fairly common **FORE** prefix, brings us to the seven-letter word.

- We got there mainly by technique, but with just that last little mental jump to finish the job.

A E I N O S T

- Now this looks good. Six of our **RETAINS** letters, and the seventh is a fairly acceptable **O**.
- A slight excess of vowels, but we have an S and there are prefixes and suffixes galore: **–(I)EST**, **–ATE**, **–ISE**, **–TION**, **–SION**, **IN–**, **EN–**, **ANTI–**.
- So what's the word? Well, there is one, but you could probably shuffle your tiles for ever and you wouldn't find it. It's **ATONIES**, the plural of **ATONY**, which means lack of muscle tone. It's an awkward, obscure word which not one person in a hundred will come across outside the confines of a Scrabble board. But **ATONY** is in *Collins Scrabble Lists*, and since the rule used in compiling *Collins Scrabble Lists* is that all nouns have a plural, that means **ATONIES** gets in as well.

Learning bonus words

And that brings us on to one more method of getting bonuses. It might not sound much fun, it might not be your idea of the spirit of a game, but there are many words which will keep coming up on your rack because they are composed of the common letters, and you just have to learn them. Sometimes games do require a bit of work. Ask a chess player who's memorized 50 standard openings up to the 20th move. Ask a footballer who's just completed a punishing two-hour training session in a downpour.

So the next two chapters will cut through the tips, techniques and strategies, and quite simply give you a whole batch of seven- and eight-letter words which, if you can learn them, will help you play bonus after bonus and really get your game moving up through the gears. You won't learn them all today, or tomorrow, but make a start, and come back to them as often as you can and learn a few more. You learnt the twos (or I hope you did) and some of the threes. You may well find sevens and eights easier because the words have a more familiar structure and may just seem less unlikely. It's a bit of a blow to the ego to be told there are so many two- and three-letter words you don't know, but it's easier to accept the existence of these longer words which you have never come across.

The words are divided into logical groups, and the lists are not exhaustive; many others could have been included, but at this stage you would be wise to concentrate on a manageable number. When a combination of seven or eight letters makes more than one word, these are sometimes shown, but not always. Even when more than one word is shown, there may be others with the same letters. But what is there is plenty to be getting on with. So make yourself a nice cup of tea, get your brain in gear, and start the next chapter.

8 Some seven-letter lists

Seven-letter words not only get you bonus scores, but they also help open up the board. You know now that, where possible and where it doesn't prevent you from getting a worthwhile score, you keep the letters **N R S T** and **A E I** to help you towards getting a bonus word.

The letters **A E I N R S T** make several seven-letter words:

RETAINS	**RETINAS**	**NASTIER**
STAINER	**RETSINA**	**STEARIN**

There are more, but they are rather obscure, and that selection should be enough to enable you to play a bonus on all but the most blocked of boards. The good news is that if you've got any six of the **R E T A I N S** letters and one other, you've probably got a bonus already.

'6 + 1' lists

These lists give all the seven-letter words that can be formed by adding one letter to a particular combination of six letters. Club players will learn these '6 + 1' lists so that once they have six of the seven letters, they can mentally flick through the appropriate list and come up with the bonus word. It's well worthwhile getting to grips with these lists, so they have been set out here for you.

> *Scrabble facts* – *Statistically, the seven-letter word you are most likely to pick out of a standard bag of tiles is* **OTARINE**, *the adjective from* **OTARY**. *An otary is any member of the seal family with ears.*

Often a combination will make more than one word, but I haven't included every anagram, and a couple of less likely combinations have been excluded. But there are plenty of words for you to get to grips with, and familiarising yourself with them will dramatically increase the number of bonuses you play. The lists start with **A E I N R S +** and shows the words that can be made by adding particular letters. Other examples follow on.

A E I N R S +

C	ARSENIC	CERASIN	
D	SANDIER	SARDINE	
F	INFARES	SERAFIN	
G	SEARING	REGAINS	
H	HERNIAS	ARSHINE	
I	SENARII		
J	INJERAS		
K	SNAKIER		
L	NAILERS	RENAILS	
M	REMAINS	SEMINAR	
N	INSANER	INSNARE	
O	ERASION		
P	PANIERS	RAPINES	
R	SIERRAN	SNARIER	
S	SARNIES	ARSINES	
T	RETAINS	RETINAS	NASTIER
	STAINER	RETSINA	STEARIN
V	RAVINES	AVENIRS	

B	ATEBRIN		
C	CERTAIN	NACRITE	
D	TRAINED	DETRAIN	
E	RETINAE	TRAINEE	
F	FAINTER	FENITAR	
G	TEARING	GRANITE	
H	HAIRNET	INEARTH	
I	INERTIA		
J	NARTJIE	JANTIER	
K	KERATIN		
L	LATRINE	RELIANT	
M	MINARET	RAIMENT	
N	ENTRAIN	TRANNIE	
O	OTARINE		
P	PAINTER	REPAINT	
R	TRAINER	RETRAIN	
S	RETAINS	RETINAS	NASTIER
	STAINER	RETSINA	STEARIN
T	NATTIER	NITRATE	
U	URINATE	TAURINE	
W	TAWNIER	TINWARE	

A	ENTASIA	TAENIAS	
B	BESAINT	BASINET	
C	CANIEST	CINEAST	
D	STAINED	INSTEAD	
E	ETESIAN		
F	FAINEST	NAIFEST	
G	TEASING	INGATES	
H	SHEITAN	STHENIA	
I	ISATINE		
J	JANTIES	TAJINES	
K	INTAKES	TANKIES	
L	ENTAILS	SALIENT	
M	INMATES	MAINEST	
N	INANEST	STANINE	
O	ATONIES		
P	SAPIENT	PANTIES	
R	RETAINS	RETINAS	NASTIER
	STAINER	RETSINA	STEARIN
S	NASTIES	SESTINA	
T	INSTATE	SATINET	
U	AUNTIES	SINUATE	
V	VAINEST	NATIVES	
W	TAWNIES	AWNIEST	
X	ANTISEX	SEXTAIN	
Z	ZANIEST	ZEATINS	

A	ASTERIA	ATRESIA	
B	BAITERS	REBAITS	
C	RACIEST	STEARIC	
D	TIRADES	ASTRIDE	
E	AERIEST	SERIATE	
F	FAIREST		
G	GAITERS	STAGIER	
H	HASTIER	SHERIAT	
I	AIRIEST	IRISATE	
K	ARKITES	KARITES	
L	RETAILS	REALIST	
M	MISRATE	SMARTIE	
N	RETAINS	RETINAS	NASTIER
	STAINER	RETSINA	STEARIN
O	OARIEST	OTARIES	
P	PARTIES	PIRATES	
R	TARRIES	ARTSIER	
S	SATIRES	TIRASSE	
T	ARTISTE	TASTIER	
V	VASTIER	TAIVERS	
W	WAITERS	WARIEST	

A	ANESTRA		
B	BANTERS		
C	CANTERS	TRANCES	
D	STANDER	ENDARTS	
E	EASTERN	NEAREST	
G	STRANGE	GARNETS	
H	ANTHERS	THENARS	
I	RETAINS	RETINAS	NASTIER
	STAINER	RETSINA	STEARIN
K	TANKERS	RANKEST	
L	RENTALS	ANTLERS	
M	SMARTEN	MARTENS	
N	TANNERS		
O	SENATOR	TREASON	
P	PARENTS	ENTRAPS	
R	ERRANTS	RANTERS	
S	SARSNET	TRANSES	
T	NATTERS	RATTENS	
U	NATURES	SAUNTER	
V	SERVANT	TAVERNS	
W	WANTERS	STRAWEN	
Y	TRAYNES		

A I N R S T +

A	ARTISAN	TSARINA	
B	BRISANT		
C	NARCIST		
D	INDARTS		
E	RETAINS	RETINAS	NASTIER
	STAINER	RETSINA	STEARIN
G	RATINGS	STARING	
H	TARNISH		
L	RATLINS		
M	MARTINS		
N	RATIONS	AROINTS	
P	SPIRANT	SPRAINT	
Q	QINTARS		
S	STRAINS	INSTARS	
T	TRANSIT	STRAINT	
U	NUTRIAS		

A	RETAINS	RETINAS	NASTIER
	STAINER	RETSINA	STEARIN
C	CISTERN	CRETINS	
D	TINDERS		
E	ENTRIES	TRENISE	
F	SNIFTER		
G	RESTING	STINGER	
H	HINTERS		
K	STINKER	TINKERS	
L	LINTERS	SNIRTLE	
M	MINSTER	ENTRISM	
N	INTERNS	TINNERS	
O	STONIER	ORIENTS	
P	NIPTERS	PTERINS	
S	INSERTS	SINTERS	
T	TINTERS	ENTRIST	
U	UNITERS	NUTSIER	
V	INVERTS	STRIVEN	
W	WINTERS	TWINERS	
Y	SINTERY		

You may have noticed that **A I N R S T** is by far the shortest of these lists, handicapped as it is by the lack of an **E**. The **A E I N R T** list is not nearly so held back by the absence of an **S**. **A I N R S T** does, however, have the saving grace of being the only one to combine with a **Q**.

Players who are used to dealing with these lists tend to refer to them as the **RETAIN** list, the **SARNIE** list, the **SANTER** list and so on. Note that **SANTER** isn't actually a word, it's just a convenient way of referring to the list. 'The **ASTERN** list' doesn't seem to have caught on, for some reason.

There are other lists which are just as good. **RAINED** and **TORIES** are both excellent six-letter combinations for forming sevens, as you can see below.

R A I N E D +

A	ARANEID	
B	BRAINED	BANDIER
C	CAIRNED	DANCIER
D	DRAINED	DANDIER
F	FRIANDE	
G	READING	GRAINED
H	HANDIER	
I	DENARII	
M	ADERMIN	INARMED
N	NARDINE	
O	ANEROID	
P	PARDINE	
R	DRAINER	RANDIER
S	SARDINE	SANDIER
T	TRAINED	DETRAIN
U	UNAIRED	URANIDE
V	INVADER	RAVINED

TORIES +

A	OARIEST	OTARIES
B	ORBIEST	SORBITE
C	EROTICS	TERCIOS
D	EDITORS	STEROID
E	EROTISE	
F	FORTIES	FOISTER
G	GOITRES	GORIEST
H	HOISTER	SHORTIE
I	RIOTISE	
K	ROKIEST	
L	LOITERS	TOILERS
M	MOISTER	EROTISM
N	STONIER	ORIENTS
O	SOOTIER	OORIEST
P	RIPOSTE	ROPIEST
R	ROISTER	RIOTERS
S	STORIES	ROSIEST
T	STOITER	
U	TOUSIER	OURIEST
V	TORSIVE	
W	OWRIEST	TOWSIER

There are lots of these '6 + 1' lists that are worth knowing, and, once you are familiar with a few, some of the seven-letter words will be known to you already from previous lists. For instance, **R A I N E D** + **D** is the same as **R E T A I N** + **D** (**TRAINED**, **DETRAIN** and the more unusual **ANTIRED**), while **T O R I E S** + **N** equals **I N T E R S** + **O** (**STONIER**, **ORIENTS** and a couple of others).

> *Scrabble facts* – *Among the least likely sevens to show up on your rack, most of which need one or even both blanks, are* **PIZAZZY** *(full of pizazz),* **MUUMUUS** *(loose dress worn in Hawaii),* **JAZZMAN** *and* **ZYZZYVA** *(American weevil).*

Lists by prefixes and suffixes

Another way of listing words is by going back to those prefixes and suffixes. It's useful to learn some of the more likely sevens that could come up with each of them.

Selection of seven-letter words listed by prefix

ANTI:	**ANTIFLU, ANTIFOG, ANTILOG, ANTIPOT, ANTISAG**
CON:	**CONFEST, CONGREE, CONGRUE, CONSEIL, CONURES**
DE:	**DEALATE, DEBRIDE, DEGAMES, DEMEANE, DEPAINT**
EN:	**ENARMED, ENFLAME, ENLIGHT, ENRANKS, ENTAYLE**
IN:	**INDENES, INFAUST, INHUMER, INQUERE, INTURNS**
MIS:	**MISDRAW, MISEDIT, MISKEEP, MISMATE, MISPART**
OUT:	**OUTDARE, OUTEARN, OUTLAND, OUTPORT, OUTWEAR**
OVER:	**OVERAGE, OVERDOG, OVERHOT, OVERMEN, OVERWET**
PRE:	**PREAGED, PRECOOL, PRENAME, PREORAL, PRERACE**
PRO:	**PROETTE, PROLANS, PROLINE, PRONAOS, PROOTIC**
SUB:	**SUBAREA, SUBDEAN, SUBHEAD, SUBLINE, SUBRENT**
UP:	**UPCOILS, UPDRIED, UPLEAPT, UPSTARE, UPTRAIN**

There are too many **RE**– and **UN**– words to give just five examples, so we have listed almost an alphabet of words for each one.

Seven-letter words starting with **RE–**

REARISE	**REINTER**	**REQUITE**
REBREED	**REJONES**	**RERAILS**
RECHEAT	**REKEYED**	**RESPELL**
REDREAM	**RELABEL**	**RETUNDS**
REENDOW	**REMERGE**	**REUNIFY**
REFLAGS	**RENESTS**	**REVOTES**
REGRATE	**REOILED**	**REWAKEN**
REHEARS	**REPURES**	**REZONES**

Seven-letter words starting with **UN–**

UNALIVE	**UNJADED**	**UNROOTS**
UNBARES	**UNKINGS**	**UNSOBER**
UNCAPED	**UNLEADS**	**UNTENTY**
UNDEALT	**UNMITRE**	**UNURGED**
UNEAGER	**UNNOBLE**	**UNVISOR**
UNFAIRS	**UNOFTEN**	**UNWATER**
UNGIRDS	**UNPAINT**	**UNYOKES**
UNHEALS	**UNQUIET**	**UNZONED**
UNIDEAL		

Some of the **UN**– words in particular are fairly unexpected; it's a bit hard to see how you can **UNWATER** or **UNPAINT** something, and isn't the opposite of **NOBLE IGNOBLE**? It might seem from looking at these lists that you can put **UN** at the front of almost anything, and maybe **RE** as well. You can't. It's a hard lesson that all Scrabble players learn sooner or later.

But back to our lists, and where there are prefixes, can suffixes be far behind? Here are some words from those useful suffixes which we looked at previously.

Selection of seven-letter words listed by suffix

ABLE:	**CITABLE, FRIABLE, HIDABLE, SEEABLE, TUNABLE**
AGE:	**CORDAGE, LISTAGE, PEONAGE, PIERAGE, SPINAGE**
ANT:	**FLOTANT, ITERANT, PERSANT, REPTANT, SEALANT**
ATE:	**CITRATE, DEALATE, EPILATE, PELTATE, SERIATE**
ENT:	**CONCENT, EXIGENT, FULGENT, MORDENT,**
	PENDENT
IER:	**BALDIER, HERBIER, LINTIER, RUNTIER, SEDGIER**
IEST:	**AWNIEST, BABIEST, LINIEST, MINIEST, RICIEST**
ISE/IZE:	**ADONISE/IZE, EROTISE/IZE, IRONISE/IZE,**
	POETISE/IZE, RIOTISE/IZE
ISH:	**ALUMISH, DEAFISH, FLEMISH, MAIDISH, PIGFISH**
IST:	**ABLEIST, DADAIST, ELOGIST, LEFTIST, TUBAIST**
LESS:	**BITLESS, EGOLESS, HATLESS, NAPLESS, TIPLESS**
LIKE:	**BEELIKE, FATLIKE, NETLIKE, RATLIKE, TINLIKE**
LY:	**DATEDLY, GAUNTLY, OBESELY, STAIDLY, USEABLY**
MAN/	**BEDEMAN/MEN, GUDEMAN/MEN, LINEMAN/MEN,**
MEN:	**ODDSMAN/MEN, TOPSMAN/MEN**
NESS:	**ALLNESS, FARNESS, HOTNESS, OUTNESS, SHINESS**
TION:	**ELUTION, ENATION, LECTION, PACTION, RECTION**

It's worth repeating what was said in the last chapter that the four-letter prefixes and suffixes (or affixes, as they're collectively known) often don't make quite as many sevens as you might think. **TION**, for example, is not great for ending seven-letter words. You really need to have scope on the board to make an eight-letter word to get the best out of these slightly longer affixes.

There are too many –**ING** and –**ED** words to make it worth picking out five examples of each, so here are a few –**ING** sevens that can take **S**.

BOLTING(S) HALTING(S) SEALING(S)

COOKING(S) HOSTING(S) SEELING(S)

DANCING(S) KEEPING(S) SHARING(S)

FOILING(S) LIMPING(S) STEWING(S)

GASPING(S) NESTING(S) TILTING(S)

GETTING(S) PIECING(S) WANTING(S)

GREYING(S) RUSTING(S)

'High probability' seven-letter words

There are a lot of 'high probability' seven-letter words, so-called because they are composed mainly of common letters and are therefore more likely to come up on your rack. However, they don't fit easily into any of our categories such as containing six of the **R E T A I N S** letters, or being formed from a prefix or suffix. Here are some sevens, only a few of which you are likely to be familiar with, but which are well worth knowing, and which we haven't managed to shoehorn into previous lists (or in one or two cases we have, but this list has some anagrams of them). We'll start with some with four or more vowels, since it's nice to have a few at your fingertips for when you have more vowels than would otherwise be ideal.

Seven-letter words with five vowels

AEOLIAN ETAERIO OLEARIA TAENIAE

Seven-letter words with four vowels (with anagrams grouped together)

ADONISE/ANODISE/SODAINE   AEDILES/DEISEAL
AILERON/ALERION/ALIENOR   AIRDATE/TIARAED
AIRLINE   ALIENER   ALUNITE
AMNIOTE   ANEROID   ANISOLE
ANTLIAE   ARANEID   ARENOSE
ARENOUS   ATELIER/REALTIE
AUDIENT   AUDILES/DEASIUL
DARIOLE   DEASOIL/ISOLEAD
ELATION/TOENAIL   ELOINER
EMAILED/LIMEADE   EROTICA
GOATIER   GODETIA   INEDITA
IODATES/TOADIES   ISOLATE
LEIPOAS   LINEATE   MORAINE/
                           ROMAINE
NIOBATE   OCEANID   ORDINEE
ORIGANE   RADIATE   RAINOUT
REGINAE   ROADIES/SOREDIA
ROSEATE   TROELIE   URALITE

Seven-letter words with four or five consonants (with anagrams grouped together)

AGRISED   AIDLESS/DEASILS
ALBERTS/BLASTER/STABLER
ALBITES/BLASTIE/LIBATES
AMORETS   ANGELIC/ANGLICE
ANGERED/DERANGE/ENRAGED/GRANDEE/GRENADE
ASTHORE/EARSHOT/HAROSET
ATINGLE/ELATING/GELATIN/GENITAL

BALDIES/DISABLE DRANGLE BRANTLE
CANTLES/LANCETS CARMINE
CENTERS/CENTRES/TENRECS CIGARET
CONSTER/CORNETS/CRESTON
COPIERS/PERSICO
DESMINE DOLINES/INDOLES/SONDELI
DISCOER DONSIER/INDORSE/ROSINED
DUNITES ESPARTO/PROTEAS/SEAPORT
ETALONS GALORES/GAOLERS
GENITOR GRECIAN HISTONE
HOGTIES
ISLEMAN/MALINES/MENIALS/SEMINAL
KINGLES KINGLET LESBIAN
LINOCUT LINSEED
LISENTE/SETLINE/TENSILE
MAILERS/REALISM/REMAILS
MANTOES MILTERS
MINERAL/RAILMEN
NAGARIS/SANGRIA/SARANGI
NAMASTE NEUTRAL NUTMEAL
OGREISH ONSTAGE ORGANIC
ORGEATS/STORAGE/TOERAGS
PALSIER/PARLIES PAROLES/REPOSAL
PERIOST/REPOSIT/RIPOSTE/ROPIEST
PERSONA PIOLETS/PISTOLE
SAPROBE SEARATS SOLERAS
STEDING/STINGED SYRINGE TELAMON
TENOURS/TONSURE
TEOPANS TERTIAL TONEARM

Notice how these lists are a mixture of the familiar, like **NEUTRAL**, the semi-familiar that you might not think of, like **NUTMEAL** and **PERSONA**, and the (almost certainly) unfamiliar, like **BRANSLE** and **BRANTLE** (variant spellings of an old French dance) and **SAPROBE** (an organism that lives in foul water). That's what makes these lists less alarming than they at first appear – you always have a head start with the words you know already.

You know what words can be made from **E E D I L N S** and **E G I N R S Y**; it's just a case of getting into your mind that when they appear on your rack you will change them into **LINSEED** and **SYRINGE**. In the same way, you will start to recognise the likes of **A C E I M N R** and **E H I N O S T**. Looking at the letters just sets off that little light-bulb in your head, and, with a bit of practice, it comes to you – **CARMINE** and **HISTONE**.

A FEW TEASERS

Try to find the seven-letter words from these combinations. They have
been graded according to how easy or difficult you are likely to find them:

1 *Almost-RETAINS words:*

11-Plus:	**AEIMNRS**	**EINRSTW**
GCSE Level:	**AEGNRST**	**AENRSTV**
A Level:	**AEIMNRT**	**AINRSTT**
Degree:	**AEHINRT**	**EILNRST**
Doctorate:	**ABEINRT**	**AEHINST**

2 *Words with affixes:*

Dopy:	**ABEEELS**	**ADILSTY**
Dozy:	**AEIKLRT**	**EINQTUU**
Doughty:	**ABDENSU**	**DEEEKRY**
Deadly:	**ANOOPRS**	**EGILOST**

3 *Other useful words:*

Clown's car:	**ADEEGNR**	**AEILNOT**
Family car:	**ACGINOR**	**ADEEILM**
Sports car:	**ACEGIRT**	**ADEINOR**
Racing car:	**AEIMNOT**	**CILNOTU**

Answers are given at the back of the book.

9 Some eight-letter lists

You might not always be able to play a seven-letter word. In this chapter we look at some tips and lists to help you on your way to playing eight-letter words.

Unblocking a game

Every Scrabble game develops in a slightly different way. Sometimes there are lots of short words played parallel to each other, so the board ends up in an angry little knot of tiles clustered round the centre. If the words on the outside of this knot are 'blockers' (words which don't take any hooks either at the front or the end), it can get to a stage where it's very difficult to add anything at all.

A blocked opening to a game.

There isn't likely to be a bonus played with the next move on this first board. It's not impossible – there are eight-letter words ending in **U**, such as **HAUSFRAU**, **THANKYOU** and the rather unlikely **SUCURUJU**, or you might even come up with a nine-letter word using two on the board, like **CHLAMYDIA**, but, realistically, this won't happen.

A slight change to the opening makes all the difference.

On the second board (above), a seven-letter word can easily be played, using hooks such as **ITS**, **ITA**, **ABA**, **OBA**, **LAMA** or any two-letter word ending in **A**.

On the third board (on the next page), it looks like a bonus has been played already. It may not – the opening move might have been **QUAKE** or various other words (**WONDER**, **AKE**, **DE**, though none of these seems very likely to have produced the board as shown). Bonuses are certainly playable onto this board, but probably not a seven-letter word. You will have to use one of the free letters on the board (a '*floater*', in Scrabble jargon) to make an eight-letter word.

A board with a completely different kind of beginning.

Using floaters to make eight-letter words

There are plenty to choose from: **W**, **O**, **N**, **S**, **U**, **A** and, if you're feeling very clever, **Q**, are all in the middle of the board, and if you can combine any of them with the seven on your rack, you will be able to play a bonus. The **D** and the **R** are also possible to use, although they are restricted, and the **K** is just about possible, but hemmed in by other letters.

If you want to maximize the number of bonuses you play, you really need to be at home with eights as well as sevens. This chapter will put an army of high-probability eight-letter words at your disposal, all ready for you to slam down on the board for those longed-for 50 bonus points.

Learning about eight-letter words

Where to start? On the basis that you are still keeping those **RETAINS** letters from the last chapter, you could start with some eights containing those letters – the **RETAINS** + 1 list. Of course, a lot of them will be sevens from the **RETAIN** list with an **S** on the end: **DETRAINS**, **HAIRNETS**,

MINARETS, **TRANNIES** and many more. There seems little point in listing them – go back to the **RETAIN** list in the previous chapter and try to work them out for yourself.

However, there are a few more which aren't quite so simple. Here are a few **RETAINS** + 1 eights you might not know, or might not think of so easily.

A selection of **RETAINS** *+ 1 words*

A	ANTISERA	ARTESIAN	RATANIES	RESINATA	SEATRAIN
B	BANISTER	BARNIEST			
C	CANISTER	CARNIEST	CISTERNA	SCANTIER	
D	RANDIEST	STRAINED			
E	ARSENITE	RESINATE	STEARINE		
G	ASTRINGE	GANISTER	GANTRIES	RANGIEST	STEARING
I	RAINIEST				
K	NARKIEST				
O	ANOESTRI	ARSONITE	NOTARIES	ROSINATE	SENORITA
P	PANTRIES	PINASTER	PRISTANE		
R	RESTRAIN	STRAINER	TRANSIRE		
S	ARTINESS	SNARIEST			
T	STRAITEN				

Of course, you don't need to have **RETAINS** on your rack to play these; if you have six of **RETAINS**, and the seventh is 'floating' on the board, you effectively have the same thing and may well be able to play a **RETAINS** + 1 word.

Using floating letters to make an eight

It's also handy to know eights you can make from sets of seven common letters plus one other, when the seven letters don't make a bonus word. Few racks are more annoying than the ones with good letters you don't want to break up, but which don't make a bonus yet. With a rack like **A A E I N R T** (**RETAIN** + **A**), getting a good score can be difficult even playing five or six tiles. Just to play the **A** will probably get you a single-figure score, and while you might get the bonus next time, you might just pick the **Q** or the **X**, or another **A**.

But using a floating letter on the board you can solve the problem by conjuring up an eight. Here are some examples.

R E T A I N A +

B	**RABATINE**	
C	**CARINATE**	**CRANIATE**
D	**DENTARIA**	**RAINDATE**
G	**AERATING**	
M	**ANIMATER**	**MARINATE**
O	**AERATION**	
P	**ANTIRAPE**	
S	*See below*	
T	**ATTAINER**	**REATTAIN**
U	**INAURATE**	
W	**ANTIWEAR**	
Z	**ATRAZINE**	

It's a bit of an oddity that despite **RETAINA** not making a seven, there are a lot of eights you can make from **RETAINA** + **S**: you saw them in the **RETAINS** + 1 list:

ANTISERA	**ARTESIAN**	**RATANIES**
RESINATA	**SEATRAIN**	

Here are some more eights from good-looking but unproductive sevens (**A E E I N R S**, **A E I L O R S** and **D E E I N R T**).

AEEINRS+

C	CINEREAS	INCREASE	RESIANCE	
D	ARSENIDE	DENARIES	DRAISENE	NEARSIDE
G	ANERGIES	GESNERIA		
H	INHEARSE			
K	SNEAKIER			
L	ALIENERS			
M	REMANIES			
N	ANSERINE			
P	NAPERIES			
R	REARISEN			
S	SENARIES			
T	ARENITES	ARSENITE	RESINATE	STEARINE
	TRAINEES			
U	UNEASIER			

AEILORS+

A	OLEARIAS		
C	CALORIES	CARIOLES	
D	DARIOLES	SOLIDARE	SOREDIAL
F	FORESAIL		
G	GASOLIER	GIRASOLE	SERAGLIO
H	AIRHOLES	SHOALIER	
M	MORALISE		
N	AILERONS	ALERIONS	ALIENORS

P	PELORIAS	POLARISE		
S	SOLARISE			
T	SOTERIAL			
V	OVERSAIL	VALORISE	VARIOLES	VOLARIES
Y	ROYALISE			
Z	SOLARIZE			

The list for **A E I L O R S** + above shows that any letter can be useful in the right circumstances; most people hate picking a **V** – perhaps club players more than most, because they know it's the only letter that doesn't make a two-letter word and so are instinctively scared of it. But if you're drawing an eighth letter to **A E I L O R S**, the best letter of all is **V**, forming four anagrams.

D E E I N R T +

A	DETAINER	RETAINED		
B	INTERBED			
D	DENDRITE			
K	TINKERED			
M	REMINTED			
N	INDENTER	INTENDER	INTERNED	
O	ORIENTED			
R	INTERRED	TRENDIER		
S	INSERTED	NERDIEST	RESIDENT	SINTERED
	TRENDIES			
T	RETINTED			
U	RETINUED	REUNITED		
V	INVERTED			
W	WINTERED			
X	DEXTRINE			

Eight-letter words using prefixes and suffixes

You can use prefixes and suffixes for eights just as much as for sevens – more so, as we have already noted, in the case of some of the four-letter affixes. So here's a selection of useful eights, with a selection of prefixes first.

Selection of eight-letter words listed by prefix

ANTI:	ANTIDOTE, ANTIFOAM, ANTIHERO, ANTIMERE, ANTIPORN
CON:	CONGLOBE, CONGREET, CONTANGO, CONTRAIL, CONURBAN
DE:	DEAERATE, DEBRUISE, DEGREASE, DERATTED, DESINING
DIS:	DISANNUL, DISCOURE, DISGAVEL, DISLEAVE, DISPLANT
EN:	ENCRADLE, ENHALOES, ENLARGEN, ENSAMPLE, ENSOULED
IN:	INDARTED, INFRUGAL, INNATIVE, INSEEMED, INSTABLE
MIS:	MISDREAD, MISGRAFT, MISLEARN, MISPLANT, MISTRACE
OUT:	OUTDRESS, OUTHOMER, OUTRANGE, OUTSMILE, OUTWEARY
OVER:	OVERDOER, OVERGILT, OVERMELT, OVERSALE, OVERWISE
PRE:	PREBLESS, PRECURSE, PRELIMIT, PRERINSE, PRETRIMS
PRO:	PROGRADE, PROMETAL, PROSTYLE, PROTONIC, PROVIRAL
SUB:	SUBAGENT, SUBCASTE, SUBGENUS, SUBLEASE, SUBTIDAL
UP:	UPBEARER, UPGATHER, UPGROWTH, UPSETTER, UPSTROKE

Eight-letter words starting with **RE–**

REASCENT	REINDUCT	REQUIGHT
REBODIES	REJACKET	REREWARD
RECANTER	REKINDLE	RESALUTE
REDECIDE	RELUMINE	RETARGET
REEMBODY	REMELTED	REUTTERS
REFRINGE	RENATURE	REVETTED
REGELATE	REOBTAIN	REWIDENS
REHARDEN	REPERUSE	REZONING

Eight-letter words starting with **UN–**

UNALLIED	UNJOINTS	UNREINED
UNBEREFT	UNKOSHER	UNSEARED
UNCHASTE	UNLETHAL	UNTAILED
UNDOCILE	UNMODISH	UNUNITED
UNELATED	UNNATIVE	UNVEILER
UNFEUDAL	UNORNATE	UNWINDER
UNGENIAL	UNPOETIC	UNYEANED
UNHAIRED	UNQUIETS	UNZIPPED
UNIDEAED		

Moving on to the suffixes, get your head round a few of these:

Selection of eight-letter words listed by suffix

ABLE: ATONABLE, FINDABLE, LAPSABLE, NAMEABLE, SENDABLE

AGE: BARONAGE, DIALLAGE, INTERAGE, PILOTAGE, STERNAGE

ANT: COSECANT, GALIVANT, PENCHANT, RELEVANT, STAGNANT

ATE: CORELATE, GEMINATE, LEVIRATE, OBTURATE, TITIVATE

ENT: ERUMPENT, FECULENT, PLANGENT, PRURIENT, SCANDENT

IER: BLUESIER, BRICKIER, CRUMMIER, FROGGIER, YOUTHIER

IEST: DULLIEST, LAWNIEST, MOORIEST, RUGGIEST, WHITIEST

ISE/ CAPONISE/IZE, FABULISE/IZE, INFAMISE/IZE, IZE: PTYALISE/IZE, SOBERISE/IZE

ISH: CAMELISH, FLIRTISH, POKERISH, SNEAKISH, TILEFISH

IST: CANOEIST, CREOLIST, LUTENIST, PARODIST, TENORIST

LESS: BATHLESS, CODELESS, HOOFLESS RIFTLESS, WARTLESS

LIKE: CORDLIKE, EPICLIKE, MASTLIKE, SALTLIKE, VESTLIKE

LY: BADGERLY, DATIVELY, GOLDENLY, PLAGUILY, TONISHLY

MAN/ CORPSMAN/MEN, HOTELMAN/MEN, LODESMAN/MEN, MEN: POINTMAN/MEN, SHIREMAN/MEN

NESS: AWAYNESS, HERENESS, LONGNESS, NULLNESS, THATNESS

TION: GELATION, LIBATION, NUDATION, PUNITION, SWAPTION

Using '6 + 2' lists

Coming back to the common letters, you need to know a good number of eights with six **RETAINS** letters and two others. Of course, we have seen a lot already – all the **RETAINS** + 1 and **RETAINA** + 1 words, to start with. However, it can do no harm to look at a few more. But setting out the **ATEBRIN** + 1 list, the **CINEAST** + 1 list and so on, would give a long and tedious series of lists, more likely to put readers off than engage their enthusiasm. It also has large numbers of duplicates – **ATEBRIN** + **C** = **CERTAIN** + **B**, and so on. (**BACTERIN**, in case you're wondering.)

Likewise, setting them out as '6 + 2' lists could give us some dauntingly long lists – there are 576 combinations of two letters (**AA**, **AB** and so on, through to **ZZ**) that could go with any six-letter set to form an eight. Obviously, no six letters go with all 576 or even get close, but there comes a time for most people when learning words to improve your game tips over from being interesting to just a chore. Some of you may feel you've passed that stage already.

But just to set out pages of words in no particular order, or even alphabetically, doesn't seem to be any improvement. So take a look at these '6 + 2' lists, which have been limited so as not to try the average reader's patience to exhaustion. Only about 30 two-letter combinations are given for any set of six letters. A maximum of two anagrams are given for any resulting eight-letter combination. And simple **s** endings on sevens we've already met have been excluded, as have eight-letter words we've seen already in other lists.

	AEINRS+	
AC	CANARIES	CESARIAN
AG	ANGARIES	ARGINASE
BL	RINSABLE	
BM	MIRBANES	
BU	ANBURIES	URBANISE
CK	SKINCARE	
DL	ISLANDER	
DY	SYNEDRIA	
FO	FARINOSE	
FP	FIREPANS	PANFRIES
FS	FAIRNESS	SANSERIF
GK	SKEARING	
GY	RESAYING	SYNERGIA
HP	PARISHEN	SERAPHIN
IK	KAISERIN	
IN	SIRENIAN	
IY	YERSINIA	
KM	RAMEKINS	
KP	RANPIKES	
LV	RAVELINS	
LX	RELAXINS	
MU	ANEURISM	
MY	SEMINARY	
NO	RAISONNE	
NW	SWANNIER	
SU	ANURESIS	SENARIUS
SX	XERANSIS	
UZ	AZURINES	SUZERAIN

	AEINRT+	
BC	BACTERIN	
CC	ACENTRIC	
CU	ANURETIC	
CV	NAVICERT	
DH	ANTHERID	
DP	DIPTERAN	
EH	ATHERINE	HERNIATE
EI	INERTIAE	
GM	EMIGRANT	REMATING
GV	GRIEVANT	VINTAGER
HP	PERIANTH	
HU	HAURIENT	
IL	INERTIAL	
LN	INTERNAL	
LO	ORIENTAL	RELATION
LP	TRAPLINE	TRIPLANE
MN	TRAINMEN	
MT	MARTINET	
MU	RUMINATE	
MW	WARIMENT	
MY	TYRAMINE	
OP	ATROPINE	
OR	ANTERIOR	
OT	TENTORIA	
PU	PAINTURE	
RW	INTERWAR	

AB	BASANITE
AC	ESTANCIA
AF	FANTASIE
AH	ASTHENIA
AT	ASTATINE TANAISTE
BH	ABSINTHE
CM	AMNESTIC SEMANTIC
CV	CISTVAEN VESICANT
DY	DESYATIN
EV	NAIVETES
FM	MANIFEST
GU	SAUTEING UNITAGES
GZ	TZIGANES
IP	PIANISTE
KU	UNAKITES
KV	KISTVAEN
MO	SOMNIATE
OV	STOVAINE
OX	SAXONITE
PS	STEAPSIN
PY	EPINASTY
TV	TASTEVIN
UV	SUIVANTE

AH	HETAIRAS
AT	ARIETTAS ARISTATE
BO	SABOTIER
CD	ACRIDEST
CH	STICHERA THERIACS
DI	IRISATED
DK	STRAIKED
DO	ASTEROID
DP	DIPTERAS TARSIPED
EE	EATERIES
EP	PARIETES PETARIES
EV	EVIRATES
GT	STRIGATE
HP	TRIPHASE
HU	THESAURI
HY	HYSTERIA
IM	AIRTIMES SERIATIM
IX	SEXTARII
LO	SOTERIAL
MU	MURIATES SEMITAUR
MV	VITAMERS
MW	WARTIMES
MY	SYMITARE
PW	WIRETAPS
PY	ASPERITY
SV	TRAVISES
VY	VESTIARY

AENRST+

AB	ANTBEARS	RATSBANE
AE	ARSENATE	SERENATA
AG	STARAGEN	TANAGERS
AL	ASTERNAL	
AM	SARMENTA	SEMANTRA
AO	ANOESTRA	
AV	TAVERNAS	TSAREVNA
BD	BANDSTER	BARTENDS
BG	BANGSTER	
CD	CANTREDS	
CE	CENTARES	SARCENET
DO	TORNADES	
EE	SERENATE	
EF	FENESTRA	
EJ	SERJEANT	
EO	EARSTONE	RESONATE
EU	SAUTERNE	
FO	SEAFRONT	
GO	RAGSTONE	STONERAG
GU	STRAUNGE	
OR	ANTRORSE	
OW	STONERAW	
PT	TRANSEPT	TRAPNEST

AINRST+

AD	INTRADAS	RADIANTS
AG	GRANITAS	
AI	INTARSIA	
AM	MARTIANS	TAMARINS
AP	ASPIRANT	PARTISAN
AZ	TZARINAS	
BD	ANTBIRDS	
BG	BRASTING	
BO	TABORINS	
CO	CANTORIS	
DK	STINKARD	
DO	DIATRONS	INTRADOS
DR	TRIDARNS	
DU	UNITARDS	
GK	KARTINGS	STARKING
GW	RINGTAWS	WRASTING
GY	STINGRAY	STRAYING
HO	TRAHISON	
KO	SKIATRON	
LO	TONSILAR	
OP	ATROPINS	
OS	ARSONIST	
OT	STRONTIA	
OU	RAINOUTS	SUTORIAN

EINRST+

CE	ENTERICS	SECRETIN	GV	STERVING		
DD	STRIDDEN		IL	NIRLIEST	NITRILES	
DO	DRONIEST		IO	IRONIEST		
EE	ETERNISE	TEENSIER	IU	NEURITIS		
EI	ERINITES	NITERIES	KL	LINKSTER	STRINKLE	
EO	ONERIEST	SEROTINE	LU	INSULTER	LUSTRINE	
EX	INTERSEX		LY	TINSELRY		
EY	SERENITY		OR	INTRORSE	SNORTIER	
FI	SNIFTIER		OY	TYROSINE		
GH	RIGHTENS		OZ	TRIZONES		
GL	LINGSTER	TRINGLES	TY	ENTRYIST		
GT	GITTERNS		UV	UNRIVETS	VENTURIS	

Some purists will be unhappy that I have chosen to give only selections of each of these lists, but this is not a book of word lists only. I have tried to achieve a balance between the lists and the rest of the book, and did not want to overwhelm newcomers to this side of the game with vast unlearnable numbers of new words. For those who want to see full lists from which these are a selection, other books and sources are available.

I have tried to include words which are likely to appear on your rack, and which are also memorable in some way. Perhaps you have been struck by the dependable rhythm of **BEELIKE**, **FATLIKE**, **NETLIKE**, **RATLIKE**, **TINLIKE**, the unexpected poetry of **GASOLIER**, **GIRASOLE**, **SERAGLIO** or the sheer serendipitousness of discovering that the anagram of **FAIRNESS** is **SANSERIF**. Playing words like **KINGLET**, **STONERAW** and **ERUMPENT** will bring a wow factor to your game that everyday words will never match.

> **Scrabble tip** – Memorable anagrams are fun and a great way of getting words to stick. Here are some good eight-letter anagrams:
>
> **LAMPPOST / PALMTOPS**
>
> **HANDOUTS / THOUSAND**
>
> **LAKELETS / SKELETAL**
>
> **EPITAPHS / HAPPIEST**
>
> **LICKSPIT / LIPSTICK**
>
> **STEWPANS / WASPNEST**
>
> But my favourite eight-letter anagram has to be the two words from the letters **ABEGMNOY**. They are both common 5–3 compound words. Can you get them?
>
> Of course... **BOGEYMAN** and **MONEYBAG**.

So do try and learn as many of these words as you can, even if only a few at a time. Your three-letter words, your clever little parallel plays, and your sticking down **EX** for 36 points are all very well, but it is the bonuses that will lift your game to a new level. Learn them, use them, treasure them.

SOME GREAT PUZZLES TO TRY

Find as many eight-letter words as you can on these boards with the
racks shown.

1. Your rack:
A E I N R S T

2. Your rack:
A E E I N R S

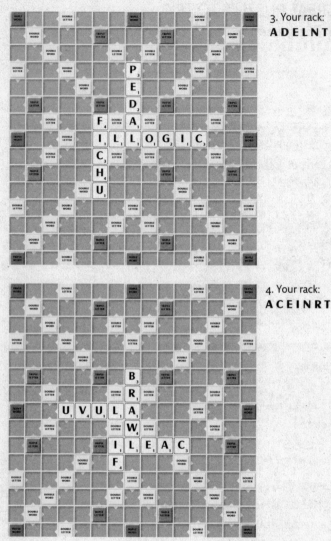

3. Your rack:
ADELNTU

4. Your rack:
ACEINRT

10 Help with unusual letter combinations

A challenge that every Scrabble player faces at some point in almost every game is dealing with an unpromising combination of letters on their rack. Having too many of the same letter, too many vowels or too many consonants can put you in a situation where it is very difficult to come up with a viable word, let alone a high-scoring one.

This section contains various lists that may prove useful in dealing with an awkward combination of tiles, because they consist of words with unusual letter combinations.

Words from World English

One method of dealing with the awkward tile combinations that inevitably appear on your rack at some point in a game is to memorize a wide selection of words outside the core vocabulary of English. As the most widely spoken language in the world, English is rich in loan-words from other languages, and the versatility of the Roman alphabet and of English pronunciation means that these words tend to be assimilated without much corruption of their original sound. This means that there are many words in English that use 'foreign' letter combinations, which are ideal for Scrabble players. The following lists contain words from Australia, Canada, New Zealand and South Africa, as well as words from the main languages of the Indian Subcontinent – Hindi and Urdu – which have entered British English.

Australian words

Australian English is distinguished not only by the numerous Aboriginal terms for Australia's flora and fauna, but also by a great many shortened forms of commonplace English words. The Australian propensity to slang and short informal words is extremely useful to Scrabble players, especially as many of these words end in **O**, one of the most common tiles in the game. If you spot an **O** on the board when you have a difficult set of letters on your rack, there's a good chance that you'll be able to form an informal Aussie word. Native Australian words provide a range of unusual letter combinations, as well as a tendency to include double **O**s – ideal for rack balancing. Double **R**s are also common in Australian English, as are **K**s and **Y**s, so it's well worth acquiring some Antipodean vocabulary.

ADJIGO	yam plant	**BOAB**	baobab tree
ALF	an uncultivated Australian	**BODGIE**	unruly or uncouth man
ARVO	afternoon	**BOGAN**	fool
ASPRO	associate professor	**BOOBOOK**	small spotted brown owl
BARRO	embarrassing		
BAUERA	small evergreen shrub	**BOOFY**	strong but stupid
		BOONG	*offensive word* for a Black person
BEAUT	outstanding person or thing		
		BOOSHIT	very good
BELAH	casuarina tree	**BORA**	native Australian coming-of-age ceremony
BERKO	berserk		
BIFFO	fighting or aggressive behaviour		
		BORAK	rubbish or nonsense
BILBY	burrowing marsupial	**BRASCO**	lavatory
BIZZO	empty and irrelevant talk	**BROLGA**	large grey crane with red-and-green head

BRUMBY	wild horse
BUNYA	tall dome-shaped coniferous tree
BUNYIP	legendary monster
CADAGI	tropical eucalyptus tree
CARBY	carburettor
CHEWIE	chewing gum
CHIACK	tease or banter
CHOCO	conscript or militiaman
CHOOK	hen or chicken
CHOOM	Englishman
COMMO	communist
COMPO	compensation
CORREA	evergreen shrub
COUCAL	long-legged bird
COUGAN	rowdy person
CRONK	unfit or unsound
CROOL	spoil
CROWEA	pink-flowered shrub
DACK	forcibly remove someone's trousers
DADAH	illegal drugs
DAGGY	untidy or dishevelled
DASYURE	small carnivorous marsupial
DELO	delegate
DERRO	vagrant
DINGO	wild dog
DINKUM	genuine or right
DOCO	documentary
DONGA	steep-sided gully
DORBA	stupid, inept or clumsy person
DRACK	unattractive
DRONGO	slow-witted person
DROOB	pathetic person
DUBBO	stupid
DUGITE	venomous snake
DURRY	cigarette
EARBASH	talk incessantly
EMU	large flightless bird
EUMUNG	type of acacia
EVO	evening
EXO	excellent
FASTIE	deceitful act
FESTY	dirty or smelly
FIBRO	house built of fibro-cement
FIGJAM	very conceited person
FIZGIG	frivolous or flirtatious girl
FOULIE	bad mood
FRIB	short heavy-conditioned piece of wool
FUNDIE	fundamentalist Christian

FURPHY	rumour or fictitious story	**JUMBUCK**	sheep
GALAH	grey-and-pink cockatoo	**KARRI**	type of eucalyptus tree
GARBO	dustman	**KOALA**	slow-moving arboreal marsupial
GEEBUNG	tree with edible but tasteless fruit	**KOORI**	native Australian
GIDGEE	small acacia tree that sometimes emits an unpleasant smell	**KYBO**	temporary lavatory
		KYLIE	boomerang that is flat on one side and convex on the other
GILGAI	natural water hole	**LOPPY**	man employed to do maintenance work on a ranch
GING	child's catapult		
GNOW	ground-dwelling bird		
GOANNA	monitor lizard	**LOWAN**	ground-dwelling bird
GOOG	egg	**LUBRA**	Aboriginal woman
GOOLIE	stone or pebble	**MALLEE**	low shrubby eucalyptus tree
GUNYAH	bush hut or shelter		
GYMPIE	tall tree with stinging hairs on its leaves	**MARRI**	type of eucalyptus
		MIDDY	middle-sized glass of beer
HAKEA	type of shrub or tree		
HOSTIE	air hostess	**MILKO**	milkman
HOVEA	plant with purple flowers	**MOLOCH**	spiny lizard
		MOPOKE	small spotted owl
HUTCHIE	groundsheet draped over an upright stick as a temporary shelter	**MOZ**	hoodoo or hex
		MUGGA	eucalyptus tree with pink flowers and dark bark
JARRAH	type of eucalyptus tree	**MULGA**	acacia shrub
JEFF	downsize or close down an organization	**MULLOCK**	waste material from a mine

MURREE	native Australian	**POON**	stupid or ineffectual person
MURRI	native Australian		
MUSO	musician	**POONCE**	male homosexual
MYALL	native Australian living independently of society	**POSSIE**	position
		PRELOVED	second-hand
		QUOKKA	small wallaby
MYXO	myxomatosis	**QUOLL**	native cat
NANA	head	**RAZOO**	imaginary coin
NARDOO	cloverlike fern	**REFFO**	*offensive term* for a European refugee after World War Two
NEDDY	horse		
NOAH	shark		
NONG	stupid or incompetent person	**REGO**	registration of a motor vehicle
NORK	female breast	**RESTO**	restored antique, vintage car, etc
NUDDY	in the nude		
NUMBAT	small marsupial with long snout	**ROO**	kangaroo
		ROUGHIE	something unfair, especially a trick
OCKER	uncultivated or boorish Australian	**SANGER**	sandwich
		SANGO	sandwich
PIKER	wild bullock	**SCOZZA**	rowdy person
PINDAN	desert region of Western Australia	**SCUNGY**	miserable, sordid or dirty
PITURI	shrub with narcotic leaves	**SHARPIE**	member of a teenage group with short hair and distinctive clothes
PLONKO	alcoholic, especially one who drinks wine		
		SHERANG	boss
PLURRY	*euphemism* for bloody	**SHYPOO**	liquor of poor quality
		SITELLA	small black-and-white bird
PODDY	handfed calf or lamb		
POKIE	poker machine		

SKEG	rear fin on the underside of a surfboard	**VEGO**	vegetarian
SKITE	boast	**VIGORO**	women's game similar to cricket
SMOKO	cigarette break	**WADDY**	heavy wooden club used by native Australians
SMOODGE	smooch		
SPAG	*offensive term* for an Italian	**WAGGA**	blanket made of sacks stitched together
SPRUIK	speak in public		
SWAGGIE	vagrant worker	**WALLABY**	marsupial resembling a small kangaroo
SWAGMAN	vagrant worker		
SWY	gambling game	**WANDOO**	eucalyptus tree with white bark
TONK	effeminate man		
TOOSHIE	angry or upset	**WARATAH**	shrub with dark green leaves and crimson flowers
TRIELLA	three horse races nominated for a bet		
TROPPO	mentally affected by a tropical climate	**WARB**	dirty or insignificant person
TRUCKIE	truck driver	**WHARFIE**	wharf labourer
TRUGO	game similar to croquet	**WIDGIE**	female bodgie
		WILGA	small drought-resistant tree
TUAN	flying phalanger		
TUART	type of eucalyptus tree	**WIRILDA**	acacia tree with edible seeds
UMPIE	umpire	**WIRRAH**	saltwater fish with bright blue spots
UNCO	awkward or clumsy		
UPTA	of poor quality	**WOF**	fool or idiot
UPTER	of poor quality	**WOMBAT**	burrowing marsupial
UTE	utility	**WOOMERA**	spear-throwing stick
VAG	vagrant	**WURLEY**	Aboriginal hut

YABBER	talk or jabber	**YIKE**	argument, squabble or fight
YABBY	small freshwater crayfish	**YUCKO**	disgusting
YACCA	grass tree	**YUMMO**	delicious
YACKA	grass tree	**ZAMBUCK**	St John Ambulance attendant
YARRAN	small hardy tree		
YATE	small eucalyptus tree	**ZIFF**	beard

Canadian words

Canadian English combines a broad range of British and US terms with words derived from Inuit, as well as from other Native American languages such as Algonquin. Canadian English incorporates many Canadian French words from Québec, and there are also a number of recently coined Canadian terms. Inuit words can be helpful to Scrabble players because they tend to be quite vowel-heavy. **K** occurs frequently in Inuit terms, and sometimes appears twice. Such words require a blank tile for the second **K** if they are to be played during a game.

AGLOO	breathing hole made in ice by a seal	**BABICHE**	thongs or lacings of rawhide
AGLU	breathing hole made in ice by a seal	**BARACHOIS**	shallow lagoon formed by a sand bar
AMAUT	hood on an Inuit woman's parka for carrying a child	**BATEAU**	light flat-bottomed boat
AMOWT	hood on an Inuit woman's parka for carrying a child	**BEIGNET**	deep-fried pastry
		BOGAN	sluggish side stream
ATIGI	Inuit parka	**BREWIS**	Newfoundland cod stew

BUTTE	isolated steep-sided flat-topped hill	**KAMIK**	Inuit boot made of caribou hide or sealskin
CABOOSE	mobile bunkhouse used by lumbermen	**KLOOCH**	North American Indian woman
CANOLA	cooking oil extracted from a variety of Canadian rapeseed	**KLOOTCH**	North American Indian woman
CAYUSE	small Native American pony used by cowboys	**KUDLIK**	Inuit soapstone seal-oil lamp
		LOGAN	backwater
COULEE	dry stream valley	**LOONIE**	Canadian dollar coin with loon bird on one face
CUSK	gadoid food fish		
DEKE	act or instance of feinting in ice hockey		
		MUCKAMUCK food	
GROWLER	small iceberg that has broken off from a larger iceberg or glacier	**MUKTUK**	beluga skin used as food
		NANOOK	polar bear
		PARFLECHE	dried rawhide
HONKER	Canada goose	**PARKADE**	building used as a car park
HOSER	unsophisticated rural person		
		PARKETTE	small public park
ICEWINE	dessert wine made from frozen grapes	**PLEW**	beaver skin used as standard unit in fur trading
JIGGER	device used when setting a gill net beneath ice		
		POGEY	financial relief for the unemployed
JOUAL	nonstandard Canadian French dialect	**POGY**	financial relief for the unemployed
		POKELOGAN	backwater

POUTINE	chipped potatoes topped with curd cheese and tomato sauce	SWILER	seal hunter
		TILLICUM	friend
		TOONIE	Canadian two-dollar coin
PUNG	horse-drawn sleigh	TULLIBEE	whitefish found in the Great Lakes
REDEYE	drink incorporating beer and tomato juice		
		TUPEK	Inuit tent of animal skins
RUBABOO	soup made by boiling pemmican		
		TUPIK	Inuit tent of animal skins
RUBBY	rubbing alcohol mixed with cheap wine for drinking		
		TWONIE	Canadian two-dollar coin
SKOOKUM	strong or brave		
SNYE	side channel of a river	WAWA	speech or language
SPLAKE	hybrid trout bred by Canadian zoologists	WENDIGO	evil spirit or cannibal

Hindi words

After Chinese, Hindi, the dominant language of India, is the most widely spoken language in the world. Many Hindi words entered British English during the Raj, and some have become everyday terms – **BUNGALOW** and **PUNDIT**, for example. Others are less common, but are useful to Scrabble players because they provide unusual letter combinations and thus solutions to difficult racks. Combinations such as **BH**, **DH** and **KH** are common in Hindi-derived words, and the preponderance of **A**s, **I**s and **U**s can be very helpful in trying to balance a vowel-heavy rack. Above all, Hindi words are useful because they are quite unusual, and so provide a range of options for Scrabble players that aren't immediately obvious – front-hooking onto **HANG** with a **B**, for example, or end-hooking onto **PUNK** with an **A**. Committing some Hindi-derived words to memory will help to keep your opponents on their toes.

AKHARA	gymnasium
ALAP	vocal music without words
AMBARY	tropical plant
ANKUS	elephant goad
ANNA	old copper coin
ARTI	Hindu ritual
AYAH	maidservant or nursemaid
BABU	Mr
BAEL	spiny tree
BAHADUR	title for distinguished Indians during the Raj
BANDH	general strike
BANYAN	tree with aerial roots
BHAJI	deep-fried vegetable savoury
BHANG	psychoactive drug made of hemp
BHANGRA	music combining traditional Punjabi music with Western pop
BHAVAN	large house or building
BHEESTY	water-carrier
BHINDI	okra used in cooking
BHISHTI	water-carrier
BINDI	decorative dot in middle of forehead
BOBBERY	mixed pack of hunting dogs
BUND	embankment
CHAI	tea, especially with added spices
CHAMPAC	tree with fragrant yellow flowers
CHAPATI	flat coarse unleavened bread
CHAPPAL	sandal
CHARAS	hashish
CHARKHA	spinning wheel
CHEETAH	large swift feline mammal
CHETAH	large swift feline mammal
CHELA	disciple of a religious teacher
CHICHI	person of mixed British and Indian descent
CHILLUM	pipe for smoking cannabis
CHINTZ	printed cotton with glazed finish
CHITAL	large, spotted deer
CHOKEY	prison
CHOLI	short-sleeved bodice
CHOWK	marketplace
CHUDDAR	large shawl or veil
CHUDDIES	underpants

CHUKAR	Indian partridge	**DHAL**	curry made from lentils
CHUKKA	period of play in polo	**DHARNA**	method of obtaining justice by fasting
CHUTNEY	Indian pickle		
COOLIE	cheaply hired unskilled labourer	**DHOBI**	washerman
		DHOTI	loincloth
COOLY	cheaply hired unskilled labourer	**DUPATTA**	scarf
		DURBAR	court of an Indian ruler
COWAGE	tropical climbing plant with stinging pods		
		DURRIE	cotton carpet
		DURZI	Indian tailor
COWHAGE	tropical climbing plant with stinging pods	**GANJA**	potent form of cannabis
		GAUR	large wild cow
CRORE	ten million	**GARIAL**	fish-eating crocodilian with long slender snout
CUSHY	comfortable		
DACOIT	a member of a gang of armed robbers		
		GAVIAL	fish-eating crocodilian with long slender snout
DACOITY	robbery by an armed gang		
DAK	system of mail delivery	**GHARIAL**	fish-eating crocodilian with long slender snout
DAL	split grain		
DATURA	plant with trumpet-shaped flowers	**GHARRI**	horse-drawn vehicle for hire
		GHARRY	horse-drawn vehicle for hire
DEKKO	look or glance		
DEODAR	Himalayan cedar	**GHAT**	stairs or passage leading down to a river
DEWAN	chief minister of an Indian princedom		
DHAK	tropical tree with red flowers	**GHEE**	clarified butter

GHERAO	industrial action in which workers imprison their employers	**KRAIT**	brightly coloured venomous snake
GINGILI	oil obtained from sesame seeds	**KUKRI**	Gurkha knife
GORAL	small goat antelope	**KULFI**	Indian dessert
GUAR	plant that produces gum	**KURTA**	long loose garment like a shirt without a collar
GUNNY	coarse fabric used for sacks	**LAC**	resinous substance secreted by insects
GURU	Hindu or Sikh religious teacher	**LAKH**	100,000
HARTAL	act of closing shop or stopping work as a political protest	**LANGUR**	arboreal monkey
		LASSI	yoghurt drink
		LATHI	long heavy stick used as a weapon
HOWDAH	seat for riding on an elephant's back	**LUNGI**	long piece of cloth worn as loincloth or turban
JAGGERY	coarse brown sugar	**MACHAN**	platform used in tiger hunting
JAI	victory		
KHADDAR	cotton cloth	**MAHOUT**	elephant driver
KHEDA	enclosure for captured elephants	**MAHSEER**	large freshwater fish
		MANDI	big market
KHEDAH	enclosure for captured elephants	**MANDIR**	Hindu or Jain temple
		MAUND	unit of weight
KHEDDAH	enclosure for captured elephants	**MEHNDI**	practice of painting designs on the hands and feet using henna
KOEL	parasitic cuckoo	**MELA**	cultural or religious festival
KOS	Indian unit of distance	**MOHUR**	old gold coin

MONAL	Asian pheasant	**PUNKA**	fan made of palm leaves
MORCHA	hostile demonstration against the government	**PUNKAH**	fan made of palm leaves
		PURDA	custom of keeping women secluded
MRIDANG	drum used in Indian music	**PURDAH**	custom of keeping women secluded
MYNAH	tropical starling	**PURI**	unleavened flaky bread
NAUCH	intricate Indian dance		
NAUTCH	intricate Indian dance	**PUTTEE**	strip of cloth wound around the leg
NAWAB	Muslim prince in India	**RAGGEE**	cereal grass
		RAGI	cereal grass
NEEM	large tree	**RAITA**	yoghurt-and-vegetable dish served with curry
NILGAI	large Indian antelope		
NULLAH	stream or drain		
NUMDAH	coarse felt	**RAJ**	government
OONT	camel	**RAJAH**	ruler or landlord
PACHISI	game resembling backgammon	**RAMTIL**	African plant grown in India
PAISA	one hundredth of a rupee	**RANEE**	queen or princess
		RANI	queen or princess
PAKORA	dish of deep-fried chicken or vegetables	**RATHA**	four-wheeled carriage drawn by horses or bullocks
PANEER	soft white cheese		
PARATHA	flat unleavened bread	**ROTI**	type of unleavened bread
PEEPUL	tree similar to the banyan	**RUPEE**	standard monetary unit of India

RUPIAH	standard monetary unit of Indonesia
RYOT	peasant or tenant farmer
SAMBAR	deer with three-tined antlers
SAMITI	political association
SAMOSA	triangular pastry containing spiced vegetables or meat
SARANGI	stringed instrument played with a bow
SARDAR	Sikh title
SARI	traditional dress of Indian women
SAROD	Indian stringed instrument
SWAMI	title for a Hindu saint or religious teacher
TABLA	pair of drums whose pitches can be varied
THALI	meal consisting of several small dishes
TIL	sesame
TOLA	unit of weight
TONGA	light two-wheeled vehicle
TOPEE	pith helmet
TOPI	pith helmet
URD	bean plant
VAHANA	vehicle in Indian myth
VANDA	type of orchid
VINA	stringed musical instrument
WALLAH	person in charge of a specific thing
ZENANA	part of a house reserved for women and girls
ZILA	administrative district in India
ZILLA	administrative district in India
ZILLAH	administrative district in India

New Zealand words

While New Zealand and Australian English have many words in common, the Kiwi lexicon is greatly enriched by New Zealand's Maori heritage. Maori-derived words are a marvellous resource for the Scrabble player, providing a wealth of unusual vowel combinations, and frequently using consonants that are rarer in European words, such as **K**, **W** and **H**. Maori words are especially good for balancing vowel-heavy racks, as many words use several **A**s, **U**s or **I**s – sometimes with three vowels in a row. Relatively high-scoring consonants are also very common, especially **K** and **H**. Unfortunately, there is only one **K** in Scrabble, so many Maori words with two **K**s are less useful than they might initially appear. Don't forget blank tiles, however: if you have a blank, a **K** and a couple of vowels on your rack, there's a good chance that you can find a New Zealand word to play profitably. There are also some unusual words that have entered the vocabulary of New Zealanders from European or Asian languages.

ATUA	spirit or demon
BOOHAI	thoroughly lost
COOTIE	body louse
GOORIE	mongrel dog
GRAUNCH	crush or destroy
HAKA	war dance
HANGI	open-air cooking pit
HAPU	subtribe
HAPUKA	large fish
HAPUKU	large fish
HEITIKI	neck ornament
HIKOI	protest march
HOKONUI	illicit whisky
HONGI	nose-touching greeting
HUHU	hairy beetle
HUI	conference or meeting
HUIA	extinct New Zealand bird
JAFA	*offensive term* for someone from Auckland
JANOLA	household bleach
KAHAWAI	large fish
KAI	food
KAIK	village
KAINGA	village
KAKA	long-billed parrot
KAKAPO	ground-dwelling parrot
KARAKIA	prayer
KARANGA	call or chant of welcome
KATIPO	small venomous spider
KAUPAPA	strategy, policy or cause
KAURI	coniferous tree
KAWA	protocol or etiquette
KIEKIE	climbing bush plant
KIWI	flightless bird with long beak and no tail
KOHA	gift or donation
KOKAKO	long-tailed crow
KONEKE	farm vehicle

KORU	curved pattern	**POI**	ball of woven flax
KOWHAI	small tree	**PONGA**	tall tree fern
KUIA	female elder	**PORAE**	edible sea fish
KURI	mongrel dog	**PORANGI**	crazy
KUTU	body louse	**PORINA**	moth larva
MANUKA	myrtaceous tree	**POTAE**	hat
MATAI	evergreen tree	**POWHIRI**	welcoming ceremony
MIHI	ceremonial greeting	**PUGGY**	sticky
MOA	extinct large flightless bird	**PUHA**	sow thistle
		PUKEKO	wading bird
MOKI	edible sea fish	**PURIRI**	forest tree
MOKO	Maori tattoo or tattoo pattern	**RAHUI**	Maori prohibition
		RATA	myrtaceous forest tree
MOOLOO	person from Waikato		
MOPOKE	small spotted owl	**RAUPATU**	seizure of land
MUNGA	army canteen	**RAURIKI**	sow thistle
NGAIO	small tree	**SHEEPO**	person who brings sheep to the catching pen for shearing
NGATI	tribe or clan		
NIKAU	palm tree		
PAKAHI	acid soil or land	**TAIAHA**	ceremonial fighting staff
PAKAPOO	Chinese lottery		
PAKOKO	small freshwater fish	**TAIHOA**	hold on!
PAUA	edible abalone	**TAKAHE**	rare flightless bird
PERFING	early retirement from the police force with financial compensation	**TANGI**	Maori funeral ceremony
		TANIWHA	legendary monster
		TAONGA	treasure
PIKAU	rucksack	**TAPU**	sacred or forbidden
PIPI	shellfish	**TARSEAL**	bitumen surface of a road
PIUPIU	leaf skirt		

TAUIWI	non-Maori people of New Zealand		**WEKA**	flightless bird
TIKANGA	Maori customs		**WERO**	warrior's challenge
TOETOE	type of tall grass		**WETA**	long-legged wingless insect
TOITOI	type of tall grass		**WHANAU**	family
TWINK	white correction fluid		**WHENAU**	native land
WAKA	Maori canoe			

South African words

South African English includes words from Nguni languages such as Xhosa and Zulu, as well as Afrikaans, amongst other languages. For Scrabble players, South African English offers a host of useful words for balancing vowel-heavy racks. Many Afrikaans-derived words contain a double **A**, while Nguni words often contain two or three **A**s. It's a good idea, therefore, to have some South African words up your sleeve for when you find yourself with two or more **A**s on your rack. There are also a lot of **K** words in South African English. As **K** can be an awkward letter to use effectively, these can come in very handy, as can the Afrikaans-derived words containing **V**, which are most helpful in trying to use a difficult tile.

AMADODA	grown men		**BUNDU**	wild, remote region
AMANDLA	political slogan calling for power to the Black population		**DAGGA**	marijuana
			DWAAL	state of befuddlement
			GEELBEK	yellow-jawed fish
BAAS	boss		**HAMBA**	go away
BABALAS	drunk or hung over		**JA**	yes
BAKKIE	small truck		**JAAP**	simpleton
BRAAI	grill or roast meat		**JEREPIGO**	heavy desert wine
BRAAIVLEIS	barbecue		**JONG**	friend

KAAL	naked	**ROOIKAT**	lynx
KEREL	chap or fellow	**SCAMTO**	argot of urban
KRAAL	stockaded village		South African
KWAITO	type of pop music		Blacks
LEGUAAN	large monitor lizard	**SKOLLY**	hooligan
MEERKAT	sociable mongoose	**SNOEK**	edible marine fish
MENEER	Mr or Sir	**SPEK**	bacon, fat or fatty
MEVROU	Mrs or Madam		pork
MOOI	pleasing	**STEEN**	variety of white
MUTI	herbal medicine		grape
NAARTJIE	tangerine	**STOKVEL**	savings pool or
NEK	mountain pass		syndicate
NKOSI	master or chief	**VLEI**	area of marshy
OKE	man		ground
OOM	title of respect	**VOEMA**	vigour or energy
OUBAAS	person senior in	**VOETSEK**	expression of
	rank or years		dismissal or
PADKOS	snacks for a long		rejection
	journey	**VROU**	woman or wife
PLAAS	farm	**YEBO**	yes

Urdu words

Urdu, the official language of Pakistan and one of the official languages of India, is closely related to Hindi. Urdu, however, contains many more words derived from Arabic and Persian, and also uses a different system of writing from Hindi, lending a different character to the words that have entered English. Many Urdu culinary terms will be familiar to British Scrabble players from Indian restaurants, while most Anglo-Indian military vocabulary also derives from Urdu rather than Hindi. As with Hindi, the variant spellings of many Urdu words provide opportunities for Scrabble players, as does the frequency of the letter **K**.

BAGH	garden		**KEBAB**	dish of meat, onions, etc, grilled on skewers
BALTI	spicy Indian dish stewed until most liquid has evaporated		**KHAKI**	dull yellowish-brown colour
BASTI	slum		**KHARIF**	crop harvested at beginning of winter
BEGUM	woman of high rank		**KHAYAL**	kind of Indian classical vocal music
BIRIANI	Indian dish of highly flavoured rice mixed with meat or fish		**KINCOB**	fine silk fabric embroidered with gold or silver threads
BIRYANI	Indian dish of highly flavoured rice mixed with meat or fish		**KOFTA**	Indian dish of seasoned minced meat shaped into balls
BUSTEE	slum			
BUSTI	slum		**KOFTGAR**	person skilled in inlaying steel with gold
CHARPAI	bedstead of woven webbing on a wooden frame		**KOFTGARI**	art of inlaying steel with gold
CHARPOY	bedstead of woven webbing on a wooden frame		**KORMA**	Indian dish of meat or vegetables braised with yoghurt or cream
DAROGHA	manager			
DHANSAK	Indian dish of meat or vegetables braised with lentils			
INQILAB	revolution		**LASCAR**	sailor from the East Indies
IZZAT	honour or prestige		**MAIDAN**	open space used for meetings and sports
JACONET	light cotton fabric			
JEMADAR	officer in the Indian police			
KAMEEZ	long tunic			

MASALA	mixed spices ground into a paste		**SHIKAR**	hunting
MOOLVI	Muslim doctor of the law		**SHIKAREE**	hunter
			SHIKARI	hunter
MOOLVIE	Muslim doctor of the law		**SICE**	servant who looks after horses
MURDABAD	down with; death to		**SUBADAH**	chief native office in a company of sepoys
MUSTH	frenzied sexual excitement in male elephants		**SUBADAR**	chief native office in a company of sepoys
NUMDAH	coarse felt		**SUBAH**	chief native office in a company of sepoys
QORMA	Indian dish of meat or vegetables braised with yoghurt or cream		**SYCE**	servant who looks after horses
			TAHSIL	administrative division
RABI	crop harvested at the end of winter		**TALOOKA**	subdivision of a district
SAHIB	title placed after a man's name		**TALUK**	subdivision of a district
SAICE	servant who looks after horses		**TALUKA**	subdivision of a district
SARPANCH	head of a village council		**TAMASHA**	show or entertainment
SEPOY	Indian soldier in the service of the British		**TANDOORI**	method of cooking on a spit in a clay oven
SHALWAR	loose-fitting trousers			

11 Ending the game

So, you've learned your twos, most of your threes, and some useful fours. You've got maximum value from whatever high-value tiles you picked up, you've used your new-found confidence in finding sevens and eights, especially with an **s** or a blank, to make a couple of bonus words, and you have increased your vocabulary from the great variety of world English. The only problem is, your opponent, being one of those annoying people, has done the exact same thing.

Final pointers

You are now approaching the end of the game, and the scores are close. Whether it's about 200 each or 400 each doesn't matter. Your score as such has become irrelevant. You want to win the game.

It won't always happen this way. In a game between two evenly matched players, one can get all the luck, or just that little bit when it matters, and run out the winner by 200 or 300 points. A weaker player can often beat a stronger one over one game. That's why tournament players always like to settle important tournaments over a number of matches – not necessarily all against the same player, but against a number of players of similar standard. Then the cream tends to rise to the top. A one-off win proves nothing.

But let's assume you are playing a game now and, with few or no tiles left in the bag, the scores are close. How do you find that vital edge?

Essentially, what you are now trying to do is not just maximize your own score but also minimize your opponent's. And to do that, you need to know what letters your opponent has got, or know as nearly as is possible. You do this by tile-tracking.

The need for tile-tracking

Back at the beginning of the book we talked about counting up whether more **A**s or **I**s had been played. If given a choice, you could then play whichever there were more of left in the bag, making you less likely to be left with an awkward duplicate. *Tile-tracking* is an extension of this tactic, and relies on the fact that you know exactly how many of each letter were in the bag at the start of the game. You also know what's been played – it's all there in front of you. And you know what's on your rack. It's simple arithmetic to work out what's left – and that must be what is on your opponent's rack or still in the bag.

I'll repeat again what I said about the **A**s and **I**s. A card player – such as in bridge or poker – will always try to remember what cards have been turned over and are therefore not in the hands of the other players or still in the pack to be dealt. It's an accepted – indeed essential – part of good play. So it is in Scrabble, but with the advantage that all that tough memory work is eliminated. Everything that's been played in Scrabble is face up. It's hard enough remembering over 200,000 allowable words without remembering whether or not somebody played the second **F** twenty minutes ago. Fortunately you don't have to. Just look at the board.

Using a tile-tracking sheet

Even better, look at your tile-tracking sheet. A tile-tracking sheet is a pre-prepared list or grid of letters, which you cross off as each tile is played. At the end of the game, what you haven't crossed off is what's still to come.

Different people use different types of tracking sheet. Some list the letters **A–Z**, plus blank, down one side of the sheet, and mark a tick against each as it is played (see Tile-Tracking Sheet 1 opposite). Towards the end of the game, if there are only eight ticks against the letter **A**, you know there is one to come, as there are nine in the set.

Some make the relevant number of ticks against each letter at the start of the game and then cross them off, so the number of ticks left is the number of that letter still to be played (see Tile-Tracking Sheet 2 on the next page). Some write out all hundred letters and cross them through as they are played (see Tile-Tracking Sheet 3 on the next page).

Three different styles of tile-tracking sheet, each shown part way through a game are shown.

Tile-Tracking Sheet 1

A	✓✓✓✓✓✓	O	✓✓✓✓✓
B	✓	P	✓✓
C	✓✓	Q	✓
D	✓✓✓	R	✓✓✓✓
E	✓✓✓✓✓✓✓✓	S	✓✓
F	✓	T	✓✓✓✓✓
G	✓	U	✓✓✓
H	✓✓	V	
I	✓✓✓✓	W	✓✓
J	✓	X	✓
K		Y	✓
L	✓✓✓	Z	✓
M	✓	?	✓
N	✓✓✓✓		

Tile-Tracking Sheet 2

A ~~AAAAA~~ ✓✓✓✓	O ~~OOOO~~ ✓✓✓✓
B ~~B~~ ✓	P ~~P~~ ✓
C ~~C~~ ✓	Q ~~Q~~
D ~~DDD~~ ✓	R ~~RRR~~ ✓✓✓
E ~~EEEEEE~~ ✓✓✓✓✓✓	S ~~S~~ ✓✓✓
F ✓✓	T ~~TT~~ ✓✓✓✓
G ~~GG~~ ✓	U ~~UU~~ ✓✓
H ~~HH~~	V ~~V~~ ✓
I ~~IIIII~~ ✓✓✓✓	W ~~WW~~
J ✓	X ✓
K ~~K~~	Y ~~Y~~ ✓
L ~~LL~~ ✓✓	Z ✓
M ~~MM~~	? ~~??~~
N ~~NNN~~ ✓✓✓	

Tile-Tracking Sheet 3

~~AAAAAA~~AA	J ~~K~~ ~~Q~~ X ~~Z~~
~~EEEEEEEE~~EEE	~~B~~B ~~CC~~ ~~DDD~~D
~~IIIIII~~III	~~F~~F ~~GG~~G ~~HH~~
~~OOOOO~~OOO	~~LL~~LL MM ~~NNNN~~NN
~~UUU~~U	~~P~~P
	~~RRRR~~RR
	~~SSS~~S
	~~TTT~~TTT
	VV WW ~~YY~~
	~~ZZ~~

Of course, if you have access to a computer or photocopier, you only need to write or type your tracking sheet out once and then print off a whole batch of them.

Many people still think of tile-tracking as somehow cheating. Coming back to the cards analogy, it has been pointed out that you can't pre-prepare a grid of cards and cross them off as they are played. I certainly wouldn't try it in the local bridge club or poker casino. But in Scrabble, given that you have pen and paper in front of you to keep the score, it would be perverse not to allow it. If I've got seven tiles left on my rack and you've got the last five, there is a far greater level of skill attached to winning the game if each of us knows what the other is holding, rather than both just shooting in the dark.

Note that you shouldn't cross tiles off your tracking sheet when you pick them; you may decide to change, so only eliminate them when they are actually played. If tile-tracking is new to you, you may find you forget to track the occasional move – usually after a bonus – but with the majority crossed off, you can usually rescue the situation with a quick count. If both the **B**s have been played and you discover you have only crossed off one, chances are that it's one of the moves in which a **B** was played that you forgot about.

Predicting what your opponent will do

So, you know what your opponent has on his final rack. (To avoid a lot of tiresome uses of 'he or she' and 'his or her', let's say in this instance that the opponent is male.) Try to work out what his highest move is, especially if he has a high-scoring tile. If his next-highest move is substantially less, play something to block the high-scoring move – unless by doing so you deny yourself a sufficiently high score for your own highest move. Do the arithmetic. If I score 16 here, he gets 32 there. But if I block his 32, even though it only scores me 12 (so I'm 'down four'), he can only get 20, so he's 'down 12'. So it must be worth it to block his 32 point move.

Playing out

The other main consideration in endgame play is playing out (i.e. getting rid of all your tiles to finish the game) as quickly as possible. When you're down to your final tiles, try to play a move which will allow you to play all your remaining tiles in the next move. That means you need two places to play out, so that even if your opponent blocks one, you still have the other. Conversely, you must look to see if your opponent only has one place to play out – and if so, block it.

It's surprising how often it's worth accepting a score that might be lower than your optimal score by quite a few points, if it enables you to play out at your next move. You deny your opponent another score, and get the value of his remaining tiles added to your score, and he gets the same value deducted. That usually adds up to a sizable swing that can make all the difference in a tight game.

Playing an end game

Have a look at the board opposite from my good friend and Scrabble genius Phil Appleby. You are 13 points behind, and, having tile-tracked, you know your opponent has **D E K O R**. What points do you need to consider for your next move? What would you play? Take a few minutes to examine the board and decide what you would do.

Your opponent has one place to play out – by playing **FORKED** using the floating **F** near the bottom left-hand corner. You must block this play, and play something that will enable you to play out in the following move. Look for his next-best score, and work out whether you can score enough to win the game. If not, look again.

Assuming your opponent has a good knowledge of three- and four-letter words, he can play **KEB** or **KOB** on the top left Triple Word square, for 27. **DREK** or **DEEK**, using the **E** of **OYEZ** and also making **KO**, notches up 25. His best score is **ROED**, played directly under the **AINE** of **MORAINE**, also making **AR**, **IO**, **NE** and **JOBED**, which scores 33.

Your rack: **I I N O S S T**

Endgame problems can get very complex, and computer power (not available during a real game, obviously) has to be harnessed to be sure of getting the optimal path for each player. One good play for you would be **MOIST**, using the **M** of **MORAINE** and making four two-letter words. That scores you 27, and blocks your opponent's **FORKED**. If he now plays his next-best **ROED**, you go down to the bottom-right Triple Word square and play out with **SIN/WARDENS/GI**, which would give you a 14-point win.

If your opponent, rather than playing **ROED**, blocks your **SIN** outplay, such as by playing **GO/OD**, he gets a much smaller score and you can win by playing **SIN** elsewhere, such as making **SIN/JOBES**.

The two important things here are that you blocked his **FORKED**, and you left yourself more than one place to play out your remaining letters. And unlike other Scrabble situations, where the best move is all about the balance of probabilities, maximizing your chances, seeing which way the wind's blowing and hoping for the best, the working out of a winning endgame can, if you can find the right path, give you a guaranteed win without trusting to luck. It's an immensely satisfying feeling to get it right and know you've won a game that, with a little less care, you could have lost.

> *Scrabble facts* – *Tournaments and most clubs use special timers to limit the length of time a game can last. You generally get 25 minutes each to play all your moves – the timer has two clock-faces (or, these days, digital displays), one for each player, and your own side is only ticking while it's your turn. This means you can't hold everyone up by sitting for an hour working out your endgame strategy. If you go to a club where timers are used, they will be fully explained to you before you play, so don't be fazed by them.*

Developing endgame strategy

Endgames need a lot of practice. As you can see in the example above, they also need a good knowledge of the shorter words. And one further difficulty – it's much harder working out what your opponent might do, even if you know what tiles he is holding, when you can't physically see those tiles in front of you.

In a recent game, I worked out that my opponent's final tiles were **D E E E M R T**, and duly blocked what I thought was her best score (probably something like **ME** for 20) while making sure I could play out next move. What I completely missed was that she had the word **METERED**, which she duly played with great glee for around 70 points to win the game. I wouldn't have missed **METERED** if I'd had those tiles in front of me on my own rack (or at least I hope I wouldn't), but it's that much harder when you're looking at the letters scribbled in a corner of a crowded piece of paper.

There are other elements to endgame strategy. For example, if you have a high-scoring tile which you can't score much with on the board as it stands, you might be able to set yourself up an unblockable high score with it next time.

Your rack: **A A C D E I X**

Opponent's rack: **N R U Y**

Without showing the whole board, let's assume there is nowhere for you to score much with your **X**. If you play **ACID** in the second-top row, also making **AA** and **CH**, you can then play out in the next move with **AXE** along the top row, also making **ACH/XI/ED** and scoring 66 points. If your opponent uses the **D** to make **DUN** or **DRY**, you still get 60 for **AX** – not an outplay, but probably enough to win even a semi-close game.

The outcome from preparing an unblockable high score.

It will rarely, if ever, work out quite as neatly as that, but always see if you can use your perfect knowledge of your opponent's rack to set yourself up a move like this if you have a high-scoring tile on your rack at the endgame.

12 Other forms of Scrabble

Over the years, some players have taken to experimenting with other ways of playing Scrabble, apart from sitting facing your opponent across a table and playing to the standard rules of the game. Various ideas have come and gone. Some take hold and become popular alternatives, others vanish almost as soon as they appear.

Junior Scrabble

Many people will have had their first introduction to the game in the form of Junior Scrabble or some other children's version of the game. Junior Scrabble has a board with preprinted words in a Scrabble game format, and players have to pick tiles which match the letters on the board and play them in the appropriate squares. The back of the board has yet another version of the game, somewhat more challenging than Junior Scrabble but not quite up to the complexity of the real thing.

Simpsons Scrabble

Mattel currently produce a range of Scrabble games for younger players, including Simpsons Scrabble, which involves among other things Bart stealing Triple Word squares from an ever more exasperated Homer. This author has not had the pleasure of playing Simpsons Scrabble yet, but it sounds immense fun.

Computer Scrabble

No game would be complete today without its computer version. There are various forms of Computer Scrabble for sale, most of which have features such as allowing you to play the computer at different levels, thus putting your opponent at a standard of anything from beginner to expert. You can set the computer to tell you what it would have played with your letters, and, being a computer, it has the annoying property, when set at the top level, of never missing a seven-letter word or other good play, thus gradually shredding your confidence as it points out all the bonuses you missed. Happily you can always switch it off, an option I would dearly love to have with certain human opponents I can think of.

Duplicate Scrabble

Another way of playing the game is Duplicate Scrabble. This is a method used for large tournaments, and involves all the players sitting at their own individual table with their own set. You do not have an opponent – or rather, everyone else in the room is your opponent. A Master of Ceremonies will draw seven tiles, and all players then have a set time to come up with the highest-scoring move they can make with those tiles. Each player scores according to his or her move, but then the highest-scoring move is announced, and all the players who did not play that move remove their own play from their board, and substitute the highest-scoring move.

Play continues with the MC drawing as many tiles as are necessary to replenish the rack to seven in the normal way, and all the players, using the tiles which are already on the board and their new rack of seven tiles, again have to find the highest-scoring move they can. This process goes on until all the tiles have been used or no further plays are possible, with the player achieving the highest total for the game being the winner.

Pros and cons of Duplicate Scrabble

The advantage of Duplicate is that the luck element is eliminated; every player has the exact same rack and the exact same board at every move; thus, in theory, the best player should always win. While this is a big advantage, there are a number of downsides to Duplicate. The skills of rack management, such as accepting a lower score this time in the hope of a much higher one next time, do not apply. You are simply looking for the highest score you can every time; if you can get one extra point for adding an **S**, you do so. There is no question of playing in certain positions to try to open up the board or close it off. Only the score for that move is important.

Duplicate Scrabble also loses an important social aspect of the game. There is less to talk about afterwards. The 'If-only-I'd-played-this-you-wouldn't-have-been-able-to-play-that' type of conversation so beloved of Scrabble players doesn't take place. No clever play such as holding back a **U** because there are only half a dozen tiles left in the bag and the **Q** has not yet been played. If you need that **U** to obtain the highest possible score now, you have to play it.

Duplicate is the form of the game used for tournaments in France. It has been tried a few times in the UK but has never proved popular, and you will be most unlikely to come across it unless you cross the Channel (where they will sneakily place you at the additional disadvantage of having to play in French).

If Only

A few other unofficial variations of Scrabble have emerged. If Only allows you to turn one of your tiles over each shot and use it as a blank, as long as you score at least 50. You can then replace that 'blank' later with the letter it represents, and reuse the original tile. For instance, you play **SQUEEZE** with the **Z** represented by a tile turned over to look like a blank. You, but not your opponent, know that the tile is really a **K**. Later in the game, your rack reads **J H U C Z L E**. You place the **Z**, right way up, in **SQUEEZE**, lifting the **K**. Then you turn your **J** over to look like a blank, call it a **C**, and hey presto – the semantic mishmash of **J H U C Z L E** becomes **CHUCKLE**.

, If Only is a fast, open form of the game with bonuses aplenty and very high scores. It's useful for honing your bonus-finding skills, and as players generally enjoy this aspect of the game more than the board-blocking negative side, If Only friendlies are often played at tournaments at the end of the day as a wind-down from the rigours of the official games.

Super Scrabble

Some time ago, an Australian player came up with **Super Scrabble**. He cut a number of Scrabble boards into sections and created a larger board, something like 25 x 25 as against the standard 15 x 15. He added Quadruple and even Quintuple Letter and Word squares, and played with two or perhaps three full sets of tiles. I believe there was even a 'wrap-around' option, where, if you came to the end of the row or bottom of the column, you could continue your word by going back to the beginning of the row or top of the column, if the space was free. A version of Super Scrabble is available but not in most shops. It's best to master the standard game before you worry about going Super.

Scrabble Poker

Finally, I can add my own modest creation to the panoply of Scrabble-related games with Scrabble Poker, a combination of Scrabble and my other favourite game, though one at which I remain distressingly and impoverishingly inept, poker. Each player picks, or is dealt, two tiles face down and one face up. There is then a round of betting in normal poker fashion, with each player calling, raising or folding as he or she sees fit. Another four tiles are dealt to each player, face up, with a further round of betting at the conclusion of each round of dealing.

When each player has seven tiles, five open and the other two known only to the holder, there is a final round of betting. The winner is the player who can make the longest word from his or her seven tiles (unlike real poker, you can use all seven to make your hand, not just your best five). In the event of two or more players making words of equal length, the winner is the one whose word has the highest face value.

It may never take the casinos or the on-line poker sites by storm, but I and a few of my friends like it as an occasional alternative to the Full Scrabble Monty, as it were. The civilizing influence of Scrabble tends to ensure stakes stay as pennies rather than pounds, and it's another good exercise in bonus-spotting, as well as giving practice in five- and six-letter words, which can sometimes get rather swept aside in the real game in the rush to master twos, threes, and fours, and to learn large numbers of ever more unlikely sevens.

None of these alternatives will ever usurp the genuine article from its position of supremacy, remaining rather the boisterous offspring of a serene and untroubled mother. Difficult enough to be challenging, yet not so arcane as to be open only to a select few, sociable, with the right combination of luck and skill, it can be tinkered with, but not improved upon. It is a tribute to the original game that it can admit so many other versions yet still remain effortlessly superior to all of them.

13 Taking it further

So, you've had your appetite whetted for trying to move your Scrabble game up a level or two. You want to squeeze more points out of every move with neat little parallel plays using two- and three-letter words, you want to play some impressive bonuses, and then eke out a win with a well-thought-out endgame. The only problem is, if your Scrabble-playing friends and relatives don't want to come on this journey with you, you are pitched into an endless round of 'What does that mean?' and 'That's not a proper word'.

Even showing Auntie Mary that **XU**, **JIZ** or **ETESIAN** is there in black and white in the *Collins Scrabble Lists* is unlikely to appease her. Learning useful words and good techniques to improve your game is seen as unsportsmanlike, almost cheating. So your next move has to be to take a deep breath and move into the wonderful world of your local Scrabble club.

Clubs and tournaments

People can have some odd ideas about Scrabble clubs – that's if they realize they exist at all. They are assumed to be patronized solely by either elderly ladies in pink cardigans or geeky guys taking an evening off from working out the square root of minus one. While I can't quite guarantee you won't meet anyone at all like that, most Scrabble club members are normal, well-adjusted people who want nothing more than a sociable evening out and a good game of Scrabble.

> **Scrabble facts** – There are about 330 Scrabble clubs in Britain, and a further 200 or so in schools.

You can find the whereabouts of your local Scrabble club by writing to:

Scrabble Clubs UK
Mattel House
Vanwall Business Park
Vanwall Road
Maidenhead
Berkshire
SL6 4UB.

Or if you're of a more technological turn of mind, try putting 'Scrabble' and your home town into your internet search engine and see what comes up.

What happens at a Scrabble Club?

It's impossible to be definitive, as each will be run in a slightly different way. Some will have a very informal approach, where you just turn up and play anyone else who is waiting for a game. Others are more structured, where you all start at the same time and the organizer tells you who to play. Others again have a league table where you have to play everyone, or everyone in your division, once or twice in a season (however long a season may be), but within that you arrange your own games at times to suit.

However, a few things are pretty much universal at any Scrabble club in the country (and, I imagine, the world). There will be a meeting place and a regular evening when the club meets (although the large and venerable London Scrabble League, of which I have had the honour of being chairman, arranges four-player fixtures in members' homes). There will either be tables about the size of card tables for individual games, or longer trestle tables that can accommodate a few games at a time.

Players generally supply their own Scrabble sets and other paraphernalia, so take yours if possible. Crucially, tea and coffee will be supplied either as part of your entry fee or subscription, or for a small charge.

There are a few other ways in which playing at a club may be different from how you are used to playing at home.

De luxe sets

Most clubs insist on, or at least give preference to, de luxe sets; these have boards which are on a turntable so that they can be moved to face each player, and tiles that click into the square on which they are played so that they don't move around when the board is turned, accidentally nudged or otherwise moved. Nothing detracts more from the pleasure of the game than continually having to realign the tiles so that you can read the words properly, or having to twist your neck to try to read the board upside-down. You don't read a book or newspaper upside-down, so why try to do it with a Scrabble board?

Smooth tiles

As you now know, the most valuable tiles in the bag are the blanks. For that reason, it is slightly unsatisfactory that you can sometimes, accidentally or deliberately, feel that a tile in the bag is a blank. Smooth tiles prevent any suspicion that a player has been feeling in the bag for a blank tile. The newest sets do contain smooth tiles. However, there are many older sets around which do not contain smooth tiles. Some Clubs insist that you play with smooth tiles.

Playing one opponent at a time

Quite simply, Scrabble is a game for two players. The rules that come with your set may say you can play with up to four, but the two-person game is far superior. You cannot form a strategy, nor can you plan ahead in any way, if there are two or even three more people to play between your last turn and your next one. Apart from that, it's just boring playing with three or four players – you are only involved in the game a third or a quarter of the time, and if one or two of your opponents are slow, you can have an interminable wait till it comes round to you again. Sure, you can be looking for what you might play when it eventually becomes your turn, but only to a limited extent. You have no way of knowing if your opponents' plays will drive a coach and horses through the place you were going to make your move – or if they might give you a better one.

In club and tournament play, if the numbers are odd, one person will sit out for a round. Alternatively, one player may take on two players at once, but in two completely separate games on two separate boards. This is an excellent way of sharpening up your Scrabble reflexes, rather like a chess simul, a form of chess match where one (usually superior) player takes on a number of others simultaneously.

Use of *Collins Scrabble Lists* for all adjudications

It's very annoying when you play a word, only to have it disallowed – especially if, the week before, you were allowed to play it. It's even more maddening if your opponent the week before was allowed to play it. Many clubs use *Collins Scrabble Lists* to adjudicate on any challenges. This lists every allowable word in strict alphabetical order except that very long words, those with 10 letters or more, are confined to a separate section at the end. For more on allowable word forms see the back of this book.

Creating your own list of words

If you are not using *Collins Scrabble Lists*, then the second-best solution is to start your own list. If you allow, say, **NUBILER**, put it on an 'allowed' list and keep it with your set or tuck it into your dictionary. Similarly, if you decide that **EDIBLER** is a comparative too far, it goes on your 'disallowed list'. Then, when the word comes up next week or next year, you can at least be consistent. But you still have the problem of deciding which list it goes on in the first place – and when one of you has played the word and there are only the two of you there, a one-each stalemate on whether the word should be valid is almost inevitable. The best solution is to buy *Collins Scrabble Lists*. If it's in there, the word is valid; if it ain't, it ain't.

Playing to win

As I've emphasized throughout this book, it's not what you score that counts, it's whether you score more than your opponent. It's a statement of the obvious, surely. Don't we always play a game to win?

In the early days of the National Scrabble Championship (NSC), the winner was the person with the highest total score over a set number of games. It didn't matter whether you actually won the games or not. So if you could score 500 points or so in all your games, even if you lost one or two, this was better than plodding along scoring 300–400 but making sure you always won. This led to a highly artificial form of the game where your opponent effectively became your partner where you played a very open game, which means you tried to make lots of places on the board where bonus words would fit in.

Matchplay Scrabble

Eventually most players realized this was a silly way to play, and what was called Matchplay Scrabble took over. Quite simply, this meant playing to win: scoring 500 is pointless if your opponent gets 501. At the end of the tournament, the player who had won the most games was the winner.

Having said that, you can't afford to neglect the possibility of high scores, because players on the same number of wins are ranked according to their 'spread'. This is the total points scored by you minus the total points scored by all your opponents – the equivalent of goal difference in football. So, at least at the beginning of a tournament or club competition, and at the end if you're in contention, it's nice to stick in a really high score, as long as your opponent doesn't score almost as much (or even more). Note that spread is a very different thing from score. Spread takes into account not just your score but also what your opponent scores against you, so you must always be alert to denying chances to your opponent as well as getting a good score yourself.

So what all that boils down to for you is this. Don't just think of your move as a score of a certain number of points. See how it affects the board before you play it. Check if it opens up any high-scoring opportunities, which your opponent is almost bound to take. If it does, try to find an alternative, less risky move elsewhere.

The playing of **CARE** would be a risky move here, as you have opened a triple-word chance for your opponent if he has an **S**, **D**, **R**, **T** or even **X** for **CAREX**.

Both players keep the score

If you are playing to win, it follows that you need to know whether you are winning or losing, and by how much, at any particular time. If you're behind, you may need to take a bit of a risk and make some openings. If you're ahead, you should be trying to close things up. So make sure you keep the score. If your opponent is of a like mind – fine, both of you can then keep the score. In any case, it's useful to have a check – mistakes are easily made.

When you try all these things for yourself at a club, as well as involving yourself in the higher standard of play, you will be rewarded by finding Scrabble suddenly just feels like a better game.

Differences between club and home play

There are a few other ways in which club play and home play differ. The moment when your shot is over is defined carefully. If timers are being used, it's the moment you press the button to stop your own timer and start your opponent's; without timers, it's the moment you announce your score. Until that point of no return is passed, you can take your tiles back and change your mind.

Challenging

From this, it follows that you shouldn't challenge your opponent's move until he has pressed the timer or announced that score; by doing so, you alert him to the fact that you think the word is wrong, and he may take the opportunity to think again.

Lifting the tile-bag

Another thing newcomers to a club find quite odd is the sight of players lifting the bag well clear of the table when they pick new tiles. The rule is that the bag should be lifted to shoulder height, thus precluding any possibility of cheating by having a sly look in the bag as it lies on the table. As with the 'feelable blanks', this is not to say that cheating was rife before this rule was introduced; merely that it is better to eliminate the possibility of cheating rather than having any unwarranted suspicions lingering around the name of an honest player.

No late changes
Apart from a few details introduced mainly to facilitate the use of timers, the actual rules of the game at a club are exactly the same as you are used to at home – with one exception: you can't change when there are fewer than seven tiles left in the bag.

This rule was introduced back in the dark days when a **Q** picked late in the game was likely to be unplayable. It prevented a player throwing a **Q** back into the bag at the last moment, in an attempt to foist it on his opponent. Nowadays, with **QI**, **QAT** and so on at our disposal, a last-minute **Q** is not such a nightmare, but the rule persists. It may be fair to say that you shouldn't be allowed to put a **Q**, a **J**, a **V**, or some other unplayable letter back in the bag at the very end, forcing your opponent to pick it if he wants to make a move. On the other hand, a more hard-nosed player may think it should all be part of the game. At the moment, once there are six tiles in the bag or fewer, whatever you've got on your rack is what you're stuck with.

Tournament play
This has the same rules as club play, but it's a difference of atmosphere more than anything else. Everyone is trying that bit harder and their play is that bit sharper.

Tournaments are generally divided into divisions, so that you play people roughly of your own standard. Also, tournaments are usually played under the Swiss system, which means that, as far as possible, you play someone on the same number of wins as yourself. However they are arranged, everyone plays in every round, so there is no danger of travelling half the length of the country and only playing one game because you lose in the first round.

A one-day tournament will normally be held over six rounds. Weekend tournaments over two days can have between 11 and 16 rounds. Sometimes, usually on a holiday weekend, they are played over three days, with between 17 and 19 rounds. Occasionally there are even weeklong tournaments. If you fancy having a go at a tournament, get in touch with the Association of British Scrabble Players. The ABSP regulates tournament play in the UK, and you'll find a very useful calendar of events on their website, **www.absp.org.uk**

Reaching for the top

One of the best aspects of getting involved in the Scrabble club and tournament scene is that, even if you don't immediately feel ready to take on the very best players, you can still mix with them, get to know them, and learn from them. With most competitions being divided into divisions, you can rub shoulders with the top players without the risk to your ego of actually having to play them. Go along to some tournaments, especially the bigger ones and you will find that restaurant, bar, and tea-room are a mix of potential world champions, the greenest of newcomers, and everything in between.

Once you've taken that first step of venturing along to a local club, the whole vista of how to get more out of Scrabble starts to open out for you. You will find out where to get hold of the better equipment that adds so much to the game but may not be available in your local shops. Many players now have personalized boards made to their own design (so much classier than a personalized number plate). Round boards, which can be turned without knocking over racks, cups of tea, etc., are particularly popular. Someone will tell you about computer programs, electronic pocket gizmos of various kinds, or even good old-fashioned books, any or all of which you can use to improve your word power and check where you might have done better in an actual game.

At this stage in developing your Scrabble skills, don't worry about tournaments but just concentrate on getting a good grip of some of the basics in this book, such as the twos, the threes, making good use of **JQXZ**, trying for bonuses by balancing your rack between vowels and consonants, keeping those bonus-friendly tiles (especially blank and **S**) and learning some of the sevens and eights that they make. Then either get your regular opponents to do the same, or join a Scrabble club. I wish you many hours of happy and stimulating Scrabble playing.

Allowable word forms

If you haven't, or haven't yet, got *Collins Scrabble Lists*, you and your fellow-players will have to do a bit of adjudicating from time to time. A dictionary will generally list only a base word, such as **TABLE**. It will not specifically show **TABLES**, **TABLED**, **TABLING** or **TABLINGS**. Before starting play it's worth agreeing a few guidelines as to what you're going to allow and what you aren't.

Plurals

Nouns, fairly obviously, have a plural. But all nouns? If you watch *Countdown* you will have become familiar with the concept of 'count nouns' and 'mass nouns'. A count noun is something you can have more than one of, and therefore the noun takes a plural. **MAN**, **HORSE** and **BANANA** are all count nouns with obvious plurals. It needn't be a thing you can touch – **DAY**, **LIE** and **FEELING** are also count nouns.

The problems start, if you allow them to, with the mass noun. Can you pluralize words like **TENNIS**, **CALCITE** and **FLU**? *Countdown* will often say 'no', declaring that they are mass nouns, so you can't have more than one of them. My advice about this is – forget it. Any noun can have a plural. Go ahead and allow **TENNISES**, **CALCITES** and **FLUS**. *Collins Scrabble Lists* certainly does.

What is not always so easy to work out is what the plural actually is. We know that it is usually formed by adding **-s**. There are some well-known exceptions – so well-known, in fact, that you barely register them. Nouns ending in **-s**, **-ch** or **-sh** all add **-es**, for example **TENNISES**, **CHURCHES** and **BRUSHES**. (As usual, there are exceptions to the exceptions – words ending in the Scottish **ch**, like **LOCH**, just add **-s** in the plural).

Words ending in **-y** preceded by a consonant change the **-y** to **-ies**, so we have **FLIES**, **BERRIES**, etc. And of course we have **MEN**, **MICE**, **SHEEP** and plenty of other common irregular plurals.

But what is the plural of **TROUT**? Usually it would just be **TROUT**, as in 'I caught six trout.' But could it ever be valid to say **TROUTS**? Remember **TROUT** has an informal meaning of a silly or unpleasant person. 'The neighbours round here are a right bunch of trout'. That sounds odd. 'A right bunch of trouts', surely. And sometimes you need a bit more technical knowledge. Is **RADIUSES** an acceptable alternative to **RADII** as the plural of **RADIUS**? It's at moments like these that you do need to go to the dictionary – preferably always the same one. For the record, *Collins Scrabble Lists* allows **TROUTS** and **RADIUSES**.

Verbs

What about verbs? Again, it's fairly simple on the face of it. We have the **-s**, **-ed** and **-ing** endings; thus **CONTAIN** leads to **CONTAINS**, **CONTAINED** and **CONTAINING**. If the verb ends in **-e**, drop the **e** before adding **-ed** or **-ing**, as in **STROKED**, **STROKING**. And we have a similar **-y** adjustment to the one we have with nouns, as in **MARRIES**, **MARRIED**. Then there is the doubling, in certain circumstances, of a final consonant before **-ed** and **-ing**, as in **STRUMMED**, **STRUMMING**. That's quite a few exceptions already, all of which we handle in normal speech and writing without a moment's thought. But if we think of short, simple verbs, there seem to be more exceptions than adherents to the rule – **RUN**, **SWIM**, **BUILD**, **TAKE**, **GO**, **DO**, **SPEAK**, **PAY**, **EAT**, **DRINK** and **MAKE** all deviate from the **-ed** form. Again, there is no substitute for a good dictionary if you want to be sure of the irregularities.

Adjectives

Now for the adjectives. Before the advent of *Collins Scrabble Lists*, no element of word adjudication caused more problems than whether you could add **-er** and **-est** to an adjective. **POLITER**, **STERILEST**, **WHOLER**, **HONESTEST**, **UNFITTER**, **LIVEST**, **DEADEST** – these and many like them caused hours of harmless merriment, and the occasional tantrum, as their acceptability or otherwise was debated. There is no doubt now which ones are not allowed (**STERILEST** and **WHOLER**).

Glossary of terms

Only terms used in this book are included.

ABSP The Association of British Scrabble Players, the official organization which regulates tournament play and carries out other associated functions.

affix A prefix or suffix.

anagram A word which comprises the same letters as another word, but in a different order.

big tiles The high-scoring tiles – **J**, **Q**, **X** and **Z**. In some contexts also includes the **S**s and blanks.

blank One of two tiles in the set which the holder may use to represent any letter.

block To play a move which prevents an opponent from playing in that part of the board.

blocked board *or* **game** A board with few positions where moves are possible. Opposite of open board or game.

blocker A move which prevents an opponent from playing, either a specific move or in a particular part of the board; a word which cannot be extended either at the front or the back.

bonus The extra 50 points awarded for playing all seven tiles in one move; or a move which achieves this.

break up To play some of a promising combination of letters.

challenge To query the validity of a word played by an opponent. The word must then be checked in a dictionary or *Collins Scrabble Lists*.

change To use one's turn by putting unwanted tiles back into the bag and picking new ones, rather than by placing a move on the board.

combination Any stated group of letters.

common letter A low-scoring letter of which there are several in the set; or a letter which is part of a word on the board both horizontally and vertically.

compound word A word made out of two smaller words, which combines the meanings of both of them.

consonant-heavy Describes a rack with too many consonants.

contraction A word formed from a longer word, but with some of the letters omitted, although the meaning is unchanged.

count noun A noun representing something of which there can be one or more than one, e.g. table. *Opposite* of mass noun.

Criss-Crosswords The name of an early version of Scrabble.

crosswise play The playing of a move which creates only one new word on the board. *Opposite* of parallel play.

discard (tiles) To replace unwanted tiles in the bag, in order to draw new ones.

distribution The frequency with which each letter appears in a standard set of tiles.

Double Letter square (score) A square, on most boards coloured light blue, which doubles the point value of any tile played on it.

Double Word square (score) A square, on most boards coloured pink, which doubles the point value of any word which has one of its letters on it.

draw (tiles) To pick tiles from the bag.

duplicate The same letter appearing two or more times on the same rack.

endgame The final stages of a game, when knowledge of the letters which are or may be on an opponent's rack affects the moves a player makes.

end hook A letter which can be placed at the end of a word to make another word.

face value The number of points scored by any tile, word or move, unaffected by Premium squares.

floater A tile on the board, in such a position that it can be used as part of another word.

frequency The number of times a given letter appears in a standard set.

front hook A letter which can be placed at the beginning of a word to make another word.

hook A letter which can be placed at the beginning or end of a word to make another word; to play a move which uses a letter in this way.

interlocking Joining tiles to those already on the board to make new words; all moves in a game except the opening move must be interlocking.

It The name of an early version of Scrabble.

leave (the) The tiles left on a player's rack, after playing a move but before picking fresh tiles from the bag.

Lexiko The name of the original version of Scrabble.

mass noun A noun representing something which cannot be counted, e.g. fairness. *Opposite* of count noun.

Matchplay Playing solely to win the game, without relevance to the score achieved.

one-pointer A tile worth one point, i.e. the commonest letters most useful for making bonus words – **A E I L N O R S T U**.

open board *or* **game** A board with several positions where moves, especially high-scoring moves, are possible. *Opposite of* blocked board or game.

outplay A move which enables a player to play all his or her remaining tiles, there being no more tiles left in the bag – therefore, the last move of the game.

parallel play A move in which a word is placed parallel to another word or words on the board, thus also forming one or more vertical words if the main word is played horizontally, and vice versa. *Opposite of crosswise play.*

play out To play all one's remaining tiles, there being no more tiles left in the bag, thus playing the last move of the game.

point value The number of points scored by a given tile.

prefix A combination of letters which can often be found at the beginning of a word.

Premium square A square on the board which awards more than face value to a letter or word played on it – a Double Letter, Double Word, Triple Letter, or Triple Word score.

rack The wooden or plastic stand on which a player places his or her tiles; the letters held by a player at any particular time.

rack management The playing of tiles in such a way as to increase one's chances of having a bonus word, or other high-scoring move, on the next or subsequent turn.

'six plus one' list A list of seven-letter words which can be formed by the addition of one other letter to a particular combination of six letters. Similarly 'six plus two' list or 'seven plus one' list.

spread In a game or tournament, the total number of points scored by a player, minus the total points scored against him or her. A spread may therefore be positive or negative.

suffix A combination of letters which can often be found at the end of a word.

Swiss system A method of organizing fixtures at large tournaments, where each player is, as far as possible, matched against another on the same number of wins.

synergy The property of certain combinations of letters of combining well with each other to form words.

take A word is said to take a particular letter when that letter can be added to the word to form another word. A word may take a letter at the front or at the end.

tile Any of the one hundred pieces, each (except the two blanks) representing a letter, which are used to play the game by forming words on the board.

tile-tracking Noting which tiles have been played, and modifying one's play accordingly to take account of which tiles are likely to be picked or which tiles the opponent is, or may be, holding.

Triple Letter square (score) A square, on most boards coloured dark blue, which triples the point value of any letter played on it.

Triple Word square (score) A square, on most boards coloured red, which triples the point value of any word which has one of its letters on it.

vowel–consonant balance *or* **vowel–consonant split** The number of vowels and consonants on the rack, or remaining in the bag, at any particular time.

vowel-heavy Describes a rack with too many vowels.

Z-three A three-letter word containing a **Z**.

Answers to puzzles

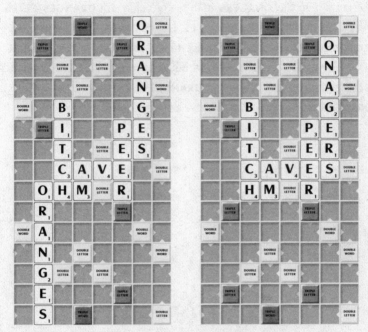

Your rack is **A E G N O R S**

Finding **ORANGES** should not have presented you with too much of a problem. But the importance of the two- and three-letter words is shown by the fact that you can't fit **ORANGES** in without either remembering **PE** and **ES**, or noticing that unlikely hook of turning **HM** into **OHM**.

Incidentally, both those moves put a letter in an outer row of the board, and thus open up a possible nine-timer – a word stretching from one Triple Word square to the next, thus having its score multiplied by nine as well as scoring the extra 50, probably scoring about 150 for one move.

This is undesirable, because your opponent gets first crack at it, and if your opponent has also been nursing his or her rack towards a bonus, they might just be ready to step in. That shouldn't stop you from playing **ORANGES** if it's the only bonus you can see, but you'd be better, if you know it, to play **ONAGERS**, in the same column as **ORANGES/PE/ES** but one square down, also making **PE**, **ER** and **CAVES**. That not only scores more but also, and more importantly, doesn't open the nine-timer.

An **onager** is a type of wild ass, but what you should try to remember is the fact that it's an anagram of **ORANGES**, so that next time you find **ORANGES** on your rack, you will have a bigger choice of moves to play.

Your rack is **DEIJNOS**

Notice how the short word comfortably outscores the longer one, and, in this case, also prevents your opponent from getting much profit out of the Triple Word squares in the top row.

CHALLENGE NO. 3

Your rack is **A E L M Q S U**

Playing **QUALM** opens a bonus spot along the bottom row, and it may be better to forego 10 points by restricting your play to **QUA**. If your opponent's last move was just playing an **N** after **PI** to make **PIN** for six points, it looks like he or she is close to a bonus so **QUA** might be more sensible. Indeed, taking out one of the high-scoring bonus spots by playing **QUALMS** or **SQUEAL** might be more sensible still. If, on the other hand, your opponent has just played **ZO/HO** for 27, he or she probably played for the points and is less likely to have a bonus rack now.

Your move will depend on how defensive you want to be, how good you think your opponent is and what sort of a feeling you've got about the whole position.

CHALLENGE NO. 4

1 **ALLURES**, **LAURELS**

2 **ALLURES** goes in the second column from the right, also making **AR**, **NE** and **NEEDLESS**. **LAURELS** goes in the second row from the bottom, also making **AL**, **TA** and **HILLOCKS**.

Playing **ALLURES**

Playing **LAURELS**

3 **SQUALLER** goes round the **Q**, also making **ST** and **UN**.

Playing **SQUALLER**

CHALLENGE NO. 5

The blank is pretty clearly going to have to be a vowel, and **E** is the most likely, especially with the duplicate **R**. Note that, even if your opponent played **QUINE** and you didn't know it, you do know **EQUINE**, and you're every bit as entitled to play it as old smarty-pants on the other side of the table.

Your rack: **B D O R R S ?**

CHAPTER 7
A BONUS WORD CHALLENGE

Twenty teasers

The unexpected 'hooks' are shown in brackets.

ASPIRIN (ASPIRING)

NIGHTJAR

ENCHANT (PENCHANT)

PASTRAMI

PARQUET OVERTHIN (OVERTHINK)

AWFULLY (LAWFULLY)

LAVISHES (LAVISHEST)

FLAMING (FLAMINGO)

EXPLOITS

ATISHOO

WORDPLAY (SWORDPLAY)

CHATEAU

HEREUPON (THEREUPON/WHEREUPON)

GAZELLE

MULTIPLE (MULTIPLEX)

DIPLOMA

REHEATED (PREHEATED)

RAVIOLI

REFREEZE

CHAPTER 8
A FEW TEASERS

1   You can check the answers. in the appropriate list (**A E I N R S**, etc).

2   **SEEABLE, STAIDLY, RATLIKE, UNQUIET, SUBDEAN, REKEYED, PRONAOS, ELOGIST**

3   **ANGERED** (+ anagrams), **ELATION/TOENAIL, ORGANIC, EMAILED/LIMEADE, CIGARET, ANEROID, AMNIOTE, LINOCUT**

CHAPTER 9
SOME GREAT PUZZLES TO TRY

1 Through the floating **G**: **ASTRINGE, REASTING, STEARING, TASERING**
Through the **N**: **TRANNIES**
Through the **T**: **INTREATS, NITRATES, STRAITEN, TARTINES, TERTIANS**
Through the **O**: **ANOESTRI, ARSONITE, NOTARIES, NOTARISE, ROSINATE, SENORITA**
Through the **R**: **STRAINER**

2 Through the **K**: **SNEAKIER**
Through the **U**: **UNEASIER**
Through the **P**: **NAPERIES**
Through the **N**: **ANSERINE** (making **MANA** or **MANI**)
Through the **D**: **ARSENIDE, DENARIES, DRAISENE, NEARSIDE**

3 Through the **E**: **UNELATED**
Through the **I**: **UNTAILED**
Through the **U**: **UNDULATE**

4 Through the **B**: **BACTERIN**
Through the **U**: **ANURETIC**
Through the **V**: **NAVICERT**
Through the **A**: **CARINATE, CRANIATE**
Through the **C**: **ACENTRIC**

A-Z GUIDE TO
SCRABBLE
WORDS

A

Essential info
Value: 1 point
Number in set: 9

A is a common tile and is very useful for forming short words to squeeze into tight corners, as it can be added easily to the majority of other tiles to form two-letter words. A can even be added to itself (to form AA, a Hawaiian word for rough volcanic rock, 2 points). A is also very helpful for short, high-scoring words such as AXE (10 points, or 9 points with its US variant AX). Some more unusual examples of three-letter words include AAL (an Asian shrub, 3 points), APO (a type of protein, 5 points) and the high-scoring ADZ (a tool for cutting roof tiles, 13 points). A is one of the letters of the RETAIN set and is therefore a good letter to keep if trying to get a bonus word.

Two-letter words beginning with A

AA	AG	AM	AT
AB	AH	AN	AW
AD	AI	AR	AX
AE	AL	AS	AY

Some three-letter words beginning with A

AAH	AFF	ALA	ANA	ASP
AAL	AGA	ALB	ANE	ASS
ABA	AGO	ALF	ANI	ATT
ABB	AHA	ALP	ANN	AWA
ABO	AHI	ALT	APO	AWL
ABY	AIA	AMA	ARB	AWN
ACH	AIN	AMI	ARD	AYE
ADO	AIT	AMP	ARF	AYU
ADZ	AKA	AMU	ARY	AZO

Hooks

Hooking requires a player to look at words already on the board without being distracted by their pronunciation. This can lead to simple hooking solutions being overlooked. Fortunately, A is one of the easier tiles to play as a hook or a tag and it can be front-hooked to many words as their negating form (e.g. MORAL can be changed to AMORAL).

Some front-hooks
Two letters to three

A-AH	A-GO	A-LA	A-PO
A-AL	A-HA	A-MA	A-RE
A-AS	A-HI	A-MI	A-SH
A-BA	A-ID	A-MU	A-TE
A-BO	A-IN	A-NA	A-WE
A-BY	A-IS	A-NE	A-YE
A-CH	A-IT	A-NY	A-YU
A-DO	A-KA	A-PE	A-ZO

Three letters to four

A-BED	A-HOY	A-NAN	A-SEA
A-BET	A-IDE	A-NEW	A-SHY
A-BID	A-JAR	A-NIL	A-TAP
A-BUT	A-KIN	A-NON	A-TOP
A-BYE	A-LAP	A-NOW	A-VOW
A-DRY	A-LAY	A-PAY	A-WAY
A-FAR	A-LEE	A-POD	A-WED
A-GAS	A-LIT	A-RED	A-WEE
A-GIN	A-LOW	A-RID	A-WRY
A-HEM	A-MEN	A-ROW	A-YES
A-HIS	A-MID	A-RUM	

Four letters to five

A-BACK	A-BUZZ	A-GAZE	A-ISLE
A-BAND	A-COLD	A-GENE	A-ITCH
A-BASE	A-CORN	A-GENT	A-KING
A-BASH	A-CUTE	A-GIST	A-LACK
A-BASK	A-DOWN	A-GLEE	A-LAND
A-BEAM	A-DOZE	A-GLOW	A-LANE
A-BEAR	A-DUST	A-GONE	A-LANT
A-BIDE	A-FEAR	A-GOOD	A-LATE
A-BLED	A-FIRE	A-GRIN	A-LEFT
A-BLOW	A-FOOT	A-HEAD	A-LIEN
A-BODE	A-FORE	A-HEAP	A-LIKE
A-BOIL	A-FOUL	A-HIGH	A-LINE
A-BORE	A-GAIN	A-HIND	A-LIST
A-BOUT	A-GAPE	A-HINT	A-LIVE
A-BRAY	A-GATE	A-HOLD	A-LOFT
A-BRIM	A-GAVE	A-HULL	A-LONE

A-LONG   A-NEAR   A-RISE   A-VALE

A-LOUD   A-NIGH   A-ROSE   A-VAST

A-LURE   A-NODE   A-SCOT   A-VINE

A-MAIN   A-PACE   A-SHED   A-VOID

A-MASS   A-PAGE   A-SIDE   A-WAIT

A-MATE   A-PAID   A-SKEW   A-WAKE

A-MAZE   A-PART   A-STIR   A-WARD

A-MEND   A-PEAK   A-STUN   A-WARE

A-MICE   A-PEEK   A-SWAY   A-WARN

A-MINE   A-PERT   A-SWIM   A-WASH

A-MISS   A-PING   A-TILT   A-WAVE

A-MOLE   A-PORT   A-TOLL   A-WING

A-MOVE   A-READ   A-TONE   A-WOKE

A-MUCK   A-REAL   A-TRIP   A-WORK

A-MUSE   A-REAR   A-VAIL   A-YELP

Five letters to six

A-BASED   A-BOUND   A-ETHER

A-BASER   A-BRAID   A-FIELD

A-BATED   A-BROAD   A-FLAME

A-BIDED   A-BURST   A-FLOAT

A-BIDER   A-BUSED   A-FRESH

A-BLATE   A-CATER   A-FRONT

A-BLAZE   A-CIDER   A-GAZED

A-BLING   A-CRAWL   A-GEIST

A-BLOOM   A-CROSS   A-GHAST

A-BLUSH   A-CUTER   A-GLARE

A-BOARD   A-DREAD   A-GLEAM

A-BODED   A-DRIFT   A-GOING

A-BORNE   A-DROIT   A-GREED

A-GUISE

A-HORSE

A-LIGHT

A-LINED

A-LINER

A-MATED

A-MAZED

A-MIDST

A-MORAL

A-MOUNT

A-MOVED

A-MUSED

A-MUSER

A-NEATH

A-NIGHT

A-PIECE

A-RAISE

A-REACH

A-RIDER

A-RIGHT

A-RILED

A-RISEN

A-ROUND

A-ROUSE

A-SCEND

A-SCENT

A-SHAKE

A-SHAME

A-SHIER

A-SHINE

A-SHORE

A-SLAKE

A-SLANT

A-SLEEP

A-SLOPE

A-SLOSH

A-SMEAR

A-SPINE

A-SPIRE

A-SPORT

A-SPOUT

A-SQUAT

A-STARE

A-START

A-STERN

A-STONE

A-STONY

A-STOOP

A-STRAY

A-STRUT

A-SWARM

A-SWING

A-SWIRL

A-SWOON

A-TONAL

A-TONED

A-TONER

A-TONIC

A-TOPIC

A-TRIAL

A-TWAIN

A-TWEEL

A-TWEEN

A-TWIXT

A-TYPIC

A-UNTIE

A-VAUNT

A-VENGE

A-VENUE

A-VERSE

A-VISED

A-VITAL

A-VOUCH

A-VOWED

A-VOWER

A-WAKED

A-WAKEN

A-WATCH

A-WEARY

A-WEIGH

A-WHEEL

A-WHILE

A-WHIRL

A-WOKEN

A-WRACK

A-WRONG

A-ZONAL

Six letters to seven

A-BANDED

A-BASHED

A-BASING

A-BATING

A-BETTED

A-BETTER

A-BIDING

A-BIOTIC

A-BODING

A-BOUGHT

A-BRAYED

A-BRIDGE

A-BROACH

A-BUBBLE

A-BUTTED

A-BUTTER

A-CLINIC

A-CORNED

A-CUTELY

A-CUTEST

A-CYCLIC

A-DEEMED

A-DUSTED

A-FEARED

A-GENTRY

A-GROUND

A-LAYING

A-LENGTH

A-LINING

A-LONELY

A-MASSED

A-MAZING

A-MENDED

A-MENDER

A-MENTAL

A-MOTION

A-MOVING

A-MUSING

A-NEARED

A-NOTHER

A-PAYING

A-PLENTY

A-QUIVER

A-RAISED

A-REALLY

A-RIPPLE

A-RISING

A-SCARED

A-SCONCE

A-SCRIBE

A-SEPTIC

A-SHAMED

A-SHIEST

A-SHIVER

A-SOCIAL

A-SPIRED

A-SPRAWL

A-SPREAD

A-SPROUT

A-SQUINT

A-STABLE

A-STATIC

A-STONED

A-STOUND

A-STRAND

A-STRICT

A-STRIDE

A-SUDDEN

A-SUNDER

A-THIRST

A-THRILL

A-TINGLE

A-TONING

A-TROPHY

A-VAILED

A-VENGED

A-VENGER

A-VERTED

A-VOIDED

A-VOIDER

A-VOWING

A-WAITED

A-WAITER

A-WAKING

A-WARDED

A-WARDER

A-WARNED

Seven letters to eight

A-BANDING

A-BASHING

A-BATABLE

A-BEARING

A-BEGGING

A-BETTING

A-BOUNDED

A-BRAIDED

A-BRAYING

A-BRIDGED

A-BROOKED

A-BUTTING

A-CENTRIC

A-CERATED

A-CHROMIC

A-COSMISM

A-COSMIST

A-DEEMING

A-DREADED

A-DUSTING

A-DYNAMIC

A-ESTHETE

A-ESTIVAL

A-ETHERIC

A-FEARING

A-FEBRILE

A-FLUTTER

A-GENESIS

A-GENETIC

A-GLIMMER

A-GLITTER

A-GNOSTIC

A-GRAPHIC

A-GREEING

A-GRISING

A-GUISING

A-KINESES

A-KINESIS

A-KINETIC

A-LEGGING

A-LIGHTED

A-LOGICAL

A-MASSING

A-MAZEDLY

A-MEIOSIS

A-MENAGED

A-MENDING

A-MIDMOST

A-MIDSHIP

A-MISSING

A-MITOSIS

A-MITOTIC

A-MORALLY

A-MORTISE

A-MOUNTED

A-NEARING

A-NEURISM

A-NODALLY

A-NOINTED

A-NOINTER

A-PIARIST

A-PLASTIC

A-PRACTIC

A-PYRETIC

A-PYREXIA

A-RAISING

A-REACHED

A-READING

A-RETTING

A-SCENDED

A-SCRIBED

A-SEISMIC

A-SEPTATE

A-SHAMING

A-SHINESS

A-SLAKING

A-SOCIALS

A-SPARKLE

A-SPERSED

A-SPHERIC

A-SPIRANT

A-SPIRING

A-SPORTED

A-STARTED

A-STERNAL

A-STEROID

A-STONIED

A-STONING A-TROPISM A-VOUCHED

A-STONISH A-TWITTER A-VOUCHER

A-STUNNED A-TYPICAL A-WAITING

A-SYNERGY A-VAILING A-WAKENED

A-SYSTOLE A-VAUNTED A-WAKENER

A-TECHNIC A-VENGING A-WANTING

A-TONALLY A-VENTURE A-WARDING

A-TREMBLE A-VERSION A-WARNING

A-TROPHIC A-VERTING A-WEARIED

A-TROPINE A-VOIDING A-WEATHER

Handy Hint: The Challenge

Never be afraid to challenge a word which looks unusual, misspelled or which you do not recognise. Many a word has slipped through the net this way, and you have nothing to lose by challenging your opponent. DO NOT BE INTIMIDATED. Gamesmanship occurs in Scrabble too and your opponent may be hoping you will let their mistakes or guesses go unnoticed or unchallenged.

Some end-hooks
Two letters to three

AB-A	BA-A	IT-A	PI-A
AG-A	BO-A	KO-A	PO-A
AH-A	CH-A	MA-A	SH-A
AI-A	ER-A	MO-A	TE-A
AL-A	ET-A	OB-A	UT-A
AM-A	FA-A	OD-A	YE-A
AN-A	GO-A	OR-A	ZO-A
AW-A	HO-A	PE-A	

Three letters to four

ALB-A	KAT-A	RAJ-A
ARE-A	KOR-A	RAT-A
BET-A	LAM-A	ROM-A
BON-A	LAV-A	ROT-A
COD-A	MAL-A	SAG-A
COL-A	MAM-A	SOD-A
DAD-A	MAY-A	SOM-A
DIV-A	MEG-A	SOY-A
DOP-A	MES-A	TOG-A
FET-A	MON-A	TOR-A
FIL-A	NAN-A	TUB-A
GAG-A	ORC-A	TUN-A
GAL-A	PAP-A	VEG-A
GAM-A	PIC-A	VIN-A
GIG-A	PIN-A	VIS-A
HAH-A	PIT-A	WET-A
IDE-A	PUP-A	

Four letters to five

BALS-A	HOND-A	PUCK-A
BURK-A	HYEN-A	PUNK-A
CHIN-A	KANG-A	RAGG-A
COCO-A	LAIK-A	RAIT-A
COMM-A	LOOF-A	RAST-A
COST-A	MANG-A	SALS-A
DELT-A	MANI-A	SUNN-A
DERM-A	MOCH-A	TAIG-A
DICT-A	MOOL-A	TIAR-A
DOON-A	MULL-A	TONK-A
DRAM-A	MURR-A	VEST-A
FAUN-A	PAND-A	VILL-A
FELL-A	PARK-A	VIOL-A
FETT-A	PASH-A	VOLT-A
FLOR-A	PAST-A	
GAMB-A	POLK-A	
GUAN-A	PRIM-A	

Five letters to six

CREST-A	NYMPH-A	SENOR-A
FASCI-A	ORBIT-A	SHISH-A
FAVEL-A	ORGAN-A	SPIRE-A
FIEST-A	PAGOD-A	STELL-A
GRAMP-A	PATIN-A	STERN-A
KORUN-A	PLASM-A	TALUK-A
LORIC-A	QUANT-A	TAPET-A
MAXIM-A	RHUMB-A	TARSI-A
MIASM-A	SATYR-A	TUNIC-A
MINIM-A	SCARP-A	VALET-A

Six letters to seven

ADDEND-A	DRACHM-A	PROPYL-A
ALUMIN-A	EMBLEM-A	QUININ-A
ANALOG-A	EXOTIC-A	ROBUST-A
ANONYM-A	FAVELL-A	ROSACE-A
ARABIC-A	FORMIC-A	ROTUND-A
ASHRAM-A	GALLET-A	SCHISM-A
BUZUKI-A	GALLIC-A	SECRET-A
CANDID-A	GUNNER-A	SELECT-A
CANTAL-A	INFANT-A	SEQUEL-A
CEMENT-A	INGEST-A	SERING-A
CHIASM-A	KHALIF-A	SHEIKH-A
CHIMER-A	LAVOLT-A	SIGNOR-A
CHOLER-A	LOCUST-A	SULTAN-A
CODEIN-A	MADRAS-A	TAMBUR-A
CORTIN-A	MOMENT-A	TARTAN-A
CURIOS-A	PAISAN-A	TAVERN-A
CYATHI-A	PERSON-A	TEMPER-A
DEJECT-A	PLACIT-A	
DEODAR-A	POTASS-A	

Seven letters to eight

ANGELIC-A
ANTEFIX-A
ARBORET-A
AUTOMAT-A
BASILIC-A
BOTANIC-A
BRONCHI-A
BROUGHT-A
CHAMPAC-A
CHARISM-A
CISTERN-A
CONSULT-A
DEMENTI-A
DIASTEM-A
DULCIAN-A

EPITHEM-A
EXCERPT-A
FASCIST-A
HEPATIC-A
JAVELIN-A
MANDIOC-A
MARCHES-A
MARINER-A
MATADOR-A
MELODIC-A
MOLLUSC-A
MONSTER-A
NYMPHAE-A
PERFECT-A
PIGNOLI-A

QUILLAI-A
RAKSHAS-A
SALICET-A
SARMENT-A
SCIATIC-A
SIGNORI-A
STROBIL-A
SYNTAGM-A
TAMANDU-A
TAMBOUR-A
THERIAC-A
TORMENT-A
TOURIST-A
UNGUENT-A

Handy Hint: say AA

If you have too many vowels on your rack, some useful short words beginning with A and using no consonants are: AA, AE and AI (2 points each). It is also worthwhile remembering common words which feature many vowels such as ADIEU (6 points), EERIE (5 points) and COOKIE (12 points).

> **Blockers**
>
> It is useful to know which words are blockers and can't therefore be extended before or after. You may want to play a blocker that your opponent can't extend, or you may want to avoid playing a blocker because you want to keep the board open.

Three-letter blocker beginning with A
AUE

Some four-letter blockers beginning with A

ABLY	AHOY	ALSO	AROW
ACHY	AJAR	ANEW	ASEA
ADRY	AJEE	ANOW	AWRY
AESC	ALAE	APEX	AXAL
AGLY	ALEE	AREG	
AHEM	ALIT	AREW	

Some five-letter blockers beginning with A
(except words ending in '-ED', '-J', '-S', '-X', '-Y' or '-Z')

AARGH	ABRIM	AFOUL
ABACK	ACERB	AGAIN
ABASH	ACHOO	AGAST
ABASK	ACRID	AGLEE
ABEAM	ADOZE	AGLOW
ABLOW	AFIRE	AGOOD
ABOIL	AFOOT	AHEAD
ABORE	AFORE	AHEAP
AHIGH	ALTHO	ASTIR

ALACK	AMAIN	ASWIM
ALGAE	AMINO	ATILT
ALGAL	APACE	AURAL
ALGID	APAGE	AVAST
ALIKE	APAID	AWASH
ALIVE	APART	AWAVE
ALOFT	APIAN	AWORK
ALONE	AREAR	AXIAL
ALOOF	AROSE	
ALOUD	ASKEW	

Some six-letter blockers beginning with A (except words ending in '-ED', '-J', '-S', '-X', '-Y' or '-Z')

ABLAZE	AFIELD	AKIMBO	APEMAN
ABLEST	AFLAME	ALBEIT	APEMEN
ABLOOM	AFLOAT	ALMOST	APIECE
ABLUSH	AFRAID	ALUMNI	APTEST
ABOARD	AFRESH	AMBUSH	APTING
ABORNE	AFRONT	AMEBIC	ARCANE
ABURST	AGHAST	AMIDST	ARDENT
ACETIC	AGILER	AMMINO	AREACH
ACHIER	AGLARE	AMORAL	ARISEN
ACIDER	AGLEAM	ANEATH	AROUND
ACIDIC	AIDMAN	ANEMIC	ASHAKE
ACRAWL	AIDMEN	ANOXIC	ASHINE
ACUTER	AIMFUL	ANYHOW	ASHORE
ADRIFT	AIRMAN	AORTAL	ASLANT
ADROIT	AIRMEN	AORTIC	ASLEEP
ASLOPE	ATOPIC	AWATCH	AWSOME
ASTERN	ATWIXT	AWEIGH	AXEMAN

ASTOOP	AUDIAL	AWEING	AXEMEN
ASTRUT	AVERSE	AWHILE	AXONIC
ASWARM	AVIDER	AWHIRL	AZONAL
ASWING	AVITAL	AWOKEN	
ASWIRL	AVOUCH	AWRACK	
ATONAL	AWARER	AWRONG	

Bonus Words

Bonus words on your rack can be hard to spot, especially for the less experienced player. One way to help find them is by using prefixes and suffixes.

Many longer words include a common prefix or suffix – remembering these and using them where you can is a good way to discover any longer words on your rack, including any potential bonus words. The key prefixes to remember beginning with A are AB-, AD-, AIR- and the key suffixes are -ABLE, -AGE, -ANCE, -ANCY and -ARCH.

Some words beginning with AB-

Seven-letter words

AB-ASHED
AB-ASHES
AB-DUCTS
AB-JOINT
AB-LATED
AB-LINGS
AB-LUTED
AB-OUGHT
AB-RAIDS

AB-REACT
AB-REAST
AB-RIDGE
AB-ROACH
AB-ROADS
AB-SEILS
AB-SENTS
AB-SOLVE
AB-SORBS

AB-STAIN
AB-SURDS
AB-THANE
AB-USAGE
AB-USERS
AB-USING
AB-UTTER

Eight-letter words

AB-ASHING
AB-DUCTED
AB-EARING
AB-EGGING
AB-ERRANT
AB-ESSIVE
AB-LEGATE
AB-NEGATE
AB-NORMAL

AB-ORALLY
AB-ORIGIN
AB-RAIDED
AB-RAYING
AB-RIDGED
AB-RIDGER
AB-ROOKED
AB-SEILED
AB-SENTED

AB-SOLUTE
AB-SOLVED
AB-SOLVER
AB-SOLVES
AB-SONANT
AB-SORBED
AB-STRICT
AB-USABLE

Some words beginning with AD-
Seven-letter words

AD-AGIOS

AD-APTED

AD-APTER

AD-AWING

AD-DICTS

AD-DRESS

AD-DUCES

AD-DUCTS

AD-HERES

AD-JOINS

AD-JOINT

AD-JUDGE

AD-JUROR

AD-JUSTS

AD-LANDS

AD-MIRED

AD-MIRES

AD-MIXED

AD-MIXES

AD-NOUNS

AD-OPTED

AD-OPTER

AD-PRESS

AD-READS

AD-RENAL

AD-SORBS

AD-VENTS

AD-VERBS

AD-VERSE

AD-VERTS

AD-VICES

AD-VISED

AD-VISES

AD-VISOR

AD-WARDS

AD-WARES

AD-WOMAN

AD-WOMEN

Eight-letter words

AD-APTING

AD-DEBTED

AD-DEEMED

AD-DICTED

AD-DOOMED

AD-DUCTED

AD-EQUATE

AD-ESSIVE

AD-JACENT

AD-JOINED

AD-JUDGED

AD-JUSTED

AD-JUSTER

AD-MASSES

AD-MIRING

AD-MIXING

AD-MONISH

AD-NATION

AD-OPTING

AD-OPTION

AD-SCRIPT

AD-SORBED

AD-UMBRAL

AD-UNCATE

AD-VERSER

AD-VERTED

AD-VISING

AD-WARDED

Some words beginning with AIR-

Seven-letter words

A

AIR-BAGS   AIR-HOLE   AIR-SHIP

AIR-BASE   AIR-LESS   AIR-SHOT

AIR-BOAT   AIR-LIFT   AIR-SHOW

AIR-CREW   AIR-LIKE   AIR-SICK

AIR-DATE   AIR-LINE   AIR-SIDE

AIR-DROP   AIR-LOCK   AIR-STOP

AIR-FARE   AIR-MAIL   AIR-TIME

AIR-FLOW   AIR-PARK   AIR-TING

AIR-FOIL   AIR-PLAY   AIR-WARD

AIR-GAPS   AIR-PORT   AIR-WAVE

AIR-GLOW   AIR-POST   AIR-WAYS

AIR-HEAD   AIR-SHED   AIR-WISE

Eight-letter words

AIR-BASES   AIR-DROME   AIR-PROOF

AIR-BOATS   AIR-DROPS   AIR-SCAPE

AIR-BORNE   AIR-FARES   AIR-SCREW

AIR-BOUND   AIR-FIELD   AIR-SHAFT

AIR-BRICK   AIR-FRAME   AIR-SPACE

AIR-BRUSH   AIR-GLOWS   AIR-SPEED

AIR-BURST   AIR-GRAPH   AIR-STRIP

AIR-BUSES   AIR-HOLES   AIR-THING

AIR-CHECK   AIR-LIFTS   AIR-TIGHT

AIR-COACH   AIR-LINER   AIR-WAVES

AIR-CRAFT   AIR-PLANE   AIR-WOMAN

AIR-DRAWN   AIR-POWER   AIR-WOMEN

Some words ending with -ABLE
Seven-letter words

ACT-ABLE HAT-ABLE SAL-ABLE
ADD-ABLE HEW-ABLE SAV-ABLE
AFF-ABLE HID-ABLE SAY-ABLE
AMI-ABLE HIR-ABLE SEE-ABLE
BAT-ABLE LIK-ABLE SEW-ABLE
BUY-ABLE LIN-ABLE SIZ-ABLE
CAP-ABLE LIV-ABLE SKI-ABLE
CIT-ABLE LOS-ABLE SOW-ABLE
COD-ABLE LOV-ABLE SUE-ABLE
CUR-ABLE MAK-ABLE TAK-ABLE
DAT-ABLE MIN-ABLE TAM-ABLE
DIS-ABLE MIR-ABLE TAX-ABLE
DRY-ABLE MIX-ABLE TEN-ABLE
DUP-ABLE MOV-ABLE TOT-ABLE
DUR-ABLE MUT-ABLE TOW-ABLE
DYE-ABLE NAM-ABLE TRI-ABLE
EAT-ABLE NOT-ABLE TUN-ABLE
EQU-ABLE OWN-ABLE TYP-ABLE
EYE-ABLE PAR-ABLE UNH-ABLE
FIX-ABLE PAY-ABLE USE-ABLE
FLY-ABLE PLI-ABLE VAT-ABLE
FRI-ABLE POK-ABLE VOC-ABLE
FRY-ABLE POS-ABLE VOL-ABLE
GEL-ABLE POT-ABLE VOT-ABLE
GET-ABLE RAT-ABLE WAD-ABLE
GIV-ABLE ROW-ABLE WAX-ABLE

Eight-letter words

ADOR-ABLE	EDUC-ABLE	KNOW-ABLE
AGIT-ABLE	ENVI-ABLE	LAUD-ABLE
AMEN-ABLE	ERAS-ABLE	LEAS-ABLE
AMIC-ABLE	EROD-ABLE	LEND-ABLE
ARGU-ABLE	EVAD-ABLE	LIKE-ABLE
ATON-ABLE	FACE-ABLE	LIVE-ABLE
BAIL-ABLE	FARM-ABLE	LOCK-ABLE
BANK-ABLE	FEED-ABLE	LOVE-ABLE
BEAR-ABLE	FILE-ABLE	MAIL-ABLE
BEAT-ABLE	FILM-ABLE	MEND-ABLE
BEND-ABLE	FOLD-ABLE	MISS-ABLE
BILL-ABLE	FUND-ABLE	MOVE-ABLE
BITE-ABLE	GAIN-ABLE	NAME-ABLE
BLAM-ABLE	GETT-ABLE	OPEN-ABLE
BRIB-ABLE	GIVE-ABLE	OPER-ABLE
CASH-ABLE	GRAD-ABLE	PALP-ABLE
CAUS-ABLE	GROW-ABLE	PASS-ABLE
CHEW-ABLE	GUID-ABLE	PICK-ABLE
CITE-ABLE	HEAR-ABLE	PITI-ABLE
CLOS-ABLE	HEAT-ABLE	PLAY-ABLE
COIN-ABLE	HOLD-ABLE	PORT-ABLE
COOK-ABLE	HUNT-ABLE	POSE-ABLE
COPY-ABLE	IMIT-ABLE	POUR-ABLE
CULP-ABLE	INVI-ABLE	PROB-ABLE
CUTT-ABLE	JOIN-ABLE	PROV-ABLE
DENI-ABLE	JUMP-ABLE	QUOT-ABLE
DRAW-ABLE	KICK-ABLE	RATE-ABLE
DRIV-ABLE	KILL-ABLE	READ-ABLE

EDIT-ABLE | KISS-ABLE | REAP-ABLE
RELI-ABLE | SING-ABLE | TRAD-ABLE
RENT-ABLE | SINK-ABLE | TURN-ABLE
REUS-ABLE | SIZE-ABLE | UNST-ABLE
RINS-ABLE | SMOK-ABLE | VALU-ABLE
RIPP-ABLE | SOCI-ABLE | VARI-ABLE
SACK-ABLE | SOLV-ABLE | VIEW-ABLE
SALE-ABLE | SORT-ABLE | VIOL-ABLE
SAVE-ABLE | SUIT-ABLE | VOID-ABLE
SEAL-ABLE | SURF-ABLE | VOTE-ABLE
SEIZ-ABLE | SWAY-ABLE | WALK-ABLE
SELL-ABLE | SYLL-ABLE | WASH-ABLE
SEND-ABLE | TAKE-ABLE | WEAR-ABLE
SERV-ABLE | TALK-ABLE | WINN-ABLE
SHAK-ABLE | TAME-ABLE | WORK-ABLE
SHAM-ABLE | TEAR-ABLE | WRIT-ABLE
SHOW-ABLE | TEAS-ABLE |

Some words ending with -AGE
Seven-letter words

ACRE-AGE | CARN-AGE | HAUL-AGE
ASSU-AGE | COIN-AGE | HERB-AGE
AVER-AGE | COLL-AGE | HOST-AGE
BAGG-AGE | CORS-AGE | LEAK-AGE
BAND-AGE | COTT-AGE | LINE-AGE
BARR-AGE | COUR-AGE | LINK-AGE
BEER-AGE | FLOW-AGE | LUGG-AGE
BREW-AGE | FOLI-AGE | MASS-AGE
BULK-AGE | FOOT-AGE | MESS-AGE
BUOY-AGE | FROM-AGE | MILE-AGE
CABB-AGE | GARB-AGE | MONT-AGE

ONST-AGE
OUTR-AGE
OVER-AGE
PACK-AGE
PASS-AGE
PEER-AGE
PLUM-AGE
POST-AGE
POTT-AGE
PRES-AGE
RAMP-AGE

RIBC-AGE
RIFF-AGE
RUMM-AGE
SALV-AGE
SAUS-AGE
SEEP-AGE
SIGN-AGE
SOIL-AGE
STOR-AGE
TEEN-AGE
TONN-AGE

UMBR-AGE
UPST-AGE
VANT-AGE
VILL-AGE
VINT-AGE
VOLT-AGE
WARP-AGE
WAST-AGE
WATT-AGE
WEBP-AGE
YARD-AGE

Eight-letter words

AMPER-AGE
BARON-AGE
BEVER-AGE
BIRDC-AGE
BLOCK-AGE
BREAK-AGE
CARRI-AGE
CLEAR-AGE
COVER-AGE
CREEP-AGE
CRIBB-AGE
DRAIN-AGE
DRESS-AGE
ENVIS-AGE
FRONT-AGE
FUSEL-AGE

GRAIN-AGE
GROUP-AGE
HERIT-AGE
HOMEP-AGE
LANGU-AGE
LEVER-AGE
MARRI-AGE
METER-AGE
MISUS-AGE
MORTG-AGE
OFFST-AGE
OVERP-AGE
PILOT-AGE
PLANT-AGE
PUPIL-AGE
ROUGH-AGE

SABOT-AGE
SEWER-AGE
SHORT-AGE
SLIPP-AGE
SPILL-AGE
SPOIL-AGE
STEER-AGE
STOPP-AGE
SUFFR-AGE
TRACK-AGE
TUTEL-AGE
TUTOR-AGE
UNDER-AGE
VAUNT-AGE
VERBI-AGE
VICAR-AGE

Some words ending with -ANCE
Seven-letter words

ADV-ANCE	DUR-ANCE	ROM-ANCE
AID-ANCE	ENH-ANCE	SON-ANCE
ASK-ANCE	FIN-ANCE	SUR-ANCE
BAL-ANCE	JOY-ANCE	VAC-ANCE
CRE-ANCE	PEN-ANCE	VAL-ANCE

Eight-letter words

ABEY-ANCE	ELEG-ANCE	PAST-ANCE
ABID-ANCE	ENTR-ANCE	PIQU-ANCE
ACUT-ANCE	EXIT-ANCE	PITT-ANCE
ADAM-ANCE	FEAS-ANCE	PORT-ANCE
AFFI-ANCE	GUID-ANCE	RADI-ANCE
ALLI-ANCE	INST-ANCE	RELI-ANCE
AMBI-ANCE	ISSU-ANCE	RESI-ANCE
AMOR-ANCE	ITER-ANCE	RIDD-ANCE
BECH-ANCE	LAIT-ANCE	SORT-ANCE
BRIS-ANCE	NOND-ANCE	TADV-ANCE
BUOY-ANCE	NUIS-ANCE	TEND-ANCE
CREP-ANCE	ORDN-ANCE	VALI-ANCE
DEFI-ANCE	OUTD-ANCE	VARI-ANCE
DEVI-ANCE	OUTR-ANCE	VIBR-ANCE
DIST-ANCE	PARL-ANCE	VOID-ANCE

Some words ending with -ANCY

Seven-letter words

ERR-ANCY	SON-ANCY	UNF-ANCY
INF-ANCY	TEN-ANCY	VAC-ANCY
PLI-ANCY	TRU-ANCY	

Eight-letter words

ABEY-ANCY	GEOM-ANCY	RADI-ANCY
ADAM-ANCY	IMIT-ANCY	RAMP-ANCY
BLAT-ANCY	INST-ANCY	REGN-ANCY
BUOY-ANCY	MORD-ANCY	UNCH-ANCY
CLAM-ANCY	MYOM-ANCY	VAGR-ANCY
DEVI-ANCY	PECC-ANCY	VALI-ANCY
DORM-ANCY	PERN-ANCY	VERD-ANCY
ELEG-ANCY	PIQU-ANCY	VIBR-ANCY

Some words ending with -ARCH

Seven-letter words

AUT-ARCH	MON-ARCH	TRI-ARCH
END-ARCH	NAV-ARCH	XER-ARCH
HEX-ARCH	NOM-ARCH	
MES-ARCH	TOP-ARCH	

Eight-letter words

ETHN-ARCH	OMNI-ARCH	POLY-ARCH
HEPT-ARCH	OUTM-ARCH	RESE-ARCH
HIER-ARCH	OVER-ARCH	TAXI-ARCH
HIPP-ARCH	PENT-ARCH	TETR-ARCH
OLIG-ARCH	PHYL-ARCH	UNST-ARCH

Unusual letter combinations

If you find you have a preponderance of vowels on your rack, a few words from World English can come in handy. Fortunately, there are many from which to choose.

A

Australian words

ADJIGO	yam plant
ALF	an uncultivated Australian
ARVO	afternoon
ASPRO	associate professor

Canadian words

AGLOO	breathing hole made in ice by a seal
AMAUT	hood on an Inuit woman's parka for carrying a child
ATIGI	Inuit parka

Hindi words

AKHARA	gymnasium
ALAP	vocal music without words
AMBARY	tropical plant
ANKUS	elephant goad
ANNA	old copper coin
ARTI	Hindu ritual
AYAH	maidservant or nursemaid

New Zealand words

New Zealand English features a great variety of words adopted from the Maori language. Many of these words use two (and sometimes three) As but are often also dependent on a consonant such as K or T.

ATUA	spirit or demon
HAKA	war dance
KAUPAPA	strategy, policy or cause
TAIAHA	ceremonial fighting staff
WAKA	Maori canoe

South African words

South African English is fed into by various different languages, including Afrikaans and Nguni languages such as Zulu and Xhosa. Afrikaans-derived words often feature a double A and Nguni words frequently contain two or three.

AMADODA	grown men
AMANDLA	political slogan calling for power to the Black population
BABALAS	drunk or hungover
KRAAL	stockaded village
PLAAS	farm

B 3

Essential info
Value: 3 points
Number in set: 2

B can form a two-letter word with every vowel except for U. If you have a letter B you can form various short everyday words, some of which can be high-scoring such as BOX (12 points), BAY (8 points), BOW (8 points), BUY (8 points) and BYE (also 8). Some more unusual three-letter words beginning with B are BEY (an official in the Ottoman Empire, 8 points) and BEZ (the second spike of a deer's antler, 14 points).

Two-letter words beginning with B

BA   BE   BI   BO   BY

Some three-letter words beginning with B

BAA	BEL	BOA	BOP
BAC	BEN	BOD	BOR
BAH	BEY	BOH	BOT
BAL	BEZ	BOI	BUR
BAM	BIO	BOK	
BAP	BIZ	BON	

B

Hooks

Hooking requires a subtle change in a player's thought process, in that they must look at words already on the board without becoming distracted by their pronunciation.

Some front-hooks
Two letters to three

B-AA	B-AT	B-IN	B-OO	B-UN
B-AD	B-AY	B-IO	B-OP	B-UR
B-AG	B-ED	B-IS	B-OR	B-US
B-AH	B-EE	B-IT	B-OS	B-UT
B-AL	B-EL	B-OB	B-OW	B-YE
B-AM	B-EN	B-OD	B-OX	
B-AN	B-ES	B-OH	B-OY	
B-AR	B-ET	B-OI	B-UG	
B-AS	B-ID	B-ON	B-UM	

Three letters to four

B-AFT	B-AUK	B-ILK
B-AIL	B-AYE	B-ILL
B-ALE	B-EAR	B-INK
B-ALL	B-EAT	B-IRK
B-AND	B-EAU	B-ISH
B-ANT	B-EGO	B-LAB
B-ARE	B-END	B-LAD
B-ARK	B-EST	B-LAG
B-ARM	B-HAT	B-LAW
B-ASH	B-HUT	B-LAY
B-ASK	B-ICE	B-LED
B-ATE	B-IDE	B-LET

B-LEY   B-OLD   B-RAY
B-LIP   B-ONE   B-RED
B-LOB   B-OOH   B-RIG
B-LOG   B-ORE   B-RIM
B-LOT   B-OUT   B-ROD
B-LOW   B-OWL   B-ROO
B-OAR   B-OXY   B-ROW
B-OAT   B-RAG   B-RUT
B-ODE   B-RAN   B-URN
B-OFF   B-RAT   B-YES
B-OIL   B-RAW

Four letters to five

B-ALAS   B-IOTA   B-LENT
B-ALKY   B-LACK   B-LESS
B-ALLY   B-LADE   B-LEST
B-ALMS   B-LADY   B-LIMP
B-ARMY   B-LAME   B-LIMY
B-EACH   B-LAND   B-LINK
B-EARD   B-LANK   B-LIST
B-EAST   B-LARE   B-LITE
B-EAUX   B-LASH   B-LIVE
B-EGAD   B-LAST   B-LOCK
B-EVER   B-LATE   B-LOOM
B-HAJI   B-LAUD   B-LOOP
B-HANG   B-LAWN   B-LORE
B-HOOT   B-LAZE   B-LUSH
B-IFFY   B-LEAK   B-OGLE
B-IGGS   B-LEND   B-OINK

B

B-ONCE
B-ONUS
B-OOZE
B-ORAL
B-OWED
B-OWER
B-OXEN
B-RACE
B-RAID
B-RAIL
B-RAIN
B-RAKE
B-RANK
B-RANT

B-RASH
B-RAVE
B-RAZE
B-READ
B-REAM
B-REED
B-RENT
B-RICK
B-RIDE
B-RING
B-RINK
B-RISE
B-RISK
B-ROAD

B-ROCK
B-ROOK
B-ROOM
B-ROSE
B-ROSY
B-RUIN
B-RULE
B-RUNG
B-RUNT
B-RUSH
B-RUSK
B-RUST
B-USED

Five letters to six

B-ACHED
B-ADDER
B-ADMAN
B-AILED
B-ALLOT
B-ALLOW
B-ANGER
B-ANGLE
B-ARROW
B-ASHED
B-ASKED
B-ASSET
B-EAGLE

B-EARED
B-EATEN
B-EATER
B-EGGED
B-ELATE
B-ENDED
B-ENDER
B-IONIC
B-LAMER
B-LANKY
B-LATER
B-LAWED
B-LAZED

B-LEACH
B-LEAKY
B-LEARY
B-LIGHT
B-LIMEY
B-LITHE
B-LOBBY
B-LOTTO
B-LOUSE
B-LOUSY
B-LOWED
B-LOWER

B-LUNGE	B-RACED	B-REACH
B-OAKED	B-RACER	B-READY
B-OATER	B-RAGGY	B-RIDGE
B-OFFED	B-RAINY	B-RIGHT
B-OILED	B-RAISE	B-RISKY
B-OILER	B-RAKED	B-ROACH
B-OLDEN	B-RANCH	B-ROGUE
B-OLDER	B-RANDY	B-ROOMY
B-ORATE	B-RATTY	B-ROUGH
B-ORDER	B-RAVED	B-ROWED
B-OTHER	B-RAVER	B-UDDER
B-OUGHT	B-RAWER	B-UNION
B-OUNCE	B-RAWLY	B-URNED
B-OVATE	B-RAYED	B-USHER
B-OWING	B-RAZED	B-UTTER
B-OWNED	B-RAZER	

Six letters to seven

B-ACHING	B-ELATED	B-LATTER
B-AILING	B-ENDING	B-LAUDED
B-ANGLED	B-INNING	B-LAZING
B-ASHING	B-LACKED	B-LEAKER
B-ASKING	B-LADDER	B-LENDER
B-ASSIST	B-LADING	B-LESSER
B-ATONED	B-LAGGED	B-LETTED
B-EAGLED	B-LANDER	B-LINGER
B-EATING	B-LASTED	B-LINKED
B-EERIER	B-LASTER	B-LINKER
B-EERILY	B-LATEST	B-LISTER
B-EGGING	B-LATHER	

B-LOBBED

B-LOCKED

B-LOCKER

B-LOGGER

B-LOOMED

B-LOOPED

B-LOOPER

B-LOUSED

B-LOWING

B-LOWSED

B-LUBBER

B-LUNGED

B-LUNGER

B-LUSTER

B-OFFING

B-OILING

B-OINKED

B-OLDEST

B-OOZILY

B-OOZING

B-ORATED

B-OWNING

B-OXLIKE

B-RABBLE

B-RACING

B-RACKET

B-RAGGED

B-RAIDED

B-RAIDER

B-RAILED

B-RAINED

B-RAISED

B-RAKING

B-RAMBLE

B-RANKED

B-RASHER

B-RASHLY

B-RATTLE

B-RAUNCH

B-RAVING

B-RAWEST

B-RAYING

B-RAZING

B-REAMED

B-RIDGED

B-RIDING

B-RINGER

B-RISKED

B-RISKER

B-ROCKED

B-ROCKET

B-ROOKIE

B-ROOMED

B-RUSHED

B-RUSHER

Seven letters to eight

B-AILMENT

B-ARTISAN

B-ASHLESS

B-ATONING

B-EAGLING

B-EARDING

B-EARLIKE

B-EATABLE

B-EERIEST

B-ELATING

B-ENDWISE

B-ESPOUSE

B-LACKING

B-LAGGING

B-LASTING

B-LAUDING

B-LEACHED

B-LEACHER

B-LENDING

B-LETTING

B-LIGHTED

B-LIGHTER

B-LINKING

B-LITHELY

B-LOGGING

B-LOOMING

B-LOOPING

B-LOUSIER

B-LOUSILY

B-LOWDOWN

B-LUNGING

B-OLDNESS

B-ORATING

B-ORDERED

B-ORDERER

B-RABBLER

B-RAGGIER

B-RAGGING

B-RAIDING

B-RAILING

B-RAINIER

B-RAINILY

B-RAINING

B-RAISING

B-RAMBLED

B-RANCHED

B-RANCHER

B-RANDING

B-RANKING

B-RASHEST

B-RATPACK

B-RATTIER

B-RATTISH

B-RATTLED

B-REACHED

B-REACHER

B-REACHES

B-READING

B-REEDING

B-RIDGING

B-RIGHTEN

B-RIGHTER

B-RIGHTLY

B-RIMLESS

B-RINGING

B-RISKING

B-ROACHED

B-ROADWAY

B-ROGUISH

B-ROILING

B-ROOMING

B-RUSHIER

B-RUSHING

B-UTTERED

Handy Hint

The more difficult or uncommon words you remember, the greater your chances of clearing your rack and achieving a high score. You could even be lucky enough to have two power tiles at your disposal to be able to play some rare high-scoring gems. Some excellent examples beginning with B are BANJAX (to ruin something, 22 points) and BEZIQUE (a card game, 27 points).

B

Some end-hooks
Two letters to three

AB-B	DI-B	JA-B	MI-B	RE-B
AL-B	DO-B	JO-B	MO-B	SI-B
AR-B	FA-B	KA-B	NA-B	SO-B
BI-B	GI-B	KO-B	NE-B	TA-B
BO-B	GO-B	LA-B	NO-B	UR-B
DA-B	GU-B	LI-B	NU-B	WE-B
DE-B	HO-B	LO-B	OR-B	YO-B

Three letters to four

BAR-B	COB-B	FOR-B	LAM-B
BIB-B	CUR-B	GAM-B	NIM-B
BOA-B	DIE-B	GAR-B	PRO-B
BUR-B	DOR-B	HER-B	TOM-B
CAR-B	FEE-B	JAM-B	WAR-B
CHI-B	FLU-B	JIB-B	

Four letters to five

ACER-B	DEMO-B	THRO-B
BLUR-B	PLUM-B	ZEBU-B
CUBE-B	SLUR-B	

Five letters to six

SCRAM-B	SUPER-B

Six letters to seven

POTHER-B	PROVER-B	REPLUM-B

Blockers

It is useful to know which words are blockers and can't therefore be extended before or after. You may want to play a blocker that your opponent can't extend, or you may want to avoid playing a blocker because you want to keep the board open.

Three-letter blocker beginning with B

BEZ

Some four-letter blockers beginning with B

BABY	BEVY	BUBO
BADE	BLEW	BURY
BEEN	BODY	BUSY

Some five-letter blockers beginning with B
(except words ending in '-ED', '-J', '-S', '-X', '-Y' or '-Z')

BANAL	BELCH	BRUNG
BARER	BIRCH	BUILT
BATCH	BLASÉ	BURNT
BEGAN	BLOWN	BUTCH
BEGAT	BLUER	BUXOM
BEGOT	BOXEN	

Some six-letter blockers beginning with B
(except words ending in '-ED', '-J', '-S', '-X', '-Y' or '-Z')

BADDER	BEHALF	BOOING
BADMAN	BEHELD	BOWMAN
BAGMAN	BENIGN	BOXIER
BALDER	BEREFT	BOYING
BALING	BIFOLD	BOYISH
BANISH	BIFORM	BREACH
BAREST	BIGGER	BREECH
BARFUL	BINMAN	BRICHT
BARING	BITTEN	BROKEN
BARISH	BLANCH	BROOCH
BARMAN	BLEACH	BRUNCH
BASEST	BLUEST	BRUTAL
BATMAN	BLUIER	BUSIER
BAYMAN	BLUISH	BUSMAN
BEATEN	BOGMAN	BUYING
BECAME	BOLDER	BYPAST
BEFORE	BONIER	
BEGONE	BONZER	

Bonus words

Bonus words on your rack can be hard to spot, especially for the less experienced player. One way to help find them is by using prefixes and suffixes.

Many larger words include a common prefix or suffix – remembering these and using them where you can is a good way to discover any longer words on your rack, including any potential bonus words. The key prefixes to remember beginning with B are BE- and BI- and the key suffixes are -BACK, -BALL, -BAND and -BIRD.

Some words beginning with BE-
Seven-letter words

BE-ACHED	BE-HAVER	BE-NEATH
BE-ARISH	BE-HEADS	BE-QUEST
BE-AVERS	BE-HINDS	BE-RATED
BE-CAUSE	BE-HOLDS	BE-REAVE
BE-COMES	BE-HOOFS	BE-SIDES
BE-DECKS	BE-JEWEL	BE-SIEGE
BE-DEVIL	BE-LATED	BE-SPOKE
BE-DRAIL	BE-LAYED	BE-STOWS
BE-DROLL	BE-LIEFS	BE-TIDES
BE-ECHES	BE-LONGS	BE-TRAYS
BE-FALLS	BE-LOVED	BE-TWEEN
BE-FOULS	BE-MOANS	BE-TWIXT
BE-GUILE	BE-MUSED	BE-WITCH

Eight-letter words

BE-ACHING	BE-GRUDGE	BE-MUSING
BE-ARABLE	BE-GUILED	BE-RATING
BE-BOPPED	BE-HAVING	BE-REAVED
BE-CALMED	BE-HAVIOR	BE-REAVER
BE-CHANCE	BE-HEADED	BE-SIEGED
BE-COMING	BE-HEADER	BE-SIEGER
BE-CURSED	BE-HOLDEN	BE-SMIRCH
BE-DAUBED	BE-HOLDER	BE-SPOKEN
BE-DAZZLE	BE-HOOVED	BE-STOWED
BE-DECKED	BE-HOVING	BE-STREWN
BE-FOULED	BE-KNIGHT	BE-SUITED
BE-FRIEND	BE-LAYING	BE-TIDING
BE-FUDDLE	BE-LIEVER	BE-TITLED
BE-GETTER	BE-LITTLE	BE-WARING
BE-GINNER	BE-LONGED	BE-WIGGED
BE-GOTTEN	BE-LONGER	BE-WILDER

Some words beginning with BI-
Seven-letter words

BI-AXIAL	BI-LEVEL	BI-SECTS
BI-BLESS	BI-MODAL	BI-SHOPS
BI-BLIST	BI-OLOGY	BI-TABLE
BI-CARBS	BI-OPTIC	BI-TINGS
BI-CYCLE	BI-PARTY	BI-TONAL
BI-DINGS	BI-PEDAL	BI-VALVE
BI-FOCAL	BI-PLANE	BI-VINYL
BI-KINGS	BI-POLAR	BI-ZONAL

Eight-letter words

BI-ANNUAL	BI-FACIAL	BI-RADIAL
BI-CHROME	BI-FORMED	BI-STABLE
BI-COLOUR	BI-HOURLY	BI-TEWING
BI-CONVEX	BI-LINEAR	BI-TINGLY
BI-CUSPID	BI-MANUAL	BI-UNIQUE
BI-CYCLED	BI-METHYL	BI-VALVED
BI-CYCLER	BI-PARTED	BI-WEEKLY
BI-CYCLIC	BI-PHASIC	BI-YEARLY

Some words ending with -BACK

Seven-letter words

BUY-BACK	FLY-BACK	SET-BACK
CUT-BACK	LAY-BACK	SUN-BACK
DIE-BACK	OUT-BACK	TIE-BACK
FAT-BACK	PAY-BACK	
FIN-BACK	RED-BACK	

Eight-letter words

BARE-BACK	FEED-BACK	PLAY-BACK
BLOW-BACK	FLAT-BACK	PULL-BACK
BLUE-BACK	FULL-BACK	ROLL-BACK
CALL-BACK	GREY-BACK	SEAT-BACK
CASH-BACK	HALF-BACK	SNAP-BACK
CLAW-BACK	HOLD-BACK	TAIL-BACK
COME-BACK	HUMP-BACK	TALK-BACK
DRAW-BACK	KICK-BACK	TURN-BACK
FALL-BACK	LIFT-BACK	WING-BACK
FAST-BACK	LOAN-BACK	

B

Some words ending with -BALL
Seven-letter words

EYE-BALL	LOW-BALL	ODD-BALL
GUM-BALL	NET-BALL	PIN-BALL

Eight-letter words

BASE-BALL	FOOT-BALL	MEAT-BALL
BLUE-BALL	GOOF-BALL	MOTH-BALL
CORN-BALL	HAIR-BALL	PUFF-BALL
FAST-BALL	HAND-BALL	SNOW-BALL
FIRE-BALL	HARD-BALL	SOFT-BALL
FISH-BALL	HIGH-BALL	SPIT-BALL
FOOS-BALL	KICK-BALL	

Some words ending with -BAND
Seven-letter words

ARM-BAND	HAT-BAND	HUS-BAND
DIS-BAND		

Eight-letter words

BACK-BAND	HEAD-BAND	SARA-BAND
BASE-BAND	NECK-BAND	SIDE-BAND
BROW-BAND	NOSE-BAND	WAVE-BAND
HAIR-BAND	RAIN-BAND	WIDE-BAND

Some words ending with -BIRD
Seven-letter words

ANT-BIRD	COW-BIRD	OIL-BIRD
AXE-BIRD	FAT-BIRD	RED-BIRD
BOO-BIRD	JAY-BIRD	SEA-BIRD
CAT-BIRD	MAY-BIRD	SUN-BIRD

Eight-letter words

BELL-BIRD	KING-BIRD	REED-BIRD
BLUE-BIRD	LADY-BIRD	RICE-BIRD
CAGE-BIRD	LOVE-BIRD	SNOW-BIRD
FERN-BIRD	LYRE-BIRD	SONG-BIRD
FIRE-BIRD	OVEN-BIRD	SURF-BIRD
GAOL-BIRD	PUFF-BIRD	WHIP-BIRD
HANG-BIRD	RAIL-BIRD	YARD-BIRD
JAIL-BIRD	RAIN-BIRD	

Handy Hint: Blank Tiles

A blank tile is, by its nature, incredibly versatile as it can be substituted for any other letter. Although it scores no points in itself, the blank tile can make forming bonus words that much easier and players should never, ever change a blank tile should they be lucky enough to find one on their rack.

Unusual letter combinations

If you have an unusual combination of letters on your rack, or want to impress your opponent with an unusual word, a few words from World English can come in handy.

Australian words

BARRO	embarrassing
BAUERA	small evergreen shrub
BEAUT	outstanding person or thing
BELAH	casuarina tree
BERKO	berserk
BIFFO	fighting or aggressive behaviour
BILBY	burrowing marsupial
BIZZO	empty and irrelevant talk
BOAB	baobab tree
BODGIE	unruly or uncouth man
BOGAN	youth who dresses and behaves rebelliously
BOOBOOK	small spotted brown owl
BOOFY	strong but stupid
BORA	native Australian coming-of-age ceremony
BORAK	rubbish or nonsense
BRASCO	lavatory
BROLGA	large grey crane with a trumpeting call
BRUMBY	wild horse
BUNYA	tall dome-shaped coniferous tree
BUNYIP	legendary monster

Canadian words

BABICHE	thongs or lacings of rawhide
BARACHOIS	shallow lagoon formed by a sand bar
BATEAU	light flat-bottomed boat
BEIGNET	deep-fried pastry
BREWIS	bread soaked in broth, gravy, etc
BUTTE	isolated steep-sided flat-topped hill

Hindi words

BABU	Mr
BAEL	spiny tree
BAHADUR	title for distinguished Indian during the Raj
BANDH	general strike
BANYAN	tree whose branches grow down into the soil
BHAJI	deep-fried vegetable savoury
BHANGRA	music combining traditional Punjabi music with Western pop
BHAVAN	large house or building
BHISHTI	water-carrier
BINDI	decorative dot in middle of forehead
BOBBERY	mixed pack of hunting dogs
BUND	embankment

New Zealand words

BOOHAI	thoroughly lost

South African words

~~BAAS~~	boss
BABALAS	drunk or hungover
~~BAKKIE~~	small truck
~~BRAAI~~	grill or roast meat
BRAAIVLEIS	barbecue
	wild, remote region

Urdu words

~~BAGH~~	garden
BALTI	spicy Indian dish stewed until most liquid has evaporated
~~BASTI~~	slum
BEGUM	woman of high rank
BIRYANI	Indian dish of highly flavoured rice mixed with meat or fish

Essential info
Value: 3 points
Number in set: 2

C can be a difficult letter to play (for example, it only forms one two-letter word: CH, an old dialect word for I, 7 points). However, it does form some good three-letter words including CAW, COW and COY (all 8 points) and also CAZ (short form of casual, 14 points). Worth remembering also are the short words which don't use any vowels: CLY (a word for steal, 8 points) and CWM (a Welsh word for valley, 10 points).

Two-letter word beginning with C

CH

Some three-letter words beginning with C

CAA	CEE	CIS	COX
CAG	CEL	CIT	COZ
CAM	CHA	CLY	CUM
CAW	CHE	COO	CUR
CAY	CHI	COR	CUZ
CAZ	CID	COS	CWM

Hooks

...ing requires a subtle change in a player's thought process, in that they must look at words already on the board without becoming distracted by their pronunciation.

Some front-hooks

..o letters to three

C-AA	C-AW	C-IS	C-OS
C-AB	C-AY	C-IT	C-OW
C-AD	C-EE	C-OB	C-OX
C-AG	C-EL	C-OD	C-OY
	C-HA	C-ON	C-UM
C-AN	C-HE	C-OO	C-UP
C-AR	C-HI	C-OP	C-UR
	C-ID	C-OR	C-UT

Three letters to four

C-AGE	C-ARK	C-HID	C-IDE
C-AID	C-ART	C-HIP	C-ILL
	C-ASH	C-HIS	C-ION
C-ALF	C-ASK	C-HIT	C-IRE
C-ALL	C-ATE	C-HOG	C-LAD
	C-HAD	C-HOP	C-LAM
C-AMP	C-HAM	C-HOW	C-LAP
C-ANT	C-HAT	C-HUB	C-LAW
C-ANY	C-HAY	C-HUG	C-LAY
C-APE	C-HER	C-HUM	C-LEG
C-ARE	C-HEW	C-HUT	C-LIP

C-LOD	C-OCH	C-ONS	C-RED
C-LOG	C-ODA	C-ORE	C-RIB
C-LOP	C-ODE	C-OUR	C-RIM
C-LOT	C-OFF	C-OWL	C-ROW
C-LOW	C-OFT	C-RAG	C-RUE
C-LOY	C-OHO	C-RAM	C-URN
C-OAT	C-OIL	C-RAN	C-UTE
C-OBS	C-OLD	C-RAW	
C-OCA	C-ONE	C-RAY	

Four letters to five

C-ABLE	C-HATS	C-HORE
C-ACHE	C-HAVE	C-HOSE
C-AGED	C-HEAP	C-HOUT
C-AGER	C-HEAT	C-HOWK
C-AIRN	C-HECK	C-HUCK
C-AKED	C-HELP	C-HUFF
C-ANON	C-HERE	C-HUMP
C-APED	C-HEST	C-HUNK
C-APER	C-HICK	C-HURL
C-ARED	C-HIDE	C-INCH
C-AULD	C-HILD	C-LACK
C-AVER	C-HILI	C-LAME
C-AWED	C-HILL	C-LAMP
C-EASE	C-HIVE	C-LAMS
C-HAFF	C-HOCK	C-LANG
C-HAIN	C-HOKE	C-LANK
C-HAIR	C-HOOF	C-LASH
C-HARM	C-HOOK	C-LASS
C-HART	C-HOPS	C-LAST

C-LEAN   C-OAST   C-RAVE
C-LEAR   C-OMER   C-RAZE
C-LEFT   C-OPED   C-REAM
C-LICK   C-ORAL   C-REDO
C-LIMB   C-OUCH   C-REED
C-LING   C-OVEN   C-REEK
C-LOCK   C-OVER   C-REEL
C-LONE   C-OWED   C-REST
C-LOSE   C-RACK   C-RIPE
C-LOUD   C-RAFT   C-RISE
C-LOUT   C-RAKE   C-ROCK
C-LOVE   C-RAMP   C-ROOK
C-LOWN   C-RANK   C-RUCK
C-LUCK   C-RARE   C-RUDE
C-LUMP   C-RASH   C-RUSH
C-LUNG   C-RATE   C-RUST

Five letters to six

C-ABLED   C-HAPPY   C-LEAVE
C-ABLER   C-HASTE   C-LONER
C-ACHED   C-HEWED   C-LOSED
C-AGING   C-HIDER   C-LOSER
C-ALLOW   C-HILLY   C-LOVER
C-AMBER   C-HIPPY   C-LUCKY
C-AMPED   C-HOKEY   C-LUMPY
C-AMPLY   C-HOPPY   C-ODDER
C-APING   C-HUBBY   C-OILED
C-ASKED   C-HUFFY   C-OLDER
C-AUGHT   C-HUNKY   C-OVERT

C-EASED

C-RAGGY

C-RATED

C-RATER

C-RAVED

C-RAVEN

C-LANKY

C-RAYON

C-RAZED

C-ROWED

C-RUDER

C-RUMMY

C-RAGGY

C-RUSTY

C-UMBER

C-UPPED

C-UPPER

C-UTTER

Six letters to seven

C-ABLING

C-ACHING

C-AMPING

C-ANGLED

C-AROUSE

C-ARTFUL

C-ASHIER

C-ASHING

C-ASKING

C-ASTRAL

C-AULDER

C-EASING

C-ENSURE

C-HACKED

C-HAIRED

C-HAMPER

C-HANGED

C-HANGER

C-HARING

C-HARKED

C-HARMED

C-HARMER

C-HASTEN

C-HATTED

C-HATTER

C-HAWING

C-HEAPER

C-HEATED

C-HEATER

C-HELPED

C-HEWING

C-HIDING

C-HILLED

C-HILLER

C-HIPPED

C-HIPPER

C-HIPPIE

C-HITTER

C-HOPPED

C-HOPPER

C-HUCKLE

C-HUFFED

C-HUFFER

C-HUGGED

C-HUGGER

C-HUMMED

C-HUNTER

C-INCHED

C-LACKED

C-LACKER

C-LAMBER

C-LAMMED

C-LAMMER

C-LAMPED

C-LAMPER

C-LANGER

C-LANKED

C-LAPPED

C-LAPPER

C-LASHED

C-LASHER

C-LATTER

C-LEANED

C-LEANER

C-LEANLY

C-LEARED

C-LEAVED

C-LEAVER

C-LICKED

C-LICKER

C-LIMBED

C-LIMBER

C-LINGER

C-LINKED

C-LINKER

C-LIPPED

C-LIPPER

C-LITTER

C-LOBBER

C-LOCKED

C-LOCKER

C-LOGGED

C-LOGGER

C-LOPPED

C-LOSING

C-LOTTED

C-LUBBER

C-LUCKED

C-LUMPED

C-LUMPER

C-LUNKER

C-LUSTER

C-OILING

C-OLDEST

C-OLDISH

C-ORACLE

C-RACKED

C-RACKER

C-RAFTED

C-RAFTER

C-RAGGED

C-RAMMED

C-RAMPED

C-RANKED

C-RASHED

C-RASHER

C-RAVING

C-REAKED

C-REAMED

C-RESTED

C-RIBBED

C-RIBBER

C-RICKED

C-RINGED

C-RINGER

C-RIPPLE

C-ROCKED

C-ROCKET

C-ROOKED

C-ROSIER

C-ROWING

C-RUDELY

C-RUDEST

C-RUMBLE

C-RUMPLE

C-RUSHED

C-RUSHER

C-RUSTED

C-UPPING

Highest Word Score

The highest-scoring word ever played in a Scrabble game was CAZIQUES, which achieved an enormous total of 392 points. It was played by Karl Khoshnaw of Richmond, Surrey.

Seven letters to eight

C-AMBERED
C-ANGLING
C-ASHLESS
C-ENSURED
C-ENTERED
C-HAIRING
C-HANDLER
C-HANGING
C-HANTING
C-HAPLESS
C-HAPPIER
C-HARMFUL
C-HARMING
C-HATTING
C-HEATING
C-HELPING
C-HEWABLE
C-HICKORY
C-HILDING
C-HILLIER
C-HOPPING
C-HUFFING
C-HUGGERS
C-HUGGING
C-HUMMING
C-HUMPING
C-HUNKIER
C-INCHING
C-LACKING

C-LAGGING
C-LAMMING
C-LAMPING
C-LANKIER
C-LANKING
C-LAPPING
C-LASHING
C-LATCHED
C-LAWLESS
C-LAWLIKE
C-LEANEST
C-LEANING
C-LEARING
C-LEAVING
C-LICKING
C-LIMBING
C-LINGIER
C-LINKING
C-LIPPING
C-LOCKING
C-LOGGING
C-LOPPING
C-LOSABLE
C-LOTTING
C-LOUTING
C-LUCKIER
C-LUCKING
C-LUMPIER
C-LUMPING

C-LUMPISH
C-OFFERED
C-OLDNESS
C-OTTERED
C-OVERAGE
C-OVERALL
C-OVERTLY
C-RACKING
C-RAFTING
C-RAGGIER
C-RAMMING
C-RAMPING
C-RANKING
C-RASHING
C-REAMING
C-REELING
C-RESTING
C-RIBBING
C-RICKING
C-RIMPLED
C-RINGING
C-RIPPLED
C-RIPPLER
C-ROCKERY
C-RUMBLED
C-RUMPLED
C-RUSHING
C-RUSTIER
C-RUSTILY

Some end-hooks

Two letters to three

AR-C	MI-C	RE-C
BA-C	MO-C	SI-C
DO-C	MY-C	SO-C
HI-C	OR-C	TE-C
HO-C	PA-C	TI-C
LA-C	PE-C	TO-C
MA-C	PI-C	

Three letters to four

ABA-C	DIS-C	SYN-C
ALE-C	HUI-C	TOR-C
BAN-C	MAR-C	ZIN-C
CHI-C	SAI-C	

Four letters to five

ANTI-C	ILIA-C	SERA-C
ARTI-C	LOTI-C	TARO-C
CODE-C	MAGI-C	TOPI-C
CONI-C	MALI-C	TORI-C
DURO-C	MANI-C	TRON-C
ILEA-C	RABI-C	YOGI-C

Five letters to six

ACINI-C	FILMI-C	MANIA-C
AGAMI-C	FUNDI-C	MYTHI-C
CHOLI-C	FUNGI-C	PARSE-C
CULTI-C	LIMBI-C	TRAGI-C

Six letters to seven

ALKALI-C	EMBOLI-C	SCORIA-C
CARDIA-C	NUCLEI-C	THALLI-C
COLONI-C	RHOMBI-C	TROPHI-C

Seven letters to eight

AMMONIA-C	CHIASMI-C	SYLLABI-C
AMNESIA-C	DACTYLI-C	TSUNAMI-C
BULIMIA-C	RHYTHMI-C	TYMPANI-C

Blockers

It is useful to know which words are blockers and can't therefore be extended before or after. You may want to play a blocker that your opponent can't extend, or you may want to avoid playing a blocker because you want to keep the board open.

Some three-letter blockers beginning with C

CAZ	CLY	CUZ

Some four-letter blockers beginning with C

CASH	COAX	COZY
CAVY	COPY	CRUX
CHEZ	COSH	CUED
CITY	COSY	CURT

Some five-letter blockers beginning with C
(except words ending in '-ED', '-J', '-S', '-X', '-Y' or '-Z')

CACTI	CLASH	CREPT
CAJUN	CLUNG	CRUSH
CINCH	COULD	CUING
CIVIL	CRASH	CYBER

Some six-letter blockers beginning with C
(except words ending in '-ED', '-J', '-S', '-X', '-Y' or '-Z')

CAGIER	CHEVAL	CONING
CAGING	CHOSEN	COSMIC
CALCIC	CISTIC	COXING
CALMER	CITING	COYEST
CANIER	CITRIC	CROUCH
CANNOT	CLENCH	CRUDER
CARDIO	CLINCH	CRUTCH
CARMAN	CLONAL	CURING
CARMEN	CLOVEN	CURTER
CATTLE	CLUING	CYANIC
CAUGHT	COGENT	CYSTIC
CAUSEN	COITAL	
CEDING	COMETH	

Bonus words

Bonus words on your rack can be hard to spot, especially for the less experienced player. One way to help find them is by using prefixes and suffixes.

Many larger words include a common prefix or suffix – remembering these and using them where you can is a good way to discover any longer words on your rack, including any potential bonus words. The key prefixes to remember beginning with C are COM- and CON-.

Some words beginning with COM-
Seven-letter words

COM-BATS	COM-MENT	COM-PERE
COM-BINE	COM-MODE	COM-PILE
COM-BING	COM-MONS	COM-PLEX
COM-BUST	COM-MUTE	COM-PORT
COM-FIER	COM-PACT	COM-POSE
COM-FORT	COM-PARE	COM-POST
COM-MAND	COM-PASS	COM-POTE
COM-MEND	COM-PEND	COM-RADE

Eight-letter words

COM-BATED	COM-PADRE	COM-PLIER
COM-BINER	COM-PARED	COM-POSED
COM-BINES	COM-PILED	COM-POSER
COM-FIEST	COM-PILER	COM-POUND
COM-MONER	COM-PLAIN	COM-PRESS
COM-MUTED	COM-PLEAT	COM-PRISE
COM-MUTER	COM-PLIED	

Some words beginning with CON-
Seven-letter words

CON-CAVE	CON-FIRM	CON-SOLE
CON-CEDE	CON-FORM	CON-SORT
CON-CERT	CON-FUSE	CON-TACT
CON-CORD	CON-GEAL	CON-TAIN
CON-CUSS	CON-GEST	CON-TEND
CON-DOLE	CON-JOIN	CON-TENT
CON-DONE	CON-JURE	CON-TEST
CON-DUCE	CON-JURY	CON-TEXT
CON-DUCT	CON-NOTE	CON-TORT
CON-DUIT	CON-SENT	CON-TOUR
CON-FESS	CON-SIGN	CON-VENT
CON-FINE	CON-SIST	CON-VERT

Eight-letter words

CON-CAVED	CON-FRONT	CON-SOLED
CON-CEDED	CON-FUSED	CON-SOLER
CON-CEDER	CON-GENIC	CON-SPIRE
CON-CLAVE	CON-JOINT	CON-TEMPT
CON-DENSE	CON-JUGAL	CON-TRACT
CON-DOLED	CON-JUROR	CON-TRITE
CON-DONER	CON-QUEST	CON-VERGE
CON-FINED	CON-SERVE	CON-VERSE
CON-FOUND	CON-SIDER	CON-VEXED

Unusual letter combinations

If you have an unusual combination of letters on your rack, or want to impress your opponent with an unusual word, a few words from World English can come in handy.

Australian words

CADAGI	tropical eucalyptus tree
CARBY	carburettor
CHEWI	chewing gum
CHIACK	tease or banter
CHOOK	hen or chicken
CHOOM	Englishman
COMPO	compensation
CORREA	evergreen shrub
COUCAL	long-legged bird
COUGAN	rowdy person

CRONK	unfit or unsound
CROOL	spoil
CROWEA	pink-flowered shrub

Canadian words

CABOOSE	mobile bunkhouse used by lumbermen
CANOLA	cooking oil extracted from a variety of rapeseed developed in Canada
CAYUSE	small Native American pony used by cowboys
CUSK	gadoid food fish

Hindi words

CHAI	tea, especially with added spices
CHAMPAC	tree with fragrant yellow flowers
CHAPATI	flat coarse unleavened bread
CHAPPAL	sandal
CHARKHA	spinning wheel
CHEETAH	large swift feline mammal
CHELA	disciple of a religious teacher
CHINTZ	printed cotton with glazed finish
CHITAL	type of deer
CHOKEY	prison
CHOLI	short-sleeved bodice
CHOWK	marketplace
CHUDDAR	large shawl or veil
CHUDDIES	underpants
CHUKAR	Indian partridge

CHUKKA	period of play in polo
COWAGE	tropical climbing plant with stinging pods
CRORE	ten million
CUSHY	comfortable

New Zealand words

| COOTIE | body louse |

Urdu words

| CHARPAI | bedstead of woven webbing on a wooden frame |

C

D 2

Essential info
Value: 2 points
Number in set: 4

D can begin a two-letter word alongside every vowel except for U. It also forms many three-letter words, especially in combination with W or Y: DAY, DYE and DEW are all worth 7 points.

Two-letter words beginning with D

DA   DE   DI   DO

Some three-letter words beginning with D

DAE	DEV	DOM
DAG	DEX	DOO
DAH	DEY	DOP
DAK	DIB	DOR
DAL	DIF	DOW
DAN	DIS	DOY
DAP	DIT	DSO
DAW	DIV	DUH
DEB	DOB	DUN
DEE	DOC	DUP
DEF	DOD	DUX
DEG	DOF	DZO
DEI	DOH	
DEL	DOL	

Hooks

Hooking requires a subtle change in a player's thought process, in that they must look at words already on the board without becoming distracted by their pronunciation. D benefits from the past participle form of many words, providing many options when it comes to end-hooking.

Some front-hooks
Two letters to three

D-AB	D-AW	D-IN	D-ON	D-UH
D-AD	D-AY	D-IS	D-OO	D-UN
D-AE	D-EE	D-IT	D-OP	D-UP
D-AG	D-EF	D-OB	D-OR	D-YE
D-AH	D-EL	D-OD	D-OS	D-ZO
D-AL	D-EN	D-OE	D-OW	
D-AM	D-EX	D-OF	D-OY	
D-AN	D-ID	D-OH	D-SO	
D-AS	D-IF	D-OM	D-UG	

Three letters to four

D-AFT	D-EAN	D-IRE
D-ALE	D-EAR	D-IRK
D-AMP	D-ECO	D-ISH
D-ARE	D-EFT	D-OFF
D-ARK	D-ELL	D-OLE
D-ART	D-EMO	D-ONE
D-ASH	D-HOW	D-OOR
D-ATE	D-ICE	D-OPE
D-AWN	D-ILL	D-OSE

D-OUR   D-RAT   D-ROW
D-OWL   D-RAW   D-RUB
D-OWN   D-RAY   D-RUG
D-RAG   D-REW   D-RUM
D-RAM   D-RIP   D-ZHO

Four letters to five

D-AIRY   D-OILY   D-REAM
D-ALLY   D-ONER   D-RIFT
D-AUNT   D-OOZY   D-RILL
D-EVIL   D-RAFT   D-RINK
D-ICED   D-RAIN   D-ROLL
D-ICKY   D-RAKE   D-WELL
D-INKY   D-RANK   D-WELT
D-ITCH   D-RAWN
D-JINN   D-READ

Five letters to six

D-AFTER   D-EJECT   D-OFFER
D-AMPLY   D-ELUDE   D-OWNED
D-ANGER   D-EMOTE   D-OWNER
D-ANGLE   D-ICIER   D-RAYED
D-APPLE   D-ICING   D-RIVEN
D-ASHED   D-IMPLY   D-ROGUE
D-AWNED   D-INNER   D-ROVER
D-EARLY   D-OCKER   D-UMBER
D-EARTH   D-OFFED

Six letters to seven

D-ALLIED

D-AMPING

D-ANGLED

D-ANGLER

D-ASHING

D-AWNING

D-ELATED

D-ELUDED

D-EMOTED

D-EVOLVE

D-ICIEST

D-INKIER

D-ITCHED

D-OFFING

D-OWNING

D-RAFTED

D-RAGGED

D-RAINED

D-RAWING

D-REAMED

D-REAMER

D-RIFTED

D-RILLED

D-RIPPED

D-RIPPER

D-ROLLER

D-RUBBED

D-RUBBER

D-RUGGED

D-RUMMER

D-WELLED

Seven letters to eight

D-ALLYING

D-ANGERED

D-ANGLING

D-EJECTED

D-ELUDING

D-ELUSION

D-EMERGED

D-EMOTING

D-EMOTION

D-ENOUNCE

D-EVOLVED

D-INKIEST

D-ITCHING

D-RAFTING

D-RAGGING

D-RAINING

D-READING

D-REAMING

D-RIFTING

D-RUBBING

D-RUGGING

D-WELLING

D-WINDLED

Some end-hooks

Two letters to three

AD-D	EN-D	MA-D	PO-D
AI-D	FA-D	ME-D	RE-D
AN-D	FE-D	MI-D	SO-D
AR-D	GI-D	MO-D	TA-D
BA-D	GO-D	MU-D	TE-D
BE-D	HA-D	NE-D	TI-D
BI-D	HI-D	NO-D	TO-D
BO-D	HO-D	OD-D	UR-D
DA-D	KI-D	OR-D	WE-D
DI-D	LA-D	OU-D	YA-D
DO-D	LI-D	PA-D	YO-D
EL-D	LO-D	PE-D	

Three letters to four

ACE-D	BOR-D	DOW-D
AGE-D	BRO-D	DUE-D
AKE-D	BUN-D	DYE-D
AMI-D	BUR-D	EAR-D
APE-D	CAR-D	ECO-D
ARE-D	CHA-D	EKE-D
AWE-D	CHI-D	ERE-D
AXE-D	COL-D	EYE-D
BAL-D	CON-D	FAN-D
BAN-D	COR-D	FAR-D
BAR-D	CRU-D	FEE-D
BEN-D	CUE-D	FEN-D
BIN-D	CUR-D	FEU-D
BON-D	DIE-D	FIN-D

FON-D	LIN-D	SEE-D
FOR-D	LOR-D	SEL-D
FOU-D	LOU-D	SEN-D
FUN-D	MAN-D	SHE-D
GAE-D	MEL-D	SIN-D
GAU-D	MEN-D	SKI-D
GEE-D	MIL-D	SOL-D
GEL-D	MOL-D	SUD-D
GIE-D	MOO-D	SUE-D
GOA-D	NEE-D	SUR-D
GOO-D	OPE-D	TAE-D
HAE-D	OWE-D	TEA-D
HAN-D	PAN-D	TEE-D
HEN-D	PAR-D	TEL-D
HER-D	PEN-D	TEN-D
HIE-D	PIE-D	TIE-D
HIN-D	PRO-D	TIN-D
HOE-D	QUA-D	TOE-D
HOO-D	RAI-D	TYE-D
HUE-D	RAN-D	USE-D
ICE-D	RED-D	VIE-D
IRE-D	REE-D	WAI-D
KIN-D	REN-D	WAN-D
KON-D	RIN-D	WAR-D
LAR-D	ROE-D	WEE-D
LEA-D	RUE-D	WEN-D
LEE-D	RUN-D	WIN-D
LEU-D	SAI-D	WOO-D
LEW-D	SAN-D	WYN-D
LIE-D	SAR-D	YAR-D

Four letters to five

ABLE-D	CLUE-D	FAKE-D
ACHE-D	CODE-D	FAME-D
ACNE-D	COKE-D	FARE-D
ACRE-D	CONE-D	FATE-D
AIDE-D	COPE-D	FAZE-D
AMEN-D	CORE-D	FETE-D
AXLE-D	COVE-D	FILE-D
BAKE-D	COZE-D	FINE-D
BALE-D	CROW-D	FIRE-D
BARE-D	CUBE-D	FRAU-D
BASE-D	CURE-D	FREE-D
BEAR-D	DARE-D	FUME-D
BIDE-D	DATE-D	FUSE-D
BIKE-D	DAZE-D	GAME-D
BLUE-D	DICE-D	GAPE-D
BOAR-D	DINE-D	GATE-D
BODE-D	DIVE-D	GAZE-D
BONE-D	DOLE-D	GLUE-D
BORE-D	DOME-D	GORE-D
BRAN-D	DOPE-D	GRAN-D
CAGE-D	DOSE-D	GRIN-D
CAKE-D	DOTE-D	GUAR-D
CANE-D	DOZE-D	HARE-D
CAPE-D	DUKE-D	HATE-D
CARE-D	DUPE-D	HAZE-D
CASE-D	EASE-D	HEAR-D
CAVE-D	EDGE-D	HIKE-D
CEDE-D	FACE-D	HIRE-D
CITE-D	FADE-D	HOLE-D

HOME-D	MIME-D	RAKE-D
HONE-D	MINE-D	RARE-D
HOPE-D	MIRE-D	RATE-D
HOSE-D	MOPE-D	RAVE-D
HYPE-D	MOVE-D	RAZE-D
IDLE-D	MUSE-D	RILE-D
JADE-D	MUTE-D	ROBE-D
JAPE-D	NAME-D	ROPE-D
JIBE-D	NOSE-D	ROSE-D
JIVE-D	NOTE-D	ROVE-D
JOKE-D	NUKE-D	RULE-D
KNEE-D	OGLE-D	RUNE-D
LACE-D	OOZE-D	SATE-D
LAIR-D	PACE-D	SAVE-D
LAZE-D	PAGE-D	SHOE-D
LIKE-D	PALE-D	SIDE-D
LIME-D	PARE-D	SIRE-D
LINE-D	PAVE-D	SITE-D
LIVE-D	PIKE-D	SIZE-D
LOPE-D	PILE-D	SPIE-D
LOVE-D	PINE-D	SURE-D
LOWE-D	PIPE-D	TAME-D
LUGE-D	PLEA-D	TAPE-D
LURE-D	PLIE-D	TILE-D
LUTE-D	POKE-D	TIME-D
MACE-D	PORE-D	TIRE-D
MATE-D	POSE-D	TONE-D
MAZE-D	RABI-D	TREE-D
METE-D	RACE-D	TRIE-D
MIKE-D	RAGE-D	TUNE-D

D

TWEE-D   WANE-D   WIRE-D
TYPE-D   WAVE-D   YOKE-D
URGE-D   WEIR-D   ZONE-D
VOTE-D   WINE-D
WADE-D   WIPE-D

Five letters to six

ABASE-D   BRAKE-D   DANCE-D
ABATE-D   BRAVE-D   DELVE-D
ABIDE-D   BRIBE-D   DEUCE-D
ABUSE-D   BUDGE-D   DODGE-D
ADDLE-D   BUGLE-D   DOUSE-D
ADORE-D   BULGE-D   DOWSE-D
AGREE-D   CABLE-D   DRAPE-D
AMAZE-D   CACHE-D   DRONE-D
AMBLE-D   CARTE-D   ELATE-D
AMUSE-D   CARVE-D   ELOPE-D
ANGLE-D   CAUSE-D   ELUDE-D
ANKLE-D   CEASE-D   EMOTE-D
ARGUE-D   CHASE-D   ENSUE-D
ATONE-D   CHIME-D   ERASE-D
BARGE-D   CHOKE-D   ERODE-D
BASTE-D   CLONE-D   EVADE-D
BELIE-D   CLOSE-D   EVOKE-D
BINGE-D   CRANE-D   EXILE-D
BLAME-D   CRAVE-D   FABLE-D
BLARE-D   CRAZE-D   FENCE-D
BLAZE-D   CURSE-D   FLAKE-D
BOOZE-D   CURVE-D   FLAME-D
BRACE-D   CYCLE-D   FLARE-D

FLUKE-D	JUICE-D	PULSE-D
FORCE-D	KNIFE-D	PURGE-D
FORGE-D	LADLE-D	QUAKE-D
FRAME-D	LANCE-D	QUEUE-D
GAUGE-D	LAPSE-D	QUOTE-D
GLARE-D	LEASE-D	RAISE-D
GLAZE-D	LEAVE-D	RANGE-D
GLIDE-D	LEDGE-D	REAVE-D
GLOVE-D	LODGE-D	RETRO-D
GORGE-D	LOOSE-D	RHYME-D
GOUGE-D	LUNGE-D	RIDGE-D
GRACE-D	MERGE-D	RIFLE-D
GRADE-D	MINCE-D	RINSE-D
GRAPE-D	NUDGE-D	ROGUE-D
GRATE-D	NURSE-D	ROUTE-D
GRAVE-D	PASTE-D	SALVE-D
GRAZE-D	PAUSE-D	SAUTE-D
GRIPE-D	PHASE-D	SCALE-D
GROPE-D	PHONE-D	SCARE-D
GROVE-D	PIECE-D	SCOPE-D
GUIDE-D	PLACE-D	SCORE-D
HASTE-D	PLANE-D	SEIZE-D
HEAVE-D	POISE-D	SENSE-D
HEDGE-D	PRICE-D	SHADE-D
HINGE-D	PRIDE-D	SHAKE-D
HORSE-D	PRIME-D	SHAPE-D
HOUSE-D	PRISE-D	SHAVE-D
IMAGE-D	PROBE-D	SHINE-D
ISSUE-D	PROVE-D	SHORE-D
JUDGE-D	PRUNE-D	SHOVE-D

SHREW-D   SPICE-D   TRACE-D

SIDLE-D   SPIKE-D   TRADE-D

SIEGE-D   STAGE-D   TRUCE-D

SIEVE-D   STAKE-D   TWINE-D

SINGE-D   STALE-D   UNITE-D

SKATE-D   STARE-D   UNTIE-D

SLATE-D   STATE-D   VALUE-D

SLAVE-D   STOKE-D   VERGE-D

SLICE-D   STONE-D   VERSE-D

SLIME-D   STORE-D   VOICE-D

SLOPE-D   STYLE-D   WAIVE-D

SMILE-D   SURGE-D   WASTE-D

SMOKE-D   SWIPE-D   WEAVE-D

SNAKE-D   TABLE-D   WEDGE-D

SNARE-D   TASTE-D   WHALE-D

SNIPE-D   TEASE-D   WHINE-D

SNORE-D   TENSE-D   WHITE-D

SOLVE-D   THEME-D   WINCE-D

SPACE-D   TINGE-D

SPARE-D   TITLE-D

Six letters to seven

ACCRUE-D   ASHAME-D   BEHAVE-D

ACCUSE-D   ASSUME-D   BELATE-D

ADHERE-D   ASSURE-D   BELOVE-D

ADMIRE-D   AVENGE-D   BEMUSE-D

ADVISE-D   BABBLE-D   BERATE-D

ALLUDE-D   BAFFLE-D   BOGGLE-D

ALLURE-D   BATTLE-D   BOTTLE-D

ARRIVE-D   BEETLE-D   BOUNCE-D

BREEZE-D	CRUISE-D	DEPOSE-D
BRIDGE-D	CUDDLE-D	DERIDE-D
BRIDLE-D	CURDLE-D	DERIVE-D
BRONZE-D	DAMAGE-D	DESIRE-D
BROWSE-D	DANGLE-D	DETUNE-D
BRUISE-D	DAPPLE-D	DEVISE-D
BUCKLE-D	DAWDLE-D	DEVOTE-D
BUNDLE-D	DAZZLE-D	DILATE-D
BUNGLE-D	DEBASE-D	DILUTE-D
BURBLE-D	DEBATE-D	DISUSE-D
BURGLE-D	DECIDE-D	DIVIDE-D
BUSTLE-D	DECODE-D	DIVINE-D
CACKLE-D	DECREE-D	DONATE-D
CASTLE-D	DEDUCE-D	DOODLE-D
CENTRE-D	DEFACE-D	DOUBLE-D
CHANCE-D	DEFAME-D	DREDGE-D
CHANGE-D	DEFILE-D	DRUDGE-D
CHARGE-D	DEFINE-D	ELAPSE-D
CHEESE-D	DEFUSE-D	EMERGE-D
CIRCLE-D	DEGREE-D	ENABLE-D
CLEAVE-D	DELATE-D	ENCASE-D
CLICHE-D	DELETE-D	ENCODE-D
COERCE-D	DELUDE-D	ENCORE-D
CORPSE-D	DELUGE-D	ENDURE-D
COUPLE-D	DEMISE-D	ENGAGE-D
COURSE-D	DEMODE-D	ENGINE-D
CRADLE-D	DEMOTE-D	ENRAGE-D
CREASE-D	DEMURE-D	ENSURE-D
CREATE-D	DENOTE-D	ENTICE-D
CRINGE-D	DENUDE-D	EQUATE-D

D

ESCAPE-D	GRUDGE-D	JOSTLE-D
ESTATE-D	GUZZLE-D	JUGGLE-D
EVOLVE-D	GYRATE-D	JUMBLE-D
EXCISE-D	HANDLE-D	LIAISE-D
EXCITE-D	HECKLE-D	LOATHE-D
EXCUSE-D	HOMAGE-D	LOCATE-D
EXHALE-D	HUDDLE-D	LOUNGE-D
EXHUME-D	HUMBLE-D	MANAGE-D
EXPIRE-D	HURDLE-D	MANGLE-D
EXPOSE-D	HURTLE-D	MANURE-D
FETTLE-D	HUSTLE-D	MARBLE-D
FIDDLE-D	ICICLE-D	MATURE-D
FIGURE-D	IGNITE-D	MENACE-D
FISSLE-D	IGNORE-D	MINGLE-D
FIZZLE-D	IMPALE-D	MINUTE-D
FLEDGE-D	IMPEDE-D	MISUSE-D
FLEECE-D	IMPOSE-D	MUDDLE-D
FONDLE-D	INCITE-D	MUFFLE-D
FORAGE-D	INDUCE-D	MUMBLE-D
FRIDGE-D	INFAME-D	MUSCLE-D
FUMBLE-D	INFUSE-D	MUTATE-D
GARBLE-D	INHALE-D	MUZZLE-D
GARGLE-D	INJURE-D	NEEDLE-D
GENTLE-D	INVADE-D	NEGATE-D
GIGGLE-D	INVITE-D	NESTLE-D
GLANCE-D	INVOKE-D	NIBBLE-D
GOBBLE-D	IONISE-D	NOTICE-D
GREASE-D	JANGLE-D	NUANCE-D
GRIEVE-D	JIGGLE-D	OBLIGE-D
GROOVE-D	JINGLE-D	OPPOSE-D

PADDLE-D	RECEDE-D	SAMPLE-D
PALACE-D	RECITE-D	SAVAGE-D
PARADE-D	REDUCE-D	SCHEME-D
PAROLE-D	REFINE-D	SCRAPE-D
PEDDLE-D	REFUSE-D	SCYTHE-D
PEOPLE-D	REGALE-D	SECEDE-D
PERUSE-D	REHIRE-D	SECURE-D
PHRASE-D	RELATE-D	SEDATE-D
PICKLE-D	RELINE-D	SEDUCE-D
PIERCE-D	REMOVE-D	SEETHE-D
PIRATE-D	RENEGE-D	SEVERE-D
PLAGUE-D	REPUTE-D	SNOOZE-D
PLEASE-D	RESCUE-D	SOMBRE-D
PLEDGE-D	RESIDE-D	SOURCE-D
PLUNGE-D	RESIZE-D	SPONGE-D
POLICE-D	RESUME-D	SQUIRE-D
POOTLE-D	RETIRE-D	STABLE-D
POUNCE-D	REVERE-D	STAPLE-D
PRAISE-D	REVILE-D	STARVE-D
PRANCE-D	REVISE-D	STATUE-D
PSYCHE-D	REVIVE-D	STRIPE-D
PUDDLE-D	REVOKE-D	STRIVE-D
PUPATE-D	RIDDLE-D	STROBE-D
PURSUE-D	ROTATE-D	STROKE-D
PUZZLE-D	RUBBLE-D	SUBDUE-D
RAFFLE-D	RUFFLE-D	SUCKLE-D
RAMBLE-D	RUMBLE-D	SUPPLE-D
RATTLE-D	RUSTLE-D	SWATHE-D
RAVAGE-D	SADDLE-D	SWERVE-D
REBUKE-D	SALUTE-D	TACKLE-D

TICKLE-D
TINGLE-D
TIPTOE-D
TITTLE-D
TONGUE-D
TOPPLE-D
TORQUE-D
TOUCHE-D
TOUSLE-D
TRANCE-D

TREBLE-D
TRIFLE-D
TRIPLE-D
TRUDGE-D
TUMBLE-D
TUSSLE-D
UMPIRE-D
UNDATE-D
UNLIKE-D
UNLOVE-D

UNSURE-D
UPDATE-D
VOYAGE-D
WABBLE-D
WHINGE-D
WIGGLE-D
WINKLE-D
WOBBLE-D

Seven letters to eight

ABRIDGE-D
ABSOLVE-D
ACCURSE-D
ACHIEVE-D
ACQUIRE-D
ADVANCE-D
AGITATE-D
AGONISE-D
ALLEDGE-D
ANALYSE-D
ANIMATE-D
APPROVE-D
ARCHIVE-D
ARRANGE-D
ARTICLE-D
ATOMISE-D
ATTACHE-D
AVERAGE-D

BALANCE-D
BANDAGE-D
BEGUILE-D
BELIEVE-D
BEREAVE-D
BRIGADE-D
CAPSIZE-D
CAPTURE-D
CHORTLE-D
CHUCKLE-D
COLLATE-D
COLLIDE-D
COLLUDE-D
COMBINE-D
COMMUTE-D
COMPARE-D
COMPERE-D
COMPETE-D

COMPILE-D
COMPOSE-D
COMPUTE-D
CONCEDE-D
CONCISE-D
CONFIDE-D
CONFUSE-D
CONJURE-D
CONSOLE-D
CONSUME-D
CONVENE-D
CORRODE-D
COSTUME-D
CRACKLE-D
CREMATE-D
CRINKLE-D
CRIPPLE-D
CRUMBLE-D

D

CRUMPLE-D

CRUSADE-D

CULTURE-D

DECEASE-D

DECEIVE-D

DECLARE-D

DECLINE-D

DEGRADE-D

DEPRAVE-D

DEPRIVE-D

DESERVE-D

DESPISE-D

DESTINE-D

DEVALUE-D

DEVIATE-D

DICTATE-D

DIFFUSE-D

DISABLE-D

DISEASE-D

DISLIKE-D

DISPOSE-D

DISPUTE-D

DIVERGE-D

DIVORCE-D

DRIBBLE-D

EDUCATE-D

ELEVATE-D

EMANATE-D

EMBRACE-D

EMULATE-D

ENCLOSE-D

ENDORSE-D

ENFORCE-D

ENGRAVE-D

ENHANCE-D

ENLARGE-D

ENTHUSE-D

ENTITLE-D

EXAMINE-D

EXCLUDE-D

EXECUTE-D

EXPLODE-D

EXPLORE-D

FATIGUE-D

FEATURE-D

FINANCE-D

FLOUNCE-D

GESTATE-D

GESTURE-D

GRUNTLE-D

HYDRATE-D

IDOLISE-D

IMAGINE-D

IMITATE-D

IMMERSE-D

IMPLODE-D

IMPLORE-D

IMPROVE-D

INCLUDE-D

INDULGE-D

INFLAME-D

INFLATE-D

INSPIRE-D

INVOLVE-D

LICENCE-D

LICENSE-D

MANACLE-D

MANDATE-D

MASSAGE-D

MEASURE-D

MESSAGE-D

MIGRATE-D

MISTIME-D

OBSCURE-D

OBSERVE-D

OPERATE-D

OUTLINE-D

OUTRAGE-D

OUTSIZE-D

OVERUSE-D

OZONIZE-D

PACKAGE-D

PICTURE-D

PILLAGE-D

PLACATE-D

POLLUTE-D

PRECEDE-D

PREFACE-D

PREPARE-D

PRESUME-D

PRODUCE-D   RESERVE-D   SURVIVE-D

PROFILE-D   REVENGE-D   SUSPIRE-D

PROMISE-D   REVERSE-D   TEXTURE-D

PROMOTE-D   REVOLVE-D   TRAMPLE-D

PROPOSE-D   SALVAGE-D   TROUBLE-D

PROVIDE-D   SCUFFLE-D   UNHINGE-D

RAMPAGE-D   SERVICE-D   UNNERVE-D

REALISE-D   SHUFFLE-D   UPGRADE-D

REALIZE-D   SILENCE-D   UPSTAGE-D

RECEIVE-D   SMUGGLE-D   VENTURE-D

RECYCLE-D   SPARKLE-D   VIBRATE-D

REJOICE-D   SQUEEZE-D   VIOLATE-D

RELAPSE-D   STUBBLE-D   WELCOME-D

RELEASE-D   STUMBLE-D   WHISTLE-D

RELIEVE-D   SUBSIDE-D   WHITTLE-D

REPLACE-D   SUFFICE-D   WREATHE-D

REPULSE-D   SUPPOSE-D   WRESTLE-D

REQUIRE-D   SURFACE-D   WRIGGLE-D

Handy Hint

Some unusual short words it is worth remembering are
DA (a Burmese knife, 3 points), DAW (a shortened form of
jackdaw, 7 points), DEY (an Ottoman governor, 7 points)
and DOW (an Arab ship, also 7).

Blockers

It is useful to know which words are blockers and can't therefore be extended before or after. You may want to play a blocker that your opponent can't extend, or you may want to avoid playing a blocker because you want to keep the board open.

Some three-letter blockers beginning with D

DUH   DUX

Some four-letter blockers beginning with D

DAFT	DEXY	DOMY	DOWF
DAVY	DIDY	DOPY	DOXY
DEAF	DIED	DORY	DOZY
DEFT	DIEL	DOSH	DREW
DEFY	DIPT	DOSS	DUED
DEMY	DISS	DOST	DULY
DENY	DIXY	DOTH	DUSH
DESI	DOBY	DOTY	DUTY
DEUS	DOEN	DOUN	DYED
DEWY	DOGY	DOUX	

Some five-letter blockers beginning with D
(except words ending in '-ED', '-J', '-S', '-X', '-Y' or '-Z')

DEALT	DOEST	DRIPT
DIACT	DONER	DUNNO
DICTA	DORIC	DURST
DINGO	DRACO	DUTCH
DINNA	DRANK	DWELT
DIRER	DRAWN	
DITCH	DREST	

Some six-letter blockers beginning with D
(except words ending in '-ED', '-J', '-S', '-X', '-Y' or '-Z')

DAFTER	DEVOID	DOZIER
DANISH	DEVOUT	DREAMT
DANKER	DEWIER	DREICH
DARKER	DEWING	DRENCH
DAYLIT	DEXTRO	DRIEST
DAZING	DICIER	DRIVEN
DEAFER	DINING	DROLER
DEARER	DIREST	DRYEST
DECENT	DOABLE	DRYISH
DEEPER	DOGMAN	DUEFUL
DEFTER	DOLING	DUKING
DELISH	DOMING	DULLER
DELUXE	DOPIER	DUMBER
DENSER	DOSING	DUPING
DERMAL	DOURER	DURING
DETACH	DOVING	DYABLE

D

Some words beginning with DE-
Seven-letter words

DE-ADMAN	DE-FENCE	DE-MERIT
DE-BASED	DE-FILED	DE-NOTED
DE-BASER	DE-FINED	DE-PARTS
DE-BATED	DE-FORMS	DE-PLOYS
DE-BONED	DE-FRAUD	DE-PORTS
DE-BRIEF	DE-FROST	DE-POSED
DE-CADES	DE-FUSED	DE-POSIT
DE-CODED	DE-GRADE	DE-PRESS
DE-COYED	DE-ICING	DE-RAILS
DE-CREED	DE-LAYED	DE-RIDER
DE-CRIED	DE-LIGHT	DE-SCENT
DE-CRYPT	DE-LIVER	DE-SIGNS
DE-FACED	DE-LUGED	DE-SIRED
DE-FAULT	DE-MEANS	DE-SPITE

DE-TAILS   DE-TRACT   DE-VOTED
DE-TESTS   DE-VALUE
DE-TOURS   DE-VICES

Eight-letter words

DE-AERATE   DE-FINITE   DE-RAILED
DE-BASING   DE-FOREST   DE-RANGED
DE-BUGGED   DE-FORMED   DE-RIDING
DE-BUNKED   DE-GRADED   DE-SCRIBE
DE-CANTER   DE-LAYING   DE-SELECT
DE-CEASED   DE-MISTED   DE-SERVED
DE-CIPHER   DE-MOTION   DE-SIGNED
DE-CODING   DE-NOTING   DE-TAILED
DE-CRYING   DE-PARTED   DE-VOLVED
DE-DUCTED   DE-PENDED
DE-FACING   DE-PORTED

Some words beginning with DIS-
Seven-letter words

DIS-ABLE   DIS-GUST   DIS-POSE
DIS-ARMS   DIS-LIKE   DIS-SECT
DIS-BAND   DIS-MISS   DIS-SENT
DIS-CARD   DIS-OBEY   DIS-TILL
DIS-CUSS   DIS-OWNS   DIS-TORT
DIS-EASE   DIS-PLAY   DIS-USED

Eight-letter words

DIS-AGREE	DIS-GUISE	DIS-PLACE
DIS-ALLOW	DIS-HONOR	DIS-PROVE
DIS-APPLY	DIS-JOINT	DIS-QUIET
DIS-ARRAY	DIS-LOYAL	DIS-SOLVE
DIS-CLOSE	DIS-MOUNT	DIS-TASTE
DIS-COLOR	DIS-ORDER	DIS-TRACT
DIS-COVER	DIS-OWNED	DIS-TRUST
DIS-GORGE	DIS-PATCH	DIS-UNITY
DIS-GRACE	DIS-PERSE	

Some words ending with -DOM

Seven-letter words

BORE-DOM	FIEF-DOM	PAPA-DOM
DUKE-DOM	FREE-DOM	SERF-DOM
EARL-DOM	KING-DOM	STAR-DOM

Eight-letter words

CHIEF-DOM	LIEGE-DOM	SHEIK-DOM
CLERK-DOM	PAPPA-DOM	THANE-DOM
DEVIL-DOM	POPPA-DOM	THRAL-DOM
DUNCE-DOM	QUEEN-DOM	UNWIS-DOM
HOTEL-DOM	SAINT-DOM	

D

Unusual letter combinations

If you have an unusual combination of letters on your rack, or want to impress your opponent with an unusual word, a few words from World English can come in handy.

D

Australian words

DASYURE	small carnivorous marsupial
DELO	delegate
DERRO	vagrant
DINGO	wild dog
DINKUM	genuine or right
DOCO	documentary
DONGA	steep-sided gully
DORBA	stupid, inept, or clumsy person
DRACK	unattractive
DRONGO	slow-witted person
DROOB	pathetic person
DUBBO	stupid
DUGITE	venomous snake
DURRY	cigarette

Canadian words

DEKE	act or instance of feinting in ice hockey

Hindi words

DACOIT	member of a gang of armed robbers
DACOITY	robbery by an armed gang

DAK	system of mail delivery
DAL	split grain
DATURA	plant with trumpet-shaped flowers
DEKKO	look or glance
DEODAR	Himalayan cedar
DEWAN	chief minister of an Indian princedom
DHAK	tropical tree with red flowers
DHAL	curry made from lentils
DHARNA	method of obtaining justice by fasting
DHOBI	washerman
DHOTI	loincloth
DUPATTA	scarf
DURRIE	cotton carpet
DURZI	Indian tailor

D

South African words
DWAAL	state of befuddlement

Urdu words
DAROGHA	manager
DHANSAK	Indian dish of meat or vegetables braised with lentils

Essential info

Value: 1 point

Number in set: 12

E may be worth only one point, but it is extremely useful as it is the most common letter in the Scrabble set. Many words contain more than one E and it is worthwhile keeping these in mind, as there is a good chance you will find yourself with more than one E on your rack. Three-letter words formed by E on either side of a consonant include EYE, EWE, EVE (6 points) and EKE (7 points). E and K combine well to form a selection of other three-letter words, including ELK, EEK (7 points) and EWK (a dialect word for itch, 10 points). E is also helpful for getting rid of double consonants with words such as EGG (5 points) or EBB (7 points). E is one of the letters of the RETAIN set and is therefore a good letter to keep if trying to get a bonus word.

Two-letter words beginning with E

EA	EF	EM	ES
ED	EH	EN	ET
EE	EL	ER	EX

Some three-letter words beginning with E

EAN	EGO	ENG	EST
EAU	ELD	EON	ETA
ECH	ELL	ERE	ETH
EDH	ELT	ERF	EWK
EEK	EME	ERG	EXO
EEN	EMO	ERK	
EFF	EMU	ERN	
EFT	ENE	ESS	

Hooks

Hooking requires a subtle change in a player's thought process, in that they must look at words already on the board without becoming distracted by their pronunciation.

Some front-hooks
Two letters to three

E-AN	E-EN	E-ON
E-AR	E-GO	E-RE
E-AS	E-ME	E-ST
E-AT	E-MO	E-TA
E-CH	E-MU	E-WE
E-EL	E-NE	E-YE

Three letters to four

E-ACH	E-NOW	E-THE
E-ARD	E-PIC	E-TIC
E-AVE	E-RED	E-TUI
E-DIT	E-RES	E-UGH
E-GAD	E-REV	E-VET
E-GAL	E-SKY	E-VOE
E-KED	E-SPY	E-YEN
E-MIR	E-TAT	
E-NEW	E-TEN	

Four letters to five

E-AGER	E-LITE	E-NORM
E-ARED	E-LOGE	E-PACT
E-BONY	E-LOGY	E-POXY
E-BOOK	E-LOIN	E-PROM
E-DICT	E-LOPE	E-QUID
E-DUCE	E-LUDE	E-QUIP
E-GEST	E-LUTE	E-RODE
E-HING	E-MAIL	E-STOP
E-IKON	E-MEER	E-TAPE
E-KING	E-MEND	E-VADE
E-LAIN	E-MOTE	E-VENT
E-LAND	E-MOVE	E-VERY
E-LATE	E-MULE	
E-LINT	E-NEWS	

Five letters to six

E-ASTER
E-CARTE
E-CHARD
E-DITED
E-GALLY
E-ITHER
E-LAPSE
E-LATED
E-LATER
E-LEGIT
E-LICIT

E-LOPED
E-LOPER
E-MERGE
E-METIC
E-MOTED
E-NERVE
E-NEWED
E-PRISE
E-QUATE
E-QUINE
E-RASED

E-RASER
E-SCAPE
E-SCARP
E-SCROW
E-SPIED
E-SPIER
E-SPRIT
E-STATE
E-VADED
E-VILER
E-VOLVE

Six letters to seven

E-ASTERN
E-BAYING
E-BONIST
E-CLOSED
E-COTYPE
E-DITING
E-LANCED
E-LAPSED
E-LECTOR
E-LEGIST
E-LOPING

E-MAILED
E-MERGED
E-MOTION
E-MOTIVE
E-MOVING
E-NERVED
E-RASING
E-RASURE
E-RODING
E-SCAPED
E-SPOUSE

E-SPYING
E-SQUIRE
E-STATED
E-TERNAL
E-VADING
E-VENTER
E-VILEST
E-VOLUTE
E-VOLVED

Seven letters to eight

E-LAPSING

E-LECTION

E-LEVATOR

E-MAILING

E-MENDING

E-MERGING

E-MERSION

E-MIGRANT

E-MIGRATE

E-MISSION

E-MISSIVE

E-NERVATE

E-NERVING

E-QUALITY

E-QUIPPED

E-QUIPPER

E-RADIATE

E-SCALADE

E-SCAPING

E-SCARPED

E-SCRIBED

E-SPECIAL

E-SPOUSAL

E-SQUIRED

E-STATING

E-STOPPED

E-STRANGE

E-TYPICAL

E-VACUATE

E-VALUATE

E-VENTING

E-VERSION

E-VOLVING

Handy Hint

If you find yourself with a vowel-heavy rack, handy short
words to remember which use no consonants are EA and
EE (both 2 points) or EAU (3 points). And there's always
EUOUAE (a mnemonic used in Gregorian chant, 6 points)
and EUOI (an interjection of Bacchic frenzy, 4 points).

Some end-hooks
Two letters to three

AG-E	DE-E	HI-E	NY-E	SH-E
AL-E	DI-E	HO-E	OB-E	TA-E
AN-E	DO-E	ID-E	OD-E	TE-E
AR-E	EM-E	JO-E	ON-E	TI-E
AT-E	EN-E	KA-E	OP-E	TO-E
AW-E	ER-E	KY-E	OR-E	UR-E
AX-E	FA-E	LI-E	OS-E	US-E
AY-E	FE-E	MA-E	OW-E	UT-E
BE-E	GI-E	ME-E	OY-E	WE-E
BY-E	GO-E	MO-E	PE-E	WO-E
CH-E	GU-E	NA-E	PI-E	YA-E
DA-E	HA-E	NE-E	RE-E	

Three letters to four

ACH-E	CAG-E	DAM-E
ADZ-E	CAM-E	DIM-E
AID-E	CAN-E	DIN-E
ANT-E	CAP-E	DIV-E
BAL-E	CAR-E	DOL-E
BAN-E	CIT-E	DOM-E
BAR-E	CON-E	DON-E
BAS-E	COP-E	DOP-E
BAT-E	COR-E	DOS-E
BID-E	COS-E	DOT-E
BIT-E	CUB-E	DUD-E
BON-E	CUR-E	DUN-E
BOR-E	CUT-E	DUP-E
BRA-E	DAL-E	EAS-E

ELS-E	KIT-E	MOR-E
FAD-E	LAC-E	MUS-E
FAR-E	LAM-E	MUT-E
FAT-E	LAT-E	NAM-E
FET-E	LIN-E	NAP-E
FIL-E	LIT-E	NIT-E
FIN-E	LOB-E	NOD-E
FIR-E	LOD-E	NON-E
FLU-E	LOP-E	NOS-E
FOR-E	LOR-E	NOT-E
FUM-E	LOS-E	OBO-E
GAL-E	LUD-E	PAC-E
GAM-E	LUG-E	PAL-E
GAP-E	LUR-E	PAN-E
GAT-E	MAC-E	PAR-E
GEN-E	MAD-E	PAT-E
GIB-E	MAG-E	PAV-E
GON-E	MAK-E	PIN-E
GOR-E	MAL-E	PIP-E
HAT-E	MAN-E	POL-E
HER-E	MAR-E	POP-E
HID-E	MAT-E	POS-E
HOM-E	MEM-E	PUR-E
HOP-E	MIC-E	RAG-E
HOS-E	MIL-E	RAT-E
HUG-E	MIM-E	RID-E
HYP-E	MIR-E	RIF-E
JAP-E	MOD-E	RIP-E
JIB-E	MOL-E	ROB-E
JUT-E	MOP-E	ROD-E

ROT-E
RUD-E
RUN-E
SAG-E
SAL-E
SAM-E
SAN-E
SAT-E
SAV-E
SIN-E
SIR-E
SIT-E
SOL-E
SOM-E

SUR-E
TAK-E
TAM-E
TAP-E
THE-E
TID-E
TIL-E
TIN-E
TOM-E
TON-E
TOP-E
TOT-E
TUB-E
TUN-E

VAN-E
VAR-E
VAS-E
VIN-E
VIS-E
VOL-E
WAD-E
WAG-E
WAN-E
WAR-E
WIN-E
WIS-E
WOK-E
YOK-E

Four letters to five

AMID-E
BATH-E
BING-E
BLAM-E
BOMB-E
BOOS-E
BRUT-E
CART-E
CAST-E
CHIV-E
COPS-E
COUP-E
CREW-E
CRIM-E

CURS-E
DOWS-E
ERAS-E
FLAK-E
FLIT-E
FORT-E
GEES-E
GLAD-E
GLOB-E
GRAD-E
GRIM-E
GRIP-E
HAST-E
HING-E

HIRE-E
LAPS-E
LENS-E
LOOS-E
MANS-E
PASS-E
PAST-E
PEAS-E
PLAN-E
PLAT-E
PLUM-E
PRIM-E
PROS-E
PURE-E

QUIT-E　　　　SNIP-E　　　　TEAS-E

RANG-E　　　　SPAR-E　　　　TENS-E

SCAR-E　　　　SPAT-E　　　　THEM-E

SHAM-E　　　　SPIN-E　　　　TRAD-E

SHIN-E　　　　SPIT-E　　　　TRIP-E

SING-E　　　　STAG-E　　　　TWIN-E

SLAT-E　　　　STAR-E　　　　UNIT-E

SLID-E　　　　STAT-E　　　　WHIN-E

SLIM-E　　　　SUED-E　　　　WHIT-E

SLOP-E　　　　SUIT-E　　　　WRIT-E

Five letters to six

BLOND-E　　　　LOCAL-E　　　　SCRAP-E

CLOTH-E　　　　LUPIN-E　　　　SOOTH-E

EQUIP-E　　　　MADAM-E　　　　SPARS-E

FINAL-E　　　　MORAL-E　　　　SPRIT-E

GRAND-E　　　　PETIT-E　　　　STRIP-E

HEARS-E　　　　PLEAS-E　　　　SWATH-E

HUMAN-E　　　　REGAL-E　　　　TOUCH-E

IMPED-E　　　　REPOS-E　　　　URBAN-E

LOATH-E　　　　RESIT-E

Six letters to seven

ADVISE-E	ESCAPE-E	REFUGE-E
ARTIST-E	FIANCE-E	RETIRE-E
ATTACH-E	FLAMBE-E	REVERS-E
AUGUST-E	GERMAN-E	SECRET-E
BREATH-E	HEROIN-E	TARTAR-E
CORNEA-E	IMPING-E	WREATH-E
DEVOTE-E	IMPROV-E	
DIVERS-E	OBLIGE-E	

E

Seven letters to eight

ABSINTH-E	EMPLOYE-E	LICENCE-E
ALKALIS-E	ENDORSE-E	LICENSE-E
AMPHORA-E	ENVELOP-E	NOCTURN-E
BACKBIT-E	ESCALOP-E	OUTWRIT-E
DECLASS-E	GELATIN-E	PROTEGE-E
DIVORCE-E	INHUMAN-E	SILICON-E
DOMICIL-E	INTERNE-E	

Handy Hint

A good short word which uses the X and a couple of
vowels is EXO (informal Australian term meaning excellent,
10 points). Note that the word could enable you to make a
play that involves hooking your O onto an existing EX.

Blockers

It is useful to know which words are blockers and can't therefore be extended before or after. You may want to play a blocker that your opponent can't extend, or you may want to avoid playing a blocker because you want to keep the board open.

Some four-letter blockers beginning with E

EASY	ELSE	ESPY	EYRY

Five-letter blocker beginning with E
(except words ending in '-ED', '-J', '-S', '-X', '-Y' or '-Z')

ENLIT

Some six-letter blockers beginning with E
(except words ending in '-ED', '-J', '-S', '-X', '-Y' or '-Z')

EASIER	EMDASH	ENRAPT
EFFETE	ENCASH	ENRICH
ELDEST	ENDASH	EYEING
ELVISH	ENMESH	

Bonus words

Bonus words on your rack can be hard to spot, especially for the less experienced player. One way to help find them is by using prefixes and suffixes.

Many larger words include a common prefix or suffix – remembering these and using them where you can is a good way to discover any longer words on your rack, including any potential bonus words. The key prefixes to remember beginning with E are EM-, EN- and EX- and the key suffixes are -EAUX, -ENCE, -ENCY, -EST, -ETTE and -EUR.

Some words beginning with EM-
Seven-letter words

EM-AILED	EM-IRATE	EM-PLOYS
EM-BARKS	EM-PANEL	EM-POWER
EM-BRACE	EM-PARTS	EM-PRESS
EM-BROIL	EM-PEACH	

Eight-letter words

EM-AILING	EM-BLAZED	EM-PARTED
EM-BALMED	EM-BODIED	EM-PATHIC
EM-BARKED	EM-BOLDEN	EM-PHATIC
EM-BATTLE	EM-BOSSED	EM-PLOYED
EM-BEDDED	EM-BRACED	
EM-BITTER	EM-PALING	

Some words beginning with EN-
Seven-letter words

EN-ABLED
EN-ACTED
EN-CAGED
EN-CASED
EN-CLOSE
EN-CODED
EN-CORED
EN-CRYPT

EN-DEARS
EN-FORCE
EN-GORGE
EN-RAGED
EN-SLAVE
EN-SNARE
EN-SUING
EN-SURED

EN-TAILS
EN-TIRES
EN-TITLE
EN-TRAIL
EN-TREES
EN-TRIES
EN-VYING
EN-ZYMES

Eight-letter words

EN-ABLING
EN-CAMPED
EN-CASING
EN-CHANTS
EN-CIPHER
EN-CIRCLE
EN-CLOSED
EN-CORING
EN-DANGER
EN-DEARED

EN-DURING
EN-FOLDED
EN-GENDER
EN-GORGED
EN-GRAVED
EN-GULFED
EN-JOYING
EN-LISTED
EN-QUIRED
EN-RICHED

EN-ROLLED
EN-SHRINE
EN-SIGNED
EN-SNARED
EN-SURING
EN-TAILED
EN-TITLED
EN-TRENCH
EN-VIABLE

Some words beginning with EX-
Seven-letter words

EX-ACTED

EX-AMINE

EX-CITED

EX-CLAIM

EX-PENDS

EX-PLAIN

EX-PORTS

EX-POSED

EX-PRESS

EX-TENDS

EX-TOLLS

EX-TRACT

Eight-letter words

EX-ACTING

EX-CELLED

EX-CESSES

EX-CITING

EX-PANDER

EX-PERTLY

EX-PLAINS

EX-PORTED

Some words ending with -EAUX
Seven-letter words

BAT-EAUX

BUR-EAUX

CAD-EAUX

GAT-EAUX

Eight-letter words

BAND-EAUX

BATT-EAUX

BORD-EAUX

CHAP-EAUX

CHAT-EAUX

MORC-EAUX

PLAT-EAUX

TABL-EAUX

E

Some words ending with -ENCE
Seven-letter words

ABS-ENCE

CAD-ENCE

COG-ENCE

DEF-ENCE

ESS-ENCE

FLU-ENCE

LIC-ENCE

OFF-ENCE

POT-ENCE

SCI-ENCE

SIL-ENCE

URG-ENCE

VAL-ENCE

Eight-letter words

AMBI-ENCE

AUDI-ENCE

COMM-ENCE

CRED-ENCE

DISP-ENCE

EMIN-ENCE

EVID-ENCE

LENI-ENCE

NASC-ENCE

OPUL-ENCE

PATI-ENCE

PRES-ENCE

PRET-ENCE

PRUD-ENCE

SALI-ENCE

SAPI-ENCE

SENT-ENCE

SEQU-ENCE

SIXP-ENCE

TEND-ENCE

TENP-ENCE

TUPP-ENCE

VIOL-ENCE

Some words ending with -ENCY
Seven-letter words

COG-ENCY

DEC-ENCY

FLU-ENCY

POT-ENCY

REC-ENCY

REG-ENCY

URG-ENCY

VAL-ENCY

Eight-letter words

CLEM-ENCY

CURR-ENCY

FERV-ENCY

LENI-ENCY

PUNG-ENCY

SOLV-ENCY

TEND-ENCY

Some words ending with -EST
Seven-letter words

AIRI-EST

BALD-EST

BOLD-EST

DAMP-EST

DARK-EST

EARN-EST

FULL-EST

FUNF-EST

HARD-EST

KIND-EST

LONG-EST

MEEK-EST

POOR-EST

PRET-EST

PROT-EST

REQU-EST

SUBT-EST

TALL-EST

TEMP-EST

TENS-EST

WARM-EST

WILD-EST

Eight-letter words

ACRID-EST

BLACK-EST

BLOND-EST

BRIEF-EST

CLEAN-EST

CLEAR-EST

DIVIN-EST

EAGER-EST

EXACT-EST

FLASH-EST

GAUDI-EST

GRAND-EST

INERT-EST

LOVEF-EST

MINUT-EST

ORANG-EST

PEPPI-EST

QUICK-EST

REDIG-EST

SIMPL-EST

SUNNI-EST

TALKF-EST

TOUGH-EST

URBAN-EST

WASPN-EST

WRONG-EST

E

Some words ending with -ETTE
Seven-letter words

BLU-ETTE	GAZ-ETTE	PAL-ETTE
CAS-ETTE	LAD-ETTE	PIP-ETTE
DIN-ETTE	MIN-ETTE	POP-ETTE
FUM-ETTE	OCT-ETTE	ROS-ETTE

Eight-letter words

AMUS-ETTE	DISK-ETTE	ROQU-ETTE
BAGU-ETTE	JEAN-ETTE	ROUL-ETTE
BRUN-ETTE	MAQU-ETTE	SEPT-ETTE
CASS-ETTE	NOIS-ETTE	VIGN-ETTE
COQU-ETTE	PALL-ETTE	
CORV-ETTE	ROOM-ETTE	

Some words ending with -EUR
Seven-letter words

AMAT-EUR	PRIM-EUR	TRAC-EUR
LIQU-EUR	SABR-EUR	
MASS-EUR	SIGN-EUR	

Eight-letter words

CHASS-EUR	LONGU-EUR	SEIGN-EUR
COIFF-EUR	MONSI-EUR	VOYAG-EUR
GRAND-EUR	SABOT-EUR	
JONGL-EUR	SECAT-EUR	

Unusual letter combinations

If you have an unusual combination of letters on your rack, or want to impress your opponent with an unusual word, a few words from World English can come in handy.

Australian words

EARBASH	talk incessantly
EMU	large flightless bird
EUMUNG	type of acacia
EVO	evening
EXO	excellent

Essential info
Value: 4 points
Number in set: 2

F can be a useful letter for scoring with short words on premium squares. Although there are only three two-letter words beginning with F (FA and FE, 5 points each, and FY, 8 points), these are complemented with IF and OF. There are also quite a few short, high-scoring words beginning with F which use X (FAX, FIX, FOX, 13 points each), Y (FEY, FLY, FRY, 9 points each) or Z (FEZ, 15 points).

Two-letter words beginning with F

FA	FE	FY

Some three-letter words beginning with F

FAA	FEM	FOB
FAE	FEN	FOH
FAH	FER	FON
FAP	FET	FOP
FAW	FEU	FOU
FAX	FEY	FOY
FAY	FEZ	FUB
FEG	FID	FUG
FEH	FIZ	FUM

Hooks

Hooking requires a subtle change in a player's thought process, in that they must look at words already on the board without becoming distracted by their pronunciation.

Some front-hooks
Two letters to three

F-AA	F-AS	F-EM	F-OB	F-OX
F-AB	F-AT	F-EN	F-OE	F-OY
F-AD	F-AW	F-ER	F-OG	F-UG
F-AE	F-AX	F-ES	F-OH	F-UM
F-AG	F-AY	F-ET	F-ON	F-UN
F-AH	F-ED	F-ID	F-OP	F-UR
F-AN	F-EE	F-IN	F-OR	
F-AR	F-EH	F-IT	F-OU	

Three letters to four

F-ACE	F-AVE	F-ILL
F-ACT	F-AWN	F-INK
F-AFF	F-EAR	F-IRE
F-AIL	F-EAT	F-ISH
F-AIR	F-EEL	F-LAB
F-AKE	F-ELL	F-LAG
F-ALL	F-ELT	F-LAP
F-ARE	F-END	F-LAT
F-ARM	F-ERN	F-LAW
F-ASH	F-ESS	F-LAX
F-ATE	F-EST	F-LAY
F-AVA	F-ETA	F-LEA

F-LED   F-OIL   F-RAT
F-LEE   F-OLD   F-RAY
F-LEW   F-OOT   F-REE
F-LEX   F-ORD   F-RET
F-LIP   F-ORE   F-RIZ
F-LIT   F-ORT   F-ROM
F-LOG   F-OUR   F-RUG
F-LOP   F-OWL   F-USE
F-LOW   F-OXY
F-LUX   F-RAG

Four letters to five

F-ABLE   F-LAKE   F-LOWN
F-ACED   F-LAKY   F-LUFF
F-ACER   F-LAME   F-LUKE
F-AERY   F-LANK   F-LUNG
F-AIRY   F-LARE   F-LUNK
F-AKED   F-LASH   F-LUSH
F-ARED   F-LEER   F-LUTE
F-AXED   F-LEET   F-OLIO
F-AYRE   F-LICK   F-OYER
F-EAST   F-LIER   F-RAIL
F-ETCH   F-LING   F-RANK
F-EVER   F-LINT   F-REED
F-EWER   F-LITE   F-RILL
F-ILLY   F-LOCK   F-RISK
F-INCH   F-LOOR   F-RITZ
F-ITCH   F-LOSS   F-ROCK
F-LACK   F-LOUR   F-RUMP
F-LAIR   F-LOUT   F-USED

F

Five letters to six

F-ABLED
F-ACING
F-ACTOR
F-AILED
F-ALLOW
F-ALTER
F-AMINE
F-ARMED
F-ARMER
F-ARROW
F-AXING
F-EARED
F-ENDED
F-ENDER
F-ESTER

F-ICKLE
F-INNER
F-LAKED
F-LAKER
F-LAMED
F-LAMER
F-LAWED
F-LAYED
F-LAYER
F-LEDGE
F-LETCH
F-LIGHT
F-LINCH
F-LINTY
F-LOWED

F-LOWER
F-LUTED
F-LUTER
F-LYING
F-ODDER
F-OILED
F-OLDER
F-OUGHT
F-RIDGE
F-RIGHT
F-RIGID
F-RISKY
F-USING
F-UTILE

Six letters to seven

F-ABLING
F-ACTION
F-ACTUAL
F-ADDLED
F-AILING
F-AIRILY
F-AIRING
F-AIRWAY
F-ANGLED
F-ARMING
F-ATTEST
F-AWNING

F-EARFUL
F-EARING
F-EASTER
F-EATING
F-ENDING
F-ETCHED
F-ETCHER
F-ICKLER
F-INCHED
F-INNING
F-LACKED
F-LACKER

F-LAGGED
F-LAGGER
F-LAKING
F-LAMING
F-LANKER
F-LAPPED
F-LAPPER
F-LASHED
F-LASHER
F-LASKET
F-LATTER
F-LAYING

F-LEDGED F-LOPPED F-RAILER
F-LEERED F-LOPPER F-RANKED
F-LEGGED F-LOWING F-RANKER
F-LENSED F-LUBBER F-RANKLY
F-LICKED F-LUMMOX F-RAPPED
F-LICKER F-LUMPED F-RAZZLE
F-LIMPED F-LUSHED F-RIDGED
F-LINGER F-LUSTER F-RINGED
F-LIPPED F-LUTING F-RIPPER
F-LIPPER F-LUTIST F-RISKED
F-LITTER F-OILING F-RISKER
F-LOCKED F-OXLIKE F-ROCKED
F-LOGGED F-OXTAIL F-RUSHED
F-LOGGER F-RAGGED F-UNFAIR

Seven letters to eight

F-ALLOWED F-LAWLESS F-RANKING
F-ALTERED F-LETCHED F-RAPPING
F-ALTERER F-LICKING F-RIDGING
F-EARLESS F-LIGHTED F-RIGHTEN
F-EASTING F-LINTING F-RIGIDER
F-ETCHING F-LIPPING F-RIGIDLY
F-ICKLEST F-LOCKING F-RINGING
F-IRELESS F-LOGGING F-RISKIER
F-LACKING F-LOPPING F-RISKILY
F-LAGGING F-LOUTING F-RISKING
F-LAKIEST F-LOWERED F-ROCKING
F-LANKING F-LUSHEST F-UNCTION
F-LAPPING F-RAGGING F-USELESS
F-LASHING F-RANKEST F-UTILITY

Some end-hooks
Two letters to three

AL-F	ER-F	OO-F
AR-F	GI-F	OR-F
DE-F	IF-F	RE-F
DI-F	KA-F	SI-F
DO-F	KI-F	TE-F
EF-F	NE-F	WO-F
EL-F	OF-F	

Three letters to four

BAR-F	GUL-F	RIF-F
BEE-F	HOO-F	ROO-F
CHE-F	HOW-F	SEL-F
CON-F	HUM-F	SER-F
CUR-F	LEA-F	SOW-F
DIF-F	LIE-F	SUR-F
DOF-F	LOO-F	WAI-F
FIE-F	PRO-F	WOO-F
GOO-F	REE-F	

Four letters to five

BRIE-F	KALI-F	SCUR-F
GANE-F	MOTI-F	SHEA-F
GONE-F	PILA-F	SKEE-F
HOUF-F	PROO-F	SNAR-F
HOWF-F	SCAR-F	SPIF-F

F

Five letters to six

BELIE-F	GONIF-F	RELIE-F
DECAF-F	PILAF-F	

Six letters to seven

SHERIF-F

Blockers

It is useful to know which words are blockers and can't therefore be extended before or after. You may want to play a blocker that your opponent can't extend, or you may want to avoid playing a blocker because you want to keep the board open.

Some two-letter blockers beginning with F

FY

Some three-letter blockers beginning with F

FAE	FAX	FEZ	FRY
FAP	FEW	FLY	

Some four-letter blockers beginning with F

FASH	FIXT	FOXY
FAUX	FLED	FROM
FEET	FLIX	FUMY
FIFI	FLUX	FURY
FILS	FOGY	

Some five-letter blockers beginning with F
(except words ending in '-ED', '-J', '-S', '-X', '-Y' or '-Z')

FATAL	FEWER	FOCAL
FETAL	FINCH	FOLIC
FETCH	FLOWN	FUNGO
FETID	FLUNG	

Some six-letter blockers beginning with F
(except words ending in '-ED', '-J', '-S', '-X', '-Y' or '-Z')

FACEUP	FEWEST	FLYMEN
FACILE	FEYEST	FOETAL
FAIRER	FILIAL	FOETID
FAKING	FILMIC	FONDER
FALLEN	FINEST	FOREGO
FAMING	FINISH	FORGOT
FAMISH	FINITO	FOULER
FARING	FITFUL	FOXIER
FATTER	FLAXEN	FREEST
FAXING	FLETCH	FRIGID
FAZING	FLIEST	FROZEN
FECUND	FLINCH	FRUGAL
FEEING	FLORID	FUMING
FERRIC	FLUIER	FUNGIC
FERVID	FLUISH	FUNNER
FETISH	FLYEST	FUSILE
FEUDAL	FLYMAN	FUSING

Bonus words

Bonus words on your rack can be hard to spot, especially for the less experienced player. One way to help find them is by using prefixes and suffixes.

Many larger words include a common prefix or suffix – remembering these and using them where you can is a good way to discover any longer words on your rack, including any potential bonus words. The key prefixes to remember beginning with F are FOOT- and FOR- and the key suffixes are -FISH, -FORM and -FUL.

Some words beginning with FOOT-
Seven-letter words

FOOT-AGE	FOOT-ERS	FOOT-MEN
FOOT-BAG	FOOT-LED	FOOT-PAD
FOOT-BAR	FOOT-LES	FOOT-ROT
FOOT-BOY	FOOT-MAN	FOOT-WAY

Eight-letter words

FOOT-BALL	FOOT-LIKE	FOOT-SIES
FOOT-BATH	FOOT-LING	FOOT-SORE
FOOT-ERED	FOOT-MARK	FOOT-STEP
FOOT-FALL	FOOT-NOTE	FOOT-WALL
FOOT-HILL	FOOT-PATH	FOOT-WEAR
FOOT-HOLD	FOOT-RACE	FOOT-WORK
FOOT-LESS	FOOT-REST	FOOT-WORN

Some words beginning with FOR-
Seven-letter words

FOR-AGED

FOR-AGER

FOR-AGES

FOR-BADE

FOR-BEAR

FOR-BIDS

FOR-BODE

FOR-CEPS

FOR-DING

FOR-DONE

FOR-ESTS

FOR-EVER

FOR-FEND

FOR-GAVE

FOR-GETS

FOR-GING

FOR-GIVE

FOR-GOER

FOR-GOES

FOR-GONE

FOR-KIER

FOR-KING

FOR-LORN

FOR-MATS

FOR-MICA

FOR-MING

FOR-RAYS

FOR-SAID

FOR-SAKE

FOR-SOOK

FOR-TING

FOR-WARD

FOR-WARN

FOR-WENT

FOR-WORN

Eight-letter words

FOR-AGING

FOR-BODED

FOR-ESTER

FOR-GIVEN

FOR-GIVER

FOR-GOING

FOR-MATED

FOR-SOOTH

FOR-SPEAK

FOR-SPEND

FOR-SPOKE

FOR-SWEAR

FOR-SWORN

FOR-TRESS

FOR-TUNED

Some words ending with -FISH
Seven-letter words

BAT-FISH

BOX-FISH

CAT-FISH

COD-FISH

COW-FISH

DEA-FISH

DOG-FISH

FIN-FISH

FOX-FISH

GAR-FISH

GEM-FISH

HAG-FISH

HOG-FISH

HUF-FISH

MUD-FISH

OAR-FISH PUP-FISH SEL-FISH
OUT-FISH RAF-FISH SER-FISH
PAN-FISH RAT-FISH SUN-FISH
PIG-FISH RED-FISH
PIN-FISH SAW-FISH

Eight-letter words

BAIT-FISH GOLD-FISH SALT-FISH
BLOW-FISH GRAY-FISH SAND-FISH
BLUE-FISH GRUF-FISH SCAR-FISH
BONE-FISH KING-FISH SNIF-FISH
CAVE-FISH LION-FISH STAR-FISH
CRAW-FISH LUNG-FISH STIF-FISH
CRAY-FISH MONK-FISH SUCK-FISH
DEAL-FISH MOON-FISH SURF-FISH
DWAR-FISH OVER-FISH TOAD-FISH
FLAT-FISH PIPE-FISH WOLF-FISH
FOOL-FISH ROCK-FISH
FROG-FISH SAIL-FISH

Some words ending with -FORM
Seven-letter words

ACI-FORM DEI-FORM OVI-FORM
ALI-FORM DIF-FORM PER-FORM
AUS-FORM DIS-FORM PRE-FORM
AVI-FORM ISO-FORM TRI-FORM
CON-FORM MIS-FORM UNI-FORM

Eight-letter words

AERI-FORM	MANI-FORM	PYRI-FORM
CONI-FORM	OMNI-FORM	ROTI-FORM
CUBI-FORM	PALI-FORM	SLIP-FORM
FREE-FORM	PARA-FORM	TUBI-FORM
FUSI-FORM	PLAN-FORM	URSI-FORM
LAND-FORM	PLAT-FORM	VARI-FORM
LYRI-FORM	POST-FORM	WAVE-FORM

Some words ending with -FUL
Seven-letter words

ARMS-FUL	FORK-FUL	PAIN-FUL
BALE-FUL	FRET-FUL	PALM-FUL
BANE-FUL	GAIN-FUL	PITI-FUL
BASH-FUL	GLEE-FUL	PLAY-FUL
BOAT-FUL	GUTS-FUL	RAGE-FUL
BOWL-FUL	HAND-FUL	REST-FUL
BRIM-FUL	HARM-FUL	RISK-FUL
CARE-FUL	HATE-FUL	SACK-FUL
DARE-FUL	HEED-FUL	SKIL-FUL
DEED-FUL	HELP-FUL	SKIN-FUL
DIRE-FUL	HOPE-FUL	SOUL-FUL
DOLE-FUL	HURT-FUL	TACT-FUL
DUTI-FUL	LUNG-FUL	TANK-FUL
FACT-FUL	LUST-FUL	TEAR-FUL
FATE-FUL	MIND-FUL	TUNE-FUL
FEAR-FUL	NEED-FUL	WAKE-FUL
FIST-FUL	PAIL-FUL	WILL-FUL

F

Eight-letter words

BELLY-FUL	GLASS-FUL	SKILL-FUL
BLAME-FUL	GRACE-FUL	SPITE-FUL
BLISS-FUL	GRATE-FUL	SPOON-FUL
BOAST-FUL	GUILE-FUL	TASTE-FUL
CHEER-FUL	HASTE-FUL	THANK-FUL
COLOR-FUL	MERCI-FUL	TRUST-FUL
DIRGE-FUL	MIRTH-FUL	TRUTH-FUL
DOUBT-FUL	MOURN-FUL	UNLAW-FUL
DREAD-FUL	MOUTH-FUL	VENGE-FUL
EVENT-FUL	PEACE-FUL	WASTE-FUL
FAITH-FUL	PLATE-FUL	WATCH-FUL
FANCI-FUL	POWER-FUL	WRATH-FUL
FORCE-FUL	RIGHT-FUL	WRONG-FUL
FRUIT-FUL	SCORN-FUL	YOUTH-FUL
GHAST-FUL	SHAME-FUL	

Handy Hint

A useful way to visualise your options is to SHUFFLE (16 points) the tiles on your rack. If you rearrange tiles, place them in alphabetical order or try to form prefixes, suffixes or verb inflections you stand a better chance of thinking up good words to play.

Unusual letter combinations

If you have an unusual combination of letters on your rack, or want to impress your opponent with an unusual word, a few words from World English can come in handy. Here are some beginning with F.

Australian words

FASTIE	deceitful act
FESTY	dirty or smelly
FIGJAM	very conceited person
FIZGIG	frivolous or flirtatious girl
FOULIE	bad mood
FRIB	short heavy-conditioned piece of wool
FURPHY	rumour or fictitious story

F

Essential info

Value: 2 points

Number in set: 3

G begins only three two-letter words in Scrabble: GI (a suit worn by martial arts practitioners, 3 points), GO and GU (a kind of violin from Shetland, 3 points). G also combines well with Y to form quite a few short words including GAY, GEY (a Scots word for very, 7 points), GOY (a Yiddish word for a person who is not Jewish, 7 points), GUY and also GYM and GYP (9 points each).

Two-letter words beginning with G

GI   GO   GU

Some three-letter words beginning with G

GAB	GEL	GJU	GUB
GAD	GEN	GNU	GUE
GAE	GHI	GOA	GUL
GAL	GIB	GOE	GUP
GAM	GID	GON	GUR
GAN	GIE	GOO	GUV
GAR	GIF	GOR	GYM
GAT	GIO	GOV	GYP
GED	GIP	GOX	
GEE	GIT	GOY	

Hooks

Hooking requires a subtle change in a player's thought process, in that they must look at words already on the board without becoming distracted by their pronunciation.

Some front-hooks
Two letters to three

G-AB	G-AS	G-ET	G-NU	G-OX
G-AD	G-AT	G-HI	G-OB	G-OY
G-AE	G-AY	G-ID	G-OD	G-UM
G-AG	G-ED	G-IF	G-OE	G-UN
G-AL	G-EE	G-IN	G-ON	G-UP
G-AM	G-EL	G-IO	G-OO	G-UR
G-AN	G-EM	G-IS	G-OR	G-US
G-AR	G-EN	G-IT	G-OS	G-UT

Three letters to four

G-AFF	G-ASH	G-LAD
G-AGA	G-ASP	G-LAM
G-AGE	G-ATE	G-LEE
G-AIN	G-AVE	G-LIB
G-AIT	G-EAR	G-LID
G-ALA	G-EEK	G-LOB
G-ALE	G-ELD	G-LOW
G-ALL	G-ELT	G-LUG
G-APE	G-ENE	G-LUM
G-ARB	G-ILL	G-NAT

G-NAW
G-OAT
G-OES
G-OLD
G-ONE
G-OOF
G-OON
G-ORE
G-OUT

G-OWN
G-RAD
G-RAM
G-RAN
G-RAY
G-REW
G-RID
G-RIM
G-RIN

G-RIP
G-RIT
G-ROT
G-ROW
G-RUB
G-RUE
G-URN

Four letters to five

G-ABLE
G-AGED
G-AGER
G-ALLY
G-APED
G-APER
G-AUNT
G-AVEL
G-EMMY
G-HAST
G-HOST
G-ILLS
G-ILLY
G-IRON
G-LACE
G-LADE
G-LADY
G-LAND
G-LARE

G-LASS
G-LAZE
G-LAZY
G-LEAM
G-LEAN
G-LINT
G-LOAM
G-LOBE
G-LODE
G-LOOM
G-LOOP
G-LORY
G-LOSS
G-LOST
G-LOUT
G-LOVE
G-LUTE
G-NOME
G-OLDY

G-ONER
G-OOFY
G-OOSE
G-OOSY
G-RACE
G-RADE
G-RAFT
G-RAIL
G-RAIN
G-RAND
G-RANT
G-RASP
G-RATE
G-RAVE
G-RAZE
G-REED
G-REEK
G-REEN

Five letters to six

G-ABLED	G-ENDER	G-RAVER
G-ABOON	G-ENTRY	G-RAYED
G-ADDED	G-INNER	G-RAZED
G-ADDER	G-LANCE	G-REAVE
G-AGGER	G-LAZED	G-REEDY
G-AGING	G-LOBED	G-RIMED
G-ALLEY	G-LOOPY	G-RIPED
G-ALLOW	G-LOSSY	G-ROPED
G-AMBIT	G-LOVED	G-ROUND
G-AMBLE	G-LOWER	G-ROUSE
G-AMINE	G-NOMIC	G-ROVED
G-AMMON	G-OLDEN	G-ROWER
G-APING	G-OLDER	G-RUBBY
G-ARGLE	G-RACED	G-RUING
G-ASHED	G-RAINY	G-RUMPY
G-ASPER	G-RANGE	G-UNMAN
G-ASTER	G-RATED	G-URNED
G-AUGER	G-RATER	G-USHER
G-EARED	G-RAVED	G-UTTER
G-ELATE	G-RAVEL	
G-ELDER	G-RAVEN	

Six letters to seven

G-ABLING	G-LINTED	G-RIDDED
G-ADDING	G-LISTEN	G-RIDDER
G-ALLIED	G-LISTER	G-RIDDLE
G-AMBLED	G-LITTER	G-RIFTED
G-AMBLER	G-LOOMED	G-RILLED
G-ASHING	G-LOOPED	G-RIMMER
G-AUNTLY	G-LOVING	G-RINDED
G-EARING	G-LOWING	G-RIPING
G-ELATED	G-OLDEST	G-RIPPED
G-ELDING	G-OLDISH	G-RIPPER
G-ESTATE	G-OWNING	G-ROOMED
G-HOSTED	G-RACING	G-ROOMER
G-HOSTLY	G-RAFTED	G-ROPING
G-IGGING	G-RAFTER	G-ROUSED
G-IZZARD	G-RAINED	G-ROUSER
G-LACIER	G-RANGER	G-ROUTED
G-LADDER	G-RANTED	G-ROUTER
G-LANCED	G-RANTER	G-ROWING
G-LANCER	G-RAPIER	G-RUBBED
G-LAZIER	G-RAPING	G-RUBBER
G-LAZILY	G-RASPED	G-RUFFED
G-LAZING	G-RASPER	G-RUFFLY
G-LEAMED	G-RATIFY	G-RUMBLE
G-LEANED	G-RATING	G-RUMMER
G-LEANER	G-RAVING	G-RUMPED
G-LEEING	G-RAYING	G-RUNTED
G-LIBBED	G-RAZING	G-UNLESS
G-LIBBER	G-REAVED	G-UNSHOT
G-LIMMER	G-REEKED	

Seven letters to eight

G-ALLOWED	G-LITTERY	G-RAVELLY
G-AMBLING	G-LOAMING	G-REEDIER
G-ANGLING	G-LOOMING	G-REEDILY
G-ARGLING	G-LOOPIER	G-RIDDLED
G-EARLESS	G-LOOPING	G-RIEVING
G-ELASTIC	G-LOWERED	G-RIFTING
G-ELATING	G-LUGGING	G-RILLING
G-ESTATED	G-NATTIER	G-RIPPING
G-HASTING	G-OATLIKE	G-ROOMING
G-HOSTING	G-OFFERED	G-ROUNDED
G-LANCING	G-OLDENED	G-ROUNDER
G-LAZIEST	G-ONENESS	G-ROUSING
G-LEAMING	G-RAFTING	G-ROUTING
G-LEANERS	G-RAINIER	G-ROWABLE
G-LEANING	G-RAINING	G-RUMBLED
G-LIBBING	G-RANTING	G-UNMAKER
G-LINTIER	G-RANULAR	G-UNSTOCK
G-LINTING	G-RASPING	G-UTTERED

G

Handy Hint

Some unusual and high-scoring words beginning with G are GJU (a variant spelling of GU, 11 points), GOX (form of gaseous oxygen, 11 points), GUANXI (Chinese social concept based on the exchange of favours, 14 points) and GYOZA (Japanese fried dumplings, 18 points).

Some end-hooks

Two letters to three

BA-G	FA-G	MA-G	RE-G
BE-G	FE-G	ME-G	SO-G
BI-G	GI-G	MI-G	TA-G
BO-G	HA-G	MO-G	TE-G
DA-G	HO-G	MU-G	TI-G
DE-G	JA-G	NA-G	TO-G
DI-G	JO-G	NE-G	WO-G
DO-G	LA-G	NO-G	YA-G
EN-G	LI-G	PE-G	YU-G
ER-G	LO-G	PI-G	ZA-G

Three letters to four

AGO-G	FRO-G	RAN-G
BAN-G	GAN-G	RIN-G
BIN-G	GON-G	RUN-G
BIO-G	HAN-G	SAN-G
BON-G	HUN-G	SIN-G
BRA-G	KIN-G	SON-G
BUN-G	LIN-G	SUN-G
BUR-G	MAR-G	TAN-G
DAN-G	MUN-G	TIN-G
DIN-G	PAN-G	TON-G
DON-G	PIN-G	WIN-G
DUN-G	PLU-G	ZIN-G
FAN-G	PRO-G	
FRA-G	QUA-G	

Four letters to five

AGIN-G	GULA-G	THIN-G
BEIN-G	RUIN-G	THON-G
BLIN-G	SPAN-G	TYIN-G
BRIN-G	STUN-G	
CLAN-G	SWAN-G	

Five letters to six

ACTIN-G	LAWIN-G	RAVIN-G
BASIN-G	LAYIN-G	RICIN-G
BELON-G	LIKIN-G	ROBIN-G
CONIN-G	LININ-G	ROSIN-G
COVIN-G	MATIN-G	SAVIN-G
ELFIN-G	MIRIN-G	SEWIN-G
GAMIN-G	PAVIN-G	TAKIN-G
LAKIN-G	PURIN-G	TAMIN-G

Six letters to seven

BOBBIN-G	HOGGIN-G	OUTWIN-G
BUGGIN-G	JERKIN-G	OVERDO-G
BUSKIN-G	MERLIN-G	PARKIN-G
COPPIN-G	MUFFIN-G	PIPPIN-G
CUFFIN-G	MUNTIN-G	PUFFIN-G
CYCLIN-G	MURLIN-G	RAISIN-G
DENTIN-G	NOGGIN-G	RENNIN-G
DUBBIN-G	OUTRAN-G	ROBBIN-G
GRADIN-G	OUTRUN-G	TANNIN-G
GRATIN-G	OUTSIN-G	TIFFIN-G

G

Seven letters to eight

ASPIRIN-G	MAHJONG-G	RESILIN-G
CHITLIN-G	MORPHIN-G	SCULPIN-G
CREATIN-G	PUMPKIN-G	SPELDIN-G
CRISPIN-G	RATTLIN-G	SPONGIN-G
GELATIN-G	RAVELIN-G	UNDERDO-G
LITTLIN-G	RELAXIN-G	

Blockers

It is useful to know which words are blockers and can't therefore be extended before or after. You may want to play a blocker that your opponent can't extend, or you may want to avoid playing a blocker because you want to keep the board open.

Some three-letter blockers beginning with G

GEY	GOX

Some four-letter blockers beginning with G

GAGA	GAZY	GIZZ
GAMY	GEED	GORY
GASH	GEEZ	

Some five-letter blockers beginning with G
(except words ending in '-ED', '-J', '-S', '-X', '-Y' or '-Z')

GEESE	GLIAL	GOYIM
GELID	GNASH	GREEK
GENAL	GNAWN	GROWN
GEYER	GONNA	GULCH
GHEST	GONZO	GURSH
GINZO	GOTTA	GYRAL

Some six-letter blockers beginning with G
(except words ending in '-ED', '-J', '-S', '-X', '-Y' or '-Z')

GAMEST	GEEING	GOOIER
GAMIER	GEMINI	GORIER
GARDAI	GENIAL	GOTTEN
GARISH	GIBING	GRAVEN
GASHER	GIDDUP	GRAYER
GASLIT	GLOBAL	GREEBO
GASMAN	GLUIER	GREYER
GASMEN	GLUING	GRINCH
GAYEST	GNOMIC	GUNMAN
GEDDIT	GOLDER	GUNMEN

G

Bonus words

Bonus words on your rack can be hard to spot, especially for the less experienced player. One way to help finding them is by using prefixes and suffixes.

Many larger words include a common prefix or suffix – remembering these and using them where you can is a good way to discover any longer words on your rack, including any potential bonus words. The key suffixes to remember ending with G are -GEN and -GRAM.

Some words ending with -GEN

Seven-letter words

ANTI-GEN	INDI-GEN	PYRO-GEN
CRYO-GEN	LOXY-GEN	SMID-GEN
ENDO-GEN	MUTA-GEN	TRUD-GEN
HALO-GEN	ONCO-GEN	TWIG-GEN

Eight-letter words

ABORI-GEN	ENLAR-GEN	NITRO-GEN
ALLER-GEN	ESTRO-GEN	PATHO-GEN
ANDRO-GEN	HISTO-GEN	PHOTO-GEN
COLLA-GEN	HYDRO-GEN	
CYANO-GEN	MISCE-GEN	

Some words ending with -GRAM

Seven-letter words

ANA-GRAM	ISO-GRAM	TAN-GRAM
DIA-GRAM	MYO-GRAM	TRI-GRAM
EPI-GRAM	PAN-GRAM	
GRO-GRAM	PRO-GRAM	

Eight-letter words

AERO-GRAM	HEXA-GRAM	LEXI-GRAM
DECA-GRAM	HOLO-GRAM	MONO-GRAM
DECI-GRAM	IDEO-GRAM	NANO-GRAM
ETHO-GRAM	IDIO-GRAM	SONO-GRAM
GENO-GRAM	KILO-GRAM	TELE-GRAM

G

Unusual letter combinations

If you have an unusual combination of letters on your rack, or want to impress your opponent with an unusual word, a few words from World English can come in handy.

Australian words

GALAH	grey-and-pink cockatoo
GARBO	dustman
GEEBUNG	tree with edible but tasteless fruit
GIDGEE	small acacia tree that sometimes emits an unpleasant smell
GILGAI	natural water hole
GING	child's catapult

GNOW   ground-dwelling bird

GOANNA   monitor lizard

GOOG   egg

GUNYAH   bush hut or shelter

GYMPIE   tall tree with stinging hairs on its leaves

Canadian words

GROWLER   small iceberg that has broken off from a larger
              iceberg or glacier

Hindi words

GAUR   large wild cow

GARIAL   fish-eating crocodilian with long slender snout

GHARRI   horse-drawn vehicle for hire

GHAT   stairs or passage leading down to a river

GHEE   clarified butter

GHERAO   industrial action in which workers imprison
              their employers

GINGILI   oil obtained from sesame seeds

GORAL   small goat antelope

GUAR   plant that produces gum

GUNNY   coarse fabric used for sacks

New Zealand words

GRAUNCH   crush or destroy

South African words

GEELBEK   yellow-jawed fish

Essential info

Value: 4 points

Number in set: 2

H begins a two-letter word with every vowel except for U (although it can form UH, a sound that people make when they are unsure about something, 5 points), making it very useful for forming short words in different directions. As H is worth 4 points, these words can return very high scores in conjunction with premium squares despite their brevity: HA, HE, HI and HO are all worth 5 points.

H

Two-letter words beginning with H

HA	HE	HI	HM	HO

Some three-letter words beginning with H

HAE	HET	HOA	HOY
HAH	HEW	HOC	HUB
HAJ	HEX	HOD	HUH
HAN	HEY	HOH	HUN
HAO	HIC	HOI	HUP
HAP	HIE	HOM	HYE
HAW	HIN	HON	HYP
HEH	HIS	HOO	
HEP	HMM	HOX	

Hooks

Hooking requires a subtle change in a player's thought process, in that they must look at words already on the board without becoming distracted by their pronunciation.

Some front-hooks
Two letters to three

H-AD	H-EM	H-OB	H-OX
H-AE	H-EN	H-OD	H-OY
H-AG	H-ER	H-OE	H-UG
H-AH	H-ES	H-OH	H-UH
H-AM	H-ET	H-OI	H-UM
H-AN	H-EX	H-OM	H-UN
H-AS	H-ID	H-ON	H-UP
H-AT	H-IN	H-OO	H-UT
H-AW	H-IS	H-OP	H-YE
H-AY	H-IT	H-OS	
H-EH	H-MM	H-OW	

Three letters to four

H-AFT	H-ALF	H-ART
H-AHA	H-ALL	H-ASP
H-AIL	H-ALT	H-ATE
H-AIN	H-AND	H-AVE
H-AIR	H-ARD	H-EAR
H-AKA	H-ARE	H-EAT
H-AKE	H-ARK	H-EEL
H-ALE	H-ARM	H-EFT

H-ELL	H-ISH	H-OOP
H-ELM	H-OAR	H-OOT
H-ERE	H-OBO	H-OPE
H-ICK	H-OLD	H-OSE
H-IDE	H-OLE	H-OUR
H-ILL	H-ONE	H-OWL
H-IRE	H-OOF	H-UMP

Four letters to five

H-AIRY	H-EAST	H-INKY
H-ARDS	H-EATH	H-IRED
H-ARED	H-EAVE	H-ITCH
H-ASHY	H-ECHT	H-OARY
H-AULD	H-EDGE	H-OAST
H-AUNT	H-EDGY	H-ONER
H-AVER	H-EXED	H-OVEN
H-AWED	H-EXES	H-OVER
H-EARD	H-EYED	

Five letters to six

H-ACKER	H-ASHED	H-ILLER
H-AILED	H-AUGHT	H-INTER
H-AIRED	H-AWING	H-IRING
H-ALLOW	H-EARTH	H-ITCHY
H-ALTER	H-EATER	H-OLDEN
H-ANGER	H-EAVED	H-OLDER
H-ARBOR	H-EDGED	H-OTTER
H-ARMED	H-EDGER	H-OWLED
H-ARMER	H-EIGHT	H-OWLER
H-ARROW	H-EXING	H-USHER

Six letters to seven

H-AILING	H-ASHIER	H-EDGING
H-AIRIER	H-ASHING	H-EIGHTH
H-AIRING	H-AUNTER	H-ERRING
H-AMBLED	H-AUTEUR	H-INKIER
H-ARBOUR	H-EARING	H-ITCHED
H-ARKING	H-EATING	H-OVERED
H-ARMFUL	H-EAVING	H-OWLING
H-ARMING	H-EDGIER	H-UPPING

Seven letters to eight

H-AIRIEST	H-ARBORED	H-ITCHILY
H-AIRLESS	H-ARMLESS	H-ITCHING
H-AIRLIKE	H-ARROWED	H-OVERFLY
H-AIRLINE	H-EATABLE	H-OVERING
H-AIRLOCK	H-EDGIEST	H-USHERED
H-ALLOWED	H-INKIEST	
H-ALTERED	H-ITCHIER	

Some end-hooks
Two letters to three

AA-H	ET-H	LA-H	RE-H
AS-H	FA-H	NA-H	SH-H
BA-H	FE-H	NO-H	SO-H
BO-H	HA-H	OO-H	UG-H
DA-H	HE-H	PA-H	YA-H
DO-H	HO-H	PE-H	YE-H
ED-H	IS-H	PO-H	

Three letters to four

ARC-H	GAS-H	MAT-H	POS-H
BAC-H	GOS-H	MES-H	PUS-H
BAS-H	GOT-H	MET-H	RAS-H
BAT-H	GUS-H	MOS-H	SHA-H
BOO-H	HAS-H	MOT-H	SIT-H
BOT-H	HAT-H	MUS-H	SUK-H
BUS-H	HET-H	NIS-H	TAS-H
COS-H	HIS-H	NOS-H	TEC-H
DAS-H	HOG-H	OAT-H	UMP-H
DIS-H	KIT-H	PAS-H	WAS-H
DOS-H	LAS-H	PAT-H	WIS-H
DOT-H	LAT-H	PEC-H	WIT-H
EAT-H	MAC-H	PIT-H	YEA-H
FAS-H	MAS-H	POO-H	

Four letters to five

BOOT-H	HUMP-H	SOUT-H
BRAS-H	LEAS-H	SWAT-H
BRUS-H	MARC-H	SYNC-H
BUMP-H	MARS-H	TENT-H
BURG-H	MERC-H	THIG-H
CLOT-H	MYNA-H	TOOT-H
CRUS-H	NEAT-H	TORA-H
FLUS-H	PLUS-H	TORC-H
FORT-H	SCAT-H	WOOS-H
FRIT-H	SLOT-H	WORT-H
GIRT-H	SMIT-H	
HEAT-H	SOOT-H	

H

Five letters to six

COMET-H	HOOKA-H	POLIS-H
DELIS-H	HURRA-H	PUNKA-H
EIGHT-H	HUZZA-H	SHEIK-H
FATWA-H	LOOFA-H	SHIVA-H
FELLA-H	MULLA-H	SUNNA-H
FINIS-H	PARIS-H	WALLA-H
HEART-H	PERIS-H	

Six letters to seven

AARRGH-H	OUTWIT-H	SABBAT-H
HAGGIS-H	QABALA-H	

Seven letters to eight

BEGORRA-H	MADRASA-H	PEISHWA-H
HOSANNA-H	MESHUGA-H	SAVANNA-H
HYDRANT-H	NARGILE-H	SCAMPIS-H
KHALIFA-H	OCTOPUS-H	VERANDA-H

Blockers

It is useful to know which words are blockers and can't therefore be extended before or after. You may want to play a blocker that your opponent can't extend, or you may want to avoid playing a blocker because you want to keep the board open.

Some three-letter blockers beginning with H

HEX	HMM	HOX

Some four-letter blockers beginning with H

HAZY	HOAX	HUNG
HELD	HOLY	
HIYA	HUED	

Some five-letter blockers beginning with H
(except words ending in '-ED', '-J', '-S', '-X', '-Y' or '-Z')

HARSH	HOOCH	HUNCH
HAULT	HOVEN	HUTCH
HAUTE	HUGER	
HOING	HUMID	

Some six-letter blockers beginning with H
(except words ending in '-ED', '-J', '-S', '-X', '-Y' or '-Z')

HABILE	HITMEN	HOSING
HARDER	HOLDEN	HOWZAT
HATING	HOLIER	HUGEST
HAUNCH	HOOTCH	HYENIC
HAZIER	HOOVEN	HYMNIC
HIKING	HOPING	
HITMAN	HORRID	

H

Bonus words

Bonus words on your rack can be hard to spot, especially for the less experienced player. One way to help find them is by using prefixes and suffixes.

Many larger words include a common prefix or suffix – remembering these and using them where you can is a good way to discover any longer words on your rack, including any potential bonus words. The key suffixes to remember ending with H are -HOLE, -HOOD and -HORN.

Some words ending with -HOLE
Seven-letter words

AIR-HOLE	KEY-HOLE	PIN-HOLE
ARM-HOLE	LUG-HOLE	POT-HOLE
EYE-HOLE	MAN-HOLE	SPY-HOLE
FOX-HOLE	PIE-HOLE	

Eight-letter words

BLOW-HOLE	HELL-HOLE	PORT-HOLE
BOLT-HOLE	KNOT-HOLE	SINK-HOLE
BORE-HOLE	LOOP-HOLE	WELL-HOLE
BUNG-HOLE	PEEP-HOLE	WOOD-HOLE
FEED-HOLE	PLUG-HOLE	WORM-HOLE

Some words ending with -HOOD
Seven-letter words

BOY-HOOD	LAD-HOOD	SON-HOOD
GOD-HOOD	MAN-HOOD	

Eight-letter words

AUNT-HOOD	LADY-HOOD	PUMP-HOOD
BABY-HOOD	MAID-HOOD	SELF-HOOD
DOLL-HOOD	MISS-HOOD	SERF-HOOD
GIRL-HOOD	MONK-HOOD	WIFE-HOOD
IDLE-HOOD	PAGE-HOOD	WIVE-HOOD
KING-HOOD	POPE-HOOD	

Some words ending with -HORN
Seven-letter words

ALP-HORN	FOG-HORN	TIN-HORN
BET-HORN	INK-HORN	UNS-HORN
BIG-HORN	LEG-HORN	
DIS-HORN	SAX-HORN	

Eight-letter words

BOXT-HORN	DEER-HORN	RAMS-HORN
BUCK-HORN	HAWT-HORN	SHOE-HORN
BULL-HORN	LONG-HORN	STAG-HORN

H

Unusual letter combinations

If you have an unusual combination of letters on your rack, or want to impress your opponent with an unusual word, a few words from World English can come in handy.

Australian words

HAKEA	type of shrub or tree
HOVEA	plant with purple flowers
HUTCHIE	groundsheet draped over an upright stick as a shelter

Canadian words

HONKER Canada goose

Hindi words

HARTAL	act of closing shop or stopping work as a political protest
HOWDAH	seat for riding on an elephant's back

New Zealand words

Many Maori words start with the letter H, and if you have an H alongside a selection of vowels you may be able to play some of the following:

HAKA	war dance
HANGI	open-air cooking pit
HAPU	subtribe
HAPUKA	large fish
HEITIKI	neck ornament
HIKOI	protest march
HOKONUI	illicit whisky

HONGI	nose-touching greeting
HUHU	hairy beetle
HUI	conference or meeting
HUIA	extinct New Zealand bird

Handy Hint

Some short, useful words starting with H and using power tiles are HAJ (Muslim pilgrimage to Mecca, 13 points, also its variant forms HAJJ and HADJ), HAZE (16 points), HAZY (19 points), HEX (a curse or spell, 13 points) and HOX (a Shakespearean word meaning to cut a horse's hamstring, also 13).

Essential info
Value: 1 point
Number in set: 9

I can be a tricky letter to use in multiples so you need to try and use an I as soon as you can to avoid getting two of them. There are plenty of two-letter words beginning with I to help you make good-scoring parallel plays as shown below. The higher- scoring three letter words beginning with I are worth making note of, such as ICY (8 points), IVY (9 points) and IMP (7 points). The I can also be vital for reaping points with a Q or X with QI or XI. The I is also one of the letters of the RETAIN set and is therefore a good letter to keep if trying to get a bonus word.

Two-letter words beginning with I

ID   IF   IN   IO   IS   IT

Some three-letter words beginning with I

ICH	ION	ISO
ICK	IRE	ITA
IDE	ISH	
IFF	ISM	

Hooks

Hooking requires a subtle change in a player's thought process, in that they must look at words already on the board without becoming distracted by their pronunciation.

Some front-hooks
Two letters to three

I-CH	I-OS	I-SO
I-DE	I-RE	I-TA
I-ON	I-SH	

Three letters to four

I-BIS	I-KON	I-RES
I-CON	I-LEA	I-RID
I-DEE	I-LEX	I-SIT
I-DOL	I-MAM	I-SOS
I-GAD	I-MID	I-TAS
I-KAT	I-RED	I-URE

Four letters to five

I-DANT	I-MAGE	I-RATE
I-DEAL	I-MINE	I-RING
I-DEES	I-MINO	I-RONE
I-DENT	I-NANE	I-SLED
I-GAPO	I-ODIC	I-VIED
I-LEAL	I-RADE	

Five letters to six

I-CONIC	I-ODISM	I-SATIN
I-GUANA	I-ONIUM	I-SLING
I-LEXES	I-RATER	I-TEMED
I-NYALA	I-RISES	

Six letters to seven

I-MAGISM	I-RISING	I-SOLATE

Seven letters to eight

I-CONICAL	I-SLANDER
I-SABELLA	I-SOLATED

Handy Hint

If you have enough letters to form the suffix -ING, you could be well on the way to scoring a bonus word for 50 points. Look at the other letters on your rack and try to form a word ending in -ING (there are thousands!). But don't hang on to -ING at all costs, as by doing so you are restricting yourself to playing with just four letters, with the consequent likelihood of low scores.

Some end-hooks

Two letters to three

AH-I	HO-I	PO-I
AM-I	JA-I	RE-I
AN-I	KA-I	TA-I
BO-I	KO-I	UN-I
CH-I	MO-I	
DE-I	OB-I	

Three letters to four

ANT-I	HAJ-I	PEN-I
ART-I	IMP-I	PER-I
BAN-I	KAK-I	PIP-I
BEN-I	LOB-I	PUR-I
BID-I	LOT-I	QUA-I
BUD-I	MAG-I	RAG-I
CAD-I	MAL-I	RAM-I
CAP-I	MAN-I	RAN-I
CHA-I	MAX-I	ROT-I
CON-I	MID-I	SAD-I
DAL-I	MIR-I	SAR-I
DEF-I	MOD-I	SAT-I
DEL-I	MOM-I	SIR-I
DEN-I	MOT-I	TAB-I
DIV-I	MUN-I	TAX-I
FEN-I	NID-I	TIP-I
FIN-I	NOD-I	TOP-I
GAD-I	NON-I	TOR-I
GAR-I	PAD-I	

Four letters to five

BASS-I

BAST-I

BEST-I

BIND-I

BUFF-I

CAMP-I

CARD-I

CARP-I

CELL-I

COAT-I

COMB-I

CORN-I

CROC-I

CULT-I

CURL-I

DILL-I

DISC-I

FAST-I

FERM-I

FILM-I

FUND-I

FUNG-I

GLOB-I

HADJ-I

HAJJ-I

HANG-I

HONG-I

HOUR-I

JINN-I

LASS-I

LENT-I

LIMB-I

LOGO-I

LUNG-I

MACH-I

MYTH-I

PARK-I

PART-I

POOR-I

PRIM-I

PULL-I

PUTT-I

ROST-I

SENS-I

SENT-I

SWAM-I

TANG-I

TARS-I

TEMP-I

VILL-I

VOLT-I

Five letters to six

ANNUL-I

AVANT-I

CAROL-I

CHICH-I

CHILL-I

COLON-I

CUBIT-I

DENAR-I

DJINN-I

EQUAL-I

FRACT-I

GARDA-I

GLUTE-I

HAIKA-I

JEHAD-I

JIHAD-I

KAIKA-I

MANAT-I

POLYP-I

RHOMB-I

SCAMP-I

SENSE-I

SHALL-I

SILEN-I

SMALT-I

SOLID-I

STELA-I

TAPET-I

YOGIN-I

Six letters to seven

ACANTH-I	DENARI-I	REVERS-I
AFGHAN-I	HALLAL-I	RHYTHM-I
BANDAR-I	JAMPAN-I	SECOND-I
CHIASM-I	MARTIN-I	SHIKAR-I
DACTYL-I	PAESAN-I	SIGNOR-I
DEMENT-I	QAWWAL-I	TYMPAN-I

Seven letters to eight

BRAHMAN-I	CONDUCT-I	MARCHES-I
CALAMAR-I	DRACHMA-I	PARCHES-I
CAPITAN-I	FASCISM-I	PERFECT-I
CONCEPT-I	FASCIST-I	SIGNIOR-I
CONCERT-I	HETAIRA-I	TANDOOR-I

Blockers

It is useful to know which words are blockers and can't therefore be extended before or after. You may want to play a blocker that your opponent can't extend, or you may want to avoid playing a blocker because you want to keep the board open.

Some four-letter blockers beginning with I

IBIS	IDLY	INLY

Some five-letter blockers beginning with I
(except words ending in '-ED', '-J', '-S', '-X', '-Y' or '-Z')

ICTIC	IMINO	INEPT	INUST
ILEAC	IMSHI	INERM	IODIC
ILEAL	INAPT	INFRA	ISNAE
ILIAC	INBYE	INTIL	
IMIDO	INCUT	INTRA	

Some six-letter blockers beginning with I
(except words ending in '-ED', '-J', '-S', '-X', '-Y' or '-Z')

ICEMEN	INFIMA	INWITH
ICONIC	INGRAM	INWORN
IDLEST	INKJET	IRATER
INANER	INLAID	IRIDAL
INBENT	INMESH	IRIDIC
INBORN	INMOST	IRITIC
INCUBI	INRUSH	IRREAL
INFELT	INTACT	ITSELF
INFERE	INTIRE	

I

Some words beginning with IM-
Seven-letter words

IM-AGERS	IM-PALER	IM-PLIED
IM-AGING	IM-PANEL	IM-PORTS
IM-BURSE	IM-PARTS	IM-POSED
IM-MENSE	IM-PASSE	IM-POUND
IM-MORAL	IM-PEACH	IM-PRESS
IM-PACTS	IM-PEDES	IM-PRINT
IM-PAIRS	IM-PENDS	IM-PROVE
IM-PALAS	IM-PERIL	IM-PULSE
IM-PALED	IM-PLANT	IM-PURER

Eight-letter words

IM-BARKED	IM-PARTED	IM-PROPER
IM-BODIED	IM-PENDED	IM-PROVED
IM-MATURE	IM-PLYING	IM-PROVER
IM-MOBILE	IM-POLITE	IM-PUDENT
IM-MODEST	IM-PORTED	IM-PURELY
IM-MORTAL	IM-POSING	IM-PUREST
IM-PAIRED	IM-POSTER	IM-PURITY
IM-PALING	IM-POTENT	
IM-PARITY	IM-PRISON	

Some words beginning with IN-
Seven-letter words

IN-BOUND	IN-FIRMS	IN-QUIRE
IN-BUILT	IN-FLAME	IN-ROADS
IN-CASED	IN-FORCE	IN-SANER
IN-CENSE	IN-FORMS	IN-SECTS
IN-CITED	IN-FRACT	IN-SIDER
IN-COMER	IN-FUSED	IN-SIGHT
IN-DENTS	IN-GESTS	IN-SISTS
IN-DEXES	IN-GRAIN	IN-SNARE
IN-DICES	IN-GRATE	IN-SOFAR
IN-DICTS	IN-GROWN	IN-SOLES
IN-DOORS	IN-HABIT	IN-SPIRE
IN-DORSE	IN-HALED	IN-STALL
IN-DUCTS	IN-HUMAN	IN-STATE
IN-EXACT	IN-LAYER	IN-STEAD
IN-FAMED	IN-MATES	IN-STEPS
IN-FESTS	IN-NARDS	IN-STILL
IN-FIGHT	IN-QUEST	IN-SURED

IN-TAKES   IN-TONER   IN-VERSE
IN-TENDS   IN-VADED   IN-VESTS
IN-TENSE   IN-VALID   IN-VOLVE
IN-TERNS   IN-VENTS   IN-WARDS

Eight-letter words

IN-ACTION   IN-EQUITY   IN-PUTTED
IN-ACTIVE   IN-EXPERT   IN-SANELY
IN-BREEDS   IN-FAMOUS   IN-SANITY
IN-CENSED   IN-FESTER   IN-SCRIBE
IN-CITING   IN-FILLED   IN-SECURE
IN-CLOSED   IN-FINITE   IN-SHRINE
IN-COMING   IN-FIRMER   IN-SISTER
IN-CREASE   IN-FLIGHT   IN-STANCE
IN-CURRED   IN-FORMAL   IN-STATED
IN-DEBTED   IN-FORMED   IN-TERNAL
IN-DECENT   IN-FRINGE   IN-THRALL
IN-DENTED   IN-FUSION   IN-TREPID
IN-DIGEST   IN-GROUND   IN-VENTED
IN-DIRECT   IN-GROWTH   IN-VIABLE
IN-DOLENT   IN-HUMANE
IN-EDIBLE   IN-JURIES

I

Some words beginning with ISO-
Seven-letter words

ISO-BARS	ISO-LATE	ISO-TOPE
ISO-DOSE	ISO-MERE	ISO-TRON
ISO-FORM	ISO-PODS	ISO-TYPE
ISO-GRAM	ISO-TONE	

Eight-letter words

ISO-BARIC	ISO-GRAPH	ISO-TONIC
ISO-BUTYL	ISO-LATED	ISO-TOPIC
ISO-GAMIC	ISO-MORPH	ISO-TYPIC
ISO-GENIC	ISO-NOMIC	
ISO-GRAFT	ISO-THERM	

Some words ending with -IBLE
Seven-letter words

ADD-IBLE	FUS-IBLE	RIS-IBLE
AUD-IBLE	LEG-IBLE	VIS-IBLE
DEL-IBLE	MIX-IBLE	
DOC-IBLE	PAT-IBLE	

Eight-letter words

CRED-IBLE	GULL-IBLE	SENS-IBLE
CRUC-IBLE	HORR-IBLE	TANG-IBLE
ELIG-IBLE	INED-IBLE	TENS-IBLE
FALL-IBLE	MAND-IBLE	TERR-IBLE
FEAS-IBLE	POSS-IBLE	VINC-IBLE
FLEX-IBLE	RINS-IBLE	
FORC-IBLE	RUNC-IBLE	

Some words ending with -IFY

Seven-letter words

ACID-IFY	GRAT-IFY	REUN-IFY
AMPL-IFY	HORR-IFY	SACR-IFY
BEAT-IFY	JUST-IFY	SALS-IFY
CERT-IFY	LIQU-IFY	SCAR-IFY
CLAR-IFY	MAGN-IFY	SIGN-IFY
CRUC-IFY	MORT-IFY	SPEC-IFY
DIGN-IFY	NULL-IFY	TERR-IFY
FALS-IFY	PETR-IFY	TEST-IFY
FORT-IFY	QUAL-IFY	YUPP-IFY
GLOR-IFY	RECT-IFY	ZOMB-IFY

Eight-letter words

BEAUT-IFY	PRETT-IFY	SANCT-IFY
CLASS-IFY	QUANT-IFY	SIMPL-IFY
DETOX-IFY	REMOD-IFY	SOLID-IFY
EMULS-IFY	RENOT-IFY	STRAT-IFY
GENTR-IFY	REPUR-IFY	STULT-IFY
HUMID-IFY	RESIN-IFY	
IDENT-IFY	RIGID-IFY	

Some words ending with -INGS
Seven-letter words

ACH-INGS
ARM-INGS
BID-INGS
BUS-INGS
CAN-INGS
COD-INGS
COM-INGS
DAT-INGS
DRY-INGS
EAR-INGS
END-INGS

FAD-INGS
FIX-INGS
GAP-INGS
GAT-INGS
HID-INGS
INN-INGS
LAD-INGS
MER-INGS
OUT-INGS
PAR-INGS
PAY-INGS

RAG-INGS
RAT-INGS
SAY-INGS
SPY-INGS
TIM-INGS
TOY-INGS
TRY-INGS
TUB-INGS
WAD-INGS
WAN-INGS

Eight-letter words

BAIT-INGS
BANG-INGS
BEAR-INGS
BEAT-INGS
BOMB-INGS
BOND-INGS
BOWL-INGS
BUCK-INGS
CAMP-INGS
CAST-INGS
COAT-INGS
COIN-INGS
COMB-INGS
DAWN-INGS
DEAL-INGS

DRAW-INGS
EARN-INGS
EDIT-INGS
ETCH-INGS
EVEN-INGS
FAIL-INGS
FAST-INGS
FEED-INGS
FIND-INGS
FISH-INGS
FOOT-INGS
GASP-INGS
GELD-INGS
GOLF-INGS
HEAD-INGS

HEAR-INGS
HINT-INGS
HUNT-INGS
JUMP-INGS
KILL-INGS
LAND-INGS
LASH-INGS
LEAN-INGS
LIMP-INGS
LIST-INGS
LOAN-INGS
LONG-INGS
MALT-INGS
MEAN-INGS
MEET-INGS

MOOR-INGS	ROCK-INGS	TRAD-INGS
MORN-INGS	ROLL-INGS	TWIN-INGS
NEST-INGS	ROOF-INGS	UNDO-INGS
ONGO-INGS	ROUT-INGS	UNIT-INGS
OUTS-INGS	SACK-INGS	WARN-INGS
PAIR-INGS	SEAL-INGS	WASH-INGS
PARK-INGS	SEAT-INGS	WEEP-INGS
PAST-INGS	SHOW-INGS	WHIN-INGS
PELT-INGS	SIGN-INGS	WHIT-INGS
PRIM-INGS	SING-INGS	WIND-INGS
RAIL-INGS	SLID-INGS	WORK-INGS
READ-INGS	SNIP-INGS	WRIT-INGS
REEL-INGS	STAG-INGS	
RING-INGS	STAR-INGS	

Some words ending with -ISE
Seven-letter words

AGON-ISE	IRON-ISE	PREC-ISE
ATOM-ISE	ITEM-ISE	PREM-ISE
BAPT-ISE	LION-ISE	PROM-ISE
CONC-ISE	MORT-ISE	REAL-ISE
DUAL-ISE	ODOR-ISE	REPR-ISE
ICON-ISE	OXID-ISE	UNIT-ISE
IDOL-ISE	POET-ISE	

I

Eight-letter words

ACTIV-ISE
BANAL-ISE
CALOR-ISE
CANON-ISE
CIVIL-ISE
COLON-ISE
COLOR-ISE
DEMON-ISE
DEPUT-ISE
EQUAL-ISE
ETHER-ISE
EXERC-ISE

FINAL-ISE
HUMAN-ISE
IDEAL-ISE
IMMUN-ISE
LEGAL-ISE
LOCAL-ISE
MAXIM-ISE
MINIM-ISE
MORAL-ISE
MOTOR-ISE
ORGAN-ISE
PARAD-ISE

PENAL-ISE
POLAR-ISE
PRACT-ISE
SANIT-ISE
SATIR-ISE
TREAT-ISE
UNION-ISE
VAPOR-ISE
VITAL-ISE
VOCAL-ISE
VOWEL-ISE

Some words ending with -ISH

Seven-letter words

BOOK-ISH
BULL-ISH
COLD-ISH
DARK-ISH
FOOL-ISH
FOPP-ISH
GIRL-ISH
GOOD-ISH

HAWK-ISH
HOTT-ISH
LEFT-ISH
LONG-ISH
MORE-ISH
PECK-ISH
PEEV-ISH
REDD-ISH

RUBB-ISH
SELF-ISH
SLAV-ISH
SLOW-ISH
SOFT-ISH
TALL-ISH
VARN-ISH
WAIF-ISH

Eight-letter words

BLACK-ISH	FEVER-ISH	ROUGH-ISH
BLOKE-ISH	FIEND-ISH	SHARP-ISH
BLOND-ISH	GOLDF-ISH	SHEEP-ISH
BLUNT-ISH	LIGHT-ISH	SMALL-ISH
CHILD-ISH	NANNY-ISH	SWEET-ISH
CLOWN-ISH	PLAIN-ISH	THICK-ISH
DEVIL-ISH	REFIN-ISH	YOUNG-ISH

Some words ending with -ISM
Seven-letter words

BRUT-ISM	EGOT-ISM	SIZE-ISM
CULT-ISM	FASC-ISM	TOUR-ISM
DADA-ISM	IDOL-ISM	
DUAL-ISM	REAL-ISM	

Eight-letter words

ACTIV-ISM	FEMIN-ISM	NIHIL-ISM
ALARM-ISM	FUTUR-ISM	OPTIM-ISM
ALIEN-ISM	HEDON-ISM	ORGAN-ISM
ANEUR-ISM	HUMAN-ISM	PACIF-ISM
BOTUL-ISM	IDEAL-ISM	POPUL-ISM
CLASS-ISM	JINGO-ISM	ROYAL-ISM
CRONY-ISM	LOCAL-ISM	STOIC-ISM
CYNIC-ISM	LOYAL-ISM	TOKEN-ISM
DYNAM-ISM	LYRIC-ISM	UNION-ISM
EMBOL-ISM	MINIM-ISM	VEGAN-ISM
ESCAP-ISM	MORAL-ISM	
FATAL-ISM	NATIV-ISM	

I

Some words ending with -IST
Seven-letter words

ATOM-IST	DIET-IST	LEFT-IST
BASS-IST	DUAL-IST	PALM-IST
CELL-IST	DUEL-IST	PERS-IST
CHEM-IST	FLOR-IST	REAL-IST
DIAR-IST	HARP-IST	TOUR-IST

Eight-letter words

ALARM-IST	IDEAL-IST	PACIF-IST
ARSON-IST	JIHAD-IST	PANEL-IST
BANJO-IST	JINGO-IST	POPUL-IST
CANOE-IST	LOBBY-IST	PUGIL-IST
CHART-IST	LOYAL-IST	RALLY-IST
CLASS-IST	LYRIC-IST	REGAL-IST
COLOR-IST	MEDAL-IST	RIGHT-IST
ESSAY-IST	MINIM-IST	ROYAL-IST
FINAL-IST	MORAL-IST	SHOOT-IST
HOBBY-IST	MOTOR-IST	STOCK-IST
HUMAN-IST	OPTIM-IST	TOTAL-IST
HUMOR-IST	ORGAN-IST	TOTEM-IST

Some words ending with -ITY
Seven-letter words

ACID-ITY	DUAL-ITY	QUAL-ITY
AMEN-ITY	JOLL-ITY	REAL-ITY
ARID-ITY	NULL-ITY	TENS-ITY
CHAR-ITY	OBES-ITY	TRIN-ITY
DENS-ITY	PRIV-ITY	UTIL-ITY
DIGN-ITY	PROB-ITY	VACU-ITY

Eight-letter words

ACRID-ITY

ACTIV-ITY

AFFIN-ITY

BANAL-ITY

CALAM-ITY

CHAST-ITY

CONIC-ITY

CUBIC-ITY

ENORM-ITY

EQUAL-ITY

FACIL-ITY

FATAL-ITY

FIDEL-ITY

FINAL-ITY

FLUID-ITY

FUTIL-ITY

GRATU-ITY

HUMAN-ITY

HUMID-ITY

HUMIL-ITY

IDENT-ITY

IMMUN-ITY

INSAN-ITY

LEGAL-ITY

LIVID-ITY

LOCAL-ITY

LUCID-ITY

MAJOR-ITY

MINOR-ITY

MOBIL-ITY

MORAL-ITY

NATIV-ITY

POLAR-ITY

PRIOR-ITY

RABID-ITY

RAPID-ITY

REGAL-ITY

RIGID-ITY

RURAL-ITY

SANCT-ITY

SECUR-ITY

SENIL-ITY

SEREN-ITY

SEVER-ITY

SOLID-ITY

TIMID-ITY

TONAL-ITY

TONIC-ITY

TOTAL-ITY

TOXIC-ITY

VALID-ITY

VITAL-ITY

Some words ending with -IUM
Seven-letter words

CALC-IUM

CRAN-IUM

FERM-IUM

GALL-IUM

HASS-IUM

HOLM-IUM

IRID-IUM

LITH-IUM

PALL-IUM

PLAG-IUM

PREM-IUM

PROT-IUM

RHOD-IUM

STAD-IUM

TERT-IUM

TRIT-IUM

URAN-IUM

YTTR-IUM

Eight-letter words

ACTIN-IUM

AEROB-IUM

ALLUV-IUM

AMMON-IUM

AQUAR-IUM

BRACH-IUM

CHROM-IUM

CORON-IUM

DELIR-IUM

DILUV-IUM

EMPOR-IUM

EULOG-IUM

FRANC-IUM

GERAN-IUM

IMPER-IUM

INGEN-IUM

MOTOR-IUM

NOBEL-IUM

OSSAR-IUM

PHORM-IUM

POLON-IUM

REFUG-IUM

ROSAR-IUM

RUBID-IUM

SELEN-IUM

SOLAR-IUM

SOLAT-IUM

THALL-IUM

TITAN-IUM

TRILL-IUM

VIVAR-IUM

Unusual letter combinations

If you have an unusual combination of letters on your rack, or want to impress your opponent with an unusual word, a few words from World English can come in handy. Here are some beginning with I.

New Zealand words

IWI   a Maori tribe

Canadian words

ICEWINE   dessert wine made from frozen grapes

Urdu words

INQILAB   revolution

Essential info
Value: 8 points
Number in set: 1
Power Tile

J alone is worth 8 points, making it an extremely valuable tile. However, it can be difficult to play: for example, there are only two two-letter words beginning with J (JA, a South African word for yes, and JO, a Scots word for sweetheart, both 9 points). When used in conjunction with the other power tiles X and Z, however, there is scope for huge scoring, especially if words are played judiciously on double- or triple-letter squares. Good short words to remember which use J alongside X and Z include JINX (18 points) and JAZY (23 points). Remember, as there is only one J tile in the Scrabble set, you will need a blank tile to take advantage of words with two Js (e.g. HAJJ, 13 points) or indeed a J and two of the same power tile letters (e.g. JAZZES, 21 points).

Two-letter words beginning with J

JA   JO

Some three-letter words beginning with J

| JAG | JAK | JAY |
| JAI | JAP | JEE |

JEU	JIZ	JOW
JEW	JOE	JUD
JIB	JOL	JUN
JIN	JOR	JUS

Some three-letter words using J

| GJU | HAJ | RAJ | TAJ |

Some four-letter words using J

Some four-letter words using J that you may not know are
DOJO (room or hall for the practice of martial arts, 12 points),
JEHU (a fast driver, 14 points), JIAO (Chinese currency unit,
11 points) and JIRD (another word for gerbil, 12 points)

AJAR	JANE	JAZZ	JESS
DJIN	JANN	JEAN	JEST
DOJO	JAPE	JEAT	JETE
FUJI	JARK	JEDI	JEUX
HADJ	JARL	JEED	JIAO
HAJJ	JARP	JEEL	JIBB
JAAP	JASP	JEEP	JIBE
JACK	JASS	JEER	JIFF
JADE	JASY	JEEZ	JILL
JAFA	JATO	JEFE	JILT
JAGA	JAUK	JEFF	JIMP
JAGG	JAUP	JEHU	JINK
JAIL	JAVA	JELL	JINN
JAKE	JAXY	JEON	JINS
JAMB	JAZY	JERK	JINX

J

JIRD	JOLL	JUBE	JURE
JIVE	JOLT	JUCO	JURY
JIVY	JOMO	JUDO	JUST
JOBE	JONG	JUDY	JUTE
JOCK	JOOK	JUGA	JUVE
JOCO	JOSH	JUJU	JYNX
JOEY	JOSS	JUKE	KOJI
JOHN	JOTA	JUKU	MOJO
JOIN	JOUK	JUMP	RAJA
JOKE	JOUR	JUNK	SOJA
JOKY	JOWL	JUPE	
JOLE	JUBA	JURA	

Hooks

Hooking requires a subtle change in a player's thought process, in that they must look at words already on the board without becoming distracted by their pronunciation.

Some front-hooks
Two letters to three

J-AB	J-EE	J-OY
J-AG	J-ET	J-UG
J-AI	J-IN	J-UN
J-AM	J-OB	J-US
J-AR	J-OE	J-UT
J-AW	J-OR	
J-AY	J-OW	

Three letters to four

J-AGA	J-EAT	J-IVY
J-AIL	J-EEL	J-OBE
J-AKE	J-EFF	J-OKE
J-ANE	J-ELL	J-OLE
J-ANN	J-ERK	J-OUK
J-APE	J-ESS	J-OUR
J-ARK	J-EST	J-OWL
J-ASP	J-IFF	J-UDO
J-ASS	J-ILL	J-UKE
J-AUK	J-IMP	J-UMP
J-AVA	J-INK	J-URE
J-EAN	J-INN	J-UTE

Four letters to five

J-AGER	J-EMMY	J-OWED
J-ALAP	J-ESSE	J-OWLY
J-AMBO	J-IFFY	J-UMBO
J-APED	J-ILLS	J-UMPY
J-APER	J-IMMY	J-UNCO
J-AUNT	J-INGO	J-UNTO
J-AVEL	J-NANA	J-UPON
J-AWED	J-OINT	
J-EELY	J-OUST	

Five letters to six

J-ABBED	J-ASSES	J-OTTER
J-ACKER	J-AUNTY	J-OUNCE
J-AGGER	J-AWING	J-OWING
J-AILED	J-EANED	J-OWLED
J-AMBER	J-EFFED	J-OWLER
J-ANGLE	J-ESSES	J-UDDER
J-ANKER	J-ESTER	J-UGGED
J-APERY	J-IGGED	J-UMBLE
J-APING	J-IMPLY	J-UMPED
J-ARGON	J-INGLE	J-UNKED
J-ARRAH	J-INKED	J-UNKET
J-ASPER	J-INKER	

J

Six letters to seven

J-AGGIES	J-IMMIES	J-OUSTER
J-AILING	J-INGOES	J-OWLIER
J-ANGLED	J-INKING	J-OWLING
J-ANGLER	J-OCULAR	J-UGGING
J-AUNTIE	J-OINTED	J-UMPING
J-AWLESS	J-OLLIES	J-UNCATE
J-EFFING	J-OSTLER	J-UNCOES
J-IGGING	J-OUSTED	J-UNKING

Seven letters to eight

J-ANGLING	J-OUSTING	J-UNCTION
J-APERIES	J-OWLIEST	
J-OINTING	J-UDDERED	

Some end-hooks

Two letters to three

HA-J   TA-J

Three letters to four

BEN-J   HAD-J   HAJ-J

J

Blockers

It is useful to know which words are blockers and can't therefore be extended before or after. You may want to play a blocker that your opponent can't extend, or you may want to avoid playing a blocker because you want to keep the board open.

Some four-letter blockers beginning with J

JASS	JEON	JOSH
JASY	JEUX	JOSS
JAZY	JINX	JURY
JEED	JIVY	JYNX
JEEZ	JOKY	

Some five-letter blockers beginning with J
(except words ending in '-ED', '-J', '-S', '-X', '-Y' or '-Z')

| JEUNE | JIRRE | JOMON |
| JINGO | JOKOL | JURAL |

Some six-letter blockers beginning with J
(except words ending in '-ED', '-J', '-S', '-X', '-Y' or '-Z')

JACENT	JINNEE	JOLING
JADING	JIVIER	JOVIAL
JADISH	JIVING	JOWING
JEEING	JOBING	JOYFUL
JEJUNE	JOCOSE	JOYING
JIBING	JOCUND	JUBATE
JIMPER	JOKIER	JUGATE
JIMSON	JOKING	JUKING

Handy Hint

When holding a power tile try looking beyond the easy
two and three-letter words that might jump out at you.
Also look for words that might score more embedding the
power tile rather than starting with it – a few containing
a J are RAJA (11 points), MAJOR (14), CAJOLE (15), OUIJA (12),
BANJO (14).

Bonus words

Seven-letter words

JABBERS

JABBING

JACKALS

JACKASS

JACKDAW

JACKERS

JACKETS

JACKING

JACKPOT

JACKSIE

JADEDLY

JAGGERS

JAGGERY

JAGGIER

JAGGIES

JAGGING

JAGUARS

JAILERS

JAILING

JAILORS

JAMJARS

JAMLIKE

JAMMERS

JAMMIER

JAMMIES

JAMMING

JAMPOTS

JANDALS

JANGLED

JANGLER

JANGLES

JANITOR

JARFULS

JARGONS

JARGONY

JARHEAD

JARPING

JARRAHS

JARRING

JASMINE

JASPERS

JASPERY

JAUNTED

JAUNTEE

JAUNTIE

JAUPING

JAVELIN

JAWBONE

JAWINGS

JAWLESS

JAWLINE

JAYBIRD

JAYWALK

JAZZIER

JAZZILY

JAZZING

JAZZMAN

JAZZMEN

JEALOUS

JEEPERS

JEEPING

JEERERS

JEERING

JEHADIS

JELLIED

JELLIFY

JELLING

JEMIMAS

JEMMIED

JEMMIER

JEMMIES

JENNIES

JEOPARD

JERBILS

JERBOAS

JEREEDS

JERKERS

JERKIER

JERKIES

JERKILY

JERKING

JERKINS
JERRIES
JERSEYS

JESSIES
JESTEES
JESTERS
JESTFUL
JESTING
JESUITS

JETLAGS
JETLIKE
JETSAMS
JETSOMS
JETTIED
JETTIER
JETTIES
JETTING

JEWELED
JEWELER
JEWELRY

JEZEBEL

JIBBERS
JIBBING

JIFFIES

JIGGERS
JIGGIER
JIGGING
JIGGLED

JIGSAWS

JIHADIS

JILTERS
JILTING
JIMJAMS
JIMMIED
JIMMIES
JIMMINY

JINGLED
JINGLER
JINGLET
JINGOES
JINXING

JITTERS
JITTERY

JIVIEST

JOANNAS

JOBBERS
JOBBING
JOBLESS

JOCKEYS
JOCULAR

JODHPUR

JOGGERS
JOGGING

JOHNNIE
JOHNSON

JOINERS
JOINERY
JOINING
JOINTED
JOINTER
JOINTLY
JOISTED

JOJOBAS

JOKIEST

JOLLEYS
JOLLIED
JOLLIER
JOLLIES
JOLLIFY
JOLLILY
JOLLITY
JOLTILY
JOLTING

JONESED
JONESES

JOSHERS
JOSHING
JOSTLED
JOSTLER

JOTTERS
JOTTING
JOURNAL
JOURNEY

J

JOURNOS   JUGHEAD   JUMPING
JOUSTED   JUGSFUL   JUNGLED
JOUSTER   JUGULAR   JUNGLES
JOWLIER   JUICERS   JUNIORS
JOWLING   JUICIER   JUNIPER
JOYLESS   JUICILY   JUNKETS
JOYRIDE   JUICING   JUNKIER
JUBILEE   JUJITSU   JUNKMAN
JUDASES   JUJUIST   JUNKMEN
JUDDERS   JUKEBOX   JURISTS
JUDGERS   JURYING
JUDGING   JUMBLED   JURYMAN
JUDOIST   JUMBLER   JURYMEN
               JUMBUCK
JUGFULS   JUMPERS   JUSTICE
JUGGLED   JUMPIER   JUSTIFY
JUGGLER   JUMPILY   JUTTING

Eight-letter words

JABBERED   JAGGIEST   JANGLIER
JABBERER   JAILABLE   JANGLING
JACKAROO   JAILBAIT   JANITRIX
JACKBOOT   JAILBIRD   JAPANISE
JACKEROO   JAILLESS   JAPANIZE
JACKETED   JALAPENO   JAPINGLY
JADELIKE   JAMBOREE   JARGONED
JAGGEDER   JAMMABLE   JAUNDICE
JAGGEDLY   JAMMIEST   JAUNTIER

JAUNTILY
JAUNTING

JAVELINA

JAWBONED

JAWBONER

JAZZIEST

JAZZLIKE

JEALOUSY

JEANETTE

JEHADISM

JEHADIST

JELLYING

JEMMIEST

JEMMYING

JEOPARDY

JERKIEST

JEROBOAM

JERRICAN

JERRYCAN

JERSEYED

JESTBOOK

JESUITIC

JESUITRY

JIGGLIER

JIGGLING

JIGSAWED

JIHADISM

JIHADIST

JILLAROO

JIMCRACK

JIMMYING

JINGLIER

JINGLING

JINGOISM

JINGOIST

JITTERED

JOBSHARE

JOCKETTE

JOCKEYED

JOGGLING

JOINABLE

JOINTING

JOINTURE

JOISTING

JOKESOME

JOKESTER

JOKINESS

JOKINGLY

JOLLEYER

JOLLIEST

JOLLYING

JOLTHEAD

JOLTIEST

JONESING

JONGLEUR

JOSTLING

JOUNCIER

JOUNCING

JOUSTING

JOVIALLY

JOVIALTY

JOWLIEST

JOYFULLY

JOYOUSLY

JOYRIDER

JOYSTICK

JUBILANT

JUBILATE

JUDDERED

JUDGMENT

JUDICIAL

JUGGLERY

JUGGLING

JUGULATE

JUICIEST

JULIENNE

JUMBLIER

JUMBLING

JUMPABLE

J

JUMPIEST	JUNKETER	JURYMAST
JUMPSUIT	JUNKIEST	JUSTICER
JUNCTION	JUNKYARD	JUSTLING
JUNCTURE	JURASSIC	JUSTNESS
JUNGLIER	JURATORY	JUTELIKE
JUNGLIST	JURISTIC	JUTTYING
JUNKETED	JURYLESS	JUVENILE

Unusual letter combinations

If you have an unusual combination of letters on your rack, or want to impress your opponent with an unusual word, a few words from World English can come in handy.

Australian words

JARRAH	type of eucalyptus tree
JEFF	downsize or close down an organization
JUMBUCK	sheep

Canadian words

| JOUAL | nonstandard Canadian French dialect |

Hindi words

| JAGGERY | coarse brown sugar |
| JAI | victory |

K 5

Essential info
Value: 5 points
Number in set: 1

K is a valuable tile at 5 points and is particularly useful if you also have a C on your rack because of the abundance of words ending in -CK. There is a selection of useful two-letter words beginning with K: KA, KI, KO (6 points each) and KY (9 points). Three-letter words beginning with K include common words such as KEG and KID (8 points) KIP (9 points), and KEY (10 points). Others tend to be more unusual words but nevertheless very useful: KEB (9 points). KEX (14 points), KIF (10 points).

Two-letter words beginning with K

KA	KI	KO	KY

Some three-letter words beginning with K

KAB	KEA	KHI	KOP
KAE	KEB	KIF	KOR
KAF	KED	KIN	KOW
KAI	KEF	KIR	KYE
KAM	KEN	KOA	KYU
KAT	KEP	KOB	
KAW	KET	KOI	
KAY	KEX	KON	

Hooks

Hooking requires a subtle change in a player's thought process, in that they must look at words already on the board without becoming distracted by their pronunciation.

Some front-hooks
Two letters to three

K-AB	K-AW	K-ET	K-IS	K-OR
K-AE	K-AY	K-EX	K-IT	K-OS
K-AI	K-EA	K-HI	K-OB	K-OW
K-AM	K-ED	K-ID	K-OI	K-YE
K-AS	K-EF	K-IF	K-ON	K-YU
K-AT	K-ET	K-IN	K-OP	

Three letters to four

K-AGO	K-AVA	K-HET	K-NOT
K-AID	K-AWA	K-ICK	K-NOW
K-AIL	K-BAR	K-IFF	K-NUB
K-AIM	K-EEK	K-ILL	K-NUR
K-AIN	K-EEL	K-INK	K-NUT
K-AKA	K-EEN	K-IRK	K-OBO
K-ALE	K-ELL	K-ISH	K-OFF
K-AMA	K-ELT	K-IWI	K-ORA
K-AMI	K-ERF	K-LAP	K-ORE
K-ANA	K-ERN	K-NAG	K-SAR
K-ANE	K-EST	K-NAP	K-UDO
K-ANT	K-ETA	K-NEE	K-UTA
K-ARK	K-HAN	K-NEW	K-UTU
K-ART	K-HAT	K-NIT	K-YAK

Four letters to five

K-ALIF	K-INKY	K-NURL
K-ANGA	K-LANG	K-NURR
K-ARSY	K-LAPS	K-OKRA
K-ARTS	K-LICK	K-OMBU
K-AVAS	K-LONG	K-RAFT
K-AWED	K-LOOF	K-RAIT
K-EDGE	K-LUGE	K-RANG
K-EDGY	K-LUTZ	K-RILL
K-EECH	K-NAVE	K-RONE
K-EMPT	K-NEED	K-ROON
K-ERNE	K-NIFE	K-ULAN
K-ETCH	K-NISH	K-VELL
K-EVIL	K-NOCK	K-YACK
K-EYED	K-NOLL	K-YANG
K-HETH	K-NOUT	
K-ICKY	K-NOWN	

K

Five letters to six

K-AINGA	K-EGGED	K-INGLE
K-ALONG	K-EGGER	K-INKED
K-ANTAR	K-EIGHT	K-INKLE
K-ANTED	K-EMBED	K-IRKED
K-ARKED	K-ENTIA	K-ISHES
K-ARRIS	K-ERNED	K-LATCH
K-ARSEY	K-ETTLE	K-LUGED
K-AWING	K-EYING	K-NAGGY
K-EBBED	K-ICKER	K-NIGHT
K-EDGED	K-ILLER	K-RATER
K-EDGER	K-INDIE	K-VETCH

Six letters to seven

K-ANTING

K-ARKING

K-EBBING

K-EDGERS

K-EDGIER

K-EDGING

K-EECHES

K-EGGING

K-ENOSIS

K-ERNING

K-ICKIER

K-IDLING

K-INKIER

K-INKING

K-INSHIP

K-IRKING

K-LAPPED

K-LINKER

K-LISTER

K-LUGING

K-LUTZES

K-NAPPED

K-NAPPER

K-NICKER

K-NISHES

K-NOBBLE

K-NOCKED

K-NUBBLE

K-NUBBLY

K-NURLED

K-ONNING

K-RATERS

K-RIMMER

K-RISING

K-VETCHY

Seven letters to eight

K-ALEWIFE

K-EDGIEST

K-ETAMINE

K-ETCHING

K-ICKIEST

K-INKIEST

K-INSHIPS

K-LAPPING

K-LATCHES

K-NAGGIER

K-NAPPING

K-NIGHTED

K-NIGHTLY

K-NOBBIER

K-NOBBLED

K-NOCKING

K-NUBBIER

K-NUBBLED

K-NURLING

K-OSMOSES

Some end-hooks
Two letters to three

AR-K	IN-K	SI-K
AS-K	JA-K	TA-K
BO-K	KA-K	WO-K
DA-K	MA-K	YA-K
EE-K	NE-K	YO-K
EL-K	OI-K	YU-K
ER-K	OU-K	

Three letters to four

BAC-K	DIS-K	HUN-K
BAL-K	DOC-K	JAR-K
BAN-K	DOR-K	JUN-K
BAR-K	DUN-K	KIN-K
BAS-K	FAN-K	KIR-K
BON-K	FIN-K	LAC-K
BOO-K	FIR-K	LAR-K
BUN-K	FOR-K	LAW-K
BUR-K	FUN-K	LEA-K
BUS-K	GEE-K	LEE-K
CAR-K	GIN-K	LIN-K
CAW-K	GON-K	LIS-K
CHI-K	GUN-K	LOO-K
CON-K	HAN-K	LUR-K
COO-K	HIC-K	MAC-K
COR-K	HOC-K	MAR-K
COW-K	HON-K	MAS-K
DAN-K	HOO-K	MAW-K
DIN-K	HOW-K	MEE-K

K

MIL-K PIC-K SOC-K
MIR-K PIN-K SUN-K
MOC-K PUN-K TAN-K
MON-K RAN-K TAS-K
MOO-K REE-K TEA-K
MUS-K RIN-K TEE-K
NOO-K ROC-K TIC-K
NOR-K ROO-K TOC-K
PAC-K RUC-K TON-K
PAR-K SAC-K TOO-K
PEA-K SAN-K WEE-K
PEC-K SEE-K WIN-K
PEE-K SIC-K
PER-K SIN-K

Four letters to five

ABAC-K CLON-K SKIN-K
ALEC-K CRAN-K SLEE-K
BLIN-K CREE-K SMIR-K
BLOC-K CROC-K SPAN-K
BRAN-K FLAN-K SPAR-K
BRIN-K FLIC-K SPEC-K
BRIS-K FLOC-K SPIN-K
BROO-K FRIS-K STAR-K
BRUS-K GREE-K STIR-K
CHAL-K PLAN-K STUN-K
CHIC-K SCUL-K SWAN-K
CHIN-K SHAN-K THAN-K
CHOC-K SHIR-K THIN-K
CLAN-K SHOO-K TWIN-K

Five letters to six

ANTIC-K	KALPA-K	RESEE-K
ASPIC-K	MEDIC-K	SQUAW-K
BEGUN-K	MELIC-K	UMIAC-K
DEBAR-K	MUSIC-K	UNBAR-K
EMBAR-K	PACHA-K	ZEBEC-K
IMBAR-K	PANIC-K	
JAMBO-K	REBEC-K	

Six letters to seven

AMTRAC-K	FINNAC-K	OUTBAR-K
BOOBOO-K	GWEDUC-K	OUTRAN-K
CALPAC-K	LIMBEC-K	TIETAC-K
DISBAR-K	OOMIAC-K	TOMBAC-K

Seven letters to eight

ALMANAC-K	OVERRAN-K	SHOEPAC-K
BALDRIC-K	POLITIC-K	TAMARIS-K
BAUDRIC-K	PRACTIC-K	
FORERAN-K	SHELLAC-K	

K

Blockers

It is useful to know which words are blockers and can't therefore be extended before or after. You may want to play a blocker that your opponent can't extend, or you may want to avoid playing a blocker because you want to keep the board open.

Three-letter blocker beginning with K

KEX

Some four-letter blockers beginning with K

KEPT   KEWL   KILD   KISH   KNEW   KRIS

Some five-letter blockers beginning with K
(except words ending in '-ED', '-J', '-S', '-X', '-Y' or '-Z')

KEECH	KIDGE	KNISH	KRONA
KEMPT	KINDA	KORAI	
KENCH	KNELT	KOTCH	

Some six-letter blockers beginning with K
(except words ending in '-ED', '-J', '-S', '-X', '-Y' or '-Z')

KAPUTT	KIPPEN	KOTUKU
KARMIC	KIRSCH	KRONEN
KAWING	KLATCH	KRONER
KEPPIT	KNITCH	KULAKI
KEWLER	KONAKI	KUTCHA
KIBOSH	KOTARE	KYBOSH

Bonus words

Bonus words on your rack can be hard to spot, especially for the less experienced player. One way to help find them is by using prefixes and suffixes.

Many larger words include a common prefix or suffix – remembering these and using them where you can is a good way to discover any longer words on your rack, including any potential bonus words. The key suffix to remember beginning with K is -KIN.

Some words ending with -KIN
Seven-letter words

BUMP-KIN	LADY-KIN	MINI-KIN
CATS-KIN	LAMB-KIN	OILS-KIN
COWS-KIN	LORD-KIN	PIGS-KIN
DOES-KIN	LUMP-KIN	PUMP-KIN
FOXS-KIN	MANA-KIN	RAMA-KIN
GHER-KIN	MANI-KIN	WOLF-KIN

Eight-letter words

BEARS-KIN	FISHS-KIN	MUNCH-KIN
BOOTI-KIN	GOATS-KIN	SEALS-KIN
BUCKS-KIN	LAMBS-KIN	SWANS-KIN
CALFS-KIN	LARRI-KIN	TURNS-KIN
CIDER-KIN	MANNI-KIN	WINES-KIN
DEERS-KIN	MOLES-KIN	WOLFS-KIN
DEVIL-KIN	MOUSE-KIN	WOOLS-KIN

Unusual letter combinations

If you have an unusual combination of letters on your rack, or want to impress your opponent with an unusual word, a few words from World English can come in handy.

Australian words

KARRI   type of eucalyptus tree

KOALA   slow-moving arboreal marsupial

KYBO   temporary lavatory

KYLIE   boomerang that is flat on one side and convex on the other

Hindi words

KHADDAR   cotton cloth

KHEDA   enclosure for captured elephants

KOEL   parasitic cuckoo

KOS   Indian unit of distance

KRAIT   brightly coloured venomous snake

KULFI   Indian dessert

KURTA   long loose garment

New Zealand words

KAHAWAI   large fish

KAI   food

KARANGA   call or chant of welcome

KATIPO   small venomous spider

KAUPAPA   strategy, policy or cause

KAURI   coniferous tree

K

KAWA	protocol or etiquette
KIWI	flightless bird with long beak and no tail
KOHA	gift or donation
KORU	curved pattern
KOWHAI	small tree
KUIA	female elder
KURI	mongrel dog
KUTU	body louse

South African words

KEREL	chap or fellow
KRAAL	stockaded village
KWAITO	type of pop music

Urdu words

KAMEEZ	long tunic
KEBAB	dish of meat, onions, etc, grilled on skewers
KHARIF	crop harvested at beginning of winter
KHAYAL	kind of Indian classical vocal music
KINCOB	fine silk fabric embroidered with gold or silver threads
KOFTA	Indian dish of seasoned minced meat shaped into balls
KOFTGAR	person skilled in inlaying steel with gold
KOFTGARI	art of inlaying steel with gold
KORMA	Indian dish of meat or vegetables braised with yoghurt or cream

K

Handy Hint

The letter K features prominently in many variants of
World English. Along with its frequency of use in the
Maori-derived words of New Zealand English, the use of
a double K is common in Australian English (QUOKKA,
18 points), Hindi (PUKKA, 10 points), Inuit words
(MUKTUK, 11 points) and Urdu (KHAKI, 11 points).
As there is only one K in the Scrabble set, you will need
to have a handy blank tile to play these fascinating words.

K

Essential info

Value: 1 points

Number in set: 4

The **L** is a very flexible letter for playing words because it combines with many other consonants such as BL-, CL-, FL-, PL-. If you have two of them there are also many words enging in -LL to help you out. Be aware of the following two-letter words for making parallel plays involving an L: LA (in music, the sixth note of a major scale, 2 points), LI (a Chinese unit of length, 2 points) and LO (a command that means look, 2 points). There's a great selection of three-letter words for combining the L with another higher-scoring consonant such as: LAW, LAY, LOW and LYE, all worth 6 points. There are also quite a few words which use X: LAX, LEX, LOX and LUX, all worth 10 points.

L

Two-letter words beginning with L

LA   LI   LO

Some three-letter words beginning with L

LAB	LAR	LEE	LIB
LAC	LAT	LES	LIG
LAH	LAV	LEX	LIN
LAM	LEA	LEZ	LOD

LOP	LOX	LUR	LYM
LOR	LOY	LUX	
LOS	LUG	LUZ	
LOU	LUM	LYE	

Hooks

Hooking requires a subtle change in a player's thought process, in that they must look at words already on the board without becoming distracted by their pronunciation.

Some front-hooks
Two letters to three

L-AB	L-ED	L-OP
L-AD	L-EE	L-OR
L-AG	L-ES	L-OS
L-AH	L-ET	L-OU
L-AM	L-EX	L-OW
L-AR	L-ID	L-OX
L-AS	L-IN	L-OY
L-AT	L-IS	L-UG
L-AW	L-IT	L-UM
L-AX	L-OB	L-UR
L-AY	L-OD	L-YE
L-EA	L-OO	

Three letters to four

L-ACE	L-EFT	L-OON
L-AID	L-END	L-OOP
L-AIN	L-ENS	L-OOT
L-AIR	L-ESS	L-OPE
L-AKE	L-EST	L-ORD
L-ALL	L-ICE	L-ORE
L-AMP	L-ICH	L-OSE
L-ANA	L-ICK	L-OUD
L-AND	L-IMP	L-OUP
L-ANE	L-INK	L-OUR
L-ARD	L-ION	L-OUT
L-ARK	L-OAF	L-OWE
L-ASH	L-OBE	L-OWN
L-ASS	L-OBO	L-OWT
L-ATE	L-OCH	L-UDO
L-AVA	L-ODE	L-UKE
L-AWN	L-OFT	L-UMP
L-EAN	L-ONE	L-URE
L-EAR	L-OOF	L-UTE
L-EEK	L-OOM	

Four letters to five

L-ACED	L-AWED	L-EAVE
L-ACER	L-AWNY	L-EDGE
L-AGER	L-AYIN	L-EDGY
L-AIRY	L-EACH	L-EECH
L-AKED	L-EARN	L-EERY
L-ANCE	L-EASE	L-EGAL
L-APSE	L-EAST	L-EGGY

L-EISH   L-LAMA   L-OWED
L-ETCH   L-OATH   L-OWER
L-EVER   L-ONER   L-OWLY
L-INCH   L-OOSE   L-OWSE
L-INGO   L-OPED   L-UMPY
L-INKY   L-OTTO   L-USER
L-ISLE   L-OVER

Five letters to six

L-ACING   L-EASER   L-IZARD
L-ACKER   L-EAVED   L-OCKER
L-ADDER   L-EDGED   L-OCULI
L-AGGER   L-EDGER   L-OFTER
L-AIRED   L-EGGED   L-OLLER
L-AMBER   L-EGGER   L-ONELY
L-AMENT   L-ENDER   L-OOPED
L-AMPED   L-ETHAL   L-OPING
L-ANGER   L-ICKER   L-ORATE
L-ANKER   L-IGGED   L-OTHER
L-ARKED   L-IMBED   L-OTTER
L-ARVAL   L-IMPED   L-OUPED
L-ASHED   L-IMPLY   L-OUTED
L-ASTER   L-INKED   L-OWING
L-AWFUL   L-INKER   L-OWNED
L-AWING   L-INTEL   L-UGGED
L-EANED   L-INTER   L-UMBER
L-EARED   L-IRKED   L-UMPED
L-EASED   L-ITHER   L-USHER

Six letters to seven

L-AIDING	L-EDGIER	L-IONIZE
L-AIRIER	L-EECHED	L-IRKING
L-AIRING	L-EERIER	L-OCULAR
L-AMPING	L-EERILY	L-OOPING
L-ARKING	L-EFTEST	L-OUPING
L-ASHING	L-EGALLY	L-OUTING
L-AUDING	L-EGGIER	L-OVERED
L-AWLESS	L-EGGING	L-OVERLY
L-AWNIER	L-ENDING	L-OWLIER
L-EANING	L-ETCHED	L-OWNING
L-EARING	L-IGGING	L-OXYGEN
L-EARNED	L-IGNIFY	L-UGGING
L-EARNER	L-IMPING	L-ULLING
L-EASING	L-INKING	L-UMPING
L-EAVING	L-INNING	
L-ECHING	L-IONISE	

Seven letters to eight

L-ABILITY	L-EDGIEST	L-IONISER
L-ACERATE	L-EECHING	L-IONIZED
L-AIRIEST	L-EERIEST	L-IONIZER
L-AMBLING	L-EGALITY	L-ITERATE
L-ANGERED	L-EGGIEST	L-OCULATE
L-ANGUISH	L-ETCHING	L-OMENTUM
L-AUREATE	L-EVITATE	L-ONENESS
L-AWFULLY	L-IGNEOUS	L-OURIEST
L-AWNIEST	L-INCHPIN	L-OWLIEST
L-EARNING	L-IONISED	L-UMBERED

L

Some end-hooks
Two letters to three

AA-L	EE-L	OW-L
AI-L	EL-L	PA-L
AL-L	GU-L	PO-L
AW-L	JO-L	SO-L
BA-L	MA-L	TE-L
BE-L	ME-L	TI-L
DA-L	MI-L	ZO-L
DE-L	MO-L	
DO-L	OI-L	

Three letters to four

AXE-L	GAL-L	POL-L
BAL-L	GOA-L	PUL-L
BOW-L	HOW-L	PUR-L
CEL-L	JAI-L	SEA-L
COO-L	JOW-L	SOU-L
COW-L	MAL-L	TAI-L
CUR-L	MEL-L	TEA-L
DAH-L	MEW-L	TEL-L
DOL-L	MIL-L	TIL-L
DOW-L	MOL-L	TOO-L
DUE-L	NIL-L	VIA-L
EAR-L	ORA-L	WAI-L
FEE-L	OVA-L	WOO-L
FOU-L	PAL-L	YOW-L
FUR-L	PEA-L	ZEA-L

L

Four letters to five

ALKY-L	HAZE-L	QUAI-L
ALLY-L	HOTE-L	RAVE-L
ANNA-L	HOVE-L	RIVA-L
AURA-L	IDEA-L	ROTA-L
BABE-L	IDYL-L	RUBE-L
BRAW-L	KNEE-L	SCOW-L
CABA-L	LEVE-L	SHAW-L
CAME-L	LOCA-L	SNAR-L
CRAW-L	META-L	SPIE-L
CREE-L	MODE-L	UREA-L
CRUE-L	MORA-L	VASA-L
DRAW-L	MOTE-L	VENA-L
DURA-L	MURA-L	VINY-L
EASE-L	NAVE-L	VITA-L
FAVE-L	OCTA-L	WHEE-L
FETA-L	PANE-L	WHIR-L
GAVE-L	PEAR-L	YODE-L
GNAR-L	PERI-L	YOKE-L
GROW-L	PROW-L	ZONA-L
GRUE-L	PUPA-L	

Five letters to six

ANIMA-L	CAUSA-L	FACIA-L
AORTA-L	COSTA-L	FAUNA-L
APPAL-L	DERMA-L	FLORA-L
ATRIA-L	DORSA-L	FLOTE-L
BARBE-L	DRIVE-L	GRAVE-L
BARRE-L	ENROL-L	GROVE-L
CARTE-L	EXTOL-L	LARVA-L

MAMMA-L   PORTA-L   SWIVE-L
MANGE-L   PRIMA-L   TASSE-L
MEDIA-L   RECAL-L   TEASE-L
MENTA-L   REDIA-L   TIBIA-L
MONGO-L   REGNA-L   TRAVE-L
MORSE-L   SCRAW-L   VANDA-L
MUSSE-L   SEPTA-L   VESTA-L
NORMA-L   SHOVE-L   VISTA-L
PASTE-L   SIGNA-L
PETRE-L   SPINA-L

Six letters to seven

ANGINA-L   DISTIL-L   MIASMA-L
BARBEL-L   EPOCHA-L   MINIMA-L
CAMERA-L   FASCIA-L   NATURA-L
CAPITA-L   FEMORA-L   NOMINA-L
CENTRA-L   FULFIL-L   OPTIMA-L
CHANCE-L   GENERA-L   ORBITA-L
CHROMY-L   INSTAL-L   RETINA-L
COLONE-L   INSTIL-L   SALIVA-L
CORNEA-L   LATERA-L   STADIA-L
CORONA-L   LEXICA-L   STIGMA-L
CRESTA-L   LINGUA-L   TRIVIA-L
CUBICA-L   MAXIMA-L

Seven letters to eight

ALLUVIA-L   CRIMINA-L   MINUTIA-L

AMPHORA-L   ENTHRAL-L   PERINEA-L

ANTENNA-L   HYDROXY-L   PERSONA-L

BRACHIA-L   IMPERIA-L   RESIDUA-L

BRIMFUL-L   INERTIA-L   SPECTRA-L

CAROUSE-L   MALARIA-L   STAMINA-L

CEREBRA-L   MANDRIL-L   VISCERA-L

CORPORA-L   MARSHAL-L

Blockers

It is useful to know which words are blockers and can't therefore be extended before or after. You may want to play a blocker that your opponent can't extend, or you may want to avoid playing a blocker because you want to keep the board open.

L

Some three-letter blockers beginning with L

LOX   LUZ

Some four-letter blockers beginning with L

LACY   LEVY   LEWD   LYNX

Some five-letter blockers beginning with L
(except words ending in '-ED', '-J', '-S', '-X', '-Y' or '-Z')

LAXER	LEISH	LURCH
LEANT	LIVID	LURID
LEAPT	LOYAL	LYNCH
LEASH	LUCID	

Some six-letter blockers beginning with L
(except words ending in '-ED', '-J', '-S', '-X', '-Y' or '-Z')

LACTIC	LAYMAN	LINEAR
LAKISH	LAYMEN	LIVEST
LAMEST	LEARNT	LOOSER
LARGER	LEFTER	LOUCHE
LARVAE	LEGMAN	LOUDER
LARVAL	LEWDER	LUBING
LAWFUL	LIMBIC	LURING
LAWMAN	LIMPID	
LAXEST	LINEAL	

L

Bonus words

Bonus words on your rack can be hard to spot, especially for the less experienced player. One way to help find them is by using prefixes and suffixes.

Many larger words include a common prefix or suffix – remembering these and using them where you can is a good way to discover any longer words on your rack, including any potential bonus words. The key suffixes to remember beginning with L are -LAND, -LESS, -LET, -LIKE, -LOGY and -LY.

Some words ending with -LAND
Seven-letter words

BAD-LAND	HIE-LAND	NOR-LAND
BOG-LAND	HOL-LAND	OUT-LAND
DRY-LAND	LAW-LAND	SUN-LAND
FEN-LAND	LOW-LAND	WET-LAND
GAR-LAND	MID-LAND	

Eight-letter words

BACK-LAND	DUNE-LAND	HOME-LAND
BOOK-LAND	FARM-LAND	LAKE-LAND
BUSH-LAND	FLAT-LAND	MAIN-LAND
CLUB-LAND	GANG-LAND	MOOR-LAND
CROP-LAND	HEAD-LAND	OVER-LAND
DOCK-LAND	HIGH-LAND	PARK-LAND

L

PEAT-LAND	SHET-LAND	WILD-LAND
PINE-LAND	SNOW-LAND	WOOD-LAND
PORT-LAND	TIDE-LAND	YARD-LAND

Some words ending with -LESS
Seven-letter words

AGE-LESS	GOD-LESS	LEG-LESS
AIM-LESS	GUN-LESS	MAP-LESS
AIR-LESS	GUT-LESS	RIB-LESS
ARM-LESS	HAP-LESS	SEX-LESS
ART-LESS	HAT-LESS	SUN-LESS
BAG-LESS	IRE-LESS	USE-LESS
EAR-LESS	JOB-LESS	WIT-LESS
END-LESS	JOY-LESS	ZIP-LESS
EYE-LESS	LAW-LESS	

Eight-letter words

BACK-LESS	GAIN-LESS	PEER-LESS
BONE-LESS	GOAL-LESS	REST-LESS
CARE-LESS	HAIR-LESS	RUTH-LESS
CASH-LESS	HARM-LESS	SEAM-LESS
CHIN-LESS	HEAD-LESS	SEED-LESS
CLUE-LESS	HELP-LESS	SELF-LESS
CORD-LESS	LIFE-LESS	TACT-LESS
DEBT-LESS	LIST-LESS	TAIL-LESS
FACE-LESS	LOVE-LESS	TIME-LESS
FEAR-LESS	MIND-LESS	WIRE-LESS
FLAW-LESS	NAME-LESS	
FORM-LESS	PAIN-LESS	

L

Some words ending with -LET
Seven-letter words

BOOK-LET	NOTE-LET	SING-LET
COUP-LET	OVER-LET	SKIL-LET
DOUB-LET	RING-LET	STAR-LET
EPAU-LET	RIVU-LET	TART-LET
LAKE-LET	ROOT-LET	TRIO-LET
LEAF-LET	SCAR-LET	
NECK-LET	SERV-LET	

Eight-letter words

BRACE-LET	GLOBU-LET	UNDER-LET
COVER-LET	PAMPH-LET	VALVE-LET
FRUIT-LET	PISTO-LET	
GAUNT-LET	PLATE-LET	

Some words ending with -LIKE
Seven-letter words

APE-LIKE	GOD-LIKE	TOY-LIKE
BAT-LIKE	HOG-LIKE	WAR-LIKE
CAT-LIKE	MAN-LIKE	WAX-LIKE
DIS-LIKE	MIS-LIKE	WIG-LIKE
DOG-LIKE	POD-LIKE	
FAN-LIKE	SKY-LIKE	

L

Eight-letter words

AUNT-LIKE	HAWK-LIKE	REED-LIKE
BEAR-LIKE	HERD-LIKE	ROCK-LIKE
BIRD-LIKE	KING-LIKE	SILK-LIKE
CLAW-LIKE	LADY-LIKE	SWAN-LIKE
DOME-LIKE	LIFE-LIKE	TWIG-LIKE
FISH-LIKE	LORD-LIKE	VICE-LIKE
GAME-LIKE	MAZE-LIKE	WHIP-LIKE
GERM-LIKE	OVEN-LIKE	WOLF-LIKE

Some words ending with -LOGY
Seven-letter words

ANA-LOGY	GEO-LOGY	URO-LOGY
APO-LOGY	NEO-LOGY	ZOO-LOGY
BIO-LOGY	TRI-LOGY	
ECO-LOGY	UFO-LOGY	

Eight-letter words

AERO-LOGY	ONTO-LOGY	TYPO-LOGY
AUTO-LOGY	PYRO-LOGY	VENO-LOGY
HOMO-LOGY	SINO-LOGY	VIRO-LOGY
IDEO-LOGY	THEO-LOGY	
ONCO-LOGY	TOPO-LOGY	

Some words ending with -LY
Seven-letter words

ACUTE-LY

AGILE-LY

AWFUL-LY

BEAST-LY

BLACK-LY

BLANK-LY

BLUNT-LY

BRAVE-LY

BROAD-LY

CHEAP-LY

CHIEF-LY

CLEAR-LY

CRACK-LY

DAZED-LY

DEATH-LY

EAGER-LY

ELDER-LY

FAINT-LY

FALSE-LY

FLUID-LY

FRESH-LY

GHOST-LY

GREAT-LY

GROSS-LY

HARSH-LY

IDEAL-LY

INEPT-LY

JOINT-LY

LARGE-LY

LEGAL-LY

LITHE-LY

LOCAL-LY

MISER-LY

MONTH-LY

MUTED-LY

NASAL-LY

NIGHT-LY

ORDER-LY

PLAIN-LY

PRICK-LY

QUICK-LY

QUIET-LY

RAPID-LY

RIGHT-LY

ROUGH-LY

SHAPE-LY

SIGHT-LY

SMART-LY

SOUND-LY

STATE-LY

STERN-LY

TACIT-LY

TENSE-LY

TOTAL-LY

TOUGH-LY

TRICK-LY

TWINK-LY

USUAL-LY

UTTER-LY

VAGUE-LY

VIRAL-LY

WEIRD-LY

WORLD-LY

L

Eight-letter words

ABRUPT-LY	GINGER-LY	PROPER-LY
ABSURD-LY	HEATED-LY	QUAINT-LY
ACTIVE-LY	HEAVEN-LY	RECENT-LY
AUGUST-LY	INSANE-LY	REMOTE-LY
BENIGN-LY	JOYFUL-LY	SCARCE-LY
BOYISH-LY	KNIGHT-LY	SECOND-LY
BRUTAL-LY	LAWFUL-LY	SECURE-LY
CANDID-LY	MANFUL-LY	SOLEMN-LY
CASUAL-LY	MANNER-LY	TRIBAL-LY
DEMURE-LY	MANUAL-LY	TURGID-LY
DIRECT-LY	MENTAL-LY	UNEVEN-LY
ENTIRE-LY	MINUTE-LY	UNFAIR-LY
EXPERT-LY	NATIVE-LY	VERBAL-LY
FACIAL-LY	ONWARD-LY	WESTER-LY
FORMAL-LY	PATENT-LY	WINTER-LY
FRIEND-LY	PRIMAL-LY	WOODEN-LY

Unusual letter combinations

If you have an unusual combination of letters on your rack, or want to impress your opponent with an unusual word, a few words from World English can come in handy.

Australian words

LOPPY	man employed to do maintenance work on a ranch
LOWAN	ground-dwelling bird

Canadian words

LOGAN   backwater
LOONIE   Canadian dollar coin with loon bird on one face

Hindi words

LAKH   100,000
LANGUR   arboreal monkey
LASSI   yoghurt drink
LATHI   long heavy stick used as a weapon
LUNGI   long piece of cloth worn as loincloth or turban

South African words

LEGUAAN   large monitor lizard

Urdu words

LASCAR   sailor from the East Indies

L

Handy Hint: Do Your Homework

A game of Scrabble can go either way and a less prepared player will always be at a disadvantage. A few simple steps can improve your chances before even starting the game, for example:

• Learn two and three-letter words, especially those with a tile worth 4 or more points (FHJKQVWXYZ), for scoring well in tight situations and milking the premium squares

• Don't forget using all your letters at once gets you a 50-point bonus

M ₃

Essential info
Value: 3 points
Number in set: 2

M is a good letter for forming short words as it begins a two-letter word with every vowel, as well as with Y and with another M. M combines well with power tiles X and Z: MAX, MIX and MUX (an old American word meaning to make a mess of something) are all worth 12 points and MIZ (informal short form of misery) is worth 14. It is also worth remembering the three-letter words ending in W: MAW, MEW and MOW (8 points each).

Two-letter words beginning with M

MA	MI	MO	MY
ME	MM	MU	

Some three-letter words beginning with M

MAA	MED	MIC	MOC	MOT
MAC	MEE	MID	MOD	MOU
MAE	MEG	MIG	MOE	MOY
MAG	MEL	MIL	MOG	MOZ
MAK	MEM	MIM	MOI	MUN
MAL	MEU	MIR	MOL	MUT
MAM	MEW	MIZ	MOM	MUX
MAW	MHO	MNA	MON	MYC
MAX	MIB	MOA	MOR	

Hooks

Hooking requires a subtle change in a player's thought process, in that they must look at words already on the board without becoming distracted by their pronunciation.

Some front-hooks

Two letters to three

M-AA	M-EE	M-OM
M-AD	M-EL	M-ON
M-AE	M-EM	M-OO
M-AG	M-EN	M-OP
M-AL	M-ES	M-OR
M-AM	M-ET	M-OS
M-AN	M-HO	M-OU
M-AR	M-ID	M-OW
M-AS	M-IS	M-OY
M-AT	M-NA	M-UG
M-AW	M-OB	M-UM
M-AX	M-OD	M-UN
M-AY	M-OE	M-US
M-ED	M-OI	M-UT

Three letters to four

M-ACE	M-AIN	M-AMA
M-ACH	M-AIR	M-ANE
M-AGE	M-AKE	M-ANY
M-AID	M-ALE	M-ARE
M-AIL	M-ALL	M-ARK
M-AIM	M-ALT	M-ART

M-ARY	M-ESS	M-OLE
M-ASH	M-ETA	M-ONO
M-ASK	M-ETH	M-OON
M-ASS	M-ICE	M-OOR
M-ATE	M-IFF	M-OOT
M-EAN	M-ILK	M-OPE
M-EAT	M-ILL	M-ORE
M-EEK	M-INK	M-ORT
M-ELD	M-IRE	M-OWN
M-ELL	M-IRK	M-ULE
M-ELT	M-ISO	M-UMP
M-EME	M-OAT	M-UMU
M-EMO	M-ODE	M-USE
M-END	M-OKE	M-UTE
M-ERE	M-OLD	

Four letters to five

M-ACED	M-AXIS	M-ORAL
M-ACER	M-ETIC	M-OSES
M-ACHE	M-IFFY	M-OTTO
M-AGMA	M-IRED	M-OUCH
M-AMBO	M-ITCH	M-OULD
M-ANGA	M-ODAL	M-OURN
M-ANNA	M-OLDY	M-OUST
M-ANTA	M-OLLA	M-OVER
M-ARCH	M-ONER	M-OWED
M-ASHY	M-ONIE	M-OWER
M-AWED	M-OOSE	M-USED
M-AXED	M-OPED	M-USER
M-AXES	M-OPUS	

M

Five letters to six

M-ACERS	M-ASKED	M-ISLED
M-ACING	M-ASKER	M-ITHER
M-ADDED	M-ASTER	M-OCKER
M-ADDER	M-AWING	M-OILED
M-ADMAN	M-AXING	M-OILER
M-ADMEN	M-EAGER	M-OLDER
M-AGISM	M-EAGRE	M-OLLIE
M-AIDED	M-EANED	M-OPING
M-AILED	M-EASED	M-ORGAN
M-AIMED	M-EASLE	M-ORGUE
M-AIMER	M-ELDER	M-ORRIS
M-AKING	M-EMBER	M-OTHER
M-ALIGN	M-ENDED	M-OUGHT
M-ALLOW	M-ENDER	M-OUPED
M-AMMON	M-ERING	M-OUTER
M-ANGEL	M-ESSES	M-OWING
M-ANGER	M-ESTER	M-OZZIE
M-ANGLE	M-ETHOS	M-UDDER
M-ANTIC	M-ETHYL	M-UGGED
M-ANTIS	M-ETTLE	M-UMBLE
M-ANTRA	M-ICKLE	M-UMPED
M-ARKED	M-ILLER	M-UNIFY
M-ARROW	M-INGLE	M-UNITE
M-ASCOT	M-INION	M-USHER
M-ASHED	M-INTER	M-USING
M-ASHES	M-IRING	M-UTTER

M

Six letters to seven

M-ADDING	M-ASKING	M-OPUSES
M-AGNATE	M-EANING	M-ORALLY
M-AIDING	M-EARING	M-ORPHIC
M-AILING	M-EASING	M-OUCHED
M-AIMING	M-ELDING	M-OUCHES
M-ANGLED	M-ENDING	M-OULDER
M-ANGLER	M-ETHANE	M-OUPING
M-ARCHED	M-ETHOXY	M-OUSTED
M-ARCHER	M-ETTLED	M-OUTHER
M-ARCHES	M-ICKLER	M-OZZIES
M-ARGENT	M-IFFIER	M-UGGING
M-ARKING	M-ITCHED	M-ULLING
M-ARROWY	M-OILING	M-UMPING
M-ASHIER	M-OMENTA	M-UNITED
M-ASHING	M-ONEYER	M-USEFUL

Seven letters to eight

M-ACERATE	M-EAGERLY	M-OORIEST
M-ADWOMAN	M-ENOLOGY	M-ORALISM
M-ADWOMEN	M-ERISTIC	M-ORALIST
M-AGISTER	M-ETHANOL	M-ORALITY
M-AIDLESS	M-ETHOXYL	M-ORATORY
M-ALIGNED	M-ETHYLIC	M-UNIFIED
M-ALIGNER	M-ICKLEST	M-UNITING
M-ANGLING	M-IFFIEST	M-UNITION
M-ARCHING	M-ISOGAMY	M-UTTERED
M-ARRIAGE	M-ITCHING	M-UTTERER
M-ARROWED	M-OATLIKE	
M-ASHIEST	M-OMENTUM	

Some end-hooks
Two letters to three

AI-M	HE-M	MI-M	SI-M
AR-M	HI-M	MO-M	SO-M
BA-M	HM-M	MU-M	TA-M
DA-M	HO-M	NA-M	TO-M
DI-M	IS-M	NO-M	UM-M
DO-M	JA-M	OH-M	WE-M
EL-M	KA-M	OO-M	YA-M
FE-M	LA-M	PA-M	YO-M
GU-M	MA-M	PO-M	YU-M
HA-M	ME-M	RE-M	

Three letters to four

BAL-M	FIR-M	MUM-M	SOW-M
BAR-M	FOR-M	NEE-M	SPA-M
BOO-M	FRO-M	NOR-M	TEA-M
BOR-M	GAU-M	PAL-M	TEE-M
CHA-M	GOR-M	PER-M	THE-M
COO-M	HAE-M	PLU-M	TOO-M
COR-M	HAW-M	PRE-M	WAR-M
DEE-M	HER-M	PRO-M	WAS-M
DOO-M	IDE-M	ROO-M	WEE-M
DOR-M	LEA-M	SEA-M	WHA-M
FAR-M	LOO-M	SEE-M	WHO-M
FER-M	MAL-M	SHA-M	ZOO-M
FIL-M	MAR-M	SKI-M	

M

403

Four letters to five

ABRI-M	FLAM-M	MAXI-M	SATE-M
ABYS-M	FLEA-M	MINI-M	SEIS-M
ALAR-M	FORA-M	MODE-M	SHAW-M
BREE-M	GOLE-M	PASH-M	SPAS-M
BROO-M	HAKA-M	PURI-M	STUM-M
CHAR-M	HARE-M	REAL-M	THAR-M
CHAS-M	HAUL-M	REAR-M	THRU-M
DENI-M	MALA-M	RETE-M	TOTE-M

Five letters to six

BALSA-M	DODGE-M	MURRA-M	SHTUM-M
BESEE-M	LINGA-M	MUTIS-M	SPIRE-M
CENTU-M	MALIS-M	PARTI-M	TELES-M
CHIAS-M	MERIS-M	PURIS-M	YOGIS-M
CONDO-M	MESTO-M	SADIS-M	
COPAL-M	MONTE-M	SCRAW-M	

Six letters to seven

ANIMIS-M	GOPURA-M	MISTER-M
BUCKRA-M	MANTRA-M	PREWAR-M
FASCIS-M	MISSEE-M	SENSIS-M

Seven letters to eight

CLASSIS-M	FINALIS-M	JIHADIS-M
CYMBALO-M	JEHADIS-M	TITANIS-M

M

Three-letter blocker beginning with M
MUX

Some four-letter blockers beginning with M

MADE	MAZY	MONY	MOZZ
MANY	MINX	MOPY	
MARY	MIXY	MOSH	
MATY	MOBY	MOWN	

M

Some five-letter blockers beginning with M
(except words ending in '-ED', '-J', '-S', '-X', '-Y' or '-Z')

MACHI	MENSH	MUCHO
MARCH	MERCH	MULCH
MARIA	MICRA	MULSH
MAYAN	MITCH	MUNCH
MEANT	MOOSE	MUTER

Some six-letter blockers beginning with M
(except words ending in '-ED', '-J', '-S', '-X', '-Y' or '-Z')

MACING	MEEKER	MIXING
MADMAN	MEIKLE	MODISH
MADMEN	MEREST	MODULI
MAGYAR	MERMAN	MONACT
MAINER	MERMEN	MOOING
MALIBU	METING	MOPIER
MANATU	MEWING	MOPING
MANFUL	MILDER	MORBID
MANTIC	MILKEN	MORISH
MAOMAO	MIMING	MURKER
MATIER	MINIER	MUTEST
MAXING	MIRING	MUTING
MAYEST	MISDID	MYSELF
MAYHAP	MISLIT	MYTHIC
MAZIER	MITRAL	
MEAGER	MIXIER	

M is for Mnemonic

You may find it useful to use memory aids when trying to remember long lists of Scrabble words. Some more experienced players prefer to remember words in their entirety, but for beginners a mnemonic or two can be a great help. Eg, the initial letters of the words in the mnemonic: Please Don't Holler So, Be Nice For Once gives the front hooks for the two-letter word OH.

Bonus words

Bonus words on your rack can be hard to spot, especially for the less experienced player. One way to help find them is by using prefixes and suffixes.

Many larger words include a common prefix or suffix – remembering these and using them where you can is a good way to discover any longer words on your rack, including any potential bonus words. The key prefixes to remember beginning with M are MAN- and MIS- and the key suffixes are -MAN and -MEN.

Some words beginning with MAN-
Seven-letter words

MAN-AGED	MAN-HOLE	MAN-LIKE
MAN-AGER	MAN-HOOD	MAN-MADE
MAN-DATE	MAN-HUNT	MAN-TIDS
MAN-GING	MAN-JACK	MAN-TRAP
MAN-GLED	MAN-KIER	MAN-URES
MAN-GOES	MAN-KIND	MAN-WARD
MAN-GOLD	MAN-LIER	

Eight-letter words

MAN-AGING	MAN-FULLY	MAN-SWORN
MAN-DATED	MAN-GROVE	MAN-URIAL
MAN-DRAKE	MAN-POWER	
MAN-DRILL	MAN-SHIFT	

Some words beginning with MIS-

Seven-letter words

MIS-ALLY

MIS-CALL

MIS-CAST

MIS-CODE

MIS-CUED

MIS-DEED

MIS-DIAL

MIS-DOER

MIS-FILE

MIS-FIRE

MIS-FITS

MIS-GIVE

MIS-HAPS

MIS-HEAR

MIS-LAID

MIS-LEAD

MIS-MARK

MIS-NAME

MIS-READ

MIS-RULE

MIS-SILE

MIS-SING

MIS-STEP

MIS-TAKE

MIS-TIME

MIS-TING

MIS-TOOK

MIS-USED

Eight-letter words

MIS-ALIGN

MIS-APPLY

MIS-BEGOT

MIS-CARRY

MIS-CHIEF

MIS-CHOSE

MIS-COLOR

MIS-COUNT

MIS-FILED

MIS-FIRED

MIS-GIVEN

MIS-GUIDE

MIS-HEARD

MIS-JUDGE

MIS-MATCH

MIS-PLACE

MIS-PRICE

MIS-PRINT

MIS-QUOTE

MIS-RULED

MIS-SABLE

MIS-SHAPE

MIS-SPEAK

MIS-SPELL

MIS-SPEND

MIS-SPOKE

MIS-TAKEN

MIS-TIMED

MIS-TREAT

MIS-TRESS

MIS-TRIAL

MIS-TRUST

MIS-TRUTH

MIS-USAGE

MIS-USING

Some words ending with -MAN

Seven-letter words

AUTO-MAN
BATS-MAN
BIRD-MAN
BOAT-MAN
BOND-MAN
BUSH-MAN
CAVE-MAN
COAL-MAN
CREW-MAN
DEAD-MAN
DOOR-MAN
DUST-MAN
FIRE-MAN

FOOT-MAN
FORE-MAN
FREE-MAN
FROG-MAN
HANG-MAN
HARD-MAN
HEAD-MAN
JAZZ-MAN
JURY-MAN
KINS-MAN
LENS-MAN
LINE-MAN
MAIL-MAN

MILK-MAN
NEWS-MAN
OARS-MAN
OTTO-MAN
PLOW-MAN
POST-MAN
REPO-MAN
SAND-MAN
SHOW-MAN
SNOW-MAN
SWAG-MAN
WING-MAN
WORK-MAN

Eight-letter words

BAILS-MAN
BLUES-MAN
BOATS-MAN
BOGEY-MAN
BONDS-MAN
BRINK-MAN
CHAIR-MAN
CLANS-MAN
CLASS-MAN
COACH-MAN
EARTH-MAN
EVERY-MAN
FERRY-MAN

FRESH-MAN
FRONT-MAN
GAMES-MAN
HANDY-MAN
HELMS-MAN
HENCH-MAN
HERDS-MAN
HUNTS-MAN
KNIFE-MAN
LANDS-MAN
LINES-MAN
MARKS-MAN
NOBLE-MAN

POINT-MAN
RIFLE-MAN
SALES-MAN
SHORE-MAN
SOUND-MAN
SPACE-MAN
STUNT-MAN
SWORD-MAN
TALIS-MAN
TRASH-MAN
WATCH-MAN
WHEEL-MAN
WOODS-MAN

M

Some words ending with -MEN

Seven-letter words

ABDO-MEN	DOOR-MEN	LENS-MEN
ALBU-MEN	DUST-MEN	LINE-MEN
BATS-MEN	FOOT-MEN	RAIL-MEN
BIRD-MEN	FORE-MEN	REGI-MEN
BITU-MEN	FREE-MEN	REPO-MEN
BOAT-MEN	FROG-MEN	SHIP-MEN
BOOK-MEN	HANG-MEN	SHOW-MEN
BUSH-MEN	HARD-MEN	SNOW-MEN
CAVE-MEN	HEAD-MEN	SWAG-MEN
COAL-MEN	HILL-MEN	WING-MEN
CREW-MEN	JAZZ-MEN	WORK-MEN
DEAD-MEN	KINS-MEN	

Eight-letter words

BAILS-MEN	GAMES-MEN	RIFLE-MEN
BARGE-MEN	HANDY-MEN	ROADS-MEN
BLUES-MEN	HELMS-MEN	SALES-MEN
BOATS-MEN	HENCH-MEN	SHORE-MEN
BONDS-MEN	HERDS-MEN	SOUND-MEN
BOOGY-MEN	HORSE-MEN	SPACE-MEN
BRINK-MEN	HUNTS-MEN	STUNT-MEN
CHAIR-MEN	KNIFE-MEN	SUPER-MEN
CLANS-MEN	LINES-MEN	WATCH-MEN
COACH-MEN	MARKS-MEN	WHEEL-MEN
DOORS-MEN	MERRY-MEN	WOODS-MEN
EVERY-MEN	NOBLE-MEN	
FERRY-MEN	POINT-MEN	
FREED-MEN	RANCH-MEN	

Unusual letter combinations

If you have an unusual combination of letters on your rack, or want to impress your opponent with an unusual word, a few words from World English can come in handy.

Australian words

MALLEE	low shrubby eucalyptus tree
MARRI	type of eucalyptus
MIDDY	middle-sized glass of beer
MILKO	milkman
MOLOCH	spiny lizard
MOPOKE	small spotted owl
MOZ	hoodoo or hex
MUGGA	eucalyptus tree with pink flowers
MULGA	acacia shrub
MULLOCK	waste material from a mine
MUSO	musician
MYALL	acacia with hard scented wood
MYXO	myxomatosis

Canadian words

MUCKAMUCK	food
MUKTUK	beluga skin used as food

Hindi words

MACHAN	platform used in tiger hunting
MAHOUT	elephant driver
MAHSEER	large freshwater fish
MANDI	big market
MANDIR	Hindu or Jain temple
MAUND	unit of weight

M

MELA	cultural or religious festival
MOHUR	old gold coin
MONAL	Asian pheasant
MORCHA	hostile demonstration
MRIDANG	drum used in Indian music
MYNAH	tropical starling

New Zealand words

MANUKA	myrtaceous tree
MATAI	evergreen tree
MIHI	ceremonial greeting
MOA	extinct large flightless bird
MOKI	edible sea fish
MOKO	Maori tattoo or tattoo pattern
MOOLOO	person from Waikato
MOPOKE	small spotted owl
MUNGA	army canteen

South African words

MEERKAT	sociable mongoose
MENEER	Mr or Sir
MEVROU	Mrs or Madam
MOOI	pleasing
MUTI	herbal medicine

Urdu words

MAIDAN	open space used for meetings and sports
MASALA	mixed spices ground into a paste
MOOLVI	Muslim doctor of the law

Essential info

Value: 1 points

Number in set: 6

There are six **N** tiles in the Scrabble set, making it one of the most common consonants. N is very useful for short words to facilitate parallel plays as it begins a two-letter word with every vowel except I. While three-letter words beginning with N are common, there are fewer high-scoring ones than you might think. These include NAB (5 points) and NAY, NEW and NOW (all 6 points). N is one of the letters of the RETAIN set and is therefore a good letter to keep if trying to get a bonus word.

Two-letter words beginning with N

NA	NE	NO	NU	NY

Some three-letter words beginning with N

NAE	NED	NIS	NON	NUR
NAH	NEE	NIT	NOO	NYE
NAM	NEF	NIX	NOR	NYS
NAT	NEG	NOB	NOT	
NAW	NEK	NOG	NOX	
NAY	NEP	NOH	NOY	
NEB	NID	NOM	NUB	

Hooks

Hooking requires a subtle change in a player's thought process, in that they must look at words already on the board without becoming distracted by their pronunciation.

Some front-hooks
Two letters to three

N-AB	N-AT	N-ID	N-ON	N-UN
N-AE	N-AW	N-IS	N-OO	N-UR
N-AG	N-AY	N-IT	N-OR	N-US
N-AH	N-ED	N-OB	N-OS	N-UT
N-AM	N-EE	N-OD	N-OW	N-YE
N-AN	N-EF	N-OH	N-OX	
N-AS	N-ET	N-OM	N-OY	

Three letters to four

N-AFF	N-EAT	N-ODE
N-AGA	N-EON	N-ONE
N-AIL	N-ERK	N-OON
N-ANA	N-ESS	N-OPE
N-ANE	N-EST	N-OSE
N-APE	N-EUK	N-OUS
N-ARC	N-EWT	N-OUT
N-ARE	N-ICE	N-OVA
N-ARK	N-ICK	N-OWL
N-ARY	N-ILL	N-OWN
N-AVE	N-ISH	N-OWT
N-EAR	N-ITS	N-UKE

N

Four letters to five

N-ACHE
N-AILS
N-AKED
N-APED
N-ARCO
N-AUNT
N-AVAL
N-AVEL
N-EATH
N-EDDY

N-EMPT
N-EVER
N-EWER
N-ICER
N-ICKY
N-IFFY
N-ODAL
N-OILY
N-OINT
N-OMEN

N-ONCE
N-ONES
N-OOSE
N-OPAL
N-OULD
N-OUPS
N-OVEL
N-OVUM
N-OWED

Five letters to six

N-ABBED
N-AGGER
N-AILED
N-APERY
N-APING
N-APRON
N-ARKED
N-ARROW
N-AUGHT
N-EARED
N-EARLY
N-EATEN

N-EATER
N-EBBED
N-ESSES
N-ESTER
N-ETHER
N-ETTLE
N-EWEST
N-ICHED
N-ICKER
N-ICKLE
N-IMBED
N-ITHER

N-ODDER
N-OGGIN
N-OSIER
N-OTARY
N-OTHER
N-OUGHT
N-UMBER
N-UMPTY
N-UNCLE
N-UTTER

N

Six letters to seven

N-AILING	N-EMESES	N-OVATED
N-APHTHA	N-EMESIS	N-OYESES
N-ARKING	N-EOLITH	N-ULLING
N-ASCENT	N-ETTLED	N-UNDINE
N-ATRIUM	N-ICHING	N-UNHOOD
N-EARING	N-IFFIER	N-UNLIKE
N-EBBING	N-OINTED	N-UNSHIP
N-EDDISH	N-ONUSES	
N-EITHER	N-OOLOGY	

Seven letters to eight

N-AINSELL	N-EARLIER	N-OVATION
N-APERIES	N-ETTLING	N-ULLINGS
N-ARRASES	N-IFFIEST	N-UMBERED
N-ARROWED	N-OINTING	N-YAFFING
N-ATRIUMS	N-OTARIES	

Some end-hooks
Two letters to three

AI-N	DO-N	HE-N	MO-N
AN-N	EA-N	HI-N	MU-N
AW-N	EE-N	HO-N	NA-N
BA-N	ER-N	IN-N	NO-N
BE-N	FA-N	IO-N	NU-N
BI-N	FE-N	KI-N	OO-N
BO-N	GI-N	KO-N	OW-N
DA-N	GO-N	LI-N	PA-N
DE-N	GU-N	MA-N	PE-N
DI-N	HA-N	ME-N	PI-N

RE-N	TA-N	TO-N	WO-N
SI-N	TE-N	UR-N	YE-N
SO-N	TI-N	WE-N	YO-N

Three letters to four

BAR-N	GOO-N	RAI-N
BEE-N	GUR-N	SAW-N
BOO-N	HEW-N	SEE-N
BOR-N	HOO-N	SEW-N
BRA-N	JIN-N	SKI-N
BUR-N	LAW-N	SOW-N
CHI-N	LEA-N	SPA-N
COR-N	LIE-N	TEE-N
DAW-N	LOO-N	THE-N
DEE-N	MOA-N	TOO-N
DOO-N	MOO-N	TOR-N
DOW-N	MOR-N	TOW-N
EAR-N	MOW-N	UPO-N
EVE-N	NOO-N	YAR-N
FAW-N	OPE-N	YAW-N
FER-N	PAW-N	

N

Handy Hint

Use a dictionary when playing Scrabble to check the validity of words when a play is challenged (and to avoid any arguments!). We recommend Collins Official Scrabble Dictionary, where you will find the meanings for all the words listed in this book.

Four letters to five

BLOW-N	GROW-N	SARI-N
BRAW-N	HALO-N	SATI-N
BROW-N	HERO-N	SHAW-N
CHAI-N	HOSE-N	SHOW-N
CLOW-N	HUMA-N	SIRE-N
COVE-N	KNOW-N	SPAW-N
CROW-N	LADE-N	SPUR-N
DEMO-N	LEAR-N	STOW-N
DJIN-N	LIKE-N	TAKE-N
DOVE-N	LINE-N	TOKE-N
DOZE-N	LOGO-N	TWEE-N
DRAW-N	MAYA-N	VEGA-N
FLOW-N	RAVE-N	WAKE-N
FROW-N	RIPE-N	WIDE-N
GIVE-N	RISE-N	WOKE-N
GNAW-N	RIVE-N	WOVE-N
GREE-N	ROMA-N	YEAR-N

Five letters to six

ALTER-N	CARBO-N	GRAVE-N
ARISE-N	CARVE-N	HASTE-N
ASTER-N	CAVER-N	HEAVE-N
AWAKE-N	CHOSE-N	HOOVE-N
AWOKE-N	CLOVE-N	INTER-N
BABOO-N	COMMO-N	LARGE-N
BARRE-N	CRAVE-N	LEAVE-N
BITTE-N	DRIVE-N	LOOSE-N
BRAZE-N	FROZE-N	MACRO-N
BROKE-N	GLUTE-N	MEDIA-N

MICRO-N ROTTE-N STRAW-N
MODER-N SCREE-N STREW-N
NORMA-N SHAKE-N STROW-N
PHOTO-N SHAMA-N SYLVA-N
PROVE-N SHAPE-N THRAW-N
RATIO-N SHAVE-N THROW-N
RESEE-N SPOKE-N WHITE-N
RESEW-N STOLE-N WICCA-N
RESOW-N STONE-N

Six letters to seven

ACKNOW-N PATTER-N SMIDGE-N
ALKALI-N POSTER-N STONER-N
BRONZE-N PREWAR-N STRIVE-N
CAPITA-N PROTEA-N STROKE-N
CHASTE-N PROTEI-N TERTIA-N
COARSE-N REDRAW-N THRIVE-N
EASTER-N REFLOW-N TRUDGE-N
EMBRYO-N REGIME-N UNDRAW-N
ENVIRO-N REGIVE-N UNWOVE-N
GELATI-N REGROW-N UPGROW-N
HOARSE-N RERISE-N UPRISE-N
JIGSAW-N RESHOW-N UPTAKE-N
MEDUSA-N RETAKE-N URANIA-N
NUCLEI-N REWAKE-N UTOPIA-N
OUTSEE-N REWOVE-N WESTER-N
PAPAYA-N RIPSAW-N WRITHE-N
PASTER-N SIERRA-N ZITHER-N

N

Seven letters to eight

AQUARIA-N
ARCADIA-N
AURELIA-N
BEREAVE-N
BESPOKE-N
BESTREW-N
BOHEMIA-N
CODRIVE-N
COLLAGE-N
DEFROZE-N
DILUVIA-N
DISLIKE-N
ELECTRO-N
ENGRAVE-N
ENLARGE-N
FLYBLOW-N
FORESEE-N

FORGIVE-N
FORSAKE-N
HACKSAW-N
LEATHER-N
MAGNETO-N
MALARIA-N
MISDRAW-N
MISGIVE-N
MISGROW-N
MISKNOW-N
MISTAKE-N
NORTHER-N
OUTDRAW-N
OUTFLOW-N
OUTGIVE-N
OUTGROW-N
OUTTAKE-N

OVERSEE-N
PANACEA-N
PARAZOA-N
PARTAKE-N
PRESHOW-N
QUARTER-N
REAWAKE-N
REFROZE-N
REGALIA-N
RESHAVE-N
ROSARIA-N
RUBELLA-N
SLATTER-N
SOUTHER-N
UNBROKE-N
UNFROZE-N
UNSPOKE-N

N

Blockers

It is useful to know which words are blockers and can't therefore be extended before or after. You may want to play a blocker that your opponent can't extend, or you may want to avoid playing a blocker because you want to keep the board open.

Some three-letter blockers beginning with N

NAE	NOH	NTH
NAH	NOX	

Some four-letter blockers beginning with N

NAVY	NOPE	NOUS
NESS	NOSH	
NIXY	NOSY	

Some five-letter blockers beginning with N
(except words ending in '-ED', '-J', '-S', '-X', '-Y' or '-Z')

NATAL	NEWER	NOMEN
NAVAL	NICER	NUTSO
NEVER	NOHOW	

Some six-letter blockers beginning with N
(except words ending in '-ED', '-J', '-S', '-X', '-Y' or '-Z')

NAFFER	NEWEST	NONMEN
NAIFER	NEWISH	NONPAR
NAIVER	NICEST	NORDIC
NAPING	NICISH	NOSIER
NEARER	NIGHER	NOSTRO
NEATER	NITRIC	NOTING
NEBISH	NIXING	NOTOUR
NERVAL	NOBLER	NOUNAL
NETHER	NONFAT	NOWISE
NEURAL	NONMAN	NUKING

N

N

Bonus words

Bonus words on your rack can be hard to spot, especially for the less experienced player. One way to help find them is by using prefixes and suffixes.

Many larger words include a common prefix or suffix – remembering these and using them where you can is a good way to discover any longer words on your rack, including any potential bonus words. The key suffix to remember beginning with N is -NESS.

Some words ending with -NESS
Seven-letter words

APT-NESS	HIP-NESS	ONE-NESS
BAD-NESS	HOT-NESS	RAW-NESS
BIG-NESS	ICI-NESS	RED-NESS
COY-NESS	ILL-NESS	SAD-NESS
DIM-NESS	LIO-NESS	SHY-NESS
DRY-NESS	LOW-NESS	WET-NESS
FAT-NESS	MAD-NESS	WIT-NESS
FIT-NESS	NEW-NESS	WRY-NESS
FUL-NESS	ODD-NESS	
HAR-NESS	OLD-NESS	

Eight-letter words

AGED-NESS

ARCH-NESS

BALD-NESS

BARE-NESS

BOLD-NESS

BUSI-NESS

CALM-NESS

COLD-NESS

COSI-NESS

CURT-NESS

DAMP-NESS

DARK-NESS

DEAF-NESS

DEFT-NESS

DEMO-NESS

EVIL-NESS

FAIR-NESS

FIRM-NESS

FOND-NESS

GLAD-NESS

GOOD-NESS

GREY-NESS

HARD-NESS

HIGH-NESS

HUGE-NESS

IDLE-NESS

KIND-NESS

LATE-NESS

LIKE-NESS

MEAN-NESS

MILD-NESS

MUCH-NESS

NEAT-NESS

NUMB-NESS

OPEN-NESS

PALE-NESS

POSH-NESS

PURE-NESS

RARE-NESS

RIPE-NESS

SAME-NESS

SICK-NESS

SLOW-NESS

SURE-NESS

TALL-NESS

TAME-NESS

TAUT-NESS

VAST-NESS

WARM-NESS

WEAK-NESS

WELL-NESS

WILD-NESS

N

Unusual letter combinations

If you have an unusual combination of letters on your rack, or want to impress your opponent with an unusual word, a few words from World English can come in handy.

Australian words

NARDOO   cloverlike fern

NEDDY   horse

NOAH	shark
NONG	stupid or incompetent person
NUMBAT	small marsupial with long snout

Canadian words

| NANOOK | polar bear |

Hindi words

NAUCH	intricate Indian dance
NAWAB	Muslim prince in India
NEEM	large tree
NILGAI	large Indian antelope
NULLAH	stream or drain
NUMDAH	coarse felt

New Zealand words

NGAIO	small tree
NGATI	tribe or clan
NIKAU	palm tree

South African words

NAARTJIE	tangerine
NEK	mountain pass
NKOSI	master or chief

N

O

Essential info
Value: 1 point
Number in set: 8

O is a common letter in Scrabble, with eight tiles in the set. It forms a two-letter word with every other vowel except for A, and is useful when it comes to forming short words in order to score in two directions at once using premium squares, or in tight corners, or for parallel plays, for example OB, OM and OP (4 points each) and OF, OH, OW (5 points each). O also combines well with X to form short words such as OXO (10 points) and OXY (13 points).

Two-letter words beginning with O

OB	OH	OO	OU
OD	OI	OP	OW
OE	OM	OR	OX
OF	ON	OS	OY

Some three-letter words beginning with O

OBA	OHM	OOM	ORC	OUS
OBE	OHO	OON	ORD	OWT
OBI	OIK	OOP	ORF	OXO
OBO	OKA	OOR	ORT	OXY
OCH	ONO	OOT	OSE	OYE
ODA	ONY	OPE	OUD	
OFF	OOF	ORA	OUK	
OFT	OOH	ORB	OUP	

Hooks

Hooking requires a subtle change in a player's thought process, in that they must look at words already on the board without becoming distracted by their pronunciation.

Some front-hooks
Two letters to three

O-AR	O-DE	O-OF	O-RE
O-AT	O-ES	O-OH	O-UP
O-BA	O-HM	O-OM	O-UR
O-BE	O-HO	O-ON	O-US
O-BI	O-KA	O-OP	O-UT
O-BO	O-NE	O-OR	O-WE
O-CH	O-NO	O-OS	O-YE
O-DA	O-NY	O-PE	

Three letters to four

O-ARY	O-GEE	O-PEN
O-BEY	O-INK	O-PUS
O-BIT	O-KAY	O-RAD
O-CHE	O-LEA	O-RES
O-DAH	O-LES	O-SAR
O-DAL	O-LID	O-TIC
O-DOR	O-MEN	O-URN
O-DSO	O-OSE	O-VUM
O-FAY	O-PAL	O-WED
O-GAM	O-PED	O-YES

Four letters to five

O-AKED

O-ARED

O-AVES

O-BANG

O-BOLE

O-CHER

O-DOUR

O-FLAG

O-GIVE

O-GLED

O-HING

O-LIVE

O-LOGY

O-MEGA

O-OBIT

O-OHED

O-OPED

O-OSES

O-PINE

O-PING

O-PIUM

O-RACH

O-RACY

O-RANG

O-RANT

O-RATE

O-READ

O-RIEL

O-SCAR

O-UNCE

O-UNDY

O-VARY

O-VERT

O-VINE

O-VOID

O-WING

O-ZONE

Five letters to six

O-BITER

O-BLAST

O-BLATE

O-BOLUS

O-CELLI

O-EDEMA

O-GAMIC

O-GIVES

O-INKED

O-LINGO

O-LIVER

O-MENED

O-MENTA

O-OHING

O-OLOGY

O-OPING

O-OSIER

O-PALED

O-PENED

O-PINED

O-PUSES

O-RACHE

O-RALLY

O-RANGE

O-RANGY

O-RATED

O-STEAL

O-STENT

O-TITIS

O-UNCES

O-WRIER

O-YESES

O

Six letters to seven

O-CARINA

O-CELLAR

O-CREATE

O-DONATE

O-DORISE

O-DORIZE

O-ESTRAL

O-ESTRUM

O-INKING

O-KIMONO

O-LOGIES

O-MENING

O-MENTAL

O-MENTUM

O-MICRON

O-MIKRON

O-PACIFY

O-PENING

O-PINING

O-PINION

O-POSSUM

O-RANGER

O-RATING

O-RATION

O-ROTUND

O-STRICH

O-UGLIED

O-UGLIES

O-UTMOST

O-VARIES

O-VERBID

O-VERSET

O-WRIEST

O-YESSES

O-ZONATE

Seven letters to eight

O-DORISED

O-DORIZED

O-ECOLOGY

O-EDEMATA

O-ENOLOGY

O-ESTRIOL

O-ESTRONE

O-ESTROUS

O-MISSION

O-MISSIVE

O-OLOGIES

O-OLOGIST

O-RANGIER

O-STOMATE

O-UROLOGY

O-VARIOLE

O-VARIOUS

O-ZONATED

Some end-hooks

Two letters to three

AB-O	EX-O	MO-O	RE-O
AD-O	GI-O	NO-O	TA-O
AG-O	GO-O	OB-O	TO-O
BI-O	HA-O	OH-O	UP-O
BO-O	HO-O	ON-O	WO-O
DO-O	IS-O	OX-O	ZO-O
EM-O	LO-O	PO-O	

Three letters to four

ALS-O	FIN-O	MON-O
ALT-O	HER-O	MUS-O
ANN-O	HOB-O	PES-O
BIT-O	HYP-O	PIS-O
BOH-O	JUD-O	POL-O
BOY-O	KAY-O	RED-O
BUB-O	KIN-O	REG-O
BUD-O	LID-O	REP-O
CAM-O	LIN-O	ROT-O
CAP-O	LIP-O	SAD-O
CIT-O	LOB-O	SAG-O
DAD-O	LOG-O	SOH-O
DIN-O	LOT-O	SOL-O
DOC-O	LUD-O	SUM-O
DOD-O	MAK-O	TAR-O
ECH-O	MAN-O	TOP-O
ERG-O	MAY-O	TOR-O
FAR-O	MEM-O	VEG-O
FID-O	MIC-O	VET-O
FIG-O	MIL-O	VIN-O
FIL-O	MIS-O	WIN-O

O

Four letters to five

AMIN-O	CRED-O	MACH-O
BANC-O	CUFF-O	MANG-O
BARD-O	DECK-O	MENT-O
BASH-O	DING-O	METH-O
BEAN-O	DIPS-O	MEZZ-O
BENT-O	DISC-O	MILK-O
BERK-O	DITT-O	MIME-O
BIFF-O	DRAC-O	MOTT-O
BING-O	DUMB-O	MUCH-O
BOFF-O	FANG-O	NACH-O
BOMB-O	FATS-O	NARC-O
BONG-O	FUNG-O	NUTS-O
BUCK-O	GAMB-O	PANT-O
BUFF-O	GECK-O	PEST-O
BUNK-O	GISM-O	PHON-O
BURR-O	GUAN-O	PHOT-O
CACA-O	GUST-O	PIAN-O
CAME-O	HALL-O	PINK-O
CARB-O	HELL-O	PINT-O
CELL-O	HILL-O	PONG-O
CHIA-O	HOWS-O	POSH-O
CHIC-O	HULL-O	POTT-O
CHIN-O	JELL-O	PRIM-O
CHOC-O	JOCK-O	PROM-O
COMB-O	KEEN-O	PROS-O
COMM-O	LASS-O	PULA-O
COMP-O	LENT-O	PUNT-O
COND-O	LIMB-O	RODE-O
CORN-O	LING-O	RUMP-O

SANT-O	TANG-O	VIDE-O
SICK-O	TEMP-O	WACK-O
SOCK-O	TORS-O	WALD-O
STEN-O	VERS-O	WHAM-O

Five letters to six

AMMON-O	FRANC-O	REECH-O
BILLY-O	HALLO-O	RIGHT-O
BRILL-O	HOLLO-O	ROMAN-O
BRONC-O	HULLO-O	SHACK-O
CARDI-O	LIBER-O	SHEEP-O
CHARR-O	LIVED-O	SOLAN-O
CHEAP-O	MEDIC-O	SPEED-O
CHEER-O	MORPH-O	STERE-O
CHOCK-O	NYMPH-O	STINK-O
CHURR-O	PEDAL-O	THICK-O
CONCH-O	PLONK-O	TOLED-O
CRYPT-O	PREST-O	TRILL-O
DINER-O	PSEUD-O	VIGOR-O
DORAD-O	PSYCH-O	WEIRD-O
DUETT-O	QUART-O	WHACK-O
ERING-O	RABAT-O	WHATS-O
FASCI-O	RANCH-O	

O

Six letters to seven

BANDIT-O	MOMENT-O	RABBIT-O
BATTER-O	NITROS-O	REVERS-O
BRACER-O	PAESAN-O	SECOND-O
BUDGER-O	PAISAN-O	SERRAN-O
CANTIC-O	PAMPER-O	TAMARA-O
CYMBAL-O	PIMENT-O	TYMPAN-O
GRADIN-O	PRIMER-O	VERISM-O
MAGNET-O	PUMMEL-O	WHERES-O

Seven letters to eight

ARMIGER-O	FASCISM-O	PRELUDI-O
CAPITAN-O	FLAMING-O	RANCHER-O
CLASSIC-O	INTAGLI-O	SESTETT-O
COMMAND-O	LEGGIER-O	SOMBRER-O
CONCERT-O	MONTANT-O	STAMPED-O
CORNETT-O	PEEKABO-O	VIGOROS-O
COURANT-O	PERFECT-O	ZECCHIN-O
EXPRESS-O	POLITIC-O	

O

Blockers

It is useful to know which words are blockers and can't therefore be extended before or after. You may want to play a blocker that your opponent can't extend, or you may want to avoid playing a blocker because you want to keep the board open.

Three-letter blocker beginning with O

OXO

Some four-letter blockers beginning with O

OAKY	ONYX	OYEZ
OCCY	ORYX	

Some five-letter blockers beginning with O
(except words ending in '-ED', '-J', '-S', '-X', '-Y' or '-Z')

OATEN	ORGIC	OUTDO
OLEIC	OSSIA	OUTGO

O

Some six-letter blockers beginning with O
(except words ending in '-ED', '-J', '-S', '-X', '-Y' or '-Z')

OAFISH	OILMEN	OUTBYE
OAKIER	OMIGOD	OUTDID
OBESER	ONRUSH	OUTSAT
OBITER	OPTING	OUTSAW
OBTECT	ORBIER	OUTWON
OCTOPI	ORGANA	OWLISH
ODDEST	ORGIAC	OXIDIC
ODDISH	OSTEAL	OZONIC
OGRISH	OSTIAL	
OILMAN	OSTIUM	

Bonus words

Bonus words on your rack can be hard to spot, especially for the less experienced player. One way to help find them is by using prefixes and suffixes.

Many larger words include a common prefix or suffix – remembering these and using them where you can is a good way to discover any longer words on your rack, including any potential bonus words. The key prefixes to remember beginning with O are OUT- and OVER- and the key suffixes are -OID, -OR, -OUS and -OUT.

Some words beginning with OUT-

Seven-letter words

OUT-ACTS

OUT-AGES

OUT-BACK

OUT-BIDS

OUT-CAST

OUT-COME

OUT-CROP

OUT-DOER

OUT-DONE

OUT-DOOR

OUT-DRAW

OUT-EARN

OUT-FALL

OUT-FISH

OUT-FITS

OUT-FLOW

OUT-FOOT

OUT-GAVE

OUT-GOER

OUT-GROW

OUT-GUNS

OUT-GUSH

OUT-KEEP

OUT-LAID

OUT-LAND

OUT-LAST

OUT-LAWS

OUT-LAYS

OUT-LETS

OUT-LIES

OUT-LIVE

OUT-LOOK

OUT-MODE

OUT-PACE

OUT-PLAY

OUT-POST

OUT-PUTS

OUT-RAGE

OUT-RANK

OUT-RIDE

OUT-RUNS

OUT-SELL

OUT-SIDE

OUT-SING

OUT-SIZE

OUT-SOLD

OUT-SPAN

OUT-STAY

OUT-TAKE

OUT-TALK

OUT-VOTE

OUT-WAIT

OUT-WARD

OUT-WITH

OUT-WITS

O

Eight-letter words

OUT-ACTED

OUT-ARGUE

OUT-BOARD

OUT-BOUND

OUT-BREAK

OUT-CHARM

OUT-CLASS

OUT-CRIES

OUT-DANCE

OUT-DATED

OUT-DOING

OUT-DRINK

OUT-FACED

OUT-FENCE

OUT-FIELD

OUT-FLANK

OUT-FOXED

OUT-GOING

OUT-GROWN

OUT-LAWED

OUT-LINED

OUT-MATCH

OUT-PACED

OUT-PRICE

OUT-RAGED

OUT-REACH

OUT-RIDER

OUT-SCORE

OUT-SIDER

OUT-SIZED

OUT-SPEAK

OUT-SPOKE

OUT-STAND

OUT-STARE

OUT-SWEPT

OUT-THINK

OUT-VOICE

OUT-WEIGH

Some words beginning with OVER-
Seven-letter words

OVER-ACT

OVER-AGE

OVER-ALL

OVER-ATE

OVER-AWE

OVER-CUT

OVER-DID

OVER-DUB

OVER-DUE

OVER-EAT

OVER-EGG

OVER-FED

OVER-JOY

OVER-LAP

OVER-LAY

OVER-PAY

OVER-RAN

OVER-SAW

OVER-SEE

OVER-TAX

OVER-USE

Eight-letter words

OVER-ARCH	OVER-GROW	OVER-PAGE
OVER-AWED	OVER-HAND	OVER-PAID
OVER-BEAR	OVER-HANG	OVER-PLAY
OVER-BITE	OVER-HAUL	OVER-RATE
OVER-BRED	OVER-HEAR	OVER-RODE
OVER-BUSY	OVER-HEAT	OVER-RULE
OVER-CAME	OVER-HYPE	OVER-SEEN
OVER-CAST	OVER-IDLE	OVER-SELL
OVER-COAT	OVER-KEEN	OVER-SHOT
OVER-COME	OVER-KILL	OVER-SIZE
OVER-COOK	OVER-LAID	OVER-STAY
OVER-DOES	OVER-LAND	OVER-STEP
OVER-DONE	OVER-LEAF	OVER-TAKE
OVER-DOSE	OVER-LOAD	OVER-TIME
OVER-EASY	OVER-LONG	OVER-TONE
OVER-FEED	OVER-LOOK	OVER-TOOK
OVER-FILL	OVER-LORD	OVER-TURN
OVER-GOES	OVER-PACK	OVER-WORK

O

Some words ending with -OID
Seven-letter words

ADEN-OID
ANDR-OID
COSM-OID
CYST-OID
DELT-OID
DISC-OID

FACT-OID
FUNG-OID
GLOB-OID
HYDR-OID
NEUR-OID
SAUR-OID

SPOR-OID
STER-OID
TABL-OID
THYR-OID
TYPH-OID

Eight-letter words

ALKAL-OID
AMOEB-OID
BLAST-OID
CAMEL-OID
CENTR-OID
DENDR-OID
GROUP-OID
HEMAT-OID
HUMAN-OID
LEMUR-OID

LYMPH-OID
MANAT-OID
MEDUS-OID
MELAN-OID
NEMAT-OID
NUCLE-OID
PARAN-OID
PLASM-OID
POLYP-OID
PSYCH-OID

RESIN-OID
RETIN-OID
RHOMB-OID
SCHIZ-OID
SLEAZ-OID
SPHER-OID
TETAN-OID
VARIC-OID
VIRUS-OID

O

Some words ending with -OR
Seven-letter words

ADAPT-OR

ADVIS-OR

AUDIT-OR

AVIAT-OR

BICOL-OR

CREAT-OR

CURAT-OR

DEBIT-OR

DILUT-OR

EJECT-OR

ELECT-OR

EMPER-OR

ENACT-OR

EQUAT-OR

EXCIT-OR

GRANT-OR

IGNIT-OR

JANIT-OR

NEGAT-OR

OFFER-OR

QUEST-OR

REACT-OR

ROTAT-OR

SCISS-OR

SENAT-OR

SETTL-OR

SPONS-OR

SQUAL-OR

TRACT-OR

TRAIT-OR

TRUST-OR

VISIT-OR

Eight-letter words

ABDUCT-OR

ACCENT-OR

ACCEPT-OR

ADJUST-OR

AGITAT-OR

ANIMAT-OR

ASSESS-OR

ASSIGN-OR

BEHAVI-OR

BISECT-OR

CAVEAT-OR

CODEBT-OR

CONVEN-OR

CONVEY-OR

CORRID-OR

CREDIT-OR

DEFECT-OR

DEPICT-OR

DETECT-OR

DICTAT-OR

DIRECT-OR

EFFECT-OR

ELEVAT-OR

ENDEAV-OR

EXECUT-OR

GOVERN-OR

IMITAT-OR

IMPOST-OR

INFECT-OR

INJECT-OR

INVENT-OR

INVEST-OR

ISOLAT-OR

METAPH-OR

NARRAT-OR

NEIGHB-OR

OBJECT-OR

OBSESS-OR

PREDAT-OR

PROVID-OR

PURVEY-OR

RADIAT-OR

REDUCT-OR

REJECT-OR

RESIST-OR

O

SCULPT-OR	STRESS-OR	VIOLAT-OR
SECRET-OR	SURVEY-OR	
SELECT-OR	TESTAT-OR	

Some words ending with -OUS
Seven-letter words

AMOR-OUS	GIBB-OUS	POMP-OUS
ARDU-OUS	GLOB-OUS	RAUC-OUS
BILI-OUS	HEIN-OUS	RIOT-OUS
BULB-OUS	HIDE-OUS	RUIN-OUS
CALL-OUS	IGNE-OUS	TEDI-OUS
CURI-OUS	JEAL-OUS	TENU-OUS
DEVI-OUS	NITR-OUS	TIME-OUS
DUBI-OUS	NOXI-OUS	VACU-OUS
ENVI-OUS	OBVI-OUS	VARI-OUS
FATU-OUS	ODOR-OUS	VICI-OUS
FERR-OUS	OMIN-OUS	ZEAL-OUS
FIBR-OUS	ONER-OUS	
FURI-OUS	PITE-OUS	

Tile Tracking

This means being aware of what tiles have already been played and therefore what might remain in the bag or on your opponent's rack. Tile tracking can be useful to manage your expectations of what common vowels or consonants you are likely to pick from the bag, and whether there are any goodies (blanks Ss JQXZ) left. At the end of a game it could even enable you to know what your opponent is holding. This practice is more common at club and tournament level.

Eight-letter words

ARSON-OUS	GRACI-OUS	RIGOR-OUS
BIBUL-OUS	GRIEV-OUS	SENSU-OUS
CHROM-OUS	LIBEL-OUS	SQUAM-OUS
COUSC-OUS	LUMIN-OUS	STUDI-OUS
COVET-OUS	LUSCI-OUS	TIMOR-OUS
DECOR-OUS	LUSTR-OUS	TORTU-OUS
DESIR-OUS	MUTIN-OUS	ULCER-OUS
DEXTR-OUS	NITRE-OUS	UNCTU-OUS
ENORM-OUS	NUMER-OUS	VAPOR-OUS
FABUL-OUS	ORDUR-OUS	VENOM-OUS
FACTI-OUS	PERIL-OUS	VIGOR-OUS
FEVER-OUS	POPUL-OUS	VIRTU-OUS
GENER-OUS	PRECI-OUS	WONDR-OUS
GORGE-OUS	PREVI-OUS	

Some words ending with -OUT
Seven-letter words

BACK-OUT	HAND-OUT	SHUT-OUT
BAIL-OUT	HANG-OUT	SPIN-OUT
BESP-OUT	HIDE-OUT	TAKE-OUT
BLOW-OUT	LOCK-OUT	TIME-OUT
BURN-OUT	LOOK-OUT	TURN-OUT
CAMP-OUT	MISS-OUT	WALK-OUT
COOK-OUT	PASS-OUT	WASH-OUT
DROP-OUT	PULL-OUT	WITH-OUT
FADE-OUT	READ-OUT	WORK-OUT
FALL-OUT	ROLL-OUT	
FOLD-OUT	SELL-OUT	

Eight-letter words

BLACK-OUT	OUTSH-OUT	SPEAK-OUT
BREAK-OUT	PHASE-OUT	STAKE-OUT
CARRY-OUT	PRINT-OUT	STAND-OUT
CHECK-OUT	RUNAB-OUT	STICK-OUT
FLAME-OUT	SEASC-OUT	THERE-OUT
FREAK-OUT	SEATR-OUT	UNDEV-OUT
INDEV-OUT	SHAKE-OUT	WATCH-OUT
KNOCK-OUT	SHOOT-OUT	WHITE-OUT
LAYAB-OUT	SLEEP-OUT	

Unusual letter combinations

If you have an unusual combination of letters on your rack, or want to impress your opponent with an unusual word, a few words from World English can come in handy.

Australian words

OCKER   uncultivated or boorish Australian

Hindi words

OONT   camel

South African words

OKE   man
OOM   title of respect

O

P

3

There are two-letter words beginning with **P** for each vowel except U which, combined with OP and UP, make it very flexible for short words such as PE (the 17th letter in the Hebrew alphabet, 4 points) and PO (an informal word for chamber pot, also 4 points). P also combines well with X, forming three-letter words PAX, PIX and POX (12 points each) and also Z, for example the three-letter POZ (an old-fashioned short form of positive, 14 points).

Two-letter words beginning with P

PA	PE	PI	PO

Some three-letter words beginning with P

PAC	PEP	PIX	PSI
PAH	PER	POA	PST
PAM	PEW	POH	PUG
PAP	PHI	POI	PUH
PAR	PHO	POL	PUR
PAV	PHT	POM	PUS
PAX	PIA	POW	PUY
PEC	PIC	POX	PYA
PED	PIR	POZ	PYE
PEH	PIU	PRE	PYX

P

Hooks

Hooking requires a subtle change in a player's thought process, in that they must look at words already on the board without becoming distracted by their pronunciation.

Some front-hooks
Two letters to three

P-AD	P-AX	P-ET	P-OM	P-UG
P-AH	P-AY	P-HI	P-OO	P-UH
P-AL	P-EA	P-HO	P-OP	P-UN
P-AM	P-ED	P-IN	P-OS	P-UP
P-AN	P-EE	P-IS	P-OW	P-UR
P-AR	P-EH	P-IT	P-OX	P-US
P-AS	P-EN	P-OD	P-RE	P-UT
P-AT	P-ER	P-OH	P-SI	P-YA
P-AW	P-ES	P-OI	P-ST	P-YE

Three letters to four

P-ACE	P-AND	P-EAR
P-ACT	P-ANE	P-EAT
P-AGE	P-ANT	P-EEK
P-AID	P-ARE	P-EEL
P-AIL	P-ARK	P-EEN
P-AIN	P-ART	P-ELT
P-AIR	P-ASH	P-END
P-AIS	P-ASS	P-EON
P-ALE	P-ATE	P-ERE
P-ALL	P-AVE	P-ERK
P-ALP	P-AWN	P-EST

P

P-HAT	P-LOP	P-OUT
P-HEW	P-LOT	P-OXY
P-HUT	P-LOW	P-RAM
P-ICK	P-LOY	P-RAT
P-ILL	P-LUG	P-RAY
P-IMP	P-LUM	P-REP
P-INK	P-OKE	P-REZ
P-ION	P-OLE	P-RIG
P-ITA	P-ONE	P-RIM
P-LAT	P-ONY	P-ROB
P-LAY	P-OOR	P-ROD
P-LEA	P-OPE	P-ROM
P-LED	P-ORE	P-ROW
P-LEX	P-ORT	P-UKE
P-LIE	P-OSE	P-UMP
P-LOD	P-OUR	P-URE

Four letters to five

P

P-ACED	P-AVER	P-ITCH
P-ACER	P-AWED	P-LACE
P-AEON	P-EACH	P-LACK
P-AGED	P-EARL	P-LAID
P-AGER	P-EASE	P-LAIN
P-ALAS	P-EGGY	P-LANE
P-ALLY	P-ESKY	P-LANK
P-APER	P-HONE	P-LANT
P-ARCH	P-ICKY	P-LAST
P-ARED	P-INCH	P-LATE
P-ARIS	P-INKY	P-LEAD
P-ARTY	P-INTO	P-LEAT

445

P-LIED   P-RANK   P-ROLL
P-LIER   P-RAWN   P-RONG
P-LINK   P-REEN   P-ROOF
P-LUCK   P-RICE   P-ROSE
P-LUMP   P-RICY   P-ROVE
P-LUSH   P-RIDE   P-RUDE
P-OINT   P-RIMA   P-RUNE
P-OLIO   P-RIME   P-SHAW
P-OUCH   P-RISE   P-UNTO
P-OWER   P-ROBE   P-URGE
P-RANG   P-ROLE

Five letters to six

P-ACING   P-AWNED   P-INKER
P-ACKER   P-AWNER   P-INNED
P-ADDED   P-EASED   P-INNER
P-ADDER   P-EGGED   P-IRATE
P-ADDLE   P-ELVES   P-ITCHY
P-AGING   P-ENDED   P-LACED
P-AIRED   P-ESTER   P-LACER
P-AIRER   P-HONED   P-LATED
P-ALATE   P-HONER   P-LATER
P-ANTED   P-HONEY   P-LAYED
P-ARISH   P-HOOEY   P-LAYER
P-ARKED   P-ICKER   P-LEASE
P-ARLED   P-ICKLE   P-LEDGE
P-ARSON   P-IGGED   P-LODGE
P-ASHED   P-IMPLY   P-LOUGH
P-ASTER   P-INION   P-LOVER
P-AWING   P-INKED   P-LOWED

P-LOWER	P-REACH	P-RIVET
P-LUCKY	P-REACT	P-ROBED
P-LUMMY	P-REBUY	P-ROPER
P-LUMPY	P-RECUT	P-ROSED
P-LUNGE	P-REFER	P-ROTON
P-LYING	P-REFIX	P-ROVED
P-ODIUM	P-REMIX	P-ROVEN
P-OLDER	P-REPAY	P-ROVER
P-OSIER	P-RESET	P-ROWER
P-OTTER	P-RETAX	P-RUNED
P-OUNCE	P-REVUE	P-UMPED
P-OUPED	P-RICED	P-UPPED
P-OUTED	P-RICER	P-URGED
P-OUTER	P-RIEVE	P-URGER
P-RAISE	P-RIMED	P-USHER
P-RANCE	P-RIMER	P-UTTER
P-RAYED	P-RISER	

Six letters to seven

P-ADDING	P-ASHING	P-ICKIER
P-ADDLED	P-AWNING	P-ICKILY
P-AIRING	P-EANING	P-ICKLER
P-ANTHER	P-EASING	P-INCASE
P-ANTING	P-EERIER	P-INCHED
P-ANTLER	P-EGGING	P-INCHER
P-ARABLE	P-ENDING	P-INKING
P-ARCHED	P-ENFOLD	P-INNING
P-ARKING	P-HATTER	P-ITCHED
P-ARLING	P-HONIED	P-LACING
P-ARTIER	P-HONING	P-LAIDED

P-LANKED	P-OINTED	P-REPACK
P-LANNER	P-OODLES	P-REPAID
P-LASTER	P-ORCINE	P-REPONE
P-LATINA	P-OUCHED	P-RESALE
P-LATTER	P-OUTING	P-RESELL
P-LAYING	P-RAISED	P-RESENT
P-LAYOFF	P-RAISER	P-RESHIP
P-LEADED	P-RANCED	P-RESIDE
P-LEADER	P-RANGED	P-RESOLD
P-LEASED	P-RANKED	P-RESUME
P-LEASER	P-RANKLE	P-RETELL
P-LEDGED	P-RATTED	P-RETOLD
P-LEDGER	P-RATTLE	P-REVERB
P-LIABLE	P-RAYING	P-REVIEW
P-LODGED	P-REAVER	P-REWASH
P-LOTTED	P-REBILL	P-REWORN
P-LOTTER	P-REBOOK	P-RICIER
P-LOWING	P-RECAST	P-RICKLE
P-LUCKED	P-RECEDE	P-RICKLY
P-LUGGED	P-RECEPT	P-RIDING
P-LUGGER	P-RECOOK	P-RISING
P-LUMBER	P-REDATE	P-ROBING
P-LUMPED	P-REDIAL	P-RODDED
P-LUMPEN	P-REFACE	P-ROOFED
P-LUMPER	P-REFECT	P-ROOFER
P-LUNGED	P-REHEAT	P-ROSILY
P-LUNGER	P-REMADE	P-ROVING
P-LUNKER	P-REMISE	P-RUDISH
P-LUSHER	P-REMOVE	P-UPPING
P-LUSHLY	P-RENAME	P-URGING

Seven letters to eight

P-ADDLING

P-ALIMONY

P-ALTERED

P-ARCHING

P-ARTICLE

P-ARTISAN

P-ARTWORK

P-EARLIER

P-ENCHANT

P-ENLIGHT

P-ENOLOGY

P-ENTICED

P-HARMING

P-HISHING

P-HONEYED

P-ICKIEST

P-INCHING

P-INKIEST

P-ITCHIER

P-ITCHILY

P-ITCHING

P-LAIDING

P-LANKING

P-LAYBACK

P-LAYTIME

P-LEADING

P-LEASING

P-LEASURE

P-LIGHTED

P-LIGHTER

P-LOTTING

P-LUCKILY

P-LUCKING

P-LUGGING

P-LUGHOLE

P-LUMPING

P-LUMPISH

P-LUNGING

P-LUSHEST

P-LUSHIER

P-OTTERED

P-OUCHING

P-RAISING

P-RANCING

P-RANGING

P-RANKING

P-RANKISH

P-RATTLED

P-RATTLER

P-REACHED

P-REACHER

P-READAPT

P-READMIT

P-REAPPLY

P-REARMED

P-REBIRTH

P-REBOUND

P-REBUILD

P-REBUILT

P-RECEDED

P-RECITED

P-RECLEAN

P-RECURED

P-REDATED

P-REDRAFT

P-REELECT

P-REFACED

P-REFIXED

P-REGNANT

P-REJUDGE

P-REMIXED

P-REMORSE

P-REMOVED

P-REORDER

P-REPAVED

P-REPLACE

P-REPOSED

P-REPRICE

P-REPRINT

P-RESERVE

P-RESHOWN

P-RESIDED

P-RESIDER

P-RESUMED

P-RESUMER

P-RETRAIN

P-RETRIAL

P

P-RETYPED	P-REWEIGH	P-ROOFING
P-REUNION	P-REWIRED	P-ROSIEST
P-REUNITE	P-RICIEST	P-UNITIVE
P-REVALUE	P-RIGGISH	P-UTTERED
P-REVISED	P-RILLING	P-UTTERER
P-REVISIT	P-RODDING	

Some end-hooks
Two letters to three

AL-P	HE-P	NE-P	TO-P
AM-P	HI-P	OO-P	UM-P
AS-P	HO-P	OU-P	UR-P
BA-P	JA-P	PA-P	WO-P
BO-P	KI-P	PE-P	YA-P
DA-P	KO-P	PI-P	YE-P
DI-P	LA-P	PO-P	YU-P
DO-P	LI-P	RE-P	ZA-P
FA-P	LO-P	SI-P	
GI-P	MA-P	SO-P	
GU-P	MO-P	TA-P	
HA-P	NA-P	TI-P	

Celebrity Scrabble Players

include Mel Gibson, Nicole Kidman, Chris Martin, Madonna and Sting.

Three letters to four

BEE-P	HAS-P	PER-P
BUM-P	HEM-P	POM-P
BUR-P	HOO-P	PRE-P
CAM-P	HUM-P	PRO-P
CAR-P	JEE-P	PUL-P
CHA-P	LAM-P	RAM-P
CHI-P	LEA-P	RAS-P
COO-P	LEE-P	ROM-P
COW-P	LIS-P	RUM-P
DAM-P	LOO-P	SEE-P
DEE-P	LOU-P	SKI-P
FRA-P	LOW-P	SUM-P
GAS-P	LUM-P	TAR-P
GOO-P	MUM-P	WAR-P
GUL-P	PAR-P	WAS-P
GUM-P	PEE-P	WIS-P

Four letters to five

BICE-P	GRAM-P	SLEE-P
BLEE-P	GRUM-P	SLUM-P
CHAM-P	PLUM-P	SLUR-P
CHUM-P	POLY-P	STUM-P
CLAM-P	PRIM-P	SWAM-P
CRAM-P	SCAM-P	SWEE-P
CREE-P	SCAR-P	TRAM-P
CRIM-P	SCUL-P	WHOM-P
CRIS-P	SKIM-P	

Five letters to six

ESCAR-P	SCRUM-P	TRICE-P
SCRAW-P	SHLEP-P	
SCRIM-P	THREE-P	

Six letters to seven

BEDLAM-P	MANTRA-P	SCHLEP-P

Seven letters to eight

AUTOCAR-P	MINICAM-P

Blockers

It is useful to know which words are blockers and can't therefore be extended before or after. You may want to play a blocker that your opponent can't extend, or you may want to avoid playing a blocker because you want to keep the board open.

P

Some three-letter blockers beginning with P

PAX	PLY	PST
PHT	POH	PYX

Some four-letter blockers beginning with P

PFFT	PLEX	PREZ
PHAT	POCO	PSST
PHEW	POKY	PUKA
PHIZ	PONY	PUNY
PITY	POSY	

Some five-letter blockers beginning with P
(except words ending in '-ED', '-J', '-S', '-X', '-Y' or '-Z')

PACTA	PILAR	PUKKA
PADRI	PILCH	PULMO
PAISE	PINCH	PUPAE
PALER	POOCH	PUPAL
PAOLO	PORCH	PURER
PAPAL	PROST	PUTID
PENAL	PROUD	PYRAL
PERCH	PUBIC	PYRIC

P

Some six-letter blockers begining with P
(except words ending in '-ED', '-J', '-S', '-X', '-Y' or '-Z')

PACTUM	PHONAL	POTMAN
PAIRER	PHYLUM	POTMEN
PALEAL	PIEING	POXIER
PALEST	PIEMAN	POXING
PALISH	PIEMEN	PRELAW
PALLID	PIPIER	PRIMAL
PANINI	PITMEN	PROGUN
PARISH	PLACID	PRONER
PARTIM	PLANAR	PRONTO
PASSEE	PLIANT	PROWAR
PASSIM	POKIER	PROWER
PAUSAL	POLISH	PULPAL
PAWING	POLYPI	PUNIER
PENMAN	POSHER	PUNISH
PENMEN	POSIER	PUREST
PEPFUL	POTASH	PURING
PERISH	POTATO	PUTRID
PERTER	POTING	

Bonus words

Bonus words on your rack can be hard to spot, especially for the less experienced player. One way to help find them is by using prefixes and suffixes.

Many larger words include a common prefix or suffix – remembering these and using them where you can is a good way to discover any longer words on your rack, including any potential bonus words. The key prefixes to remember beginning with P are PER-, PRE- and PRO-.

Some words beginning with PER-
Seven-letter words

PER-CENT	PER-JURY	PER-TAKE
PER-CHER	PER-KING	PER-USED
PER-CUSS	PER-MING	PER-USER
PER-FORM	PER-PLEX	PER-VADE
PER-FUME	PER-SIST	PER-VERT
PER-HAPS	PER-SONS	
PER-JURE	PER-TAIN	

Eight-letter words

PER-FUMED	PER-SPIRE	PER-VADED
PER-ISHES	PER-SUING	PER-VERSE
PER-MUTED	PER-TAKEN	
PER-OXIDE	PER-USING	

P

Some words beginning with PRE-

Seven-letter words

PRE-ACHY	PRE-FACE	PRE-SENT
PRE-BOIL	PRE-LATE	PRE-SHOW
PRE-BOOK	PRE-LOAD	PRE-SIDE
PRE-CAST	PRE-LUDE	PRE-TEEN
PRE-CEDE	PRE-MADE	PRE-TEND
PRE-CODE	PRE-MISE	PRE-TERM
PRE-COOK	PRE-PACK	PRE-TEXT
PRE-DATE	PRE-PAID	PRE-VAIL
PRE-DAWN	PRE-PARE	PRE-VIEW
PRE-DIAL	PRE-PLAN	PRE-WARN
PRE-DICT	PRE-SAGE	PRE-WASH
PRE-EMPT	PRE-SALE	PRE-WORN

Eight-letter words

PRE-ADAPT	PRE-JUDGE	PRE-SIDED
PRE-AMBLE	PRE-MOLAR	PRE-SLEEP
PRE-BIRTH	PRE-ORDER	PRE-SOLVE
PRE-BUILT	PRE-OWNED	PRE-STORE
PRE-CEDED	PRE-PARED	PRE-TASTE
PRE-CITED	PRE-PLANT	PRE-TENSE
PRE-CURED	PRE-POSED	PRE-TRIAL
PRE-DATED	PRE-PRESS	PRE-TYPED
PRE-ELECT	PRE-PRINT	PRE-VALUE
PRE-EXIST	PRE-SAGER	PRE-VISED
PRE-FACED	PRE-SERVE	
PRE-FIXED	PRE-SHAPE	

Some words beginning with PRO-

Seven-letter words

PRO-BALL	PRO-FESS	PRO-PONE
PRO-BATE	PRO-FILE	PRO-POSE
PRO-BING	PRO-FUSE	PRO-SING
PRO-CESS	PRO-GRAM	PRO-TEST
PRO-CURE	PRO-LONG	PRO-VERB
PRO-DRUG	PRO-MISE	PRO-VIDE
PRO-DUCE	PRO-MOTE	PRO-WEST
PRO-DUCT	PRO-NOUN	
PRO-FANE	PRO-PANE	

Eight-letter words

PRO-BATED	PRO-MISER	PRO-STATE
PRO-CLAIM	PRO-MOTED	PRO-STYLE
PRO-CURED	PRO-MOTOR	PRO-TEASE
PRO-FILED	PRO-PHASE	PRO-TRACT
PRO-FILER	PRO-POSED	PRO-TRADE
PRO-FOUND	PRO-POUND	PRO-UNION
PRO-LAPSE	PRO-RATED	PRO-VISOR

P

Unusual letter combinations

If you have an unusual combination of letters on your rack, or want to impress your opponent with an unusual word, a few words from World English can come in handy.

Australian words

PINDAN — desert region of Western Australia

PLONKO — alcoholic, especially one who drinks wine

PODDY — handfed calf or lamb

POKIE — poker machine

POSSIE — position

PRELOVED — second-hand

Canadian words

PARFLECHE — dried rawhide

PARKADE — building used as a car park

PARKETTE — small public park

PLEW — beaver skin used as a standard unit

POGEY — financial relief for the unemployed

POKELOGAN — backwater

POUTINE — chipped potatoes topped with curd cheese and tomato sauce

PUNG — horse-drawn sleigh

Hindi words

PACHISI — game resembling backgammon

PAISA — one hundredth of a rupee

PAKORA — dish of deep-fried chicken or vegetables

PANEER — soft white cheese

PARATHA — flat unleavened bread

PEEPUL	tree similar to the banyan
PUNKAH	fan made of palm leaves
PURDAH	custom of keeping women secluded
PURI	unleavened flaky bread
PUTTEE	strip of cloth wound around the leg

New Zealand words

PAKAHI	acid soil or land
PAKOKO	small freshwater fish
PAUA	edible abalone
PIKAU	rucksack
PIPI	shellfish
PIUPIU	leaf skirt
POI	ball of woven flax
PONGA	tall tree fern
PORAE	edible sea fish
PORANGI	crazy
PORINA	moth larva
POTAE	hat
POWHIRI	welcoming ceremony
PUGGY	sticky
PUHA	sow thistle
PUKEKO	wading bird
PURIRI	forest tree

P

South African words

| PADKOS | snacks for a long journey |
| PLAAS | farm |

Essential info

Value: 10 points

Number in set: 1

Power Tile

Along with Z, **Q** is the highest-scoring letter in the Scrabble set. However, unlike Z, Q can prove difficult to use if it is not accompanied by the letter U. The best method of getting around this is to commit to memory all the short words beginning with Q which do not require a U. This is easier than it sounds, as there is only one two-letter word beginning with Q: QI (vital energy believed to circulate around the body, 11 points). There are three three-letter words (12 points each, and only one of these uses a U): QUA (in the capacity of), QAT (evergreen shrub of Africa and Asia whose leaves have narcotic properties) and QIS (plural of QI). The fourth three-letter word containing a Q is SUQ.

Two-letter word beginning with Q

QI

Three-letter words beginning with Q

QAT   QUA

Three-letter word using Q

SUQ

Four-letter words

Some four-letter words using Q with which you may not be familiar include QUAG (short form of quagmire, 14 points), QUEY (a young cow, 16 points) and WAQF (endowment in Muslim law, 19 points).

AQUA	QUAT	QUIT
QADI	QUAY	QUIZ
QAID	QUEP	QUOD
QOPH	QUEY	QUOP
QUAD	QUID	SUQS
QUAG	QUIN	WAQF
QUAI	QUIP	

Q without U

Q is dependent on U for many of its words, but there is no need to panic if you have a Q and no U. If you find yourself in this situation, some useful examples to remember are: Q (11 points), QADI (14), QAT (12), QORMA (16), FAQIR (17) and TRANQ (14).

Hooks

Hooking requires a subtle change in a player's thought process, in that they must look at words already on the board without becoming distracted by their pronunciation.

Some front-hooks
Two letters to three

Q-AT   Q-IS

Three letters to four

Q-AID   Q-UEY

Four letters to five

Q-AIDS   Q-UEYS

Some end-hooks
Four letters to five

TALA-Q

Q

Blockers

It is useful to know which words are blockers and can't therefore be extended before or after. You may want to play a blocker that your opponent can't extend, or you may want to avoid playing a blocker because you want to keep the board open.

Three-letter blocker beginning with Q
QIS

Four-letter blocker beginning with Q
QUEP

Some five-letter blockers beginning with Q
(except words ending in '-ED', '-J', '-S', '-X', '-Y' or '-Z')

QUALE	QUAYD	QURSH
QUASI	QUOAD	

Some six-letter blockers beginning with Q
(except words ending in '-ED', '-J', '-S', '-X', '-Y' or '-Z')

QUAINT	QUENCH	QUOTHA
QUALIA	QUETCH	QURUSH
QUATCH	QUINIC	
QUEINT	QUOOKE	

Q

Bonus words

Seven-letter words

QABALAH

QAWWALI

QAWWALS

QIGONGS

QINDARS

QINTARS

QUACKED

QUACKER

QUACKLE

QUADDED

QUADRAT

QUADRIC

QUAERED

QUAERES

QUAFFED

QUAFFER

QUAGGAS

QUAICHS

QUAIGHS

QUAILED

QUAKERS

QUAKIER

QUAKILY

QUAKING

QUALIFY

QUALITY

QUAMASH

QUANGOS

QUANNET

QUANTAL

QUANTED

QUANTIC

QUANTUM

QUAREST

QUARREL

QUARTAN

QUARTER

QUARTES

QUARTET

QUARTIC

QUARTOS

QUARTZY

QUASARS

QUASHED

QUASHEE

QUASHER

QUASHES

QUASHIE

QUASSIA

QUASSIN

QUATRES

QUAVERS

QUAVERY

QUAYAGE

QUEENED

QUEENIE

QUEENLY

QUEESTS

QUELLED

QUELLER

QUEMING

QUERIDA

QUERIED

QUERIER

QUERIES

QUERIST

QUESTED

QUESTER

QUESTOR

QUETZAL

QUEUERS

QUEUING

QUIBBLE

QUICHED

QUICHES

QUICKEN

QUICKER

QUICKIE

QUICKLY

QUIDAMS

QUIDDIT

Q

QUIESCE
QUIETED
QUIETEN
QUIETER
QUIETLY
QUIETUS
QUIGHTS
QUILLAI
QUILLED
QUILLET
QUILLON
QUILTED
QUILTER
QUINARY
QUINATE
QUINCES
QUINCHE
QUINELA
QUINIES
QUININA
QUININE
QUININS
QUINNAT
QUINOAS

QUINOID
QUINOLS
QUINONE
QUINTAL
QUINTAN
QUINTAR
QUINTAS
QUINTES
QUINTET
QUINTIC
QUINTIN
QUINZES
QUIPPED
QUIPPER
QUIPPUS
QUIRING
QUIRKED
QUIRTED
QUITING
QUITTAL
QUITTED
QUITTER
QUITTOR
QUIVERS

QUIVERY
QUIXOTE
QUIZZED
QUIZZER
QUIZZES

QUODDED
QUODLIN
QUOHOGS
QUOIFED
QUOINED
QUOISTS
QUOITED
QUOITER
QUOKKAS
QUOMODO
QUONDAM
QUONKED
QUOPPED
QUORATE
QUORUMS
QUOTERS
QUOTING
QUOTUMS
QWERTYS

Q

Eight-letter words

QABALISM
QABALIST
QALAMDAN
QINDARKA
QUAALUDE
QUACKERY
QUACKIER
QUACKING
QUACKISH
QUACKISM
QUACKLED
QUADDING
QUADPLEX
QUADRANT
QUADRATE
QUADRIGA
QUADROON
QUAESTOR
QUAFFING
QUAGGIER
QUAGMIRE
QUAGMIRY
QUAICHES
QUAILING
QUAINTER
QUAINTLY
QUAKIEST
QUALMIER

QUALMING
QUALMISH
QUANDANG
QUANDARY
QUANDONG
QUANTIFY
QUANTILE
QUANTING
QUANTISE
QUANTITY
QUANTIZE
QUANTONG
QUARRIAN
QUARRIED
QUARRIER
QUARRIES
QUARRION
QUARTERN
QUARTETT
QUARTIER
QUARTILE
QUARTZES
QUASHIES
QUASHING
QUASSIAS
QUATCHED
QUATORZE
QUATRAIN
QUAVERED

QUAVERER
QUAYLIKE
QUAYSIDE
QUAZZIER
QUEACHES
QUEASIER
QUEASILY
QUEAZIER
QUEENITE
QUEENLET
QUELCHED
QUELCHES
QUELLING
QUENCHED
QUENCHER
QUENCHES
QUENELLE
QUERCINE
QUERYING
QUESTANT
QUESTERS
QUESTING
QUESTION
QUETCHED
QUETCHES
QUETHING
QUEUEING

Q

QUIBBLED QUINCHED QUITCHES
QUIBBLER QUINCHES QUITRENT
QUIBBLES QUINCUNX QUITTALS
QUICHING QUINELLA QUITTERS
QUICKEST QUINIELA QUITTING
QUICKIES QUININES QUIVERED
QUICKSET QUINOIDS QUIVERER
QUIDDANY QUINOLIN QUIXOTES
QUIDDITY QUINONES QUIXOTIC
QUIDDLED QUINSIED QUIXOTRY
QUIDDLER QUINSIES QUIZZERY
QUIDNUNC QUINTAIN QUIZZIFY
QUIESCED QUINTETS QUIZZING
QUIESCES QUINTETT
QUIETEST QUINTICS QUODDING
QUIETING QUINTILE QUODLINS
QUIETISM QUIPPIER QUOIFING
QUIETIST QUIPPING QUOINING
QUIETIVE QUIPPISH QUOITERS
QUIETUDE QUIPSTER QUOITING
QUIGHTED QUIRKIER QUONKING
QUILLAIA QUIRKILY QUOPPING
QUILLAJA QUIRKING QUOTABLE
QUILLING QUIRKISH QUOTABLY
QUILLMAN QUIRTING QUOTIENT
QUILLMEN QUISLING
QUILTING QUITCHED QWERTIES

Q

Unusual letter combinations

If you have an unusual combination of letters on your rack, or want to impress your opponent with an unusual word, a few words from World English can come in handy.

Australian words

QUOKKA   small wallaby
QUOLL   native cat

Urdu words

QORMA   Indian dish of meat or vegetables braised with yoghurt or cream

QUIZ show

If you are lucky enough to have the letters Q, U, I and Z on your rack, or with one of them in a usable place on the board, the obvious choice would be to play QUIZ, an extremely useful and high-scoring word (22 points). Should your opponent be the lucky one to play QUIZ then perhaps you can then reap the benefits of front-hooking it with an S to make SQUIZ (23 points).

Essential info

Value: 1 point

Number in set: 6

R is one of the most common consonants in Scrabble but, surprisingly, only begins one two-letter word: RE (2 points). Some useful three-letter words to remember include ROW and RAY (6 points each) and there are also more unusual words such as RAX (a Scots word for stretch or extend, 10 points) and REZ (a short informal word for reservation, 12 points) which use power tiles. R is one of the letters of the RETAIN set and is therefore a good letter to keep if trying to get a bonus word.

Two-letter word beginning with R

RE

Some three-letter words beginning with R

RAD	REE	RET	RIT
RAH	REG	REW	RIZ
RAI	REH	REX	ROM
RAJ	REI	REZ	ROO
RAS	REM	RHO	RYA
RAX	REN	RHY	
REB	REO	RIF	
REC	REP	RIN	

R

Hooks

Hooking requires a subtle change in a player's thought process, in that they must look at words already on the board without becoming distracted by their pronunciation.

Some front-hooks
Two letters to three

R-AD	R-EF	R-OD
R-AG	R-EH	R-OE
R-AH	R-EM	R-OM
R-AI	R-EN	R-OO
R-AM	R-ES	R-OW
R-AN	R-ET	R-UG
R-AS	R-EX	R-UM
R-AT	R-HO	R-UN
R-AW	R-ID	R-UT
R-AX	R-IF	R-YA
R-AY	R-IN	R-YE
R-ED	R-IT	
R-EE	R-OB	

Three letters to four

R-ACE	R-ALE	R-ATE
R-AFF	R-AMP	R-AVE
R-AFT	R-AND	R-AWN
R-AGE	R-ANT	R-EAR
R-AID	R-APT	R-EEK
R-AIL	R-ARE	R-EEL
R-AIN	R-ASH	R-EFT
R-AKE	R-ASP	R-END

R

R-EST	R-INK	R-OOT
R-ICE	R-OAR	R-OPE
R-ICH	R-OBE	R-OSE
R-ICK	R-ODE	R-OUT
R-ICY	R-OIL	R-ULE
R-IDE	R-OLE	R-UMP
R-IFF	R-OOF	R-USE
R-IGG	R-OOM	R-YES

Four letters to five

R-ABID	R-AVER	R-OAST
R-ACED	R-EACH	R-OILY
R-ACER	R-EAVE	R-OPED
R-AGED	R-EDDY	R-OUST
R-AGER	R-EGAL	R-OVEN
R-AKED	R-EMIT	R-OVER
R-ALLY	R-ENEW	R-OWED
R-AMEN	R-ETCH	R-OWER
R-ARED	R-ICED	
R-AVEL	R-OARY	

R

Five letters to six

R-ABIES	R-AVINE	R-ICKLE
R-ACING	R-AZURE	R-ICTAL
R-ADDER	R-EARED	R-ICTUS
R-ADIOS	R-EAVED	R-IGGED
R-AFTER	R-EBOOK	R-INKED
R-AGING	R-EDUCE	R-OARED
R-AIDED	R-EFFED	R-OCKER
R-AIDER	R-EGRET	R-OILED
R-AILED	R-EJECT	R-OLLER
R-AKING	R-ELATE	R-OPING
R-AMBLE	R-EMAIL	R-OSIER
R-AMPED	R-EMOTE	R-OTARY
R-ANGER	R-EMOVE	R-OTTER
R-ANKER	R-ENDED	R-OUGHT
R-ANKLE	R-ENTER	R-OUNCE
R-ANTED	R-ESTER	R-OUPED
R-APPEL	R-ETAPE	R-OUTED
R-APTLY	R-EVERT	R-OUTER
R-AREFY	R-EVERY	R-OWING
R-ASHED	R-EVOKE	R-UDDER
R-ASPER	R-ICIER	R-USHER
R-AUGHT	R-ICING	R-UTTER

R

Six letters to seven

R-ABIDER	R-EFFING	R-EVOKED
R-ADDLED	R-EGALLY	R-EVOKER
R-AIDING	R-EGENCE	R-EVOLVE
R-AILING	R-EGENCY	R-ICHING
R-ALLIED	R-EGRESS	R-ICIEST
R-AMBLED	R-ELAPSE	R-IGGING
R-AMBLER	R-ELATED	R-INKING
R-AMPING	R-ELATER	R-OARING
R-ANKLED	R-EMERGE	R-OILING
R-ANTING	R-EMOTER	R-OUGHLY
R-APPORT	R-EMOVED	R-OUSTED
R-ASHING	R-ENDING	R-OUSTER
R-ASPISH	R-ENEWED	R-OUTING
R-EARING	R-EPRISE	R-OYSTER
R-EAVING	R-ESTATE	R-UGGING
R-EDDISH	R-ETCHED	R-UNLESS
R-EDUCED	R-EVILER	

R

Seven letters to eight

R-ADDLING

R-ALLYING

R-AMBLING

R-ANKLING

R-APTNESS

R-AREFIED

R-ECLOSED

R-EDUCING

R-EGALITY

R-EJECTED

R-ELAPSED

R-ELATING

R-ELATION

R-ELATIVE

R-EMAILED

R-EMERGED

R-EMITTED

R-EMITTER

R-EMOTION

R-EMOVING

R-ENEWING

R-ENFORCE

R-ENOUNCE

R-ESTATED

R-ETCHING

R-EVERTED

R-EVOKING

R-EVOLVED

R-EVOLVER

R-EVULSED

R-UNROUND

R-URALITE

Handy Hint

JAR (10 points) is an obvious word to spot on the rack. If it won't play then remember that JAR backwards makes the word RAJ which might fit in. RAJ is an Indian word for government and it also takes a useful A hook for RAJA, which then can take an H for RAJAH. Other short reversible words beginning with R are RAW/WAR (6 points) RAP/PAR (5 points) RIM/MIR (5 points).

Some end-hooks
Two letters to three

AI-R	JA-R	OO-R
BA-R	JO-R	OU-R
BO-R	KI-R	PA-R
DO-R	KO-R	PE-R
EA-R	LA-R	PI-R
ER-R	LO-R	SI-R
FA-R	MA-R	TA-R
FE-R	MI-R	TO-R
GO-R	MO-R	YA-R
GU-R	NO-R	
HE-R	NU-R	

Three letters to four

ACE-R	EWE-R	OWE-R
AGA-R	EYE-R	PEA-R
AGE-R	FEE-R	PIE-R
APE-R	FIE-R	PUR-R
AVE-R	FOU-R	SEA-R
BEE-R	GOE-R	SEE-R
BOA-R	HOA-R	SOU-R
BOO-R	HOE-R	SPA-R
BRR-R	HUE-R	SUE-R
BUR-R	ICE-R	TEA-R
CHA-R	JEE-R	TEE-R
CHE-R	LEA-R	TIE-R
DEE-R	LEE-R	USE-R
DOE-R	LIE-R	VEE-R
DOO-R	MEE-R	VIE-R
DYE-R	MOO-R	YEA-R
EVE-R	ONE-R	YOU-R

R

Four letters to five

ABLE-R	DINE-R	HOME-R
BAKE-R	DIVE-R	HOPE-R
BARE-R	DONE-R	HOVE-R
BASE-R	DOPE-R	HUGE-R
BIDE-R	DOSE-R	HYPE-R
BIKE-R	DOVE-R	IDLE-R
BITE-R	DOZE-R	JIVE-R
BLUE-R	EASE-R	JOKE-R
BORE-R	EDGE-R	LACE-R
CAGE-R	FACE-R	LAKE-R
CANE-R	FADE-R	LAME-R
CAPE-R	FAKE-R	LASE-R
CARE-R	FILE-R	LATE-R
CATE-R	FINE-R	LEVE-R
CAVE-R	FIRE-R	LIFE-R
CHAI-R	FIVE-R	LIKE-R
CIDE-R	FREE-R	LINE-R
CITE-R	FUME-R	LIVE-R
CODE-R	GAME-R	LONE-R
COME-R	GATE-R	LOSE-R
COPE-R	GAZE-R	LOVE-R
COVE-R	GIVE-R	LUGE-R
CUBE-R	GONE-R	LUNA-R
CURE-R	HATE-R	LURE-R
CUTE-R	HAVE-R	LUTE-R
DARE-R	HAZE-R	MACE-R
DATE-R	HIDE-R	MAKE-R
DECO-R	HIKE-R	MANO-R
DICE-R	HIRE-R	MATE-R

MAYO-R	RARE-R	SUPE-R
METE-R	RATE-R	SURE-R
MINE-R	RAVE-R	TAKE-R
MITE-R	RAZE-R	TAME-R
MOVE-R	RICE-R	TAPE-R
MUSE-R	RIDE-R	TIGE-R
NAME-R	RIPE-R	TIME-R
NICE-R	RISE-R	TONE-R
NOSE-R	ROPE-R	TRUE-R
NOTE-R	ROTO-R	TUBE-R
OCHE-R	ROVE-R	TUNE-R
ONCE-R	RUDE-R	UNDE-R
PACE-R	RULE-R	VILE-R
PAGE-R	SABE-R	VINE-R
PALE-R	SAFE-R	VOTE-R
PATE-R	SAGE-R	WADE-R
PIKE-R	SANE-R	WAGE-R
PIPE-R	SAVE-R	WAKE-R
POKE-R	SHOE-R	WAVE-R
POSE-R	SIDE-R	WIDE-R
PUKE-R	SIZE-R	WIPE-R
PURE-R	SOLA-R	WISE-R
RACE-R	SORE-R	ZONE-R

R

Five letters to six

ABIDE-R	CRUDE-R	HEAVE-R
ACUTE-R	CURSE-R	HOUSE-R
ADORE-R	CYCLE-R	IRATE-R
AGILE-R	DANCE-R	ISSUE-R
AMPLE-R	DENSE-R	JUDGE-R
AMUSE-R	DODGE-R	JUICE-R
ANGLE-R	DOUSE-R	KNIFE-R
ARGUE-R	DRIVE-R	LANCE-R
BADGE-R	DRONE-R	LARGE-R
BARBE-R	DROVE-R	LATHE-R
BATHE-R	EERIE-R	LATTE-R
BINGE-R	ELATE-R	LEASE-R
BLAME-R	ERASE-R	LEAVE-R
BLAZE-R	EVADE-R	LODGE-R
BOMBE-R	EXILE-R	LUNGE-R
BOOZE-R	FALSE-R	MERGE-R
BRAVE-R	FENCE-R	MINCE-R
BRIBE-R	FLAKE-R	NOOSE-R
BULGE-R	FLAME-R	PARSE-R
CARVE-R	FORCE-R	PASSE-R
CAUSE-R	GLAZE-R	PIECE-R
CHAFE-R	GLIDE-R	PLACE-R
CHASE-R	GLOVE-R	PLANE-R
CLEVE-R	GORGE-R	PRIME-R
CLONE-R	GOUGE-R	PROVE-R
CLOSE-R	GRADE-R	QUAKE-R
CLOVE-R	GRAVE-R	REAVE-R
CONDO-R	GUIDE-R	RECTO-R
CRATE-R	GUISE-R	RIFLE-R

RINSE-R	SINGE-R	TRACE-R
ROUTE-R	SLATE-R	TRADE-R
SAUCE-R	SLIDE-R	TWICE-R
SCALE-R	SPARE-R	UNITE-R
SCORE-R	SPICE-R	VAGUE-R
SERVE-R	STATE-R	VALUE-R
SHAKE-R	STONE-R	VERGE-R
SHAPE-R	SWIPE-R	WAIVE-R
SHARE-R	TASTE-R	WASTE-R
SHAVE-R	TEASE-R	WHITE-R
SHINE-R	TITLE-R	

Six letters to seven

ACCUSE-R	CRINGE-R	FLEECE-R
ADMIRE-R	CRUISE-R	FORAGE-R
ADVISE-R	DAMAGE-R	FREEZE-R
AVENGE-R	DANGLE-R	GAMBLE-R
BABBLE-R	DEBASE-R	GENTLE-R
BAFFLE-R	DEBATE-R	GROOVE-R
BOTTLE-R	DECIDE-R	GROUSE-R
BOUNCE-R	DEFINE-R	HANDLE-R
BROWSE-R	DIVIDE-R	HUDDLE-R
BUNDLE-R	DOUBLE-R	HUMBLE-R
CACKLE-R	ENABLE-R	HURDLE-R
CHANGE-R	ENCODE-R	HUSTLE-R
CHARGE-R	ENDURE-R	IGNITE-R
CHEQUE-R	ESCAPE-R	IMPALE-R
CLEAVE-R	EVOLVE-R	IMPOSE-R
COARSE-R	EXPOSE-R	IMPURE-R
CREASE-R	FIERCE-R	INCITE-R

R

INCOME-R   OBTUSE-R   SECURE-R

INHALE-R   OFFICE-R   SEDUCE-R

INSANE-R   OPPOSE-R   SNOOZE-R

INSIDE-R   PEOPLE-R   SPARSE-R

INSURE-R   PERUSE-R   SQUARE-R

INVADE-R   PICKLE-R   STRIKE-R

IONISE-R   PIERCE-R   STRIPE-R

IONIZE-R   PLEASE-R   TODDLE-R

JUGGLE-R   PLEDGE-R   TROUSE-R

KINDLE-R   POLITE-R   TRUDGE-R

LOATHE-R   PRAISE-R   TUMBLE-R

LOCATE-R   QUARTE-R   UNIQUE-R

LOUNGE-R   RAMBLE-R   UNSAFE-R

MANAGE-R   RATTLE-R   UNSURE-R

MARINE-R   REDUCE-R   UPDATE-R

MENACE-R   REFINE-R   VOYAGE-R

MINUTE-R   REMOTE-R   WAFFLE-R

MUZZLE-R   RESCUE-R   WHEEZE-R

NEEDLE-R   REVISE-R   WIGGLE-R

NOTICE-R   RUSTLE-R   WOBBLE-R

NUZZLE-R   SAMPLE-R

OBLIGE-R   SAVAGE-R

Seven letters to eight

ACHIEVE-R   BELIEVE-R   COMBINE-R

ADVANCE-R   BICYCLE-R   COMMUTE-R

AIRLINE-R   BREATHE-R   COMPUTE-R

ARRANGE-R   CAPTURE-R   CONJURE-R

BALANCE-R   CAROUSE-R   CONSUME-R

BANDAGE-R   CHUCKLE-R   DECEIVE-R

R

DECLINE-R

DIFFUSE-R

DISABLE-R

DISPOSE-R

ENDORSE-R

ENFORCE-R

ENHANCE-R

EXAMINE-R

EXECUTE-R

EXPLORE-R

FORGIVE-R

FRAGILE-R

GESTURE-R

GRAPPLE-R

GRUMBLE-R

IMAGINE-R

IMMENSE-R

IMPROVE-R

INQUIRE-R

INTRUDE-R

JOYRIDE-R

JUSTICE-R

LECTURE-R

LICENCE-R

LICENSE-R

MEASURE-R

MISTAKE-R

NARRATE-R

NEWCOME-R

NURTURE-R

OBSCURE-R

OBSERVE-R

OUTLINE-R

OUTSIDE-R

PERJURE-R

PILLAGE-R

POLLUTE-R

PRECISE-R

PREFACE-R

PREPARE-R

PRODUCE-R

PROFILE-R

PROMOTE-R

PROPOSE-R

PROVIDE-R

RECEIVE-R

RECLINE-R

RECYCLE-R

REPLACE-R

RESERVE-R

RESTORE-R

REVERSE-R

REVOLVE-R

REWRITE-R

SERVICE-R

SHUTTLE-R

SILENCE-R

SINCERE-R

STICKLE-R

STRANGE-R

SURVIVE-R

TEENAGE-R

TOASTIE-R

TOPLINE-R

TORTURE-R

TROUBLE-R

TWINKLE-R

UPGRADE-R

UPSTATE-R

VENTURE-R

VILLAGE-R

WELCOME-R

WHISTLE-R

WHITTLE-R

R

Blockers

It is useful to know which words are blockers and can't therefore be extended before or after. You may want to play a blocker that your opponent can't extend, or you may want to avoid playing a blocker because you want to keep the board open.

Some three-letter blockers beginning with R

RAX   RHY

Some four-letter blockers beginning with R

| RAZZ | RELY | ROUX |
| REFT | ROPY | RUBY |

Some five-letter blockers beginning with R
(except words ending in '-ED', '-J', '-S', '-X', '-Y' or '-Z')

RABID	REDID	RESAT
RADII	RELIT	RIFER
RARER	RENAL	RUNIC
RASTA	RERAN	

R

Some six-letter blockers beginning with R
(except words ending in '-ED', '-J', '-S', '-X', '-Y' or '-Z')

RACIAL	REDONE	RESHOD
RACIER	REDREW	RESHOT
RADDER	REFLEW	RETOOK
RADGER	REGAVE	RETORN
RADISH	REGNAL	RETROD
RAKISH	REGREW	RICHER
RANCID	REHASH	RIDDEN
RAREST	REHUNG	RIFEST
RARING	RELAID	RIPEST
RATHER	RELISH	ROPIER
RAVISH	RESAID	RUEFUL
RAWISH	RESEEN	

R

Bonus words

Bonus words on your rack can be hard to spot, especially for the less experienced player. One way to help find them is by using prefixes and suffixes.

Many larger words include a common prefix or suffix – remembering these and using them where you can is a good way to discover any longer words on your rack, including any potential bonus words. The key prefixes to remember beginning with R are RE- and RED-.

Some words beginning with RE-
Seven-letter words

RE-ACTED	RE-CITED	RE-FILLS
RE-ADAPT	RE-CLAIM	RE-FINED
RE-AGENT	RE-COILS	RE-FORMS
RE-ALIGN	RE-CORDS	RE-FRESH
RE-APING	RE-COUNT	RE-FUSED
RE-APPLY	RE-COVER	RE-GALES
RE-BATED	RE-CYCLE	RE-GENTS
RE-BIRTH	RE-DEEMS	RE-GROUP
RE-BOOTS	RE-DOUBT	RE-GROWN
RE-BOUND	RE-DRAFT	RE-HOUSE
RE-BRAND	RE-DRESS	RE-INTER
RE-BUILD	RE-DUCES	RE-ISSUE
RE-CALLS	RE-ELECT	RE-JOINS
RE-CEDED	RE-ENACT	RE-KEYED
RE-CITAL	RE-ENTRY	RE-LAPSE

RE-LAXER
RE-LEASE
RE-LIVED
RE-LOADS
RE-LYING
RE-MAINS
RE-MARKS
RE-MATCH
RE-MINDS
RE-MIXED
RE-MORSE
RE-MOVED
RE-NEWER
RE-ORDER
RE-PAINT
RE-PASTS
RE-PEALS
RE-PEATS
RE-PLACE
RE-PLAYS

RE-PLIES
RE-PORTS
RE-PRESS
RE-PRINT
RE-QUEST
RE-READS
RE-ROUTE
RE-SEALS
RE-SERVE
RE-SIDED
RE-SIGNS
RE-SISTS
RE-SOLVE
RE-SOUND
RE-SPIRE
RE-SPITE
RE-START
RE-STATE
RE-STING
RE-STORE

RE-TAILS
RE-TAPED
RE-TEACH
RE-THINK
RE-TIRED
RE-TRACT
RE-TREAD
RE-TREAT
RE-TURNS
RE-UNIFY
RE-UNION
RE-UNITE
RE-VENGE
RE-VERSE
RE-VISED
RE-VOLVE
RE-WORKS
RE-WOUND
RE-WRITE

Eight-letter words

RE-ABSORB
RE-ACTION
RE-ADJUST
RE-APPEAR
RE-ASSESS
RE-BOOTED
RE-BUFFED
RE-BUTTED

RE-CALLED
RE-CAPPED
RE-CEDING
RE-CHARGE
RE-CITING
RE-COILED
RE-COMMIT
RE-CONNED

RE-CORDED
RE-COUPED
RE-COURSE
RE-CYCLED
RE-DEEMED
RE-DEFINE
RE-DEPLOY
RE-DESIGN

R

RE-DOUBLE

RE-DUBBED

RE-EMERGE

RE-ENGAGE

RE-ENLIST

RE-FILLED

RE-FINERY

RE-FITTED

RE-FLEXED

RE-FORMAT

RE-FORMED

RE-FUELED

RE-FUNDED

RE-GAINED

RE-GROWTH

RE-HEARSE

RE-HEATED

RE-IGNITE

RE-INVENT

RE-ISSUED

RE-JOINED

RE-KINDLE

RE-LAPSED

RE-LAUNCH

RE-LAYING

RE-LEASED

RE-LIABLE

RE-LOADED

RE-LOCATE

RE-MAKING

RE-MARKED

RE-MASTER

RE-MEMBER

RE-MINDED

RE-MOVING

RE-OCCUPY

RE-OFFEND

RE-PAIRED

RE-PEALED

RE-PHRASE

RE-PLACED

RE-PORTER

RE-PRISED

RE-PUBLIC

RE-QUITED

RE-RECORD

RE-ROUTED

RE-SEALED

RE-SEARCH

RE-SECURE

RE-SIDING

RE-SISTER

RE-SOLVED

RE-SORTED

RE-STORED

RE-STRICT

RE-TAILED

RE-TIRING

RE-TRACED

RE-TURNED

RE-UNITED

RE-USABLE

RE-VALUED

RE-VERSED

RE-VIEWER

RE-VISING

RE-VISION

RE-WARDED

RE-WINDER

RE-WRITER

Some words beginning with RED-
Seven-letter words

RED-BACK	RED-EYES	RED-RAWN
RED-BIRD	RED-FISH	RED-ROOT
RED-CAPS	RED-FOOT	RED-TAIL
RED-COAT	RED-HEAD	RED-TOPS
RED-DENS	RED-LINE	RED-WING
RED-DING	RED-NECK	RED-WOOD
RED-DISH	RED-NESS	

Eight-letter words

RED-BELLY	RED-OLENT	RED-SHIRT
RED-BRICK	RED-SHANK	RED-START
RED-HORSE	RED-SHIFT	RED-WATER
RED-LINED	RED-SHIRE	

Unusual letter combinations

If you have an unusual combination of letters on your rack, or want to impress your opponent with an unusual word, a few words from World English can come in handy.

Australian words

RAZOO	imaginary coin
REGO	registration of a motor vehicle
RESTO	restored antique, vintage car, etc
ROO	kangaroo
ROUGHIE	something unfair, especially a trick

Canadian words

REDEYE	drink incorporating beer and tomato juice

R

| RUBABOO | soup made by boiling pemmican |
| RUBBY | rubbing alcohol mixed with cheap wine for drinking |

Hindi words

RAGGEE	cereal grass
RAITA	yoghurt-and-vegetable dish served with curry
RAJ	government
RAJAH	ruler or landlord
RAMTIL	African plant grown in India
RANI	queen or princess
RATHA	four-wheeled carriage drawn by horses or bullocks
ROTI	type of unleavened bread
RUPEE	standard monetary unit of India
RUPIAH	standard monetary unit of Indonesia
RYOT	peasant or tenant farmer

New Zealand words

RAHUI	Maori prohibition
RATA	myrtaceous forest tree
RAUPATU	seizure of land
RAURIKI	sow thistle

South African words

| ROOIKAT | lynx |

Urdu words

| RABI | crop harvested at the end of winter |

R

Essential info

Value: 1 point

Number in set: 4

The **S** is such a valuable letter for making longer plays, especially a seven-letter bonus word, that it ought not to be squandered in a short two-letter word play. The four twos that begin with S could assist in hooking your play onto an existing word: SH (a sound people make to request silence or quiet, 5 points) and SI, SO and ST (2 each). Quite a few three-letter words which use no vowels begin with S (although you will need a Y), including: SHY (9 points), SKY (10) and SPY (8). S also forms various three-letter words using X, one for each vowel except for U: SAX, SEX, SIX and SOX (10 points each).

Two-letter words beginning with S

SH   SI   SO   ST

Some three-letter words beginning with S

SAB	SAY	SHH	SNY	SOV
SAE	SAZ	SIB	SOC	SOX
SAI	SED	SIC	SOG	SOY
SAL	SEL	SIF	SOH	SUQ
SAM	SEN	SIK	SOL	SUR
SAN	SER	SIM	SOM	SUS
SAR	SEZ	SKA	SOT	SWY
SAX	SHA	SMA	SOU	SYE

S

Hooks

Examples of S as end hooks are not included in this book due to their ease of use as the simple plural form of the word originally played. We recommend checking the Collins Scrabble Dictionary (or the dictionary you are using) if you are in any doubt.

Some front-hooks
Two letters to three

S-AB	S-AW	S-EX	S-MA	S-OW
S-AD	S-AX	S-HA	S-NY	S-OX
S-AE	S-AY	S-HE	S-OB	S-OY
S-AG	S-EA	S-IF	S-OD	S-PA
S-AI	S-ED	S-IN	S-OH	S-UM
S-AL	S-EE	S-IS	S-OM	S-UN
S-AM	S-EL	S-IT	S-ON	S-UP
S-AN	S-EN	S-KA	S-OP	S-UR
S-AR	S-ER	S-KI	S-OS	S-US
S-AT	S-ET	S-KY	S-OU	S-YE

Three letters to four

S-ADO	S-ALE	S-ATE
S-AGA	S-ALT	S-AVE
S-AGE	S-AND	S-AWN
S-AGO	S-ANE	S-CAB
S-AID	S-ARK	S-CAG
S-AIL	S-ARS	S-CAM
S-AIR	S-ASH	S-CAN
S-AKE	S-ASS	S-CAR

S

S-CAT	S-KID	S-NOT
S-CRY	S-KIN	S-NOW
S-CUD	S-KIP	S-OAK
S-CUM	S-KIT	S-OAR
S-EAR	S-LAB	S-ODA
S-EAT	S-LAM	S-OFT
S-EEK	S-LAP	S-OIL
S-EEN	S-LAT	S-OLD
S-ELF	S-LAY	S-OLE
S-ELL	S-LED	S-OON
S-END	S-LEW	S-OOT
S-HAH	S-LID	S-ORE
S-HAM	S-LIP	S-ORT
S-HAW	S-LIT	S-OUP
S-HEW	S-LOB	S-OUR
S-HIN	S-LOG	S-OWN
S-HIP	S-LOP	S-PAM
S-HOD	S-LOT	S-PAN
S-HOE	S-LOW	S-PAR
S-HOP	S-LUG	S-PAT
S-HOT	S-LUM	S-PAY
S-HOW	S-LUR	S-PEC
S-HUN	S-MOG	S-PEW
S-HUT	S-MUG	S-PIN
S-ICK	S-MUT	S-PIT
S-IDE	S-NAG	S-POT
S-ILK	S-NAP	S-PRY
S-ILL	S-NIB	S-PUD
S-INK	S-NIP	S-PUN
S-IRE	S-NOB	S-PUR

S

S-TAB   S-TOP   S-WAG
S-TAG   S-TOT   S-WAN
S-TAR   S-TOW   S-WAP
S-TAT   S-TUB   S-WAT
S-TAY   S-TUN   S-WAY
S-TEN   S-UMP   S-WIG
S-TET   S-URE   S-WOP
S-TEW   S-WAB

Four letters to five

S-ABLE	S-CRAM	S-HARE
S-AGER	S-CRAN	S-HARK
S-ALLY	S-CREW	S-HARP
S-AUNT	S-CROW	S-HAVE
S-AVER	S-CUFF	S-HEAR
S-AWED	S-CULL	S-HELL
S-CAMP	S-EDGE	S-HERE
S-CANT	S-EVEN	S-HILL
S-CAPE	S-EVER	S-HIRE
S-CARE	S-EWER	S-HOCK
S-CART	S-EXED	S-HOED
S-COFF	S-HACK	S-HONE
S-COLD	S-HAFT	S-HOOK
S-CONE	S-HAKE	S-HOOT
S-COOP	S-HALE	S-HORN
S-COOT	S-HALL	S-HOVE
S-COPE	S-HALT	S-HUCK
S-CORE	S-HAME	S-HUNT
S-CORN	S-HANK	S-HUSH
S-COWL	S-HARD	S-IDLE

S

S-IRED	S-MOCK	S-TACK
S-KELP	S-MOKE	S-TAKE
S-KILL	S-NAIL	S-TALE
S-KINK	S-NIFF	S-TALK
S-LACK	S-OILY	S-TALL
S-LAIN	S-OWED	S-TANK
S-LAKE	S-PACE	S-TART
S-LANG	S-PAIN	S-TATE
S-LASH	S-PARE	S-TEAK
S-LATE	S-PARK	S-TEAL
S-LEEK	S-PATE	S-TEAM
S-LEET	S-PAWN	S-TEED
S-LICE	S-PEAK	S-TEEL
S-LICK	S-PEAR	S-TERN
S-LIME	S-PECK	S-TICK
S-LOAN	S-PELT	S-TIFF
S-LOPE	S-PEND	S-TILE
S-LOTH	S-PIKE	S-TILL
S-LUMP	S-PILL	S-TINT
S-LUNG	S-PINE	S-TOCK
S-LUNK	S-PLAY	S-TONE
S-LUSH	S-POKE	S-TOOK
S-MACK	S-POOL	S-TOOL
S-MALL	S-PORE	S-TOUT
S-MART	S-PORT	S-TOWN
S-MASH	S-POUT	S-TRAP
S-MELL	S-PRAY	S-TRAY
S-MELT	S-PROG	S-TRIP
S-MILE	S-QUAD	S-TUCK
S-MITE	S-QUID	S-URGE

S

S-WARM   S-WELT   S-WIPE
S-WEAR   S-WEPT   S-WISH
S-WEEP   S-WILL   S-WORD
S-WEER   S-WINE   S-WORE
S-WELL   S-WING

Five letters to six

S-ADDER	S-ELECT	S-LEDGE
S-ADDLE	S-ENDER	S-LIGHT
S-AILED	S-ENTRY	S-LIMED
S-ALLOW	S-EXIST	S-LOPED
S-ALTER	S-HANDY	S-LOWER
S-AMPLE	S-HARPY	S-LOWLY
S-AVANT	S-HAVEN	S-MIDGE
S-AWING	S-HAVER	S-MILER
S-CABBY	S-HEATH	S-MITER
S-CARED	S-HIRED	S-MOGGY
S-CATTY	S-HOVED	S-NAKED
S-COPED	S-HOVEL	S-NAPPY
S-CORED	S-HOVER	S-NATCH
S-CRAWL	S-ICKER	S-NIFFY
S-CREAM	S-ICKLE	S-OAKED
S-CREED	S-IDLED	S-OARED
S-CRIED	S-INKER	S-OFTEN
S-CRIMP	S-INNER	S-OILED
S-CURRY	S-KIDDY	S-OLDER
S-CURVY	S-KITED	S-OMBRE
S-EARED	S-LAKED	S-OUGHT
S-EATER	S-LATER	S-OUPED
S-EDUCE	S-LAYER	S-OWING

S-PACED	S-TARRY	S-TUBBY
S-PARED	S-TENCH	S-UNDER
S-PARKY	S-TICKY	S-UNLIT
S-PARSE	S-TILED	S-UPPER
S-PAYED	S-TITCH	S-URGED
S-PIKER	S-TONED	S-WAGER
S-PINED	S-TOWED	S-WAYED
S-POKED	S-TRAIN	S-WEEPY
S-PORED	S-TRIKE	S-WIPED
S-POTTY	S-TRIPE	S-WITCH
S-PRINT	S-TROLL	S-WOOSH
S-QUASH	S-TROVE	
S-TABLE	S-TRUCK	

Six letters to seven

S-ADDLED	S-CORING	S-HARKED
S-AILING	S-CORNED	S-HARPER
S-ALLIED	S-CORNER	S-HATTER
S-AMPLER	S-CRUMMY	S-HAVING
S-CABBED	S-CUDDLE	S-HIPPED
S-CAMPER	S-CUFFED	S-HOOTER
S-CANNED	S-CUPPER	S-HOPPED
S-CANTER	S-CUTTLE	S-HOVING
S-CARING	S-EATING	S-HUNTED
S-CARPER	S-EDUCED	S-HUSHED
S-COFFER	S-ELFISH	S-INKING
S-COLDER	S-ENDING	S-KIDDED
S-COOPER	S-HACKED	S-KILLED
S-COOTER	S-HALLOW	S-KIPPED
S-COPING	S-HARING	S-KIPPER

S

S-KITING	S-MELTED	S-TABLED
S-LACKED	S-MITTEN	S-TACKED
S-LAKING	S-MOCKED	S-TAGGER
S-LAMMED	S-MOLDER	S-TAKING
S-LANDER	S-MOTHER	S-TALKED
S-LAPPED	S-MUGGER	S-TALKER
S-LASHED	S-NAGGED	S-TAMPER
S-LASHER	S-NAILED	S-TEAMED
S-LAYING	S-NAPPED	S-TICKER
S-LEDGED	S-NIPPED	S-TICKLE
S-LEDGER	S-OILING	S-TILTED
S-LENDER	S-PACING	S-TINGED
S-LICKED	S-PANNER	S-TINKER
S-LIMIER	S-PARING	S-TONING
S-LINGER	S-PARKED	S-TOPPED
S-LINKED	S-PARSER	S-TUMBLE
S-LITHER	S-PATTER	S-UNLESS
S-LOGGED	S-PAWNED	S-UNLIKE
S-LOPING	S-PAYING	S-URGING
S-LOWEST	S-PLAYED	S-WAGGER
S-LUGGED	S-PONGED	S-WALLOW
S-LUMBER	S-POOLED	S-WARMED
S-LUMPED	S-PORTED	S-WAYING
S-LUSHED	S-POTTED	S-WEEPER
S-MASHED	S-PRAYED	S-WIPING
S-MATTER	S-PURRED	S-WITHER
S-MELLED	S-TABBED	S-WORDED

Seven letters to eight

S-ADDLING

S-ALLOWED

S-ALLYING

S-CANNING

S-CARLESS

S-CRAMMED

S-CRAWLED

S-CREAMED

S-CRUMPLE

S-CRUNCHY

S-CUFFING

S-CURRIED

S-EDITION

S-ELECTED

S-HACKING

S-HACKLED

S-HARKING

S-HEARING

S-HEATHER

S-HILLING

S-HIPPING

S-HOCKING

S-HOOTING

S-HOPPING

S-HUNTING

S-HUSHING

S-HUTTING

S-KIDDING

S-KILLING

S-KINLESS

S-KIPPING

S-LACKING

S-LAPPING

S-LASHING

S-LIGHTLY

S-LOWDOWN

S-LOWNESS

S-LUGGING

S-MASHING

S-MELTING

S-MOOCHED

S-MOULDER

S-NAPPING

S-NIPPING

S-OFTENER

S-PANNING

S-PARKING

S-PAWNING

S-PEAKING

S-PILLAGE

S-PILLING

S-PINNING

S-PITTING

S-PLATTER

S-PLAYING

S-POOLING

S-PORTING

S-POTTING

S-PRAYING

S-PRINTED

S-QUASHED

S-TABBING

S-TABLING

S-TACKING

S-TAKEOUT

S-TALKING

S-TEAMING

S-TICKING

S-TICKLED

S-TILTING

S-TOPPING

S-TOWAWAY

S-TRAINED

S-TRAPPED

S-TRESSED

S-TRIDENT

S-TRIPPED

S-TRUMPET

S-TUMBLED

S-UNBAKED

S-UNBLOCK

S-WADDLED

S-WARMING

S-WEEPING

S-WILLING

S-WINGING

S-WORDING

S

Some end-hooks
Two letters to three

AA-S	EM-S	LO-S	PE-S
AB-S	EN-S	MA-S	PI-S
AD-S	ER-S	MI-S	PO-S
AG-S	ES-S	ME-S	QI-S
AH-S	FA-S	MI-S	RE-S
AI-S	FE-S	MO-S	SI-S
AL-S	GI-S	MU-S	SO-S
AR-S	GO-S	NA-S	TA-S
AS-S	GU-S	NO-S	TE-S
AY-S	HA-S	NU-S	TI-S
BA-S	HE-S	NY-S	UG-S
BE-S	HI-S	OB-S	UN-S
BI-S	HO-S	OD-S	UP-S
BO-S	ID-S	OE-S	UT-S
BY-S	IF-S	OH-S	WO-S
DA-S	IN-S	OM-S	XI-S
DI-S	IO-S	ON-S	YE-S
DPO-S	IT-S	OO-S	YO-S
EA-S	KA-S	OP-S	YU-S
ED-S	KI-S	OR-S	ZA-S
EF-S	KO-S	OU-S	ZO-S
EH-S	LA-S	OY-S	
EL-S	LI-S	PA-S	

S

Blockers

It is useful to know which words are blockers and can't therefore be extended before or after. You may want to play a blocker that your opponent can't extend, or you may want to avoid playing a blocker because you want to keep the board open.

Some three-letter blockers beginning with S

SAE	SHH	SMA
SAZ	SIX	SOX
SEZ	SLY	SWY

Some four-letter blockers beginning with S

SAGY	SEWN	SOON
SASH	SEXY	SPED
SAWN	SHMO	SPRY
SCRY	SHOD	SUCH
SECO	SIZY	SUNG
SEEN	SOHO	SUSS
SESH	SOME	SWUM

Some five-letter blockers beginning with S
(except words ending in '-ED', '-J', '-S', '-X', '-Y' or '-Z')

SAFER	SHERE	SHOWN
SANER	SHEWN	SHUSH
SHALT	SHONE	SINCE
SHAWN	SHORN	SITKA

SKINT   SNUCK   STUNK

SLAIN   SOCKO   SUPRA

SLASH   SORBO   SWANG

SLEPT   SORER   SWAPT

SLIPT   SPAKE   SWEPT

SLUNG   SPENT   SWOPT

SLUNK   STAID   SWORE

SLYER   STASH   SWORN

SMASH   STEPT   SWUNG

SMOTE   STOOD

SMUSH   STUNG

Some six-letter blockers ending with S
(except words ending in '-ED', '-J', '-S', '-X', '-Y' or '-Z')

SADDER   SCORCH   SHOULD

SAFEST   SCOTCH   SHRANK

SAFING   SEAMAN   SHREWD

SAGEST   SEAMEN   SHRUNK

SAGIER   SEARCH   SHYEST

SAIRER   SEARER   SHYING

SAMIER   SEDENT   SHYISH

SANCTA   SELDOM   SICKER

SANEST   SEMPER   SINFUL

SANING   SEXIER   SIRING

SAPFUL   SHAKEN   SITING

SATING   SHAPEN   SKOOSH

SAYEST   SHAVEN   SKYING

SCOOCH   SHAZAM   SKYLIT

SCOOSH   SHEESH   SLEAZO

SLIEST   SOUGHT   STRODE

SLOWER   SOURER   STRONG

SLYEST   SPEECH   STRUCK

SLYISH   SPLOSH   STRUNG

SMOOSH   SPOILT   SUABLE

SNIDER   SPOKEN   SUAVER

SOAKEN   SPRUNG   SUBSEA

SOBFUL   SPRYER   SUNKEN

SOFTER   STALER   SUNLIT

SOLEMN   STINKO   SUPERB

SOLING   STITCH   SUREST

SORDID   STOLEN   SWOOSH

SOREST   STREWN

Handy Hint: saving the S for last

If you can earn 10 points more by playing the S then do so,
otherwise consider holding it back as an investment for
better scores later in the game. More experienced players
tend to save S tiles instead of playing them immediately.
This is because S is easy to play at the end of a six-letter
word, thus making it much easier to score a 50-point
bonus word by using all your tiles in one go.

S

Bonus words

Bonus words on your rack can be hard to spot, especially for the less experienced player. One way to help find them is by using prefixes and suffixes.

Many larger words include a common prefix or suffix – remembering these and using them where you can is a good way to discover any longer words on your rack, including any potential bonus words. The key prefixes to remember beginning with S are SEA-, SUB- and SUN- and the key suffixes are -SET, -SHIP, -SKIN, -SMAN and -SOME.

Some words beginning with SEA-
Seven-letter words

SEA-BANK	SEA-LANT	SEA-SICK
SEA-BEDS	SEA-LIFT	SEA-SIDE
SEA-BIRD	SEA-LINE	SEA-SING
SEA-DOGS	SEA-LING	SEA-SONS
SEA-FOLK	SEA-MAID	SEA-TING
SEA-FOOD	SEA-MING	SEA-WALL
SEA-FOWL	SEA-PORT	SEA-WARD
SEA-GULL	SEA-REST	SEA-WEED
SEA-HAWK	SEA-RING	SEA-ZING

Eight-letter words

SEA-BEACH

SEA-BOARD

SEA-BORNE

SEA-COAST

SEA-CRAFT

SEA-DROME

SEA-FARER

SEA-FLOOR

SEA-FRONT

SEA-GOING

SEA-HORSE

SEA-HOUND

SEA-MANLY

SEA-MOUNT

SEA-PLANE

SEA-QUAKE

SEA-SCAPE

SEA-SCOUT

SEA-SHELL

SEA-SHORE

SEA-SPEAK

SEA-TRAIN

SEA-TROUT

SEA-WATER

Some words beginning with SUB-
Seven-letter words

SUB-AQUA

SUB-ARID

SUB-ATOM

SUB-BASS

SUB-BING

SUB-CELL

SUB-CODE

SUB-CULT

SUB-DUCE

SUB-DUED

SUB-DUES

SUB-EDIT

SUB-FILE

SUB-ITEM

SUB-JOIN

SUB-LETS

SUB-LIME

SUB-MISS

SUB-PLOT

SUB-RENT

SUB-RULE

SUB-SECT

SUB-SETS

SUB-SIDE

SUB-SIST

SUB-SOIL

SUB-TASK

SUB-TEND

SUB-TEXT

SUB-TONE

SUB-TYPE

SUB-UNIT

SUB-URBS

SUB-VERT

SUB-WAYS

SUB-ZERO

S

Eight-letter words

SUB-ADULT

SUB-AGENT

SUB-BASIN

SUB-CHORD

SUB-CLAIM

SUB-CLASS

SUB-DUING

SUB-DURAL

SUB-ENTRY

SUB-EQUAL

SUB-FLOOR

SUB-GENRE

SUB-GRADE

SUB-GROUP

SUB-HUMAN

SUB-INDEX

SUB-LEASE

SUB-LEVEL

SUB-LIMED

SUB-MERGE

SUB-POLAR

SUB-SCALE

SUB-SENSE

SUB-SERVE

SUB-SIDED

SUB-SIDER

SUB-SKILL

SUB-SONIC

SUB-SPACE

SUB-STAGE

SUB-STATE

SUB-TITLE

SUB-TOPIC

SUB-TOTAL

SUB-TRACT

SUB-URBAN

SUB-URBIA

SUB-VERSE

SUB-WAYED

SUB-WORLD

Some words beginning with SUN-

Seven-letter words

SUN-BACK

SUN-BAKE

SUN-BEAM

SUN-BEDS

SUN-BELT

SUN-BURN

SUN-DIAL

SUN-DOWN

SUN-FISH

SUN-HATS

SUN-LAMP

SUN-LESS

SUN-NIES

SUN-RAYS

SUN-RISE

SUN-ROOF

SUN-SETS

SUN-SPOT

SUN-TANS

SUN-TRAP

SUN-WARD

SUN-WISE

S

Eight-letter words

SUN-BAKED	SUN-BURST	SUN-LIGHT
SUN-BATHE	SUN-DERED	SUN-PROOF
SUN-BERRY	SUN-DRESS	SUN-SHADE
SUN-BLOCK	SUN-DRILY	SUN-SHINE
SUN-BURNT	SUN-GLASS	SUN-SHINY

Some words ending with -SET

Seven-letter words

BACK-SET	HAND-SET	MOON-SET
BONE-SET	HARD-SET	OVER-SET
BRAS-SET	HEAD-SET	TOOL-SET
CHIP-SET	LOCK-SET	TWIN-SET
FILM-SET	MIND-SET	TYPE-SET

Eight-letter words

EARTH-SET	PHOTO-SET	THICK-SET
HEAVY-SET	QUICK-SET	THORN-SET
MARMO-SET	SOMER-SET	UNDER-SET

Some words ending with -SHIP

Seven-letter words

AIR-SHIP	KIN-SHIP	SON-SHIP
END-SHIP	MID-SHIP	WAR-SHIP
GOD-SHIP	PAL-SHIP	WOR-SHIP
GUN-SHIP	PRE-SHIP	

S

Eight-letter words

AMID-SHIP	HARD-SHIP	POET-SHIP
BARD-SHIP	HEAD-SHIP	POPE-SHIP
CLAN-SHIP	HEIR-SHIP	SERF-SHIP
DEAN-SHIP	HERO-SHIP	STAR-SHIP
DUKE-SHIP	KING-SHIP	TANK-SHIP
EARL-SHIP	LADY-SHIP	TOWN-SHIP
FIRE-SHIP	LONG-SHIP	TWIN-SHIP
FLAG-SHIP	LORD-SHIP	WARD-SHIP
FORE-SHIP	MATE-SHIP	

Some words ending with -SKIN

Seven-letter words

CAT-SKIN	DOG-SKIN	OIL-SKIN
COW-SKIN	FOX-SKIN	PIG-SKIN
DOE-SKIN	KID-SKIN	

Eight-letter words

BEAR-SKIN	FISH-SKIN	WINE-SKIN
BUCK-SKIN	GOAT-SKIN	WOLF-SKIN
CALF-SKIN	LAMB-SKIN	WOOL-SKIN
CAPE-SKIN	MOLE-SKIN	
DEER-SKIN	SEAL-SKIN	

S

Some words ending with -SMAN
Seven-letter words

ART-SMAN
BAT-SMAN
DAY-SMAN
KIN-SMAN
LEN-SMAN

MAG-SMAN
MES-SMAN
MOB-SMAN
NEW-SMAN
OAR-SMAN

ODD-SMAN
PAS-SMAN
ROD-SMAN
TAP-SMAN
TOP-SMAN

Eight-letter words

BAIL-SMAN
BAND-SMAN
BANK-SMAN
BLUE-SMAN
BOAT-SMAN
BOND-SMAN
CHES-SMAN
CLAN-SMAN
CLAS-SMAN
CORP-SMAN
DOOM-SMAN
DOOR-SMAN
GAME-SMAN

GANG-SMAN
GILD-SMAN
GLAS-SMAN
GOWN-SMAN
HEAD-SMAN
HELM-SMAN
HERD-SMAN
HUNT-SMAN
ISLE-SMAN
LAND-SMAN
LINE-SMAN
LINK-SMAN
LOCK-SMAN

MARK-SMAN
PRES-SMAN
PUNT-SMAN
RAFT-SMAN
RAMP-SMAN
ROAD-SMAN
SALE-SMAN
SIDE-SMAN
SWAG-SMAN
TALI-SMAN
TIDE-SMAN
TOWN-SMAN
WOOD-SMAN

S

Some words ending with -SOME
Seven-letter words

AWE-SOME

FUL-SOME

IRK-SOME

LIS-SOME

NOI-SOME

TOY-SOME

TRI-SOME

TWO-SOME

WAG-SOME

WIN-SOME

WOE-SOME

Eight-letter words

BORE-SOME

DARK-SOME

DOLE-SOME

DUEL-SOME

FEAR-SOME

FOUR-SOME

FRET-SOME

GLAD-SOME

GLEE-SOME

GRUE-SOME

HAND-SOME

JOKE-SOME

LARK-SOME

LONE-SOME

LONG-SOME

LOTH-SOME

LOVE-SOME

MURK-SOME

PLAY-SOME

PYRO-SOME

RIBO-SOME

ROOM-SOME

TEDI-SOME

TIRE-SOME

TOIL-SOME

WORK-SOME

Unusual letter combinations

If you have an unusual combination of letters on your rack, or want to impress your opponent with an unusual word, a few words from World English can come in handy.

Australian words

SANGER	sandwich
SCOZZA	rowdy person
SCUNGY	miserable, sordid or dirty person
SHARPIE	a member of a teenage group with short hair and distinctive clothes
SHERANG	boss
SHYPOO	liquor of poor quality
SITELLA	small black-and-white bird
SKEG	rear fin on the underside of a surfboard
SKITE	boast
SMOKO	cigarette break
SPRUIK	speak in public
SWAGMAN	vagrant worker
SWY	a gambling game

Canadian words

SKOOKUM	strong or brave
SNYE	side channel of a river
SPLAKE	hybrid trout bred by Canadian zoologists
SWILER	seal hunter

S

Hindi words

SAMBAR   deer with three-tined antlers

SAMITI   polictical association

SAMOSA   triangular pastry containing spiced vegetables or meat

SARANGI   stringed instrument played with a bow

SARDAR   Sikh title

SARI   traditional dress of Indian women

SAROD   Indian stringed instrument

SWAMI   title for a Hindu saint or religious teacher

New Zealand words

SHEEPO   person who brings sheep to the catching pen for shearing

South African words

SCAMTO   argot of South African Blacks

SKOLLY   hooligan

SNOEK   edible marine fish

SPEK   bacon, fat or fatty pork

STEEN   variety of white grape

STOKVEL   savings pool or syndicate

Urdu words

SAHIB   title placed after a man's name

SARPANCH   head of a village council

SHALWAR   loose-fitting trousers

SHIKAR   hunting

SICE   servant who looks after horses

S

Essential info

Value: 1 point

Number in set: 6

T is one of the most common consonants in Scrabble. Four two-letter words begin with T (all scoring 2 points), but they are easy to remember as there is one for every vowel except U. Various useful three-letter words begin with T. Some that you may not know include TAI (Chinese system of callisthenics, 3 points), TAO (in Confucian philosophy, the correct course of action, 3 points) and TEF (African grass grown for its grain, 6 points). T is one of the letters of the RETAIN set and is therefore a good letter to keep if trying to get a bonus word.

Two-letter words beginning with T

TA   TE   TI   TO

Some three-letter words beginning with T

TAD	TAU	TEG	TIG	TUM
TAE	TAV	TEL	TIL	TUN
TAI	TAW	TET	TIX	TUP
TAJ	TAY	TEW	TOC	TUT
TAK	TEC	TEX	TOD	TUX
TAM	TED	THO	TOG	TWP
TAO	TEE	TIC	TOM	TYE
TAT	TEF	TID	TOR	

T

Hooks

Hooking requires a subtle change in a player's thought process, in that they must look at words already on the board without becoming distracted by their pronunciation. Simple hooking solutions may be overlooked by a player, but things become easier with T as it is one of the most versatile letters when it comes to combining words.

When it comes to end-hooking, players often concentrate on S, as it can be easy to convert a singular word to a plural. However, T can also be highly effective and by learning a few of the hooks below, many more options present themselves to the player.

Handy Hint: Consonantitis

If you are stuck with very few vowels in your rack but you also have a letter T, it is useful to remember that T can form several words using only consonants. These are TSK (a sound uttered in disapproval, 7 points), TWP (a Welsh word meaning stupid, 8 points), TYG (a cup with more than one handle, 7 points), NTH (of an unspecified number), 6 points and PHT (expression of irritation), 8 points.

T

Some front-hooks
Two letters to three

T-AB	T-AS	T-EL	T-IS	T-OW
T-AD	T-AT	T-EN	T-IT	T-OY
T-AE	T-AW	T-ES	T-OD	T-UG
T-AG	T-AX	T-ET	T-OE	T-UM
T-AI	T-AY	T-EX	T-OM	T-UN
T-AM	T-EA	T-HE	T-ON	T-UP
T-AN	T-ED	T-HO	T-OO	T-UT
T-AP	T-EE	T-ID	T-OP	T-WO
T-AR	T-EF	T-IN	T-OR	T-YE

Three letters to four

T-ABS	T-HAT	T-OUR
T-ACT	T-HAW	T-OUT
T-AIL	T-HEM	T-OWN
T-AKE	T-HEN	T-RAD
T-ALE	T-HEY	T-RAM
T-ALL	T-HIN	T-RAP
T-APE	T-HIS	T-RAY
T-ARE	T-HUG	T-RIM
T-ART	T-ICK	T-RIP
T-ASK	T-IDE	T-ROD
T-ATE	T-ILL	T-ROT
T-EAR	T-IRE	T-RUE
T-EAT	T-OFF	T-URN
T-ELL	T-OIL	T-WEE
T-END	T-OLD	T-WIG
T-EST	T-ONE	T-WIN
T-HAN	T-OOT	T-WIT

T

Four letters to five

T-ABLE	T-HORN	T-REND
T-ACHE	T-HOSE	T-RIAL
T-ALKY	T-HUMP	T-RICK
T-ALLY	T-IMID	T-RIPS
T-APED	T-IRED	T-ROLL
T-APER	T-IRES	T-ROOP
T-AUNT	T-ITCH	T-ROUT
T-AWNY	T-OAST	T-RUCK
T-AXED	T-ONER	T-RUER
T-AXES	T-OUCH	T-RULY
T-EACH	T-OWED	T-RUST
T-EASE	T-OWER	T-RUTH
T-EDDY	T-RACE	T-WANG
T-EMPT	T-RACK	T-WEAK
T-EPEE	T-RADE	T-WEED
T-HANK	T-RAIL	T-WEET
T-HEFT	T-RAIN	T-WICE
T-HEIR	T-RAIT	T-WINE
T-HERE	T-RAMP	T-WINY
T-HICK	T-RASH	T-WIST
T-HIGH	T-READ	
T-HING	T-REES	

T

Five letters to six

T-ABBED	T-ERROR	T-OUTER
T-ABLED	T-ESTER	T-OWING
T-ABLET	T-ETHER	T-RACED
T-AILED	T-HANKS	T-RACER
T-ANGLE	T-HATCH	T-RACES
T-ANNOY	T-HAWED	T-RANCE
T-APING	T-HENCE	T-RAVEL
T-ASKED	T-HORNY	T-RIFLE
T-ASTER	T-HOUGH	T-ROUGH
T-AUGHT	T-ICKLE	T-ROWEL
T-AXING	T-INGLE	T-RUSTY
T-AXMAN	T-INNER	T-UMBLE
T-EARED	T-IRADE	T-URBAN
T-EASED	T-IRING	T-URNED
T-EASER	T-ISSUE	T-WEEDY
T-EASES	T-OASTS	T-WIGGY
T-ENDED	T-OILED	T-WINGE
T-ENDER	T-OTTER	T-WIRED
T-ENURE	T-OUTED	T-WITCH

T

Six letters to seven

T-ABLING

T-AILING

T-ALLIED

T-ANGLER

T-ASKING

T-EARFUL

T-EASING

T-EDDIES

T-ENABLE

T-ENDING

T-ENFOLD

T-ENURED

T-ISSUED

T-OILING

T-ESTATE

T-HANKER

T-HAWING

T-HEREBY

T-HEREIN

T-HUMPED

T-INNING

T-OUTING

T-RACING

T-RACKED

T-RAILER

T-RAINED

T-RAMPED

T-RAPPER

T-RASHES

T-RAVELS

T-REASON

T-RIFLES

T-RIGGER

T-RILLED

T-RIMMED

T-RIPPED

T-ROTTER

T-ROUBLE

T-RUCKED

T-RUFFLE

T-RUSTED

T-UNABLE

T-WEAKER

T-WIGGED

T-WINGED

T-WINKLE

T-WITCHY

T-WITTER

Seven letters to eight

T-ALLOWED

T-ALLYING

T-ANGLING

T-ANNOYED

T-APELIKE

T-EARDROP

T-ENFOLDS

T-ENTERED

T-HATCHED

T-HICKIES

T-HUMPING

T-ISSUING

T-RACKING

T-RAILING

T-RAINING

T-RAMMING

T-RAMPING

T-RAPPING

T-RASHING

T-RAVELER

T-READING

T-RIFLING

T-RIMMING

T-RIPPING

T-ROTTING

T-RUCKING

T-RUSTING

T-WEEDIER

T-WIGLESS

T-WINGING

T-WINKLED

T-WINNING

T-WITCHES

Some end-hooks
Two letters to three

AI-T	DO-T	HA-T	MA-T	OP-T	SO-T
AL-T	EA-T	HE-T	ME-T	OR-T	TA-T
AN-T	EF-T	HI-T	MO-T	OU-T	TE-T
AR-T	EL-T	HO-T	MU-T	OW-T	TI-T
AT-T	ES-T	JO-T	NA-T	PA-T	TO-T
BA-T	FA-T	KA-T	NE-T	PE-T	WE-T
BE-T	FE-T	KI-T	NO-T	PI-T	WO-T
BI-T	GI-T	LA-T	NU-T	PO-T	YE-T
BO-T	GO-T	LI-T	OF-T	RE-T	
DI-T	GU-T	LO-T	OO-T	SI-T	

Three letters to four

BEE-T	DOL-T	KEP-T	PAS-T	TAR-T
BEN-T	DUE-T	LAS-T	PES-T	TAU-T
BOA-T	EAS-T	LIN-T	PIN-T	TEN-T
BOO-T	FAS-T	LIS-T	POS-T	TES-T
CAN-T	FEE-T	LOS-T	RAN-T	TIN-T
CAR-T	FON-T	LOU-T	RAP-T	TOO-T
CEL-T	FOR-T	MAL-T	REN-T	UNI-T
CHA-T	GEN-T	MAS-T	RES-T	VAS-T
CHI-T	GIF-T	MEL-T	RIF-T	VOL-T
COL-T	GIS-T	MIS-T	ROO-T	WAI-T
COO-T	GOA-T	MOA-T	RUN-T	WAN-T
COS-T	GUS-T	MOO-T	SAL-T	WAT-T
CUR-T	HIN-T	MOS-T	SEA-T	WEN-T
DEB-T	HOO-T	MUS-T	SEN-T	WHA-T
DEF-T	HUN-T	NEW-T	SKI-T	WIS-T
DEN-T	JOL-T	PAC-T	SPA-T	ZOO-T
DIE-T	JUS-T	PAR-T	SUI-T	

Four letters to five

AVER-T	FACE-T	OVER-T
BEAU-T	FILE-T	PLAN-T
BLUR-T	FIRS-T	PLEA-T
BOAS-T	FLEE-T	ROOS-T
BOOS-T	GRAN-T	SHIR-T
BURN-T	GUES-T	SHOO-T
CADE-T	HEAR-T	SIGH-T
CHAR-T	ISLE-T	SPUR-T
CLEF-T	JOIN-T	STAR-T
COME-T	LEAN-T	STUN-T
COVE-T	LEAP-T	TEMP-T
DEAL-T	MEAN-T	TWEE-T
EVEN-T	NIGH-T	VALE-T

Five letters to six

BARES-T	FORES-T	PALES-T
BASAL-T	FORGE-T	PLANE-T
BASES-T	FORGO-T	PURES-T
BLUES-T	GADGE-T	RABBI-T
BONNE-T	GAMES-T	RARES-T
BOUGH-T	HONES-T	RIPES-T
BUDGE-T	IDLES-T	SAFES-T
CACHE-T	LANCE-T	SAGES-T
CLOSE-T	LAXES-T	SHIES-T
COVER-T	LEARN-T	SONNE-T
DIVER-T	LOCUS-T	SORES-T
DRIES-T	MIDGE-T	SPOIL-T
FILLE-T	MODES-T	TURBO-T
FINES-T	MUTES-T	WEIGH-T

Six letters to seven

ARCHES-T	DEARES-T	RICHES-T
ARTIES-T	EASIES-T	ROSIES-T
BRAVES-T	FALSES-T	SINGLE-T
BROUGH-T	GRAVES-T	STALES-T
BUSIES-T	HOLIES-T	TENSES-T
CLOSES-T	INANES-T	THOUGH-T
CONSUL-T	LAZIES-T	TIDIES-T
COSIES-T	LUSHES-T	TINIES-T
COUPLE-T	NAIVES-T	TRITES-T
COZIES-T	NOBLES-T	UGLIES-T
CRUDES-T	PERCEN-T	WARRAN-T
CURRAN-T	POSIES-T	WAVIES-T

Seven letters to eight

ANGRIES-T	FRESHES-T	ROOMIES-T
BAGGIES-T	FUNNIES-T	ROWDIES-T
BLONDES-T	GENTLES-T	SAVAGES-T
BULLIES-T	HARDIES-T	SECURES-T
CHOICES-T	HEAVIES-T	SHIPMEN-T
CONTRAS-T	INTERNE-T	SILLIES-T
CRAZIES-T	JOLLIES-T	SIMPLES-T
CROSSES-T	LITTLES-T	SQUARES-T
DIPLOMA-T	LUCKIES-T	STABLES-T
DIVINES-T	MATURES-T	SUNBURN-T
DIZZIES-T	MUDDIES-T	SUNNIES-T
EARLIES-T	NASTIES-T	TALKIES-T
EMPTIES-T	READIES-T	TELETEX-T
FEEBLES-T	REDREAM-T	TINNIES-T
FLAKIES-T	REGIMEN-T	UNLEARN-T
FLASHES-T	REMOTES-T	WEARIES-T

T

Blockers

It is useful to know which words are blockers and can't therefore be extended before or after. You may want to play a blocker that your opponent can't extend, or you may want to avoid playing a blocker because you want to keep the board open.

Some three-letter blockers beginning with T

TAJ	THY	TIX	TUX	TWP

Some four-letter blockers beginning with T

THAT	THIS	TIDY	TOED	TORN
THEY	THUS	TINY	TOLD	

Some five-letter blockers beginning with T
(except words ending in '-ED', '-J', '-S', '-X', '-Y' or '-Z')

TACIT	THIEF	TIDAL
TAKEN	THINE	TIMID
TEACH	THOSE	TRUER

Some six-letter blockers beginning with T
(except words ending in '-ED', '-J', '-S', '-X', '-Y' or '-Z')

TALLER	TAXMEN	THRICE	TRENCH
TAMEST	TENSER	THROWN	TRUEST
TAPING	TERGAL	TINIER	
TAUGHT	THRASH	TINMAN	
TAXMAN	THRESH	TOMATO	

Bonus words

Bonus words on your rack can be hard to spot, especially for the less experienced player. One way to help find them is by using prefixes and suffixes.

Many larger words include a common prefix or suffix – remembering these and using them where you can is a good way to discover any longer words on your rack, including any potential bonus words. The key prefix to remember beginning with T is TRI- and the key suffixes are -TION and -TIME.

Some words beginning with TRI-
Seven-letter words

TRI-ABLE	TRI-COTS	TRI-LOBE	TRI-SECT
TRI-ACID	TRI-DARN	TRI-LOGY	TRI-SEME
TRI-AGED	TRI-DENT	TRI-NARY	TRI-SHAW
TRI-AGES	TRI-DUAN	TRI-ODES	TRI-SOME
TRI-ARCH	TRI-ENES	TRI-ONES	TRI-SOMY
TRI-AXON	TRI-FLED	TRI-OSES	TRI-TEST
TRI-BADE	TRI-FOLD	TRI-OXID	TRI-TIDE
TRI-BLET	TRI-FORM	TRI-PACK	TRI-TONE
TRI-BUTE	TRI-GAMY	TRI-PART	TRI-TONS
TRI-CARS	TRI-GONS	TRI-PIER	TRI-UMPH
TRI-CEPS	TRI-GRAM	TRI-PLED	TRI-VETS
TRI-CLAD	TRI-JETS	TRI-PODS	TRI-VIAL
TRI-CORN	TRI-LITH	TRI-PSIS	TRI-ZONE

T

Eight-letter words

TRI-ACIDS

TRI-AGING

TRI-ALIST

TRI-ANGLE

TRI-AXIAL

TRI-AXONS

TRI-AZINE

TRI-AZOLE

TRI-BALLY

TRI-BASIC

TRI-BLETS

TRI-BRACH

TRI-BUTES

TRI-CHINA

TRI-CHORD

TRI-CLADS

TRI-COLOR

TRI-CORNS

TRI-CYCLE

TRI-DARNS

TRI-DENTS

TRI-ETHYL

TRI-FLING

TRI-FOCAL

TRI-GLYPH

TRI-GRAMS

TRI-GRAPH

TRI-LEMMA

TRI-LITHS

TRI-LOBED

TRI-LOBES

TRI-METER

TRI-MORPH

TRI-MOTOR

TRI-NODAL

TRI-OLEIN

TRI-OXIDE

TRI-OXIDS

TRI-PACKS

TRI-PEDAL

TRI-PHASE

TRI-PHONE

TRI-PLANE

TRI-PLIED

TRI-PLIES

TRI-PLING

TRI-PODAL

TRI-POLIS

TRI-POSES

TRI-SECTS

TRI-SEMES

TRI-SHAWS

TRI-STATE

TRI-STICH

TRI-THING

TRI-TICAL

TRI-TIDES

TRI-TONES

TRI-UNITY

TRI-VALVE

TRI-ZONAL

TRI-ZONES

T

Some words ending with -TIME
Seven-letter words

AIR-TIME	CEN-TIME	ONE-TIME	TEA-TIME
ANY-TIME	DAY-TIME	PAS-TIME	WAR-TIME
BED-TIME	LAY-TIME	RAG-TIME	
BIG-TIME	MIS-TIME	SEP-TIME	

Eight-letter words

CHOW-TIME	LONG-TIME	REAL-TIME
DOWN-TIME	MARI-TIME	SEED-TIME
FLEX-TIME	MEAL-TIME	SHOW-TIME
FORE-TIME	MEAN-TIME	SOME-TIME
GOOD-TIME	NOON-TIME	TERM-TIME
HALF-TIME	OVER-TIME	XENO-TIME
LIFE-TIME	PLAY-TIME	ZONE-TIME

Some words ending with -TION
Seven-letter words

ALA-TION	DIC-TION	MEN-TION	STA-TION
AMA-TION	EDI-TION	MIC-TION	SUC-TION
AMO-TION	ELA-TION	MIX-TION	TAC-TION
AUC-TION	ELU-TION	ORA-TION	TUI-TION
BAS-TION	EMO-TION	OVA-TION	UNC-TION
CAN-TION	EMP-TION	PAC-TION	UNI-TION
CAP-TION	ENA-TION	POR-TION	
CAU-TION	FAC-TION	REC-TION	
COC-TION	FIC-TION	RUC-TION	
COI-TION	LEC-TION	SEC-TION	

Eight-letter words

ABLA-TION	EDUC-TION	IODA-TION
ABLU-TION	EGES-TION	JOBA-TION
ABOR-TION	EJEC-TION	JUNC-TION
ADAP-TION	ELEC-TION	LAVA-TION
ADDI-TION	EMIC-TION	LEGA-TION
ADNA-TION	ENAC-TION	LENI-TION
ADOP-TION	EQUA-TION	LIBA-TION
AERA-TION	EREC-TION	LIGA-TION
AGNA-TION	ERUP-TION	LIMA-TION
AMBI-TION	EVEC-TION	LOBA-TION
AUDI-TION	EVIC-TION	LOCA-TION
AVIA-TION	EXAC-TION	LOCU-TION
BIBA-TION	EXER-TION	LUNA-TION
CIBA-TION	FETA-TION	LUXA-TION
CITA-TION	FIXA-TION	MONI-TION
COAC-TION	FLEC-TION	MUNI-TION
CONA-TION	FRAC-TION	MUTA-TION
COOP-TION	FRIC-TION	NATA-TION
CREA-TION	FRUI-TION	NEGA-TION
DELA-TION	FUNC-TION	NIDA-TION
DELE-TION	GELA-TION	NIVA-TION
DEMO-TION	GUMP-TION	NODA-TION
DERA-TION	HALA-TION	NOLI-TION
DEVO-TION	HIMA-TION	NOTA-TION
DILA-TION	IDEA-TION	NOVA-TION
DILU-TION	IGNI-TION	NUTA-TION
DONA-TION	ILLA-TION	OBLA-TION
DOTA-TION	INAC-TION	PACA-TION
DURA-TION	INUS-TION	PETI-TION

T

POSI-TION	SANC-TION	TAXA-TION
POTA-TION	SCON-TION	TRAC-TION
PUNI-TION	SEDA-TION	VACA-TION
PUPA-TION	SEDI-TION	VENA-TION
QUES-TION	SOLA-TION	VEXA-TION
REAC-TION	SOLU-TION	VOCA-TION
RELA-TION	SORP-TION	VOLI-TION
REMO-TION	STIC-TION	VOLU-TION
ROGA-TION	SUDA-TION	ZONA-TION
ROTA-TION	SWAP-TION	

Unusual letter combinations

If you have an unusual combination of letters on your rack, or want to impress your opponent with an unusual word, a few words from World English can come in handy.

Australian words

TOOSHIE	angry or upset
TRIELLA	three horse races nominated for a bet
TROPPO	mentally affected by a tropical climate
TRUCKIE	truck driver
TRUGO	game similar to croquet
TUAN	flying phalanger
TUART	type of eucalyptus tree

T

Canadian words

TILLICUM	friend
TOONIE	Canadian two-dollar coin
TULLIBEE	whitefish found in the Great Lakes
TUPEK	Inuit tent of animal skins

Hindi words

TABLA	pair of drums whose pitches can be varied
THALI	meal consisting of several small dishes
TIL	sesame
TOLA	unit of weight
TONGA	light two-wheeled vehicle
TOPEE	pith helmet

New Zealand words

TAIAHA	ceremonial fighting staff
TAIHOA	hold on!
TAKAHE	rare flightless bird
TANGI	Maori funeral ceremony
TANIWHA	legendary monster
TAONGA	treasure
TAPU	sacred or forbidden
TARSEAL	bitumen surface of a road
TAUIWI	non-Maori people of New Zealand
TIKANGA	Maori customs
TOETOE	type of tall grass
TOITOI	type of tall grass
TWINK	white correction fluid

T

Urdu words

TAHSIL	administrative division
TALOOKA	subdivision of a district
TAMASHA	show or entertainment
TANDOORI	method of cooking on a spit in a clay oven

T

Essential info

Value: 1 point

Number in set: 4

U can be a difficult tile to play effectively. In fact, there are no particularly high-scoring short words which start with U. In order to make the best of your tiles, some handy words to remember are UH (5 points), UM (4 points), UP (4 points) and UG (3 points). Also, when aiming for short words, you can save yourself some time by remembering that there are no valid three-letter words beginning with U which use Q, X or Z.

Two-letter words beginning with U

UG	UM	UP	US
UH	UN	UR	UT

Some three-letter words beginning with U

UDO	UNI	URP
UGH	UPO	UTA
UMM	URB	UTE
UMP	URD	UTU
UMU	URE	

Hooks

Hooking requires a subtle change in a player's thought process, in that they must look at words already on the board without becoming distracted by their pronunciation.

Some front-hooks
Two letters to three

U-DO	U-PO	U-TE
U-MM	U-RE	
U-MU	U-TA	

Three letters to four

U-DAL	U-NIS	U-SER
U-DON	U-NIT	U-TIS
U-LES	U-PAS	U-VAE
U-LEX	U-SED	U-VAS

Four letters to five

U-LAMA	U-RASE	U-RITE
U-NARY	U-RATE	U-SAGE
U-NITE	U-REAL	U-SING
U-PEND	U-REDO	U-SURE
U-PLAY	U-RENT	U-TILE
U-PLED	U-RIAL	U-VEAL
U-RARE	U-RINE	

U

Five letters to six

U-LEXES	U-PLEAD	U-REDIA
U-LOSES	U-PLINK	U-SABLE
U-NEATH	U-PLOOK	U-SAGER
U-NITER	U-PRATE	U-SAGES
U-NOWED	U-PREST	U-SURED
U-PASES	U-PRISE	U-SURER
U-PHANG	U-PROLL	U-SWARD
U-PLAID	U-PROSE	

Six letters to seven

U-NEARED	U-PLINKS	U-PREACH
U-NEATEN	U-PLYING	U-PRISER
U-PENDED	U-PRAISE	U-REDIAL
U-PLIGHT	U-PRATED	U-SURING

Seven letters to eight

U-PENDING	U-PRAISED	U-PRISING
U-PLAYING	U-PRAISER	U-PROLLED
U-PLINKED	U-PRATING	

U

Some end-hooks
Two letters to three

AM-U	KY-U	SO-U
AY-U	LO-U	TA-U
EA-U	ME-U	UM-U
EM-U	MO-U	UT-U
FE-U	PI-U	YO-U

Three letters to four

AIT-U	LAT-U	RAT-U
BAL-U	LEK-U	RIM-U
BAP-U	LIE-U	SUS-U
BED-U	LIT-U	TAB-U
BUB-U	MAS-U	TAP-U
EME-U	MEN-U	TAT-U
FRA-U	MOT-U	TEG-U
FUG-U	MUM-U	THO-U
GEN-U	NAM-U	TUT-U
GUR-U	PAT-U	VAT-U
HAP-U	PUD-U	WUD-U
HUH-U	PUL-U	
KOR-U	PUP-U	

U

Four letters to five

BANT-U	CORN-U	PARE-U
BATT-U	FOND-U	PEND-U
BITO-U	HAIK-U	PIKA-U
BUCK-U	JAMB-U	PILA-U
BUND-U	KAWA-U	QUIP-U
BUSS-U	LASS-U	TEND-U
CENT-U	MUNT-U	VERT-U

Five letters to six

CONGO-U	HALER-U	MANAT-U

Six letters to seven

MANITO-U	TAMARA-U
SUBMEN-U	TURACO-U

Handy Hint

UKE (7 points) is a short form of UKULELE (11 points). There are not many short high-scoring words beginning with U: UKE and UGH (a sound people make when they dislike or are disgusted by something) are the highest-scoring three-letter words at 7 points each. UMM and UMP also score 7.

U

Blockers

It is useful to know which words are blockers and can't therefore be extended before or after. You may want to play a blocker that your opponent can't extend, or you may want to avoid playing a blocker because you want to keep the board open.

Some four-letter blockers beginning with U

UNDO   UPGO   UPSY

Some five-letter blockers beginning with U
(except words ending in '-ED', '-J', '-S', '-X', '-Y' or '-Z')

UNAPT   UNHIP   UPTER
UNBID   UNMET   UREAL
UNDID   UNRID   URNAL
UNDUE   UNWET   UTERI
UNDUG   UPBYE
UNGOT   UPLIT

U

Some six-letter blockers beginning with U
(except words ending in '-ED', '-J', '-S', '-X', '-Y' or '-Z')

ULTIMO	UNLASH	UNWISH
UMBRAL	UNLOST	UNWORN
UNBENT	UNMADE	UPBLEW
UNBORE	UNMEEK	UPDREW
UNCAST	UNMEET	UPGONE
UNCHIC	UNMESH	UPGREW
UNCLAD	UNMIXT	UPGUSH
UNCOOL	UNMOWN	UPHAND
UNCUTE	UNOPEN	UPHELD
UNDEAD	UNPAID	UPHILD
UNDEAR	UNPENT	UPHOVE
UNDONE	UNPURE	UPHUNG
UNDREW	UNREAL	UPLAID
UNEVEN	UNRENT	UPMOST
UNFELT	UNSAID	UPPISH
UNFIRM	UNSAWN	UPROSE
UNFOND	UNSENT	UPRUSH
UNGAIN	UNSEWN	UPSENT
UNHEWN	UNSHOD	UPTOOK
UNHUNG	UNSOLD	UPTORE
UNHURT	UNSPUN	UPTORN
UNIFIC	UNSUNG	UPWENT
UNITAL	UNSUNK	URETIC
UNJUST	UNTOLD	URSINE
UNKEPT	UNTORN	USABLE
UNKIND	UNTROD	
UNLAID	UNWELL	

Some words beginning with UN-
Seven-letter words

UN-ACTED	UN-BOLTS	UN-CLEAN
UN-ADDED	UN-BONED	UN-CLEAR
UN-AGING	UN-BOUND	UN-CLING
UN-AIDED	UN-BOWED	UN-CLIPS
UN-AIMED	UN-BOXED	UN-CLOAK
UN-AIRED	UN-BURNT	UN-CLOGS
UN-ARMED	UN-CAGED	UN-CODED
UN-AWARE	UN-CANNY	UN-COILS
UN-BAKED	UN-CASED	UN-CORKS
UN-BEGUN	UN-CHAIN	UN-COUTH
UN-BENDS	UN-CHECK	UN-COVER
UN-BINDS	UN-CITED	UN-CUFFS
UN-BLOCK	UN-CIVIL	UN-CURED
UN-BLOWN	UN-CLASP	UN-CURLS

U

UN-DATED
UN-DEALT
UN-DOERS
UN-DOING
UN-DRAWN
UN-DRESS
UN-DRUNK
UN-DYING
UN-EAGER
UN-EARTH
UN-EATEN
UN-ENDED
UN-EQUAL
UN-FAIRS
UN-FAKED
UN-FAZED
UN-FENCE
UN-FILED
UN-FIRED
UN-FLUSH
UN-FOLDS
UN-FORMS
UN-FOUND
UN-FROCK
UN-FROZE
UN-FUNNY
UN-FUSSY
UN-GLUED
UN-GODLY
UN-GORED

UN-GROWN
UN-GUARD
UN-GULAR
UN-HANDS
UN-HAPPY
UN-HASTY
UN-HEALS
UN-HEARD
UN-HELMS
UN-HINGE
UN-HITCH
UN-HOOKS
UN-HORSE
UN-HUMAN
UN-KEMPT
UN-KNOWN
UN-LACED
UN-LADED
UN-LATCH
UN-LEARN
UN-LEASH
UN-LINED
UN-LIVED
UN-LOADS
UN-LOCKS
UN-LOVED
UN-LUCKY
UN-MAKER
UN-MANLY
UN-MASKS

UN-MIXED
UN-MORAL
UN-MOUNT
UN-MOVED
UN-NAMED
UN-NERVE
UN-OILED
UN-PACKS
UN-PAVED
UN-PICKS
UN-PLACE
UN-PLUGS
UN-POSED
UN-QUIET
UN-QUOTE
UN-RATED
UN-RAVEL
UN-READY
UN-RESTS
UN-ROBED
UN-ROLLS
UN-SAFER
UN-SATED
UN-SAVED
UN-SCARY
UN-SCREW
UN-SEATS
UN-SEWED
UN-SHELL
UN-SHOED

UN-SHORN   UN-STICK   UN-TRIED

UN-SHOWN   UN-STRAP   UN-TRUER

UN-SIGHT   UN-STUCK   UN-TRUST

UN-SIZED   UN-STUNG   UN-TRUTH

UN-SLAIN   UN-SURER   UN-TWIST

UN-SLUNG   UN-TAKEN   UN-TYING

UN-SNAGS   UN-TAMED   UN-USUAL

UN-SOLID   UN-TAXED   UN-VEILS

UN-SOUND   UN-THAWS   UN-WAGED

UN-SPENT   UN-TILED   UN-WINDS

UN-SPILT   UN-TIMED   UN-WIRED

UN-SPLIT   UN-TIRED   UN-WISER

UN-SPOOL   UN-TONED   UN-WOUND

UN-STACK   UN-TRACE   UN-WRAPS

Eight-letter words

UN-ABATED   UN-BIDDEN   UN-CANNED

UN-ACTIVE   UN-BILLED   UN-CAPPED

UN-AFRAID   UN-BITTEN   UN-CARING

UN-AGEING   UN-BOLTED   UN-CAUGHT

UN-AMUSED   UN-BONDED   UN-CHOSEN

UN-ARGUED   UN-BOOKED   UN-CLENCH

UN-ARMING   UN-BOUGHT   UN-CLOTHE

UN-AVOWED   UN-BOWING   UN-CLUTCH

UN-BAITED   UN-BRIDLE   UN-COATED

UN-BEARED   UN-BROKEN   UN-COCKED

UN-BEATEN   UN-BURDEN   UN-COILED

UN-BEGGED   UN-BURIED   UN-COMMON

UN-BELIEF   UN-BUTTON   UN-COOKED

UN-BIASED   UN-CALLED   UN-CORKED

U

UN-COUPLE	UN-GAINLY	UN-NERVED
UN-CUFFED	UN-GENTLE	UN-OPENED
UN-CURLED	UN-GIVING	UN-PACKED
UN-DARING	UN-GUIDED	UN-PAIRED
UN-DECENT	UN-HANDED	UN-PLAYED
UN-DENIED	UN-HARMED	UN-PRICED
UN-DERATE	UN-HEEDED	UN-PROVED
UN-DINTED	UN-HELPED	UN-QUOTED
UN-DOCILE	UN-HINGED	UN-REALLY
UN-DRIVEN	UN-HOLIER	UN-REASON
UN-EARNED	UN-HOOKED	UN-RESTED
UN-EASIER	UN-HORSED	UN-RINSED
UN-EASILY	UN-IRONED	UN-ROLLED
UN-EDIBLE	UN-ISSUED	UN-SAFELY
UN-EDITED	UN-JAMMED	UN-SALTED
UN-ENDING	UN-JOINED	UN-SAVORY
UN-ENVIED	UN-KINDER	UN-SEATED
UN-ERRING	UN-LAWFUL	UN-SEEING
UN-EVENLY	UN-LEADED	UN-SEEMLY
UN-FALLEN	UN-LEARNT	UN-SETTLE
UN-FAMOUS	UN-LIKELY	UN-SHAKEN
UN-FASTEN	UN-LISTED	UN-SHAVEN
UN-FENCED	UN-LOADED	UN-SIGNED
UN-FILLED	UN-LOCKED	UN-SOILED
UN-FILMED	UN-LOVING	UN-SOLVED
UN-FOLDED	UN-MANNED	UN-SPOILT
UN-FORCED	UN-MARKED	UN-SUBTLE
UN-FORMED	UN-MASKED	UN-SURELY
UN-FROZEN	UN-MENDED	UN-TAPPED
UN-FURLED	UN-MOVING	UN-THRONE

U

UN-TIDILY   UN-VERSED   UN-WIELDY
UN-TIEING   UN-VIABLE   UN-WISELY
UN-TITLED   UN-WANTED   UN-WORTHY
UN-TOWARD   UN-WARILY
UN-USABLE   UN-WASHED

Some words beginning with UP-
Seven-letter words

UP-BEATS   UP-HEAVE   UP-STAGE
UP-BRAID   UP-HOLDS   UP-STAIR
UP-BRING   UP-LIFTS   UP-STAND
UP-CHUCK   UP-LOADS   UP-START
UP-CLOSE   UP-LYING   UP-STATE
UP-COMES   UP-PINGS   UP-SURGE
UP-CURVE   UP-RAISE   UP-SWELL
UP-DATED   UP-RATED   UP-SWING
UP-DRAFT   UP-REACH   UP-TAKEN
UP-ENDED   UP-RIGHT   UP-TEMPO
UP-FIELD   UP-RISEN   UP-TIGHT
UP-FLUNG   UP-RIVER   UP-TOWNS
UP-FRONT   UP-ROOTS   UP-TURNS
UP-GOING   UP-SCALE   UP-WARDS
UP-GROWN   UP-SLOPE

U

Eight-letter words

UP-COMING
UP-DATING
UP-DIVING
UP-ENDING
UP-FLOWED
UP-FURLED
UP-GAZING
UP-GRADED
UP-GROWTH
UP-HEAPED
UP-HEAVED

UP-LANDER
UP-LIFTED
UP-LINKED
UP-LOADED
UP-LOOKED
UP-MARKET
UP-RATING
UP-RISING
UP-ROARED
UP-ROOTED
UP-SCALED

UP-SETTER
UP-SIZING
UP-SPOKEN
UP-SPRUNG
UP-STAGED
UP-STREAM
UP-STROKE
UP-SURGED
UP-TAKING
UP-THROWN
UP-TURNED

Some words ending with -URE
Seven-letter words

BRAV-URE
CAPT-URE
CENS-URE
CLOS-URE
CONJ-URE
COUT-URE
CULT-URE
DENT-URE
DISC-URE
EPIC-URE
ERAS-URE
FACT-URE
FAIL-URE
FEAT-URE

FISS-URE
FIXT-URE
FLEX-URE
GEST-URE
LEAS-URE
LECT-URE
LEIS-URE
MEAS-URE
MIXT-URE
NURT-URE
OBSC-URE
PAST-URE
PERJ-URE
PICT-URE

PREC-URE
PROC-URE
RAPT-URE
RUPT-URE
SEIS-URE
SEIZ-URE
STAT-URE
TEXT-URE
TONS-URE
TORT-URE
VENT-URE
VERD-URE
VULT-URE

Eight-letter words

ANNEX-URE	IMMAT-URE	PUNCT-URE
APERT-URE	INSEC-URE	REASS-URE
ARMAT-URE	JUNCT-URE	REFIG-URE
AVENT-URE	LIGAT-URE	REINJ-URE
BROCH-URE	MANIC-URE	REINS-URE
COIFF-URE	MOIST-URE	RENAT-URE
CREAT-URE	OVERC-URE	REPOS-URE
DENAT-URE	OVERS-URE	RESEC-URE
DOUBL-URE	OVERT-URE	SINEC-URE
EXPOS-URE	PEDIC-URE	TAINT-URE
FIXAT-URE	PLEAS-URE	TINCT-URE
FRACT-URE	PRESS-URE	TREAS-URE

Unusual letter combinations

If you have an unusual combination of letters on your rack, or want to impress your opponent with an unusual word, a few words from World English can come in handy. Some beginning with U include:

Australian words

UMPIE	umpire
UNCO	awkward or clumsy
UPTA	of poor quality
UTE	utility

Hindi word

URD	bean plant

U

Essential info

Value: 4 points

Number in set: 2

It is important to note that there are no two-letter words with the **V** which can make it a natural blocker, preventing parallel plays. Generally it is easier to play the V with vowels but watch out for some good-scoring in combination with other high-scoring consonants such as VEX (13 points), VLY (9 points), VOW (9 points), VUM (8 points).

Three-letter words beginning with V

VAC	VAW	VLY
VAE	VEE	VOE
VAG	VID	VOR
VAR	VIM	VOX
VAS	VIN	VUG
VAV	VIS	VUM

V

Hooks

Hooking requires a subtle change in a player's thought process, in that they must look at words already on the board without becoming distracted by their pronunciation.

Some front-hooks
Two letters to three

V-AE	V-EE	V-OR
V-AG	V-ET	V-OW
V-AN	V-EX	V-OX
V-AR	V-ID	V-UG
V-AS	V-IN	V-UM
V-AT	V-IS	
V-AW	V-OE	

Three letters to four

V-AIL	V-EGO	V-ILL
V-AIN	V-ELD	V-IRE
V-AIR	V-ELL	V-ITA
V-ALE	V-END	V-LEI
V-AMP	V-ERA	V-OAR
V-ANE	V-ERS	V-OLE
V-ANT	V-EST	V-ROT
V-ARE	V-ICE	V-ROW
V-ARY	V-IDE	V-UGH

V

Four letters to five

V-AGUE	V-ETCH	V-OARS
V-AIRY	V-EXED	V-OLES
V-ALES	V-EXES	V-OMER
V-ARIA	V-IBEX	V-OMIT
V-ARNA	V-ICED	V-OUCH
V-AUNT	V-IRED	V-OWED
V-EALE	V-IRID	V-OWER
V-EERY	V-ISIT	V-ROOM
V-ERST	V-LIES	

Five letters to six

V-AGILE	V-AWARD	V-EXING
V-AGUED	V-EALES	V-ICING
V-AILED	V-EGGED	V-IRING
V-ALINE	V-ELATE	V-IZARD
V-ALLEY	V-ENDED	V-ORANT
V-AMPED	V-ENDER	V-OTARY
V-ASTER	V-ENDUE	V-OWING
V-ATMAN	V-ENTER	
V-AUNTY	V-ERVEN	

V

Six letters to seven

V-ACUATE	V-ASSAIL	V-ENDING
V-ACUITY	V-AUNTER	V-ENTAIL
V-AILING	V-AUNTIE	V-ESTRAL
V-AIRIER	V-EGGING	V-OCULAR
V-ALGOID	V-ELATED	V-OUCHED
V-AMPING	V-ENATIC	V-ROOMED

Seven letters to eight

V-AGILITY	V-ENTAYLE	V-IRIDIAN
V-AIRIEST	V-ERISTIC	V-OTARIES
V-ALLEYED	V-ERMINED	V-OUCHING
V-ENATION	V-ICELESS	V-ROOMING
V-ENOLOGY	V-ICELIKE	

Some end-hooks
Two letters to three

DE-V	GU-V	RE-V
DI-V	LA-V	SO-V
GO-V	PA-V	TA-V

Three letters to four

CHA-V	DEE-V	MIR-V
CHI-V	ERE-V	PER-V

Four letters to five

GANE-V	OLLA-V	PARE-V

V

Blockers

It is useful to know which words are blockers and can't therefore be extended before or after. You may want to play a blocker that your opponent can't extend, or you may want to avoid playing a blocker because you want to keep the board open.

Some three-letter blockers beginning with V

VLY   VOX

Some four-letter blockers beginning with V

VAGI	VERD	VIAE	VIZY
VAIN	VETO	VIBS	VROT
VERA	VEXT	VIVO	

Handy Hint

If you have a V and the board is quite blocked then it is more likely that vowels on your rack, or on the board, will help you out. Look out for plays involving AVA, AVE, OVA, UVA, VAE, VAU (all 6 points). Even if you have two Vs the vowels could rescue you with VIVA VIVE VIVO (all 10 points). There is also VAV (A Hebrew letter, 9 points).

Some five-letter blockers beginning with V
(except words ending in '-ED', '-J', '-S', '-X', '-Y' or '-Z')

VACUA	VENAE	VIRID
VAGAL	VENAL	VITAE
VAIRE	VERRA	VIVID
VALID	VILDE	VOILA
VAPID	VILLI	VOLTA
VASAL	VINIC	VOLTI
VATIC	VIOLD	VULGO
VELUM	VIRAL	

Some six-letter blockers beginning with V
(except words ending in '-ED', '-J', '-S', '-X', '-Y' or '-Z')

VACANT	VENIAL	VIRENT
VAGILE	VERIER	VIRILE
VAGROM	VERMAL	VIRING
VAGUER	VERNAL	VISCID
VAINER	VIABLE	VISIVE
VALVAL	VIBIER	VISTAL
VALVAR	VICING	VOLAGE
VANMAN	VIDUAL	VOLING
VANMEN	VILLAE	VORAGO
VARSAL	VILLAR	VORANT
VASTER	VINEAL	VORPAL
VATMAN	VINIER	VOSTRO
VATMEN	VINING	

V

Unusual letter combinations

If you have an unusual combination of letters on your rack, or want to impress your opponent with an unusual word, a few words from World English can come in handy. Here are a few examples beginning with V.

Australian words

VAG	vagrant
VEGO	vegetarian
VIGORO	women's game similar to cricket

Hindi words

VAHANA	vehicle in Indian myth
VANDA	type of orchid
VINA	stringed musical instrument

South African words

VLEI	area of marshy ground
VOEMA	vigour or energy
VROU	woman or wife

V

Essential info
Value: 4 points
Number in set: 2

There are only two two-letter words beginning with **W**: WE (5 points) and WO (an old-fashioned spelling of woe, also 5). There are, however, many short, common-usage words which can return good scores such as WAX (13 points), WHO (9 points) and WOK (10 points). The highest-scoring three-letter word beginning with W is WIZ (short form of wizard, 15 points).

Two-letter words beginning with W

WE WO

Some three-letter words beginning with W

WAB	WEN	WOK
WAE	WEX	WOP
WAI	WEY	WOT
WAN	WHA	WOW
WAP	WIS	WOX
WAT	WIZ	WUS
WAW	WOF	WYE
WEM	WOG	WYN

W

Hooks

Hooking requires a subtle change in a player's thought process, in that they must look at words already on the board without becoming distracted by their pronunciation.

Some front-hooks
Two letters to three

W-AB	W-AY	W-IT
W-AD	W-ED	W-OE
W-AE	W-EE	W-OF
W-AG	W-EM	W-ON
W-AI	W-EN	W-OO
W-AN	W-ET	W-OP
W-AR	W-EX	W-OS
W-AS	W-HA	W-OW
W-AT	W-HO	W-OX
W-AW	W-IN	W-US
W-AX	W-IS	W-YE

W

Three letters to four

W-ADD	W-AWA	W-HIT
W-AFF	W-AWE	W-HOA
W-AFT	W-AWL	W-HOM
W-AGE	W-EAN	W-HOP
W-AID	W-EAR	W-HOT
W-AIL	W-EEK	W-HOW
W-AIN	W-EEL	W-HUP
W-AIR	W-EEN	W-ICE
W-AIT	W-EFT	W-ICH
W-AKE	W-ELD	W-ICK
W-ALE	W-ELK	W-IDE
W-ALL	W-ELL	W-ILL
W-AND	W-ELT	W-IMP
W-ANE	W-END	W-INK
W-ANT	W-ERE	W-INN
W-ANY	W-EST	W-IRE
W-ARB	W-ETA	W-ISH
W-ARD	W-HAE	W-OKE
W-ARE	W-HAM	W-OLD
W-ARK	W-HAP	W-OOF
W-ARM	W-HAT	W-OON
W-ART	W-HEN	W-OOT
W-ARY	W-HET	W-ORD
W-ASH	W-HEW	W-ORE
W-ASP	W-HEY	W-ORT
W-ATE	W-HID	W-RAP
W-ATT	W-HIM	W-REN
W-AUK	W-HIN	W-RIT
W-AVE	W-HIP	

Four letters to five

W-ADDY	W-HEAT	W-OMEN
W-AGED	W-HEEL	W-OOFY
W-AGER	W-HEFT	W-OOSE
W-AGON	W-HELM	W-OOZY
W-AIDE	W-HELP	W-OULD
W-AKED	W-HERE	W-OVEN
W-ALLY	W-HIPT	W-OWED
W-ANNA	W-HISH	W-OXEN
W-ARED	W-HISS	W-RACK
W-ARTY	W-HIST	W-RANG
W-ASHY	W-HIZZ	W-RAPT
W-ATAP	W-HOLE	W-RAST
W-AVER	W-HOOF	W-RATE
W-AXED	W-HOOP	W-RATH
W-EAVE	W-HOOT	W-REAK
W-ECHT	W-HOPS	W-RECK
W-EDGE	W-HORE	W-REST
W-EDGY	W-HOSE	W-RICK
W-EXED	W-HUMP	W-RING
W-EXES	W-HUPS	W-RITE
W-HACK	W-ICKY	W-ROKE
W-HALE	W-IDES	W-RONG
W-HANG	W-ILLY	W-ROOT
W-HARE	W-INCH	W-ROTE
W-HEAL	W-IRED	W-RUNG
W-HEAR	W-ITCH	

W

Five letters to six

W-ACKER
W-ADDED
W-ADDER
W-ADDLE
W-AFTER
W-AGGER
W-AGING
W-AILED
W-AIRED
W-AIVER
W-AKING
W-ALLOW
W-AMBLE
W-ANGLE
W-ANION
W-ANKER
W-ANKLE
W-ANTED
W-ARKED
W-ARMED
W-ARMER
W-ARRAY
W-ASHED
W-ASHEN
W-ASHES
W-ASTER
W-AUGHT

W-AXING
W-EANED
W-EARED
W-EASEL
W-EAVED
W-EAVES
W-EBBED
W-EDGED
W-EIGHT
W-ELDER
W-ENDED
W-ESTER
W-ETHER
W-EXING
W-HALED
W-HALER
W-HAMMY
W-HEELS
W-HEEZE
W-HENCE
W-HERRY
W-HEUGH
W-HEWED
W-HILLY
W-HINGE
W-HINNY
W-HIPPY

W-HOLLY
W-HOOSH
W-ICHES
W-ICKER
W-IGGED
W-ILLER
W-IMPED
W-INDOW
W-INKED
W-INKER
W-INKLE
W-INNED
W-INNER
W-INTER
W-IRING
W-ISHES
W-ITCHY
W-ITHER
W-IZARD
W-ONNED
W-ORMER
W-OUBIT
W-OUNDY
W-OWING
W-RASSE
W-RETCH
W-RIGHT

W

Six letters to seven

W-ADDING	W-ENDING	W-HITTER
W-ADDLED	W-HACKED	W-HIZZED
W-AILING	W-HACKER	W-HOLISM
W-AIRING	W-HALING	W-HOLIST
W-AMBLED	W-HAMMED	W-HOOFED
W-ANGLED	W-HANGED	W-HOOPED
W-ANGLER	W-HAPPED	W-HOOPER
W-ANTING	W-HEELED	W-HOOPLA
W-APPEND	W-HEELER	W-HOOTED
W-ARKING	W-HEEZED	W-HOPPED
W-ARLING	W-HELMED	W-HOPPER
W-ARMING	W-HELPED	W-HUMPED
W-ARRANT	W-HEREAT	W-HUPPED
W-ARTIER	W-HEREBY	W-IGGING
W-ASHERY	W-HEREIN	W-ILLEST
W-ASHIER	W-HEREOF	W-IMPING
W-ASHING	W-HEREON	W-IMPISH
W-ASPISH	W-HERETO	W-IMPLED
W-ASSAIL	W-HETHER	W-INCHED
W-ATTEST	W-HEWING	W-INCHER
W-AXLIKE	W-HIDDER	W-INCHES
W-EANING	W-HINGED	W-INDIGO
W-EARING	W-HINGER	W-INKING
W-EAVING	W-HIPPED	W-INKLED
W-EBBING	W-HIPPER	W-INNING
W-EDGIER	W-HISHED	W-ITCHED
W-EDGING	W-HISSED	W-ITCHES
W-EIGHTY	W-HISTED	W-ONNING
W-ELDING	W-HITHER	W-OOZIER

W-OOZILY
W-RACKED
W-RANGED
W-RAPPED
W-RAPPER
W-RASSES

W-RASSLE
W-REAKED
W-RECKED
W-RESTED
W-RESTER
W-RICKED

W-RINGED
W-RINGER
W-ROOTED
W-ROUGHT

Seven letters to eight

W-ADDLING
W-AGELESS
W-ALLEYED
W-ALLOWED
W-AMBLING
W-ANGLING
W-ANTHILL
W-ARRAYED
W-ARTIEST
W-ARTLESS
W-ASHIEST
W-ASTABLE
W-EANLING
W-EASELED
W-EDGIEST
W-HACKING
W-HAMMING
W-HANGING
W-HAPPING
W-HEELING
W-HEEZING
W-HELMING

W-HELPING
W-HERRIED
W-HINGING
W-HINNIED
W-HINNIES
W-HIPLIKE
W-HIPPIER
W-HIPPING
W-HIPSTER
W-HIRLING
W-HISHING
W-HISSING
W-HISTING
W-HIZZING
W-HOOFING
W-HOOPING
W-HOOSHED
W-HOOSHES
W-HOOTING
W-HOPPING
W-HUMPING
W-HUPPING

W-INCHING
W-INDOWED
W-INKLING
W-IRELESS
W-ITCHIER
W-ITCHING
W-OOFIEST
W-OOZIEST
W-OULDEST
W-RACKFUL
W-RACKING
W-RANGING
W-RAPPING
W-RASSLED
W-REAKING
W-RECKING
W-RESTING
W-RETCHED
W-RICKING
W-RINGING
W-ROOTING

W

Some end-hooks
Two letters to three

BO-W	KA-W	PE-W
DA-W	KO-W	PO-W
DE-W	LA-W	RE-W
DO-W	LO-W	SO-W
FA-W	MA-W	TA-W
FE-W	ME-W	TE-W
HA-W	MO-W	TO-W
HE-W	NA-W	WO-W
HO-W	NE-W	YA-W
JA-W	NO-W	YE-W
JO-W	PA-W	YO-W

Three letters to four

ALE-W	CHA-W	SHE-W
ANE-W	CHE-W	SKA-W
ARE-W	ENE-W	SPA-W
AVO-W	FRO-W	THE-W
BRA-W	PRO-W	VIE-W
BRO-W	SHA-W	WHO-W

Four letters to five

BEDE-W	PAWA-W	THRO-W
KOTO-W	PILA-W	VINE-W
NAVE-W	SINE-W	VROU-W
PAPA-W	SYBO-W	

Five letters to six

BARRO-W	MATLO-W	PURSE-W
BURRO-W	MISSA-W	REVIE-W
HALLO-W	MORRO-W	UNCLE-W
HOLLO-W	OUTRO-W	

Six letters to seven

DAYGLO-W

Seven letters to eight

BUDGERO-W	RICKSHA-W

Handy Hint

Some of the more unusual words beginning with W are WAKIKI (Melanesian shell currency, 12 points), WAMBLE (move unsteadily, 13 points), WUXIA (genre of Chinese fiction and film, concerning the adventures of sword-wielding chivalrous heroes, 15 points) and WYVERN (heraldic beast having a serpent's tail, a dragon's head and a body with wings and two legs, 15 points).

W

Blockers

It is useful to know which words are blockers and can't therefore be extended before or after. You may want to play a blocker that your opponent can't extend, or you may want to avoid playing a blocker because you want to keep the board open.

Three-letter blocker beginning with W

WOX

Some four-letter blockers beginning with W

WADY	WERT	WILY
WARY	WHAE	WIRY
WAVY	WHIO	WOST
WAXY	WHOA	WOWF
WENA	WHOT	WYCH
WERE	WICH	

W

Some five-letter blockers beginning with W
(except words ending in '-ED', '-J', '-S', '-X', '-Y' or '-Z')

WANNA	WHOSE	WOWEE
WAXEN	WHOSO	WOXEN
WELCH	WIDER	WRAPT
WELSH	WILCO	WROTE
WENCH	WINCH	WROTH
WHAMO	WISER	WRUNG
WHICH	WISHT	WRYER
WHIPT	WOMEN	

Some six-letter blockers beginning with W
(except words ending in '-ED', '-J', '-S', '-X', '-Y' or '-Z')

WANIER	WHILST	WISEST
WANKLE	WHITER	WISING
WANNER	WHOMSO	WITHAL
WARIER	WHOOSH	WITING
WARING	WIDEST	WOEFUL
WARMAN	WIDISH	WORSER
WARMEN	WIFING	WOWING
WASHEN	WILFUL	WRENCH
WASSUP	WILIER	WRETCH
WAVIER	WILING	WROKEN
WAXIER	WIMMIN	WRYEST
WHATSO	WIRIER	WRYING

W

Bonus words

Bonus words on your rack can be hard to spot, especially for the less experienced player. One way to help find them is by using prefixes and suffixes.

Many larger words include a common prefix or suffix – remembering these and using them where you can is a good way to discover any longer words on your rack, including any potential bonus words. The key prefix to remember is WAR- and the key suffixes are -WARD, -WARDS, -WAY, -WISE, -WOOD, -WORK, -WORM and -WORT.

Some words beginning with WAR-
Seven-letter words

WAR-BLED

WAR-DENS

WAR-DING

WAR-DOGS

WAR-FARE

WAR-HEAD

WAR-KING

WAR-LESS

WAR-LIKE

WAR-LING

WAR-LOCK

WAR-LORD

WAR-MING

WAR-PATH

WAR-PING

WAR-RAND

WAR-RANT

WAR-RAYS

WAR-RENS

WAR-RING

WAR-SAWS

WAR-SHIP

WAR-SLED

WAR-TIER

WAR-TIME

WAR-WOLF

WAR-WORK

WAR-WORN

WAR-ZONE

W

Eight-letter words

WAR-BLING

WAR-CRAFT

WAR-DERED

WAR-DRESS

WAR-FARED

WAR-FARER

WAR-HORSE

WAR-MAKER

WAR-MOUTH

WAR-PLANE

WAR-POWER

WAR-RAYED

WAR-SLING

Some words ending with -WARD
Seven-letter words

AIR-WARD

AWK-WARD

BED-WARD

FOR-WARD

HAY-WARD

LEE-WARD

NAY-WARD

NOR-WARD

OUT-WARD

SEA-WARD

SKY-WARD

STE-WARD

SUN-WARD

VAN-WARD

WAY-WARD

WEY-WARD

Eight-letter words

BACK-WARD

BECO-WARD

CITY-WARD

DOWN-WARD

EAST-WARD

FORE-WARD

GOAL-WARD

HEAD-WARD

HELL-WARD

HIND-WARD

HIVE-WARD

HOME-WARD

KIRK-WARD

LAND-WARD

LEFT-WARD

MOON-WARD

REAR-WARD

SELF-WARD

SIDE-WARD

UNTO-WARD

WEST-WARD

WIND-WARD

WOOD-WARD

WOOL-WARD

W

Some words ending with -WAY
Seven-letter words

ARCH-WAY	HADA-WAY	ROLL-WAY
AREA-WAY	HALF-WAY	ROPE-WAY
BELT-WAY	HALL-WAY	RUNA-WAY
BIKE-WAY	HEAD-WAY	SHIP-WAY
CART-WAY	HIGH-WAY	SIDE-WAY
CUTA-WAY	LANE-WAY	SKID-WAY
DOOR-WAY	LAYA-WAY	SLIP-WAY
FAIR-WAY	LIFE-WAY	SOME-WAY
FARA-WAY	PACK-WAY	TAXI-WAY
FISH-WAY	PARK-WAY	THRU-WAY
FLYA-WAY	PART-WAY	TIDE-WAY
FOLK-WAY	PATH-WAY	TOLL-WAY
FOOT-WAY	RACE-WAY	TOWA-WAY
FREE-WAY	RAIL-WAY	TRAM-WAY
GANG-WAY	RING-WAY	WALK-WAY
GATE-WAY	ROAD-WAY	WIND-WAY
GETA-WAY	RODE-WAY	WIRE-WAY

Eight-letter words

AISLE-WAY	GIVEA-WAY	STAIR-WAY
ALLEY-WAY	GREEN-WAY	STAYA-WAY
BROAD-WAY	GUIDE-WAY	STOWA-WAY
CABLE-WAY	HIDEA-WAY	TAKEA-WAY
CASTA-WAY	HORSE-WAY	TEARA-WAY
CAUSE-WAY	MOTOR-WAY	THATA-WAY
CLEAR-WAY	OVERS-WAY	THISA-WAY
CRAWL-WAY	RIDGE-WAY	TRACK-WAY
CROSS-WAY	RIVER-WAY	TRAIN-WAY
CYCLE-WAY	ROCKA-WAY	UNDER-WAY
DRIVE-WAY	ROLLA-WAY	WALKA-WAY
ENTRY-WAY	ROUTE-WAY	WASHA-WAY
EVERY-WAY	SLIDE-WAY	WASTE-WAY
FADEA-WAY	SOARA-WAY	WATER-WAY
FLOOD-WAY	SPEED-WAY	
FOLDA-WAY	SPILL-WAY	

Some words ending with -WISE
Seven-letter words

AIR-WISE	FAN-WISE	SUN-WISE
ANY-WISE	MAN-WISE	TAX-WISE
END-WISE	MAP-WISE	

W

Eight-letter words

ARCH-WISE
BEND-WISE
CRAB-WISE
DROP-WISE
EDGE-WISE
FLAT-WISE

LIKE-WISE
LONG-WISE
OVER-WISE
PAIR-WISE
RING-WISE
SIDE-WISE

SOME-WISE
STEP-WISE
SUCH-WISE
TEAM-WISE
TENT-WISE

Some words ending with -WOOD

Seven-letter words

BAR-WOOD
BAY-WOOD
BOG-WOOD
BOX-WOOD

DOG-WOOD
ELM-WOOD
INK-WOOD
LOG-WOOD

NUT-WOOD
PLY-WOOD
RED-WOOD
SAP-WOOD

Eight-letter words

BACK-WOOD
BASS-WOOD
BEAR-WOOD
BENT-WOOD
BLUE-WOOD
COLT-WOOD
CORD-WOOD
CORK-WOOD

DEAD-WOOD
FIRE-WOOD
FUEL-WOOD
HARD-WOOD
IRON-WOOD
KING-WOOD
MILK-WOOD
PEAR-WOOD

PINE-WOOD
ROSE-WOOD
SOFT-WOOD
SOUR-WOOD
TEAK-WOOD
WILD-WOOD
WORM-WOOD

W

Some words ending with -WORK
Seven-letter words

ART-WORK	OUT-WORK	TOP-WORK
CUT-WORK	PIN-WORK	TUT-WORK
DAY-WORK	PRE-WORK	WAR-WORK
LEG-WORK	RAG-WORK	WAX-WORK
NET-WORK	RIB-WORK	WEB-WORK
NON-WORK	TIN-WORK	

Eight-letter words

BACK-WORK	HAND-WORK	RACK-WORK
BEAD-WORK	HEAD-WORK	ROAD-WORK
BODY-WORK	HOME-WORK	ROPE-WORK
BOOK-WORK	IRON-WORK	SEAT-WORK
BUSY-WORK	LACE-WORK	STUD-WORK
CAGE-WORK	LEAD-WORK	TASK-WORK
CASE-WORK	LIFE-WORK	TEAM-WORK
FARM-WORK	MESH-WORK	TIME-WORK
FIRE-WORK	OPEN-WORK	WIRE-WORK
FOOT-WORK	OVER-WORK	WOOD-WORK
FRET-WORK	PART-WORK	YARD-WORK
HACK-WORK	PILE-WORK	
HAIR-WORK	PIPE-WORK	

W

Some words ending with -WORM
Seven-letter words

BAG-WORM

BUD-WORM

CAT-WORM

CUT-WORM

EAR-WORM

EEL-WORM

LOB-WORM

LUG-WORM

PIN-WORM

RAG-WORM

SEA-WORM

WAX-WORM

WEB-WORM

Eight-letter words

ARMY-WORM

BOLL-WORM

BOOK-WORM

CASE-WORM

CORN-WORM

FIRE-WORM

FISH-WORM

FLAT-WORM

GLOW-WORM

GRUB-WORM

HAIR-WORM

HOOK-WORM

HORN-WORM

INCH-WORM

LEAF-WORM

LUNG-WORM

MEAL-WORM

PILL-WORM

RING-WORM

SAND-WORM

SHIP-WORM

SILK-WORM

SLOW-WORM

TAPE-WORM

TUBE-WORM

WHIP-WORM

WIRE-WORM

WOOD-WORM

Some words ending with -WORT
Seven-letter words

AWL-WORT

BLA-WORT

BUG-WORT

FAN-WORT

FEL-WORT

FIG-WORT

MAD-WORT

MUD-WORT

MUG-WORT

RAG-WORT

RIB-WORT

W

Eight-letter words

BELL-WORT	HORN-WORT	PILL-WORT
COLE-WORT	LEAD-WORT	PIPE-WORT
DAME-WORT	LUNG-WORT	SALT-WORT
DANE-WORT	MILK-WORT	SAND-WORT
DROP-WORT	MODI-WORT	SOAP-WORT
FLEA-WORT	MOON-WORT	STAR-WORT
GOUT-WORT	MOOR-WORT	WALL-WORT
HONE-WORT	PILE-WORT	WART-WORT

Unusual letter combinations

If you have an unusual combination of letters on your rack, or want to impress your opponent with an unusual word, a few words from World English can come in handy.

Australian words

WADDY	heavy wooden club used by native Australians
WAGGA	blanket made of sacks stitched together
WALLABY	marsupial resembling a small kangaroo
WANDOO	eucalyptus tree with white bark
WARATAH	shrub with dark green leaves and crimson flowers
WARB	dirty or insignificant person
WHARFIE	wharf labourer
WILGA	small drought-resistant tree
WIRILDA	acacia tree with edible seeds

W

WIRRAH	saltwater fish with bright blue spots
WOMBAT	burrowing marsupial
WOOMERA	spear-throwing stick
WURLEY	Aboriginal hut

Canadian words

| WAWA | speech or language |
| WENDIGO | evil spirit or cannibal |

Hindi words

| WALLAH | person in charge of a specific thing |

New Zealand words

WAI	water
WAKA	Maori canoe
WEKA	flightless bird
WERO	warrior's challenge
WETA	long-legged wingless insect
WHANAU	family
WHENAU	native land

W

Essential info
Value: 8 points
Number in set: 1
Power Tile

X may be the most versatile of the power tiles. It is extremely useful when it comes to tagging as it forms a two-letter word with every vowel. The only two valid two-letter words starting with X are XI (14th letter in the Greek alphabet, 9 points) and XU (the Vietnamese unit of currency, also 9 points) and the only three-letter word is XIS (plural of XI). Therefore, if you have an X on your rack and are thinking of playing short words, it probably makes more sense to think of words which contain or end with X (such as AX, 9 points, or EX, also 9) rather than those which begin with it.

Two-letter words beginning with X

XI   XU

Some three-letter words using X

AXE	FAX	KEX	MIX
BOX	FIX	LAX	MUX
COX	FOX	LEX	NIX
DEX	GOX	LOX	NOX
DUX	HEX	LUX	OXO
EXO	HOX	MAX	OXY

X

PAX	SAX	TIX	WOX
PIX	SEX	TUX	YEX
POX	SIX	VEX	ZAX
PYX	SOX	VOX	ZEX
RAX	TAX	WAX	
REX	TEX	WEX	

Some four-letter words using X

Some useful four-letter words you may not know include BRUX (to grind one's teeth, 13 points), NIXY (a female water sprite, 14 points) and WEXE (obsolete form of wax, 14 points).

APEX	FAUX	NEXT
AXED	FIXT	NIXY
AXIS	FLAX	ONYX
AXLE	FLEX	ORYX
BOXY	FLUX	OXEN
BRUX	FOXY	OXER
COAX	GREX	OXID
CRUX	HOAX	PIXY
DEXY	IBEX	PLEX
DIXY	JAXY	POXY
DOUX	JEUX	ROUX
EAUX	JINX	SEXY
EXAM	JYNX	TAXI
EXEC	LYNX	TEXT
EXED	MAXI	VEXT
EXIT	MINX	WAXY
EXON	MIXT	WEXE
EXPO	MYXO	XYST

X

Hooks

Hooking requires a subtle change in a player's thought process, in that they must look at words already on the board without becoming distracted by their pronunciation.

Some front-hooks
Two letters to three
X-IS

Four letters to five
X-ERIC   X-YLEM

Five letters to six
X-YLEMS

Six letters to seven
X-EROSES   X-EROTIC

Some end-hooks
Two letters to three

BO-X	MI-X	TA-X
DE-X	MU-X	TE-X
FA-X	NO-X	TI-X
GO-X	PA-X	WE-X
HE-X	PI-X	WO-X
HO-X	PO-X	YE-X
LA-X	RE-X	ZA-X
LO-X	SI-X	
MA-X	SO-X	

X

Three letters to four

APE-X	EAU-X	JEU-X	PRE-X
BRU-X	FLU-X	JIN-X	ULE-X
CRU-X	HOA-X	ONY-X	

Four letters to five

BEAU-X	LATE-X	REDO-X
BORA-X	LIMA-X	SILE-X
CARE-X	LURE-X	SORE-X
CHOU-X	MALA-X	TELE-X
CODE-X	MIRE-X	VIBE-X
FORE-X	MURE-X	VITE-X
GALA-X	PYRE-X	

Five letters to six

ADIEU-X	BIJOU-X	BOYAU-X	DUPLE-X

Six letters to seven

BATEAU-X	GATEAU-X	SIMPLE-X
BUREAU-X	MILIEU-X	TRIPLE-X
CADEAU-X	MINIMA-X	
COTEAU-X	RESEAU-X	

Seven letters to eight

BANDEAU-X	FABLIAU-X	PONCEAU-X
BATTEAU-X	JAMBEAU-X	RONDEAU-X
BERCEAU-X	MANTEAU-X	ROULEAU-X
CAMAIEU-X	MORCEAU-X	TABLEAU-X
CHAPEAU-X	NOUVEAU-X	TONNEAU-X
CHATEAU-X	OCTUPLE-X	TRUMEAU-X
COUTEAU-X	PLATEAU-X	

X

Blockers

It is useful to know which words are blockers and can't therefore be extended before or after. You may want to play a blocker that your opponent can't extend, or you may want to avoid playing a blocker because you want to keep the board open.

Two-letter blocker beginning with X

XU

**Some five-letter blockers beginning with X
(except words ending in '-ED', '-J', '-S', '-X', '-Y' or '-Z')**

XERIC   XOANA   XYLIC   XYSTI

**Some six-letter blockers beginning with X
(except words ending in '-ED', '-J', '-S', '-X', '-Y' or '-Z')**

XENIAL   XENIUM   XOANON   XYLOID   XYSTOI

Handy Hint

Power tile letters may be less common than others in the set but there are many simple and easy-to-remember words that use them. Some examples for X include: BOX (12 points), FOX (13), WAX (13), EXAM (13), NEXT (11) and TEXT (11). You could even impress your opponent with words beginning with X such as XENIA (12 points) and XERIC (14 points).

X

Bonus words

Seven-letter words

XANTHAM
XANTHAN
XANTHIC
XANTHIN
XENOPUS
XERAFIN
XERARCH
XERASIA
XEROMAS

XEROSES
XEROSIS
XEROTES
XEROTIC
XEROXED
XEROXES
XERUSES
XIPHOID
XYLENES

XYLENOL
XYLIDIN
XYLITOL
XYLOGEN
XYLOMAS
XYLONIC
XYLOSES
XYSTERS

Eight-letter words

XANTHAMS
XANTHANS
XANTHATE
XANTHEIN
XANTHENE
XANTHINE
XANTHINS
XANTHISM
XANTHOMA
XANTHONE
XANTHOUS

XENOGAMY
XENOGENY
XENOLITH
XENOPHYA
XENOTIME
XENURINE
XERANSES
XERANSIS
XERANTIC
XERAPHIM
XEROMATA

XEROSERE
XEROXING
XYLIDINE
XYLITOLS
XYLOCARP
XYLOIDIN
XYLOLOGY
XYLOMATA
XYLONITE
XYLOTOMY

X

Essential info
Value: 4 points
Number in set: 2

Y is worth 4 points on its own, making it a tile with good scoring potential. There are four two-letter words beginning with Y but they use all the vowels except for I: YA, YE, YO and YU (5 points each). High-scoring three-letter words beginning with Y include YEW (9 points) and YOB (8 points). Y is also excellent for end hooking onto nouns for use as adjectives.

Two-letter words beginning with Y

YA	YE	YO	YU

Some three-letter words beginning with Y

YAD	YAW	YGO	YON
YAE	YAY	YID	YOW
YAG	YEA	YIN	YUG
YAH	YEH	YOD	YUK
YAM	YEP	YOK	YUM
YAR	YEX	YOM	YUP

Y

Hooks

Hooking requires a subtle change in a player's thought process, in that they must look at words already on the board without becoming distracted by their pronunciation.

Some front-hooks
Two letters to three

Y-AD	Y-AY	Y-GO	Y-OS
Y-AE	Y-EA	Y-ID	Y-OU
Y-AG	Y-EH	Y-IN	Y-OW
Y-AH	Y-EN	Y-OB	Y-UG
Y-AM	Y-ES	Y-OD	Y-UM
Y-AR	Y-ET	Y-OM	Y-UP
Y-AW	Y-EX	Y-ON	Y-US

Three letters to four

Y-AFF	Y-EGG	Y-OOF
Y-ALE	Y-ELK	Y-OOP
Y-APP	Y-ELL	Y-ORE
Y-ARD	Y-ELM	Y-OUK
Y-ARE	Y-EST	Y-OUR
Y-ARK	Y-EVE	Y-OWE
Y-ATE	Y-ILL	Y-OWL
Y-AWL	Y-IRK	Y-UKE
Y-AWN	Y-ODE	Y-ULE
Y-EAN	Y-OKE	Y-UMP
Y-EAR	Y-OLD	

Y

Four letters to five

Y-ABBA	Y-CLAD	Y-LIKE
Y-ACCA	Y-COND	Y-MOLT
Y-AGER	Y-DRAD	Y-OGEE
Y-AMEN	Y-EARD	Y-OURN
Y-ARCO	Y-EARN	Y-OWED
Y-AULD	Y-EAST	Y-ULAN
Y-AWED	Y-EVEN	Y-UPON
Y-AWNY	Y-EXED	
Y-BORE	Y-FERE	

Five letters to six

Y-ACKER	Y-BRENT	Y-IRKED
Y-AGGER	Y-CLEPT	Y-OWING
Y-ANKER	Y-EANED	Y-OWLED
Y-ANTRA	Y-EARDS	Y-OWLER
Y-ARKED	Y-EARLY	Y-PIGHT
Y-ARROW	Y-EMMER	Y-PLAST
Y-AWING	Y-ESSES	Y-SHEND
Y-AWNED	Y-ESTER	Y-SHENT
Y-AWNER	Y-EUKED	Y-UMPED
Y-BLENT	Y-EXING	Y-UMPIE
Y-BOUND	Y-ICKER	Y-WROKE

Y

Six letters to seven

Y-ARKING	Y-EARDED	Y-MOLTEN
Y-AWNERS	Y-EARNED	Y-OWLING
Y-AWNIER	Y-EARNER	Y-PLIGHT
Y-AWNING	Y-EASTED	Y-SLAKED
Y-CLEPED	Y-EUKING	Y-UMPIES
Y-EANING	Y-IRKING	Y-UMPING

Seven letters to eight

Y-ATAGHAN	Y-EANLING	Y-EASTING
Y-AWNIEST	Y-EARDING	Y-OURSELF
Y-BOUNDEN	Y-EARLIES	
Y-CLEEPED	Y-EARNING	

Handy Hint

Some useful short high-scoring words beginning with Y are YEX (Scots word for hiccup or cough, 13 points), YOK (a noisy laugh, 10 points) and YUK (a noise used to express disgust or dislike, also 10 points).

Some end-hooks

Two letters to three

AB-Y	GU-Y	NO-Y
AN-Y	HA-Y	ON-Y
AR-Y	HE-Y	OX-Y
BA-Y	HO-Y	PA-Y
BE-Y	JA-Y	SH-Y
BO-Y	JO-Y	SO-Y
DA-Y	KA-Y	ST-Y
DE-Y	LA-Y	TA-Y
DO-Y	LO-Y	TO-Y
FA-Y	MA-Y	WE-Y
FE-Y	MO-Y	YA-Y
GO-Y	NA-Y	

Three letters to four

ACH-Y	BON-Y	COW-Y
ADD-Y	BOX-Y	COX-Y
AFF-Y	BRA-Y	COZ-Y
AIR-Y	BUR-Y	DEF-Y
ALA-Y	BUS-Y	DEN-Y
ALL-Y	CAG-Y	DEW-Y
ARM-Y	CAN-Y	DEX-Y
ARS-Y	CHA-Y	DID-Y
ART-Y	CIT-Y	DOG-Y
ASH-Y	COL-Y	DOM-Y
AWA-Y	CON-Y	DOP-Y
AWN-Y	COP-Y	DOR-Y
BOD-Y	COR-Y	DOT-Y
BOG-Y	COS-Y	EAS-Y

Y

EEL-Y	MAN-Y	PUL-Y
EGG-Y	MAR-Y	PUN-Y
ELM-Y	MAT-Y	QUA-Y
FAD-Y	MIX-Y	RIM-Y
FOG-Y	MOB-Y	RUB-Y
FOX-Y	MOL-Y	SAG-Y
FRA-Y	MON-Y	SHA-Y
FUM-Y	MOP-Y	SPA-Y
FUR-Y	NIX-Y	SUM-Y
GAB-Y	NOS-Y	TAK-Y
GAM-Y	NOW-Y	TED-Y
GAP-Y	OAK-Y	THE-Y
GOB-Y	OAR-Y	TID-Y
GOE-Y	OBE-Y	TIN-Y
GOR-Y	OIL-Y	TOD-Y
GUL-Y	OKA-Y	TOE-Y
HER-Y	OLD-Y	TON-Y
HOM-Y	ORB-Y	TOR-Y
HUG-Y	OWL-Y	TOW-Y
ICK-Y	PAC-Y	TUN-Y
IFF-Y	PAL-Y	TWA-Y
ILL-Y	PAT-Y	UPS-Y
INK-Y	PIN-Y	VAR-Y
JOE-Y	PIP-Y	VIN-Y
JUD-Y	PIT-Y	WAD-Y
LAC-Y	PIX-Y	WAN-Y
LAD-Y	POL-Y	WAR-Y
LEV-Y	POS-Y	WAX-Y
LIN-Y	POX-Y	WIN-Y
LOG-Y	PRE-Y	YUK-Y

Four letters to five

ACID-Y	BONE-Y	CHEW-Y
AGON-Y	BOOK-Y	COAL-Y
ANNO-Y	BOOM-Y	COCK-Y
ANTS-Y	BOOT-Y	CONE-Y
ARTS-Y	BOSS-Y	CONK-Y
AUNT-Y	BOTH-Y	COOK-Y
BALD-Y	BRIN-Y	COPS-Y
BALM-Y	BUFF-Y	CORE-Y
BAND-Y	BULK-Y	CORK-Y
BARB-Y	BULL-Y	CORN-Y
BARK-Y	BUMP-Y	COSE-Y
BARM-Y	BUNG-Y	COVE-Y
BARN-Y	BUNN-Y	COZE-Y
BASS-Y	BUNT-Y	CULT-Y
BATT-Y	BURL-Y	CURL-Y
BAWD-Y	BURR-Y	CURR-Y
BEAD-Y	BUSH-Y	CUSH-Y
BEAK-Y	BUSK-Y	CUTE-Y
BEAN-Y	BUST-Y	DAFF-Y
BEEF-Y	BUTT-Y	DAIS-Y
BEER-Y	BUZZ-Y	DAMP-Y
BELL-Y	CAGE-Y	DEAR-Y
BEND-Y	CAKE-Y	DECO-Y
BIFF-Y	CALM-Y	DEED-Y
BILL-Y	CAMP-Y	DEIF-Y
BING-Y	CARB-Y	DELL-Y
BITS-Y	CARN-Y	DICE-Y
BLOW-Y	CARR-Y	DICK-Y
BLUE-Y	CASK-Y	DILL-Y

DING-Y	FLAK-Y	GOOS-Y
DINK-Y	FLAM-Y	GOUT-Y
DIRT-Y	FLAX-Y	GRAV-Y
DISH-Y	FLUE-Y	GRIM-Y
DITT-Y	FOAM-Y	GRIP-Y
DITZ-Y	FOLK-Y	GULL-Y
DOLL-Y	FOOD-Y	GUNG-Y
DOOM-Y	FOOT-Y	GUNK-Y
DOPE-Y	FORA-Y	GUSH-Y
DORK-Y	FORK-Y	GUST-Y
DOWD-Y	FORT-Y	GUTS-Y
DOWN-Y	FULL-Y	GYPS-Y
DUCK-Y	FUNK-Y	HAIL-Y
DUMP-Y	FUSS-Y	HAIR-Y
DUNG-Y	FUZZ-Y	HAND-Y
DUSK-Y	GAME-Y	HANK-Y
DUST-Y	GASP-Y	HARD-Y
EARL-Y	GAUD-Y	HARP-Y
EBON-Y	GAWK-Y	HAST-Y
EMPT-Y	GEEK-Y	HEAD-Y
EVER-Y	GERM-Y	HEFT-Y
FAIR-Y	GILL-Y	HERB-Y
FAWN-Y	GIMP-Y	HILL-Y
FELT-Y	GINN-Y	HISS-Y
FIER-Y	GIPS-Y	HOAR-Y
FILL-Y	GIRL-Y	HOKE-Y
FILM-Y	GLUE-Y	HOLE-Y
FISH-Y	GOLD-Y	HOME-Y
FIST-Y	GOOD-Y	HONE-Y
FIZZ-Y	GOOF-Y	HONK-Y

HOOD-Y	LEER-Y	MOOD-Y
HOOK-Y	LEFT-Y	MORA-Y
HORN-Y	LIME-Y	MOSS-Y
HUFF-Y	LOAM-Y	MUCK-Y
HULK-Y	LOFT-Y	MUMM-Y
HUNK-Y	LOLL-Y	MUMS-Y
HUSK-Y	LOON-Y	MURK-Y
HUSS-Y	LOOP-Y	MUSH-Y
IRON-Y	LORD-Y	MUSK-Y
ITCH-Y	LOUS-Y	NARK-Y
JAKE-Y	LOVE-Y	NEED-Y
JAZZ-Y	LUCK-Y	NERD-Y
JELL-Y	LUMP-Y	NIFF-Y
JERK-Y	LUST-Y	NOSE-Y
JIFF-Y	MALT-Y	PACE-Y
JIVE-Y	MANG-Y	PALL-Y
JOKE-Y	MASH-Y	PALM-Y
JOLL-Y	MATE-Y	PANS-Y
JOWL-Y	MEAL-Y	PARK-Y
JUMP-Y	MEAN-Y	PART-Y
JUNK-Y	MEAT-Y	PAST-Y
KELP-Y	MELT-Y	PATS-Y
KICK-Y	MERC-Y	PEAK-Y
KISS-Y	MESS-Y	PEAT-Y
KOOK-Y	MIFF-Y	PERK-Y
LACE-Y	MILK-Y	PHON-Y
LAIR-Y	MINT-Y	PICK-Y
LARD-Y	MISS-Y	PINE-Y
LEAF-Y	MIST-Y	PINK-Y
LEAK-Y	MOLD-Y	PITH-Y

Y

PLUM-Y	SASS-Y	TEST-Y
POKE-Y	SCAR-Y	TILL-Y
POLL-Y	SEAM-Y	TIPS-Y
PONG-Y	SEED-Y	TOAD-Y
PORK-Y	SHAD-Y	TOFF-Y
POSE-Y	SHIN-Y	TOWN-Y
PROS-Y	SHOW-Y	TWIN-Y
PUFF-Y	SILK-Y	UNIT-Y
PULP-Y	SILL-Y	VAMP-Y
PUNK-Y	SISS-Y	VEIN-Y
PUSH-Y	SLIM-Y	VIBE-Y
RAIN-Y	SLOP-Y	VIEW-Y
RANG-Y	SNOW-Y	WACK-Y
READ-Y	SOAP-Y	WALL-Y
REED-Y	SOFT-Y	WART-Y
REEK-Y	SONS-Y	WAVE-Y
REST-Y	SOOT-Y	WEAR-Y
RICE-Y	SOUP-Y	WEED-Y
RILE-Y	SPIN-Y	WELL-Y
RISK-Y	STAG-Y	WHIN-Y
RITZ-Y	STUD-Y	WHIT-Y
ROCK-Y	SULK-Y	WIFE-Y
ROOK-Y	TACK-Y	WIMP-Y
ROOM-Y	TALK-Y	WIND-Y
ROOT-Y	TALL-Y	WISP-Y
ROPE-Y	TANG-Y	WOMB-Y
RUST-Y	TATT-Y	WOOD-Y
SALT-Y	TEAR-Y	WOOL-Y
SAME-Y	TEEN-Y	WORD-Y
SAND-Y	TELL-Y	ZEST-Y

Y

Five letters to six

ANGST-Y	CHEER-Y	DROPS-Y
ARMOR-Y	CHILL-Y	EARTH-Y
AUGUR-Y	CHIRP-Y	EATER-Y
BAKER-Y	CHOKE-Y	EIGHT-Y
BARON-Y	CHUFF-Y	FAULT-Y
BEACH-Y	CHUNK-Y	FEIST-Y
BEARD-Y	CLASS-Y	FELON-Y
BEAUT-Y	CLOUD-Y	FILTH-Y
BEECH-Y	CLUCK-Y	FINER-Y
BLEAR-Y	CLUNK-Y	FLAKE-Y
BLOCK-Y	COLON-Y	FLESH-Y
BLOKE-Y	COUNT-Y	FLINT-Y
BLOOD-Y	CRAFT-Y	FLOAT-Y
BLOWS-Y	CRANK-Y	FLOSS-Y
BLUES-Y	CRAWL-Y	FLOUR-Y
BOOZE-Y	CREAK-Y	FLUFF-Y
BOWER-Y	CREAM-Y	FLUNK-Y
BRAIN-Y	CREEP-Y	FOLKS-Y
BRAND-Y	CRISP-Y	FOOTS-Y
BRASS-Y	CROAK-Y	FREAK-Y
BRAWN-Y	CRUST-Y	FRIAR-Y
BRICK-Y	CURVE-Y	FRILL-Y
BROOD-Y	CUTES-Y	FRISK-Y
BROTH-Y	DRAFT-Y	FRIZZ-Y
BROWN-Y	DRAWL-Y	FROST-Y
BRUSH-Y	DREAM-Y	FROTH-Y
CHALK-Y	DREAR-Y	FRUIT-Y
CHEAP-Y	DRESS-Y	FRUMP-Y
CHEEK-Y	DROOP-Y	GLASS-Y

Y

GLITZ-Y	PEACH-Y	SLINK-Y
GLOOM-Y	PEARL-Y	SLUSH-Y
GLOSS-Y	PHONE-Y	SMART-Y
GNARL-Y	PLUCK-Y	SMELL-Y
GRAIN-Y	POINT-Y	SMILE-Y
GRASS-Y	PRICE-Y	SMITH-Y
GREED-Y	PRIOR-Y	SMOKE-Y
GROWL-Y	PUNCH-Y	SNAKE-Y
GRUMP-Y	QUACK-Y	SNEAK-Y
GUILT-Y	QUIRK-Y	SNIFF-Y
HEART-Y	RIGHT-Y	SNOOP-Y
HERES-Y	ROOTS-Y	SPACE-Y
HORSE-Y	ROUGH-Y	SPARK-Y
HOUSE-Y	RUDER-Y	SPEED-Y
HURRA-Y	SAVOR-Y	SPICE-Y
JAPER-Y	SCARE-Y	SPIKE-Y
LEMON-Y	SCREW-Y	SPOOK-Y
LIVER-Y	SCUZZ-Y	SPORT-Y
MARSH-Y	SHAND-Y	STEAD-Y
MEDLE-Y	SHARP-Y	STEAM-Y
MEREL-Y	SHELL-Y	STEEL-Y
MIGHT-Y	SHIFT-Y	STICK-Y
MISER-Y	SHIRT-Y	STING-Y
MOULD-Y	SHORT-Y	STINK-Y
MOUTH-Y	SHOUT-Y	STOCK-Y
NIGHT-Y	SINEW-Y	STONE-Y
ONION-Y	SKANK-Y	STORE-Y
PAPER-Y	SKIMP-Y	STORM-Y
PARLE-Y	SLANG-Y	STRIP-Y
PATCH-Y	SLEEP-Y	STUFF-Y

Y

STUMP-Y

SUGAR-Y

SWAMP-Y

SWEAT-Y

SWEET-Y

SWIRL-Y

SYRUP-Y

TEENS-Y

THICK-Y

THING-Y

THORN-Y

TITCH-Y

TOAST-Y

TOOTH-Y

TOOTS-Y

TOUCH-Y

TRASH-Y

TREAT-Y

TREND-Y

TRICK-Y

TRUST-Y

TWANG-Y

TWEED-Y

TWEEN-Y

TWIRL-Y

TWIST-Y

VINER-Y

WAFER-Y

WATER-Y

WEIRD-Y

WHIFF-Y

WHIMS-Y

WHINE-Y

WHIRL-Y

WHIRR-Y

WHISK-Y

WHITE-Y

WIELD-Y

WORTH-Y

Six letters to seven

ALMOND-Y

ANALOG-Y

ANARCH-Y

ARCHER-Y

ARMOUR-Y

AUTUMN-Y

BALSAM-Y

BATTER-Y

BILLOW-Y

BLIGHT-Y

BLOTCH-Y

BRAVER-Y

BREATH-Y

BREWER-Y

BRIBER-Y

BURSAR-Y

BUTTER-Y

CARVER-Y

CHINTZ-Y

CHOOSE-Y

CITRUS-Y

CLIQUE-Y

CLOVER-Y

COOKER-Y

COPPER-Y

COTTON-Y

CRUNCH-Y

CURSOR-Y

CUTLER-Y

DODDER-Y

DRAPER-Y

DROUTH-Y

DYNAST-Y

EPONYM-Y

FACTOR-Y

FARMER-Y

FIBBER-Y

FIDDLE-Y

FIDGET-Y

FISHER-Y

FLAVOR-Y

FLIGHT-Y

FLOWER-Y

FORGER-Y

GADGET-Y

Y

GINGER-Y	NURSER-Y	SHRILL-Y
GLITCH-Y	ORANGE-Y	SILVER-Y
GOSSIP-Y	ORATOR-Y	SKETCH-Y
GRAVEL-Y	PANICK-Y	SLAVER-Y
GROCER-Y	PAUNCH-Y	SMOOTH-Y
GROUCH-Y	PEDLAR-Y	SPIDER-Y
GUNNER-Y	PEPPER-Y	SPLASH-Y
HACKER-Y	PHLEGM-Y	SPRING-Y
HAUGHT-Y	PILFER-Y	SQUASH-Y
HEALTH-Y	PILLOW-Y	SQUEAK-Y
HICCUP-Y	POTTER-Y	STARCH-Y
HONEST-Y	POWDER-Y	STREAK-Y
HOSIER-Y	PREACH-Y	STRING-Y
IMAGER-Y	QUIVER-Y	STRIPE-Y
JARGON-Y	RAGGED-Y	SURGER-Y
JITTER-Y	RAISIN-Y	TANNER-Y
JOINER-Y	RAUNCH-Y	THIRST-Y
KITSCH-Y	RECTOR-Y	THRIFT-Y
LATHER-Y	RIFLER-Y	TIMBER-Y
LECHER-Y	ROBBER-Y	TRICKS-Y
LENGTH-Y	ROCKER-Y	TWITCH-Y
LOTTER-Y	RUBBER-Y	UNREAD-Y
MARTYR-Y	SAVOUR-Y	VELVET-Y
MASTER-Y	SCRUFF-Y	VICTOR-Y
MISTER-Y	SENSOR-Y	WASHER-Y
MOCKER-Y	SERVER-Y	WEALTH-Y
MODEST-Y	SHADOW-Y	WEASEL-Y
MONGER-Y	SHIVER-Y	WEIGHT-Y
MUMMER-Y	SHLOCK-Y	WILLOW-Y
NAUGHT-Y	SHOWER-Y	WINTER-Y

Y

Seven letters to eight

ADVISOR-Y	ENTREAT-Y	PARADOX-Y
AUDITOR-Y	FEATHER-Y	PEDAGOG-Y
BISCUIT-Y	FLATTER-Y	PLASTER-Y
BLADDER-Y	FLICKER-Y	POLYGAM-Y
BLOSSOM-Y	FLUSTER-Y	POLYMER-Y
BLUSTER-Y	FRIPPER-Y	PUDDING-Y
BOULDER-Y	FRUITER-Y	QUIZZER-Y
BURGLAR-Y	GIMMICK-Y	RECOVER-Y
BUTCHER-Y	GLITTER-Y	REFINER-Y
CABBAGE-Y	GLUTTON-Y	RUBBISH-Y
CAJOLER-Y	GREENER-Y	SADDLER-Y
CALAMAR-Y	GRINDER-Y	SAVAGER-Y
CARTOON-Y	GYRATOR-Y	SCHLOCK-Y
CHANCER-Y	HATCHER-Y	SCRATCH-Y
CHEATER-Y	HEATHER-Y	SCREECH-Y
CHIFFON-Y	HOMONYM-Y	SCRUNCH-Y
CHIRRUP-Y	INCISOR-Y	SEMINAR-Y
CITATOR-Y	JEALOUS-Y	SHIMMER-Y
CLATTER-Y	JEOPARD-Y	SHMALTZ-Y
COBBLER-Y	KNACKER-Y	SLIPPER-Y
COLLIER-Y	LAMINAR-Y	SLOBBER-Y
CREAMER-Y	LEATHER-Y	SLUMBER-Y
CRYOGEN-Y	MILITAR-Y	SMOTHER-Y
CURATOR-Y	MONARCH-Y	SOLDIER-Y
CUSTARD-Y	MONITOR-Y	SPINNER-Y
DASTARD-Y	MUSTARD-Y	SPUTTER-Y
DELIVER-Y	NEGATOR-Y	SQUELCH-Y
DRAUGHT-Y	NITPICK-Y	STEALTH-Y
DRUDGER-Y	ORDINAR-Y	STUDENT-Y

Y

SYNONYM-Y	TOURIST-Y	UNWORTH-Y
TABLOID-Y	TRICKER-Y	VILLAIN-Y
THUNDER-Y	TWITTER-Y	WARRANT-Y
TITULAR-Y	UNTRUST-Y	WHISKER-Y

Blockers

It is useful to know which words are blockers and can't therefore be extended before or after. You may want to play a blocker that your opponent can't extend, or you may want to avoid playing a blocker because you want to keep the board open.

Some three-letter blockers beginning with Y

YAE	YEH	YEX

Four-letter blocker beginning with Y

YUTZ

Some five-letter blockers beginning with Y
(except words ending in '-ED', '-J', '-S', '-X', '-Y' or '-Z')

YAULD	YOKUL	YOUSE	YUCKO
YOGIC	YOURN	YUCCH	YUMMO

Some six-letter blockers beginning with Y
(except words ending in '-ED', '-J', '-S', '-X', '-Y' or '-Z')

YAKUZA	YEOMAN	YIKING
YAWING	YEOMEN	YIPPEE

Y

Bonus words

Bonus words on your rack can be hard to spot, especially for the less experienced player. One way to help find them is by using prefixes and suffixes.

Many larger words include a common prefix or suffix – remembering these and using them where you can is a good way to discover any longer words on your rack, including any potential bonus words. The key suffix to remember beginning with Y is -YARD.

Some words ending with -YARD
Seven-letter words

BEE-YARD	INN-YARD	TAN-YARD
HAL-YARD	LAN-YARD	

Eight-letter words

BACK-YARD	FEED-YARD	SALE-YARD
BALL-YARD	FORE-YARD	SAVO-YARD
BARN-YARD	HAUL-YARD	SHIP-YARD
BOAT-YARD	JUNK-YARD	SHOW-YARD
BONE-YARD	KAIL-YARD	TILT-YARD
COAL-YARD	KALE-YARD	VINE-YARD
DEER-YARD	KIRK-YARD	WHIN-YARD
DOCK-YARD	MAIN-YARD	WILL-YARD
DOOR-YARD	METE-YARD	WOOD-YARD
FARM-YARD	RICK-YARD	

Y

Unusual letter combinations

If you have an unusual combination of letters on your rack, or want to impress your opponent with an unusual word, a few words from World English can come in handy.

Australian words

YABBER	talk or jabber
YABBY	small freshwater crayfish
YACCA	grass tree
YARRAN	small hardy tree
YATE	small eucalyptus tree
YIKE	argument, squabble or fight
YUCKO	disgusting
YUMMO	delicious

South African word

YEBO	yes

Y

Essential info
Value: 10 points
Number in set: 1
Power tile

Z is one of the most valuable tiles in the Scrabble set. It is easier to use than, for example, Q, as it is not so heavily reliant on another letter (as is Q on U). Various three-letter words using Z can be remembered easily as sets of two, with another fixed consonant and alternating vowels, for example ZIG, ZAG and especially ZAX, ZEX (using two power tiles and thus potentially achieving huge scores). Sets of three are also useful to keep in mind, such as CAZ, COZ, CUZ.

Two-letter words beginning with Z

ZA   ZO

Some three-letter words beginning with Z

ZAG	ZED	ZEL	ZHO	ZIT
ZAX	ZEE	ZEP	ZIG	ZOA
ZEA	ZEK	ZEX	ZIN	ZOL

Some three-letter words using Z

ADZ	COZ	FIZ	POZ	SEZ
AZO	CUZ	LUZ	REZ	WIZ
BEZ	DZO	MIZ	RIZ	
CAZ	FEZ	MOZ	SAZ	

Some four-letter words using Z

Some interesting four-letter words using the letter Z are AZYM (unleavened bread, 18 points) and NAZE (marshy headland, 13 points). Words beginning with Z which may be unfamiliar include ZATI (a type of macaque, 13 points) and ZOEA (larva of a crab or crustacean, 13 points). Don't forget words such as JAZY (wig, 23 points) and QUIZ (22 points) as they use more than one power tile and can return relatively high scores considering their length.

ADZE	HAZE	OYEZ	YUZU	ZITE
AZAN	HAZY	PHIZ	ZACK	ZITI
AZON	IZAR	PIZE	ZANY	ZOEA
AZYM	JAZZ	PREZ	ZARF	ZOIC
BIZE	KUZU	QUIZ	ZATI	ZONA
BOZO	LAZO	RAZE	ZEAL	ZONE
BUZZ	LAZY	RAZZ	ZEBU	ZONK
CHEZ	LUTZ	RITZ	ZEIN	ZOON
CHIZ	MAZE	RIZA	ZERK	ZORI
COZE	MAZY	SITZ	ZEST	ZOUK
COZY	MEZE	SWIZ	ZETA	ZOOM
CZAR	MOZE	TIZZ	ZIFF	ZOOT
FOZY	MOZO	TOZE	ZILA	ZULU
FAZE	MZEE	TREZ	ZILL	ZUPA
FIZZ	NAZE	TZAR	ZIMB	ZURF
FUTZ	NAZI	VIZY	ZINC	ZYGA
FUZZ	OOZE	WHIZ	ZING	ZYME
GAZE	ORZO	YUTZ	ZIPS	

Hooks

By their nature, power tiles feature in fewer words than the other letters in the Scrabble set. As a result, examples of their use in hooking (especially end-hooking) can be few and far between. Bear in mind the prefix ZOO- as it features heavily in the longer examples.

Useful examples to remember are ZESTER (kitchen utensil used to scrape peel from citrus fruits, 15 points) and ZITHER (a stringed musical instrument, 18 points).

Some front-hooks
Two letters to three

Z-AG	Z-ED	Z-HO	Z-OS
Z-AS	Z-EE	Z-IN	
Z-AX	Z-EL	Z-IT	
Z-EA	Z-EX	Z-OO	

Three letters to four

Z-ARF	Z-IFF	Z-OON
Z-ERK	Z-ILL	Z-OOT
Z-ETA	Z-OBO	Z-OUK

Four letters to five

Z-AMIA	Z-HOMO	Z-OPPO
Z-ANTE	Z-INKY	Z-UPAS
Z-AYIN	Z-LOTE	

Z

Five letters to six

Z-ANANA   Z-INKED   Z-ONERS

Z-ESTER   Z-ITHER

Six letters to seven

Z-INCITE   Z-OOGENY   Z-OOLITH

Z-INKIER   Z-OOIDAL   Z-ORBING

Z-OOGAMY   Z-OOLITE

Seven   letters to eight

Z-OOLITIC   Z-OOPHYTE   Z-OOSPORE

Z-OOLOGIC   Z-OOSPERM

Handy Hint

Power tile letters may be less common than others in the set but there are many simple and easy-to-remember words that use them. Some examples for Z include: LAZY (16 points), QUIZ (22), ZERO (13), ZAP (14), ZOOM (15) and ZONE (13).

Some end-hooks
Two letters to three

AD-Z	FE-Z	PO-Z
BE-Z	MI-Z	RE-Z
BI-Z	MO-Z	

Three letters to four

CHI-Z	MOZ-Z	SIT-Z
GEE-Z	PHI-Z	
MIZ-Z	POZ-Z	

Four letters to five

BORT-Z	GREN-Z	SPIT-Z
CAPI-Z	MILT-Z	WARE-Z
CHIZ-Z	PLOT-Z	WOOT-Z

Five letters to six

QUART-Z	SPELT-Z	SPRIT-Z

Six letters to seven

SCHNOZ-Z

Z

Some three-letter blockers using Z

BEZ	SAZ	ZOA
CAZ	SEZ	ZUZ
FEZ	ZAX	
LUZ	ZEX	

Some four-letter blockers using Z

FOZY	MOZZ	TUZZ
FUTZ	PHIZ	VIZY
GAZY	PUTZ	YUTZ
JAZY	SITZ	ZITE
MAZY	SIZY	ZIZZ

Z

(the study of animals, 20 points) and the less-well-known ZOOLATRY (the worship of animals as divine beings, also 20 points).

Seven-letter words

ZABTIEH

ZACATON

ZADDICK

ZAITECH

ZAKUSKA

ZAKUSKI

ZAMARRA

ZAMARRO

ZAMBUCK

ZAMOUSE

ZAMPONE

ZAMPONI

ZANELLA

ZANIEST

ZANJERO

ZAPATEO

ZAPPIER

ZAPPING

ZAPTIAH

ZAPTIEH

ZAREEBA

ZARNICH

ZEALANT

ZEALFUL

ZEALOUS

ZESTFUL

ZESTIER

ZESTING

ZETETIC

ZEUXITE

ZEBRAIC

ZEBRINA

ZEBRINE

ZEBROID

ZEBRULA

ZEBRULE

ZECCHIN

ZEDOARY

ZELATOR

ZELKOVA

ZEMSTVA

ZEMSTVO

ZENAIDA

ZEOLITE

ZIFFIUS

ZIGANKA

ZIKURAT

ZITHERN

ZLOTYCH

ZILLION

ZIMOCCA

ZINCATE

ZINCIER

ZINCIFY

ZINCING

ZINCITE

ZINCKED

ZINCODE

ZINCOID

ZINCOUS

ZINGANI

ZINGANO

ZINGARA

ZINGARE

ZINGARI

Z

ZINGARO

ZINKIER

ZINKIFY

ZINKING

ZOARIAL

ZOARIUM

ZOCCOLO

ZOECIUM

ZOEFORM

ZOISITE

ZOMBIFY

ZONALLY

ZONATED

ZONKING

ZONULAE

ZONULAR

ZONULES

ZONULET

ZOOECIA

ZOOGAMY

ZOOGENY

ZOOGLEA

ZOOGONY

ZOOIDAL

ZOOLITE

ZOOLITH

ZOOLOGY

ZOONITE

ZOONOMY

ZOOPERY

ZOOTAXY

ZOOTOMY

ZOOTYPE

ZORBING

ZORGITE

ZORILLA

ZORILLE

ZORILLO

ZOYSIAS

ZUFFOLI

ZUFFOLO

ZYGOSIS

ZYGOTIC

ZYMOGEN

ZYMOSAN

ZYMOSIS

ZYMOTIC

ZYMURGY

Eight-letter words

ZABAIONE

ZABAJONE

ZADDIKIM

ZAIBATSU

ZAKOUSKA

ZAKOUSKI

ZAMBOMBA

ZAMINDAR

ZAMPOGNA

ZAMZAWED

ZAPPIEST

ZARATITE

ZARZUELA

ZASTRUGA

ZASTRUGI

ZEALLESS

ZEALOTRY

ZEBRINNY

ZECCHINE

ZECCHINI

ZECCHINO

ZELATRIX

ZEMINDAR

ZEMSTVOS

ZENITHAL

ZEOLITIC

Z

ZEPPELIN

ZERUMBET

ZESTIEST

ZESTLESS

ZIBELINE

ZIGGURAT

ZIGZAGGY

ZIKKURAT

ZIMOCCAS

ZINCIEST

ZINCKIER

ZINCKIFY

ZINCKING

ZINCODES

ZINDABAD

ZINGIBER

ZINGIEST

ZINKIEST

ZIRCALOY

ZIRCONIA

ZIRCONIC

ZODIACAL

ZOETROPE

ZOIATRIA

ZOMBIISM

ZOMBORUK

ZONATION

ZONELESS

ZONETIME

ZOOBLAST

ZOOCHORE

ZOOCHORY

ZOOCYTIA

ZOOECIUM

ZOOGENIC

ZOOGLEAE

ZOOGLEAL

ZOOGLOEA

ZOOGRAFT

ZOOLATER

ZOOLATRY

ZOOLITIC

ZOOLOGIC

ZOOMANCY

ZOOMANIA

ZOOMETRY

ZOOMORPH

ZOONITIC

ZOONOMIA

ZOONOMIC

ZOONOSIS

ZOONOTIC

ZOOPATHY

ZOOPERAL

ZOOPHOBE

ZOOPHORI

ZOOPHYTE

ZOOSCOPY

ZOOSPERM

ZOOSPORE

ZOOTHOME

ZOOTIEST

ZOOTOMIC

ZOOTOXIC

ZOOTOXIN

ZOOTROPE

ZOOTYPIC

ZOPILOTE

ZUCCHINI

ZUCHETTA

ZUCHETTO

ZWIEBACK

ZYGAENID

ZYGANTRA

ZYGODONT

ZYGOMATA

ZYGOSITY

ZYGOTENE

ZYLONITE

ZYMOGENE

ZYMOGENS

ZYMOGRAM

ZYMOLOGY

ZYMOTICS

Z

Unusual letter combinations

If you have an unusual combination of letters on your rack, or want to impress your opponent with an unusual word, a few words from World English can come in handy.

Australian words

ZAMBUCK   St John ambulance attendant
ZIFF   beard

Hindi words

ZENANA   part of a house reserved for women
ZILA   administrative district in India

Zho and Tell

There are various alternative spellings for ZHO (A Tibetan breed of cattle, developed by crossing the yak with common cattle). These are DSO, DZO, DZHO and ZO, all of which it is worth remembering in order to form short, high-scoring words (ZHO scores 15 points and DZO is worth 13).

Z

TWO AND THREE-LETTER WORDS

Two- and three-letter words

Two-letter words

AA   volcanic rock

AB   abdominal muscle

AD   short form of advertisement

AE   Scots word meaning one or a single

AG   agriculture

AH   expression of pleasure, pain, or sympathy

AI   the three-toed sloth

AL   Asian shrub or tree

AM   part of the verb to be

AN   the indefinite article used before an initial vowel sound

AR   the letter R

AS   while, because, since

AT   used to indicate location or position

AW   expression of disapproval, commiseration, or appeal

AX   US spelling of axe

AY   yes

BA   the soul represented as a bird with a human head

BE   exist, live

BI   short for bisexual

BO   exclamation used to startle or surprise

BY   near to, at the side of, via; a bye

CH   obsolete form of I

DA   Burmese knife

DE   of or from

DI   plural form of deus

DO   perform, complete; a party

EA   dialect word for river

ED   education

EE   Scots word for eye

EF   the letter F

EH   exclamation of surprise or inquiry

EL   elevated railway

EM   printing meaurement

EN   printing measurement

ER   expression of hesitation

ES   the letter S

ET   past tense of eat

EX   former spouse or partner

FA   variant spelling of fah

FE   charge, fee

FY   variant spelling of fie

GI   martial arts suit

GO   to move or proceed; a turn or attempt

GU	musical instrument	MI	musical term
HA	exclamation of derision, triumph, or surprise	MM	expression of satisfaction
HE	male person or animal	MO	short for moment
HI	hello	MU	12th Greek letter
HM	expression of thoughtful consideration	MY	of or belonging to the speaker or writer
HO	exclamation used to attract attention	NA	Scots word for no
ID	unconscious primitive instincts	NE	not, nor
		NO	expression of denial, refusal, etc
IF	in case that; an uncertainty or condition	NU	13th Greek letter
IN	inside, within; a way of approaching a person	NY	nigh; to approach
		OB	objection
IO	cry of joy or grief	OD	hypothetical force
IS	part of the verb to be	OE	grandchild
IT	nonhuman thing	OF	belonging to
JA	yes	OH	exclamation of surprise, pain, etc
JO	Scots word for a sweetheart	OI	exclamation used to attract attention
KA	ancient Egyptian spirit	OM	intonation chanted as a mantra
KI	Japanese martial art	ON	not off; the side of the field on which the batsman stands
KO	Maori digging-stick		
KY	Scots word for cows		
LA	variant spelling of lah	OO	Scots word for wool
LI	Chinese unit of length	OP	short for operation
LO	look!	OR	conjunction used to join alternatives; gold
MA	word for mother	OS	bone
ME	refers to the speaker or writer	OU	South African slang for a man
		OW	exclamation of pain

OX	adult castrated bull
OY	grandchild
PA	word for father
PE	17th Hebrew letter
PI	16th Greek letter
PO	chamberpot
QI	vital energy believed to circulate in the body
RE	musical term
SH	exclamation to request silence
SI	musical term
SO	variant spelling of soh
ST	exclamation to request silence
TA	thank you
TE	musical term
TI	variant spelling of te
TO	towards, in the direction of
UG	cause loathing in, hate
UH	expression of uncertainty
UM	sound of hesitation
UN	dialect variant of one
UP	in a higher place; a rise or success
UR	sound of hesitation
US	refers to the speaker or writer and another
UT	syllable used for the note C
WE	refers to the speaker or writer and another
WO	archaic spelling of woe
XI	14th Greek letter
XU	monetary unit
YA	you
YE	archaic word for you
YO	expression of greeting
YU	jade
ZA	pizza
ZO	Tibetan breed of cattle

Three-letter words

AAH exclamation of pleasure, satisfaction, etc

AAL Asian shrub or tree

AAS plural form of aa

ABA type of cloth from Syria

ABB yarn used in weaving

ABO offensive word for Aborigine

ABS plural form of ab

ABY pay the penalty for

ACE playing card

ACH Scots expression of surprise

ACT something done, deed

ADD combine

ADO fuss, trouble

ADS plural form of ad

ADZ heavy hand tool

AFF Scots word for off

AFT at or towards the rear

AGA Ottoman military commander

AGE length of time

AGO in the past

AGS plural form of ag

AHA exclamation of triumph, surprise, etc

AHI the yellowfin tuna

AHS plural form of ah

AIA nursemaid in East

AID assistance or support

AIL trouble, afflict

AIM point or direct at target

AIN Scots word for own

AIR the mixture of gases forming the earth's atmosphere

AIS plural form of ai

AIT islet, esp in a river

AKA New Zealand vine

AKE old spelling of ache

ALA wing

ALB Christian priest's robe

ALE kind of beer

ALF uncultivated Australian

ALL the whole quantity of something

ALP high mountain

ALS plural form of al

ALT musical term

AMA wet nurse

AMI male friend

AMP ampere

AMU atomic mass unit

ANA in equal quantities

AND conjunction used to express addition

ANE Scots word for one

ANI type of tropical American bird

ANN payment to a parish minister's widow

ANT small insect

ANY one or some

APE primate

APO type of protein

APP short for application program

APT suitable, appropriate

ARB short form of arbitrageur

ARC part of a circle or curve

ARD primitive plough

ARE 100 square metres

ARF barking sound

ARK the boat built by Noah

ARM upper limb

ARS plural form of ar

ART creation of works of beauty

ARY dialect form of any

ASH substance left after burning

ASK request an answer from

ASP small poisonous snake

ASS donkey

ATE part of the verb to eat

ATT old Siamese coin

AUA the yellow-eye mullet

AUE Maori exclamation of pain, distress, etc

AUF old word for oaf

AUK northern sea bird

AVA Scots word for at all

AVE welcome or farewell

AVO Macao currency unit

AWA Scots word for away

AWE wonder and respect mixed with dread

AWL pointed tool

AWN bristles growing from certain grasses

AXE tool with a sharp blade

AYE yes

AYS plural form of ay

AYU small Japanese fish

AZO chemistry term

BAA sound of a sheep

BAC baccalaureate

BAD not good

BAG flexible container

BAH expression of contempt or disgust

BAL balmoral, an ankle-high shoe

BAM cheat, hoax

BAN prohibit or forbid

BAP large soft bread roll

BAR length of metal, etc

BAS plural form of ba

BAT club used to hit the ball in sports

BAY semicircular indentation of a shoreline

BED piece of furniture

BEE insect that makes honey

BEG	solicit (money, etc)
BEL	unit for comparing two power levels
BEN	mountain peak
BES	variant of beth, 2nd Hebrew letter
BET	wager
BEY	Ottoman official
BEZ	part of deer's horn
BIB	cloth worn by babies
BID	offer to buy something, esp in competition
BIG	of considerable size, number, etc
BIN	container for rubbish
BIO	short for biography
BIS	twice
BIT	small piece or portion
BIZ	short for business
BOA	large snake
BOB	move up and down repeatedly
BOD	person
BOG	wet spongy ground
BOH	exclamation used to startle or surprise
BOI	lesbian who dresses like a boy
BOK	S African antelope
BON	good
BOO	shout of disapproval
BOP	dance to pop music

BOR	neighbour
BOS	plural form of bo
BOT	larva of a botfly
BOW	lower head as sign of respect
BOX	container
BOY	male child
BRA	brassiere
BRO	family member
BRR	used to suggest shivering
BRU	South African word for friend
BUB	youngster
BUD	swelling on a plant
BUG	insect
BUM	buttocks
BUN	sweet bread roll or cake
BUR	washer fitting around the end of a rivet
BUS	large motor vehicle
BUT	except, only
BUY	acquire by paying money
BYE	goodbye
BYS	plural form of by
CAA	Scots word for call
CAB	taxi
CAD	dishonourable man
CAG	short for cagoule
CAM	device that converts a circular motion

CAN be able to

CAP covering for the head

CAR motor vehicle

CAT furry mammal

CAW cry of a crow or raven

CAY small low island

CAZ short for casual

CEE 3rd letter of the alphabet

CEL short for celluloid

CEP another name for porcino

CHA tea

CHE dialectal form of I

CHI 22nd Greek letter

CID leader

CIG short for cigarette

CIS chemistry term

CIT town dweller

CLY to steal or seize

COB male swan

COD large food fish

COG tooth on the rim of a gearwheel

COL high mountain pass

CON deceive, swindle

COO make a soft murmuring sound

COP copper

COR exclamation of surprise or admiration

COS cosine

COT baby's bed with high sides

COW mature female bovine animal

COX coxswain

COY affectedly shy or modest

COZ archaic word for cousin

CRU vineyard

CRY shed tears

CUB the young of some animals

CUD partially digested food

CUE signal to an actor or musician to begin

CUM with

CUP drinking vessel

CUR mongrel dog

CUT divide with a sharp instrument

CUZ cousin

CWM geology term

DAB pat lightly

DAD word for father

DAE Scots word for do

DAG cut daglocks from sheep

DAH term used in Morse code

DAK system of mail delivery

DAL decalitre

DAM barrier built across a river to create a lake

DAN judo term

DAP flyfishing with a floss silk line

DAS plural form of da

DAW jackdaw

DAY period of 24 hours

DEB debutante

DEE Scots word for die

DEF very good

DEG water (a plant, etc)

DEI plural form of deus

DEL differential operator

DEN home of a wild animal

DEV Hindu god

DEW drops of water that form on the ground

DEX dextroamphetamine

DEY commanders of the Janissaries of Algiers

DIB fish with a bobbing bait

DID part of the verb to do

DIE cease living

DIF short for difference

DIG cut into earth, esp with a spade

DIM badly lit

DIN loud unpleasant noise

DIP plunge briefly into liquid

DIS treat someone with contempt

DIT term used in Morse code

DIV stupid or foolish person

DOB (as in dob in) inform against

DOC doctor

DOD cut the hair of

DOE female deer

DOF South African word for stupid

DOG domesticated four-legged mammal

DOH musical term

DOL unit of pain intensity

DOM title given to monks

DON put on (clothing)

DOO Scots word for dove

DOP tot of alcoholic drink

DOR European dung beetle

DOS plural form of do

DOT small round mark

DOW Arab vessel

DOY beloved person

DRY lacking moisture

DSO Tibetan breed of cattle

DUB give (a person or place) a name

DUD ineffectual person

DUE something owed

DUG part of the verb to dig

DUH response implying that the speaker is stupid

DUI   plural form of duo

DUN   brownish-grey

DUO   duet

DUP   open

DUX   the top pupil in a class or school

DYE   colouring substance

DZO   Tibetan breed of cattle

EAN   give birth

EAR   organ of hearing

EAS   plural form of ea

EAT   chew and swallow food

EAU   drainage channel

EBB   (of tide water) flow back

ECH   Shakespearean word for eke out

ECO   short for ecology

ECU   French coin

EDH   character of the runic alphabet

EDS   plural form of ed

EEK   expression indicating shock

EEL   snakelike fish

EEN   Scots form of eye

EFF   say the word 'fuck'

EFS   plural form of ef

EFT   newt

EGG   oval or round object laid by female birds

EGO   conscious mind of an individual

EHS   plural form of eh

EIK   Scots form of eke

EKE   increase, enlarge, or lengthen

ELD   old age

ELF   small mischievous fairy

ELK   large deer of N Europe and Asia

ELL   unit of length equal to approximately 45 inches

ELM   tree with serrated leaves

ELS   plural form of el

ELT   young female pig

EME   uncle

EMO   type of music

EMS   plural form of em

EMU   large flightless bird

END   come to a finish

ENE   variant of even

ENG   phonetics symbol

ENS   existence in the most general abstract sense

EON   long period of time

ERA   period of time

ERE   before

ERF   plot of land for building purposes

ERG   unit of work or energy

ERK   aircraftman

ERN	archaic variant of earn	FAT	having excess flesh on the body
ERR	make a mistake	FAW	gypsy
ERS	bitter vetch	FAX	electronic system for sending documents
ESS	the letter S		
EST	treatment that helps people achieve psychological growth	FAY	fairy or sprite
		FED	FBI agent
		FEE	charge
ETA	7th Greek letter	FEG	segment from an orange
ETH	character of the runic alphabet		
		FEH	Hebrew coin
EUK	itch	FEM	feminine
EVE	evening or day before an event	FEN	flat marshy land
		FER	same as far
EVO	evening	FES	plural form of fe
EWE	female sheep	FET	fetch
EWK	itch	FEU	right of use of land
EWT	archaic form of newt	FEW	not many
EXO	excellent	FEY	whimsically strange
EYE	organ of sight	FEZ	brimless tasselled cap
FAA	Scots word for fall	FIB	trivial lie
FAB	excellent	FID	spike for separating strands of rope
FAD	short-lived fashion		
FAE	Scots word for from	FIE	exclamation of disapproval
FAG	slang word for cigarette		
		FIG	soft pear-shaped fruit
FAH	musical term	FIL	Shakespearean word for the shaft of a vehicle
FAN	object used to create a current of air		
		FIN	the organs of locomotion in fish
FAP	drunk		
FAR	at, to, or from a great distance	FIR	tree
		FIT	be appropriate for
FAS	plural form of fa		

FIX   make or become firm, stable, or secure

FIZ   make a hissing sound

FLU   viral infection

FLY   move through the air on wings

FOB   short watch chain

FOE   enemy, opponent

FOG   mass of condensed water vapour in the air

FOH   expression of disgust

FON   fool

FOP   man excessively concerned with fashion

FOR   in the place of, in favour of

FOU   Scots word for full

FOX   reddish-brown bushy-tailed animal

FOY   loyalty

FRA   brother: a title given to an Italian monk or friar

FRO   back or from

FRY   cook in fat or oil

FUB   put off, fob

FUD   rabbit's tail

FUG   hot stale atmosphere

FUM   mythological phoenix

FUN   enjoyment or amusement

FUR   soft hair of a mammal

GAB   talk or chatter

GAD   go about in search of pleasure

GAE   Scots word for go

GAG   choke or retch

GA   girl

GAM   school of whales

GAN   archaic word for begin

GAP   break or opening

GAR   pike-like fish

GAS   airlike substance that is not liquid or solid

GAT   pistol or revolver

GAU   district set up by the Nazi Party

GAY   homosexual

GED   Scots word for pike

GEE   mild exclamation of surprise

GEL   jelly-like substance

GEM   precious stone or jewel

GEN   information

GEO   small fjord or gully

GET   obtain or receive

GEY   intensifier

GHI   clarified butter

GIB   metal wedge

GID   disease of sheep

GIE   Scots word for give

GIF   obsolete word for if

GIG   single performance by musicians

GIN   spirit flavoured with juniper berries

GIO gully, creek

GIP pain, torture

GIS plural form of gi

GIT contemptible person

GJU musical instrument

GNU ox-like antelope

GOA Tibetan gazelle

GOB lump of a soft substance

GOD worshipped spirit

GOE Spenserian word for go

GON geometrical grade

GOO sticky substance

GOR God!

GOS plural form of go

GOT part of the verb to get

GOV short for governor

GOX gaseous oxygen

GOY Jewish word for a non-Jew

GUB white man

GUE musical instrument

GUL oriental carpet design

GUM flesh in which the teeth are set

GUN weapon

GUP gossip

GUR unrefined cane sugar

GUS plural form of gu

GUT intestine

GUV short for governor

GUY man or boy

GYM gymnasium

GYP swindle

HAD part of the verb to have

HAE Scots form of have

HAG ugly old woman

HAH exclamation of derision, triumph, or surprise

HAJ Muslim pilgrimage

HAM meat from a pig's thigh

HAN archaic form of have

HAO monetary unit

HAP luck, chance

HAS part of the verb to have

HAT covering for the head

HAW hawthorn berry

HAY grass cut and dried as fodder

HEH exclamation of surprise

HEM bottom edge of a garment

HEN female domestic fowl

HEP fruit of the dog rose

HER refers to a female person or animal

HES plural form of he

HET short for heterosexual

HEW cut with an axe

HEX evil spell

HEY expression of surprise or for catching attention

HIC	sound of a hiccup
HID	part of the verb to hide
HIE	hurry
HIM	refers to a male person or animal
HIN	Hebrew unit of capacity
HIP	part of the body between pelvis and thigh
HIS	belonging to him
HIT	strike, touch forcefully
HMM	expression of thoughtful consideration
HOA	exclamation to attract attention
HOB	flat top part of a cooker
HOC	Latin for this
HOD	open wooden box attached to a pole
HOE	long-handled tool
HOG	castrated male pig
HOH	exclamation to attract attention
HOI	cry used to attract attention
HOM	sacred plant
HON	short for honey
HOO	expression of boisterous emotion
HOP	jump on one foot
HOS	plural form of ho

HOT	having a high temperature
HOW	in what way
HOX	hamstring
HOY	cry used to attract attention
HUB	centre of a wheel
HUE	colour
HUG	clasp tightly in the arms
HUH	exclamation of derision
HUI	meeting of Maori people
HUM	low continuous vibrating sound
HUN	member of Asiatic nomadic peoples
HUP	cry to make a horse turn
HUT	small house, shelter, or shed
HYE	hurry
HYP	hypotenuse
ICE	water in its solid state
ICH	dialect form of I
ICK	expression of disgust
ICY	very cold
IDE	silver fish
IDS	plural form of id
IFF	conjunction used in logic
IFS	plural form of if
IGG	ignore, snub

ILK	type	JAY	bird
ILL	not in good health	JEE	move a horse faster
IMP	mischievous small creature	JET	aircraft
		JEU	game
INK	coloured liquid used for writing or printing	JEW	obsolete offensive word meaning haggle
INN	pub or small hotel	JIB	triangular sail
INS	plural form of in	JIG	type of lively dance
ION	atom	JIN	Chinese unit of weight
IOS	plural form of io	JIZ	wig
IRE	anger	JOB	occupation
IRK	irritate, annoy	JOE	Scots word for a sweetheart
ISH	issue, expiry		
ISM	doctrine, system, or practice	JOG	run at a gentle pace
		JOL	party
ISO	short segment of film	JOR	movement in Indian music
ITA	type of palm		
ITS	belonging to it	JOT	write briefly
IVY	evergreen climbing plant	JOW	ring (a bell)
		JOY	feeling of great delight
IWI	Maori tribe	JUD	large block of coal
JAB	poke sharply	JUG	container for liquids
JAG	cut unevenly	JUN	monetary unit
JAI	victory (to)	JUS	right, power, or authority
JAK	South and South East Asian tree		
		JUT	project or stick out
JAM	pack tightly into a place	KAB	ancient Hebrew measure
JAP	splash, spatter	KAE	jackdaw
JAR	wide-mouthed container	KAF	letter of the Hebrew alphabet
JAW	bone in which the teeth are set	KAI	New Zealand word for food

KAK   S African offensive word for faeces

KAM   Shakespearean word for crooked

KAS   plural form of ka

KAT   shrub whose leaves have narcotic properties

KAW   cry of a crow

KAY   the letter K

KEA   large parrot

KEB   Scots word meaning miscarry a lamb

KED   (as in sheep ked) sheep tick

KEF   marijuana

KEG   small metal beer barrel

KEN   know

KEP   catch

KET   Scots word for carrion

KEX   type of plant

KEY   device for operating a lock

KHI   letter of the Greek alphabet

KID   child

KIF   marijuana

KIN   person's relatives collectively

KIP   sleep

KIR   alcoholic drink

KIS   plural form of ki

KIT   outfit or equipment

KOA   Hawaiian tree

KOB   antelope

KOI   type of carp

KON   Spenserian word for know

KOP   African hill

KOR   ancient Hebrew unit of capacity

KOS   Indian unit of distance

KOW   branch, bunch of twigs

KUE   the letter Q

KYE   Scots word for cows

KYU   judo term

LAB   laboratory

LAC   (in India and Pakistan) 100,000 rupees

LAD   boy or young man

LAG   go too slowly

LAH   musical term

LAM   thrash, beat

LAP   part between the waist and knees

LAR   boy or young man

LAS   plural form of la

LAT   former coin of Latvia

LAV   short for lavatory

LAW   rule binding on a community

LAX   not strict

LAY   part of the verb to lie

LEA   meadow

LED   part of the verb to lead

LEE   sheltered side

LEG   limb

LEI	(in Hawaii) garland of flowers	LOR	exclamation of surprise or dismay
LEK	monetary unit	LOS	approval, praise
LEP	Spenserian word for leap	LOT	great number
		LOU	Scots word for love
LES	offensive short form of lesbian	LOW	not tall or high
		LOX	smoked salmon
LET	allow, permit	LOY	narrow spade with a single footrest
LEU	monetary unit		
LEV	monetary unit	LUD	lord
LEW	tepid	LUG	carry or drag with great effort
LEX	system or body of laws		
LEY	land temporarily under grass	LUM	chimney
		LUR	musical horn
LEZ	offensive short form of lesbian	LUV	love
		LUX	unit of illumination
LIB	short for liberation	LUZ	supposedly indestructible bone
LID	movable cover		
LIE	make a deliberately false statement	LYE	caustic solution
		LYM	bloodhound
LIG	function with free refreshments	MAA	bleat
		MAC	short for macintosh
LIN	cease	MAD	mentally deranged
LIP	fleshy folds at the mouth	MAE	(as in mae west) inflatable life jacket
LIS	fleur-de-lis		
LIT	part of the verb to light	MAG	short for magazine
LOB	ball struck or thrown in a high arc	MAK	Scots word for make
		MAL	illness, pain
LOD	type of logarithm	MAM	word for mother
LOG	portion of a felled tree	MAN	adult male
LOO	word for lavatory	MAP	representation of the earth's surface
LOP	cut away (twigs and branches)		
		MAR	spoil or impair

MAS plural form of ma

MAT piece of fabric

MAW animal's mouth

MAX the full extent

MAY used to express possibility

MED doctor

MEE Malaysian noodle dish

MEG short for megabyte

MEL pure form of honey

MEM 13th letter in the Hebrew alphabet

MEN plural form of man

MES plural form of me

MET part of the verb to meet

MEU the plant spignel

MEW cry of a cat

MHO former name for siemens

MIB marble used in games

MIC short for microphone

MID intermediate

MIG marble used in games

MIL unit of length

MIM prim

MIR Russian peasant commune

MIS plural form of mi

MIX combine or blend

MIZ shortened form of misery

MNA Greek weight

MOA large extinct flightless bird

MOB disorderly crowd

MOC short for moccasin

MOD sixties youth group

MOE more

MOG short for moggy

MOI me

MOL SI unit mole

MOM word for mother

MON dialect variant of man

MOO cry of a cow

MOP cleaning device

MOR layer of acidic humus

MOS plural form of mo

MOT girl or young woman

MOU Scots word for mouth

MOW to cut grass or crops

MOY coin

MOZ hex

MUD wet soft earth

MUG large drinking cup

MUM word for mother

MUN dialect word for must

MUS plural form of mu

MUT printing measurement

MUX spoil

MYC oncogene

NAB arrest (someone)

NAE Scots word for no

NAG scold constantly

NAH no

NAM	distraint	NOH	drama of Japan
NAN	word for grandmother	NOM	name
NAP	short sleep	NON	not
NAS	has not or was not	NOO	a Scots word for now
NAT	supporter of nationalism	NOR	and not
		NOS	plural form of no
NAW	no	NOT	expressing negation
NAY	no	NOW	at or for the present time
NEB	beak of a bird		
NED	derogatory Scots word for a young working-class male	NOX	nitrogen oxide
		NOY	harass
		NTH	of an unspecified number
NEE	born		
NEF	church nave	NUB	point or gist
NEG	photographic negative	NUN	female member of a religious order
NEK	mountain pass		
NEP	catmint	NUR	knot of wood
NET	meshed fabric	NUS	plural form of nu
NEW	recently made	NUT	fruit
NIB	writing point of a pen	NYE	flock of pheasants
NID	pheasant's nest	NYS	plural form of ny
NIE	archaic spelling of nigh	OAF	stupid person
NIL	nothing	OAK	tree
NIM	game with matchsticks	OAR	pole with a broad blade
NIP	pinch		
NIS	friendly goblin	OAT	grass grown for its edible seed
NIT	egg or larva of a louse		
NIX	be careful!	OBA	Yoruba chief or ruler
NOB	person of social standing	OBE	ancient village
		OBI	Japanese sash
NOD	lower and raise (one's head)	OBO	ship carrying oil and ore
NOG	alcoholic drink	OBS	plural form of ob

OCA South American herbaceous plant

OCH expression of surprise

ODA room in a harem

ODD unusual, peculiar

ODE lyric poem

ODS plural form of od

OES plural form of oe

OFF not on; away

OFT often

OHM unit of electrical resistance

OHO exclamation of surprise or derision

OHS plural form of oh

OIK person regarded as inferior

OIL viscous liquid

OKA unit of weight

OKE unit of weight

OLD having lived for a long time

OLE exclamation of approval

OLM salamander

OMS plural form of om

ONE single

ONO Hawaiian fish

ONS plural form of on

ONY Scots word for any

OOF money

OOH exclamation of surprise

OOM title of respect

OON Scots word for oven

OOP Scots word meaning to bind

OOR Scots word for our

OOS plural form of oo

OOT Scots word for out

OPE archaic word for open

OPS plural form of op

OPT show a preference

ORA plural form of os

ORB decorated sphere

ORC whale

ORD point of a weapon

ORE mineral

ORF disease of sheep

ORS plural form of or

ORT fragment

OSE long winding ridge of gravel, sand, etc

OUD musical instrument

OUK Scots word for week

OUP Scots word meaning to bind

OUR belonging to us

OUS plural form of ou

OUT outside

OVA plural of ovum

OWE be obliged to pay money

OWL bird of prey

OWN used to indicate possession

OWT dialect word for anything

OXO (as in oxo acid) acid that contains oxygen

OXY oxygen

OYE grandchild

OYS plural form of oy

PAC soft shoe

PAD material for protection

PAH exclamation of disgust, disbelief, etc

PAL friend

PAM knave of clubs

PAN metal container for cooking

PAP soft food, mash

PAR usual or average condition

PAS dance step

PAT tap lightly

PAV short for pavlova

PAW animal's foot

PAX kiss of peace

PAY give money for goods

PEA plant, vegetable

PEC pectoral muscle

PED pannier

PEE urinate

PEG pin or clip

PEH letter in the Hebrew alphabet

PEN instrument for writing in ink

PEP high spirits

PER for each

PES technical name for foot

PET animal kept for companionship

PEW seat in a church

PHI 21st letter in the Greek alphabet

PHO noodle soup

PHT expression of irritation or reluctance

PIA pious

PIC photograph, picture

PIE pastry dish

PIG animal

PIN piece of stiff wire for fastening

PIP small seed in a fruit

PIR Sufi master

PIS plural form of pi

PIT hole in the ground

PIU musical term meaning more

PIX photographs

PLU beaver skin used as a unit of value

PLY work at (a job or trade)

POA type of grass

POD seed case of peas

POH exclamation expressing contempt

POI ball of woven flax

POL short for politician

POM short for pommy

POO defecate

POP make a small explosive sound

POS plural form of po

POT round deep container

POW sound imitative of a collision, explosion, etc

POX disease

POZ short for positive

PRE before

PRO in favour of

PRY make an impertinent inquiry

PSI 23rd letter of the Greek alphabet

PST sound to attract attention

PUB building with a licensed bar

PUD short for pudding

PUG small snub-nosed dog

PUH exclamation expressing contempt

PUL Afghan monetary unit

PUN play on words

PUP young dog

PUR obsolete form of purr

PUS yellowish fluid

PUT place in a position

PUY small volcanic cone

PYA monetary unit of Myanmar

PYE book for finding Church services

PYX receptacle for the Eucharistic Host

QAT shrub whose leaves have narcotic properties

QIS plural form of qi

QUA in the capacity of

RAD former unit of radiation

RAG fragment of cloth

RAH US word for cheer

RAI type of Algerian pop music

RAJ (in India) government

RAM male sheep

RAN part of the verb to run

RAP hit with a sharp quick blow

RAS headland

RAT long-tailed rodent

RAW uncooked

RAX stretch or extend

RAY single line of light

REB soldier in the American Civil War

REC short for recreation ground

RED colour

REE Scots word for walled enclosure

REF short for referee

REG short for registration number

REH (in India) surface crust on the soil

REI former Portuguese coin

REM dose of ionizing radiation

REN archaic variant of run

REO language

REP short for representative

RES residence

RET moisten or soak flax

REV revolution (of an engine)

REW archaic spelling of rue

REX king

REZ reservation

RHO 17th letter in the Greek alphabet

RHY archaic spelling of rye

RIA long narrow inlet of the seacoast

RIB bone

RID clear or relieve (of)

RIF discharge from military service

RIG arrange in a dishonest way

RIM edge or border

RIN Scots variant of run

RIP tear violently

RIT Scots word for cut or slit

RIZ dialectal past form of rise

ROB steal from

ROC mythological bird

ROD slender straight bar

ROE mass of eggs in a fish

ROK mythological bird

ROM male gypsy

ROO kangaroo

ROT decompose or decay

ROW straight line of people or things

RUB apply pressure and friction

RUC mythological bird

RUD redness, flush

RUE feel regret for

RUG small carpet

RUM alcoholic drink

RUN move quickly

RUT furrow made by wheels

RYA Scandinavian rug

RYE grain

SAB short for saboteur

SAC pouchlike structure in an animal

SAD sorrowful, unhappy

SAE Scots word for so

SAG sink in the middle

SAI capuchin monkey

SAL	salt
SAM	collect, gather up
SAN	short for sanatorium
SAP	fluid that circulates in plants
SAR	marine fish
SAT	part of the verb to sit
SAU	archaic past form of see
SAV	saveloy
SAW	hand tool
SAX	saxophone
SAY	speak or utter
SAZ	musical instrument
SEA	mass of salt water
SEC	short for second
SED	old spelling of said
SEE	perceive with the eyes or mind
SEG	metal stud on shoe sole
SEI	type of whale
SEL	Scots word for self
SEN	monetary unit
SER	unit of weight
SET	put in a specified position or state
SEW	join with thread
SEX	state of being male or female
SEY	Scots word for part of cow
SEZ	informal spelling of says
SHA	be quiet
SHE	female person or animal
SHH	sound made to ask for silence
SHY	not at ease in company
SIB	blood relative
SIC	so or thus
SIF	South African slang for disgusting
SIK	Australian slang for excellent
SIM	simulation game on a computer
SIN	offence or transgression
SIP	drink in small mouthfuls
SIR	polite term of address for a man
SIS	short for sister
SIT	rest one's body on the buttocks and thighs
SIX	one more than five
SKA	type of West Indian pop music
SKI	snow sport
SKY	upper atmosphere
SLY	crafty
SMA	Scots word for small
SNY	side channel of a river

SOB	weep with convulsive gasps
SOC	feudal right to hold court
SOD	(piece of) turf
SOG	soak
SOH	musical term
SOL	liquid colloidal solution
SOM	monetary unit
SON	male offspring
SOP	concession to pacify someone
SOS	plural form of so
SOT	habitual drunkard
SOU	former French coin
SOV	sovereign
SOW	scatter or plant
SOX	informal spelling of socks
SOY	(as in soy sauce) salty dark brown sauce
SPA	resort with a mineral-water spring
SPY	obtain secret information
SRI	title of respect
STY	pigpen
SUB	short for subeditor
SUD	singular form of suds
SUE	start legal proceedings against
SUI	of himself, herself, itself
SUK	open-air marketplace
SUM	result of addition, total
SUN	star around which the earth revolves
SUP	swallow liquid
SUQ	open-air marketplace
SUR	above
SUS	become aware of
SWY	gambling game
SYE	strain something
SYN	Scots word for since
TAB	small flap or projecting label
TAD	small bit or piece
TAE	Scots word for to
TAG	label bearing information
TAI	(as in tai chi chuan) Chinese system of callisthenics
TAJ	tall conical cap
TAK	Scots word for take
TAM	short for tam-o'-shanter
TAN	coloration of the skin
TAO	philosophical term
TAP	knock lightly
TAR	thick black liquid
TAS	cup, goblet, or glass
TAT	tatty or tasteless article(s)
TAU	19th letter in the Greek alphabet
TAV	22nd letter in the Hebrew alphabet

TAW	convert skins into leather	TIP	narrow or pointed end of anything
TAX	compulsory payment levied	TIS	plural form of ti
TAY	Irish dialect word for tea	TIT	small songbird
		TIX	tickets
TEA	drink	TOC	communication code for T
TEC	short for detective	TOD	unit of weight
TED	dry hay	TOE	digit of the foot
TEE	small peg for golf	TOG	unit of thermal resistance
TEF	grass grown for its grain	TOM	male cat
TEG	two-year-old sheep	TON	unit of weight
TEL	large mound formed from accumulated rubbish	TOO	also, as well
		TOP	highest point or part
TEN	one more than nine	TOR	high rocky hill
TES	plural form of te	TOT	small child
TET	9th letter of the Hebrew alphabet	TOW	drag, esp by means of a rope
TEW	toil	TOY	something designed to be played with
TEX	unit of weight	TRY	make an effort or attempt
THE	definite article	
THO	short for though	TSK	expression of disapproval
THY	of or associated with you (thou)	TUB	open round container
TIC	spasmodic muscular twitch	TUG	pull hard
		TUI	New Zealand bird
TID	girl	TUM	stomach
TIE	fasten with string	TUN	large beer cask
TIG	children's game	TUP	male sheep
TIL	another name for sesame	TUT	sound of mild reprimand
TIN	soft metallic element	

TUX short for tuxedo

TWA two

TWO one more than one

TWP stupid

TYE trough used in mining

TYG cup with two handles

UDO perennial plant

UDS 'God's' or 'God save'

UEY u-turn

UFO flying saucer

UGH exclamation of disgust

UGS plural form of ug

UKE short for ukulele

ULE rubber tree

ULU type of knife

UMM sound of hesitation

UMP short for umpire

UMU type of oven

UNI short for university

UNS plural form of un

UPO upon

UPS plural form of up

URB urban area

URD type of plant with edible seeds

URE extinct wild ox

URN container for the ashes of the dead

URP dialect word for vomit

USE put into service or action

UTA type of lizard

UTE utility vehicle

UTS plural form of ut

UTU reward

UVA grape or berry

VAC short for vacation

VAE bay or narrow creek

VAG vagrant

VAN motor vehicle for transporting goods

VAR unit of reactive power

VAS vessel or tube that carries a fluid

VAT large container for liquids

VAU sixth letter of the Hebrew alphabet

VAV sixth letter of the Hebrew alphabet

VAW Hebrew letter

VEE the letter V

VEG short for vegetable

VET check the suitability of

VEX frustrate, annoy

VIA by way of

VID video

VIE compete (with someone)

VIG interest on a loan

VIM force, energy

VIN French wine

VIS power, force, or strength

VLY low marshy ground

VOE   bay or narrow creek

VOL   short for volume

VOR   (in dialect) warn

VOW   solemn and binding promise

VOX   voice or sound

VUG   small cavity in a rock or vein

VUM   swear, vow

WAB   Scots word for web

WAD   small mass of soft material

WAE   old form of woe

WAG   move rapidly from side to side

WAI   in New Zealand, water

WAN   pale and sickly-looking

WAP   strike

WAR   fighting between nations

WAS   part of the verb to be

WAT   Thai Buddhist monastery or temple

WAW   sixth letter of the Hebrew alphabet

WAX   solid shiny fatty or oily substance

WAY   manner or method

WEB   net spun by a spider

WED   marry

WEE   small or short

WEM   womb or belly

WEN   cyst on the scalp

WET   covered or soaked with water

WEX   wax

WEY   measurement of weight

WHA   Scots word for who

WHO   which person

WHY   for what reason

WIG   artificial head of hair

WIN   come first in a competition

WIS   know or suppose

WIT   clever humour

WIZ   accomplished person, whizz

WOE   grief

WOF   fool

WOG   Australian word meaning influenza

WOK   bowl-shaped Chinese cooking pan

WON   monetary unit

WOO   seek the love or affection of

WOP   strike or beat

WOS   plural form of wo

WOT   wit, to know

WOW   exclamation of astonishment

WOX   obsolete form of the verb to wax

WRY   drily humorous

WUD   Scots word for wood

WUS   casual term of address

WYE the letter Y

WYN rune equivalent to English W

XIS plural form of xi

YAD pointer used for reading the Torah

YAE Scots word meaning one or a single

YAG artificial crystal

YAH exclamation of derision or disgust

YAK Tibetan ox with long shaggy hair

YAM tropical root vegetable

YAP bark with a high-pitched sound

YAR nimble

YAW turn from side to side while moving

YAY exclamation of approval

YEA yes

YEH yes

YEN monetary unit of Japan

YEP affirmative statement

YES expresses consent

YET up until then or now

YEW evergreen tree

YEX hiccup, belch

YGO archaic form of the verb to go

YID offensive word for a Jew

YIN Scots word for one

YIP emit a high-pitched bark

YOB bad-mannered aggressive youth

YOD 10th letter in the Hebrew alphabet

YOK chuckle

YOM day

YON that or those over there

YOS plural form of yo

YOU person or people addressed

YOW variant of ewe

YUG one of the four ages of mankind

YUK expression of dislike or disgust

YUM expression of delight

YUP informal affirmative statement

YUS plural form of yu

ZAG change direction sharply

ZAP kill (by shooting)

ZAS plural form of za

ZAX small axe for cutting slates

ZEA type of grass

ZED the letter Z

ZEE the letter Z

ZEK Soviet prisoner

ZEL Turkish cymbal

ZEP type of long sandwich

ZEX tool for cutting roofing slate

ZHO Tibetan breed of cattle

ZIG change direction sharply

ZIN short form of zinfandel

ZIP fastener with two rows of teeth

ZIT spot or pimple

ZIZ short sleep

ZOA plural form of zoon

ZOL South African slang for a cannabis cigarette

ZOO place where live animals are kept

ZOS plural form of zo

ZUZ silver coin of ancient Palestine

ZZZ informal word for sleep

Useful links

SCRABBLE is a registered trademark owned by Hasbro (US and Canada) and Mattel (rest of the world).

For more information on Scrabble products, visit:
www.scrabble.com
Association of British Scrabble Players:
www.absp.org.uk
National Scrabble Association (of North America):
www2.scrabble-assoc.com
Singapore Scrabble Association:
www.toucanet.com
Netherlands English Scrabble Club:
www.nesc.nl
South African National Scrabble Player's Association (SANSPA):
www.geocities.com/sanspa/home.html
Australian Scrabble Players Association:
www.scrabble.org.au
New Zealand Association of Scrabble Players:
www.scrabble.co.nz
Malta Scrabble Club:
www.scrabblemalta.com
Nigeria Scrabble Federation:
www.nigerianscrabble.com
Collins Official Scrabble Checker:
www.collinslanguage.com/extras/scrabble.aspx
World English-Language Scrabble Players Association:
www.wespa.org

Scrabble Dictionaries
Play to win!

Within the Scrabble range you'll find the perfect companion for all Scrabble games. Settle all those Scrabble squabbles once and for all with the ultimate authority – the Official Scrabble Dictionary range.

For the Tournament Scrabble Player

COLLINS ULTIMATE
SCRABBLE WORD LIST
£25.00

SCRABBLE LISTS
£10

SCRABBLE WORDS
£10

For those who play for fun

SCRABBLE DICTIONARY:
FRIENDS AND FAMILY EDITION
£12.99

POCKET SCRABBLE DICTIONARY
(Second edition) £9.99

COLLINS GEM
SCRABBLE DICTIONARY £4.99

Find the perfect companion for all levels of Scrabble games

To place an order for any Collins Scrabble titles call our sales team on 0870 787 1732